Contemporary Japanese Architecture

Contemporary Japanese Architecture

Its Development and Challenge

Botond Bognar

VNR Van Nostrand Reinhold Company
New York

Published by Van Nostrand Reinhold Company Inc.
135 West 50th Street
New York, New York 10020

Van Nostrand Reinhold Company Limited
Molly Millars Lane
Wokingham, Berkshire RG11 2PY, England

Van Nostrand Reinhold
480 La Trobe Street
Melbourne, Victoria 3000, Australia

Macmillan of Canada
Division of Canada Publishing Corporation
164 Commander Boulevard
Agincourt, Ontario M1S 3C7, Canada

16 15 14 13 12 11 10 9 8 7 6 5 4 3 2 1

Library of Congress Cataloging in Publication Data
Bognár, Botond, 1944-
    Contemporary Japanese architecture, its development
and challenge.

    Bibliography: p.
    Includes index.
    1. Architecture, Modern—20th century—Japan.
2. Architecture—Japan. I. Title.
NA1555.B52   1985   720'.952   84-27089
ISBN 0-442-21174-0

The photographs listed below have been furnished to me through the courtesy of the following
persons, to whom I am very grateful: Japanese
Consul General, Los Angeles: 18; Professor Kiyoshi
Seike: 66; Kenzo Tange: 92, 93; Kiyonori Kikutake:
108, 113; Kisho N. Kurokawa: 129, 131; Masato
Otaka: 147; Kijo Rokkaku: 320; Monta Mozuna:
341, 342, 358; Hiromi Fujii: 381; The Japan Architect Co. Ltd., Tokyo: 464. All other photographs
have been taken by the author. Project drawings
have been made available by the architects responsible for them.

*To my wife, Binky,
and sons, Balazs, Zsolt, and Balint*

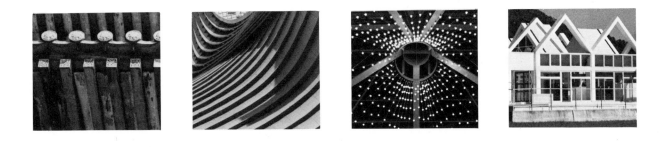

Contents

Acknowledgments

The compilation of this book would have been quite impossible without the kind help and co-operation of many people to whom I extend my deepest gratitude. Above all, I am indebted to the Japanese Ministry of Education (Mombusho) for having granted me the initial two-year scholarship to conduct my research in Japan. In addition, I wish to thank Dr. Kiyoshi Seike, professor and dean of the Tokyo Institute of Technology, who guided me in my work; Shozo Baba, editorial director, and Masayuki Fuchigami, senior editor, of *JA: The Japan Architect*, and Toshio Nakamura, editor of *A + U: Architecture and Urbanism*, for the advice and detailed information they generously furnished; Kunio Maekawa, Kenzo Tange, Kiyonori Kikutake, Kisho N. Kurokawa, Fumihiko Maki, Arata Isozaki, Minoru Takeyama, Takefumi Aida, Kazuo Shinohara, Hiromi Fujii, Toyo Ito, Monta Mozuna, Yasufumi Kijima, Kijo Rokkaku, Toyokazu Watanabe, Kunihiko Hayakawa, Hiroshi Hara, Shin Takamatsu, Itsuko Hasegawa, Yuzuru Tominaga, Kazunari Sakamoto, and Shin Toki— architects who provided me with written documents, drawings, and photos, in addition to their personal views and opinions.

Likewise, I am very grateful to the staff of Design System, Inc., and my architect friends Kazumasa Yamashita, Tadao Ando, Kazuhiro Ishii, Koji Yagi, Hideo Kubota, and Yasuhiko and Yoshiko Matsushiro, for their invaluable support and kind assistance; to Neil Sheehan and Jack Borromeo, who printed the black and white photographs with great skill and dedication.

I am also indebted to Kenneth Frampton for his editorial suggestions and support, which helped greatly in the realization of the book. With appreciation I acknowledge a grant from The Research Board of the University of Illinois that helped me in collecting some final photographic material in Japan. Last but not least, my very special thanks to my wife Binky Borromeo, who not only translated the Foreword into English, but without whose encouragement, persistent and dedicated help, and effective work throughout all the phases of compilation of the material this book could not have been completed.

Though numerous publications have shaped my views about Japan and Japanese architecture, two have been so important that they need special mention here. They are Günter Nitschke's seminal essay " 'Ma': The Japanese Sense of Place," and Chris Fawcett's book, *The New Japanese House: Ritual and Anti-Ritual Patterns of Dwelling*, an excellent introduction to the origin and aspects of Japanese residential architecture. Likewise, my understanding of the significance of architecture in general has been for quite some time extensively influenced by the works of such hermeneutical-phenomenological philosophers as Martin Heidegger, Maurice Merleau-Ponty, Gaston Bachelard, and Paul Ricoeur. These works in many ways point toward the post-Structuralist philosophies of Jacques Derrida and the so-called French deconstructionists, who seriously question the prevailing "logocentric" traditions of Western thought and metaphysics, as well as the social and ideological premises derived from these traditions. In addition, I have been influenced by the critical works of Hannah Arendt, Kenneth Frampton, Alberto Perez-Gomez, Hajime Yatsuka, and lately by the critical theories of the Frankfurt School, especially those of Jürgen Habermas.

Foreword

The Architecture of an Open-Port Japan

After investigating the history of political ideology in Japan, Professor Masao Maruyama has concluded that the ports of Japan were opened three times in the past. They were first opened during the sixteenth century when the Portuguese Christian missionaries arrived. This signified Japan's first contact with Western civilization; prior to the arrival of the missionaries, Japan's only international contact was with mainland China, with whom a relationship had existed for about ten centuries. Fifty years after this first opening to the West, however, Japan decided to close her ports, isolating herself again from the rest of the world. Because the missionaries had converted several thousand people to Christianity in a relatively short time, the shōguns began to fear that Western civilization would reduce their ability to control the people.

The ports were opened a second time during the Meiji Restoration, during the second half of the nineteenth century, commonly known as the period of modernization for Japan. All Japanese social systems, beginning with the constitution, were modified to adapt to those developed in Western Europe. Japanese culture was considerably affected by Westernization as well. Around 1930, however, Japan again turned her back on the West, becoming an almost completely closed country until World War II.

The next opening of ports came about with Japan's 1945 defeat in the war. The constitution of the Imperial System was again revised, this time into a democratic document. Once again Japan began to adopt the various facets of Western culture, now influenced primarily by the United States.

Thus, Japan's relationship with Western cultures seems to have occurred in waves of enthusiastic acceptance and complete rejection. Similar cycles of opening and closing the country can be observed as Japan imported the Chinese culture prior to the arrival of the Western missionaries.

Although the Japanese initially adopted foreign social, cultural, and political systems exactly as they were, be they Chinese or Western, as time went on they modified these systems to incorporate their own Japanese traditions. Professor Maruyama likens this phenomenon of subsequent Japanization that has followed every foreign importation to the *basso ostinato* in music. The ideology taken from China or the West forms the main melody, which is always accompanied by a repeated background strain, that of the Japanese mentality.

The development of architecture in Japan points to this same relationship between the main melody and *basso ostinato* in music. More precisely, the relationship in architecture is between the modern (primarily foreign) and the traditional (primarily Japanese). In fact, this issue can be recognized as a problem that almost every part of the world now faces. Yet the two tendencies could result in unique solutions if understood as not necessarily excluding but as mutually influencing each other. Not until the 1930s did the Japanese recognize the possibility of a successful mediation between the two, which they then declared as their architectural goal.

This mediation, with traditional Japanese architecture serving as the *basso ostinato*, nevertheless began as a clash of styles that seriously threatened modern architecture, which had become the main melody. Modern architecture, born in Western Europe, was being imported in the exact style in which it had been conceived abroad. This mirroring of Western architecture ran parallel with the social modernization process that followed the second opening of the ports. In reaction to this, a more traditional Japanese style of architecture was proposed in the early 1930s. The primarily boxlike modern structures built according to rationalized design principles were embellished with certain traditional formal and decorative elements and capped with Japanese Oriental-style roofs. This type of architecture became known as the Imperial style.

Proponents of the Imperial style advocated the expression of local or native architectural features, as opposed to the international features of modern architecture that were not identifiable with any particular country. This promotion of Japanese architectural traditions was just one facet of a growing nationalistic fervor that included strong support of the existing political system and other related ideological trends. Within a few years, Japan would form an alliance with Nazi Germany, demonstrating further her commitment to a strongly nationalistic regime. Unlike German architects, however, Japanese architects were not leaving the country for political or ideological reasons. The more conscientious architects were determined to find ways to mediate skillfully between traditional and modern architecture.

Architect Bruno Taut stimulated their search. Taut, who left Germany for Japan in 1933, praised the architecture of the Katsura Villa in Kyoto. He demonstrated how the space construction of traditional Japanese architecture was analogous to that of modern architecture and referred to Katsura as a classic that rivaled the Parthenon. Such opinion gave courage to the modernists in Japan. Many architects tried to develop an understanding and theoretical base that did not call for the wholesale elimination of modernism but rather looked for points of contact between traditional Japanese and modern architecture, thereby mediating between the two.

Sutemi Horiguchi was an early advocate of this ideology, but in his own designs he did not press for a hasty integration of the elements of the two architectures. Instead, he chose a solution that allowed his favorite *sukiya*-style architecture and early modern architecture to coexist. The man who proposed the clearest solution to this problem was Kenzo Tange, in the early 1940s. He skillfully integrated traditional architectural forms with modern architecture in a competition-winning proposal for a Japanese cultural hall in Bangkok. The spatial organization was based on the construction system of Japanese wooden architecture. With this project the foundations were laid to attract international attention to contemporary Japanese architecture after World War II and the consequent third opening of her ports.

Botond Bognar's book focuses on the developments of contemporary Japanese architecture after the 1960s. The various trends discussed in the book may appear to parallel the international developments of contemporary architecture. It is important to note, however, that when these similar trends began to develop in Japan in the 1960s, the cycle of unique mediation between modernism and traditionalism had just been completed. The sudden economic growth, urban expansion, and construction boom of the sixties continued for over ten years until the oil shock in the early 1970s, and within this period the main melody of the next cycle was being formed. New architectural technologies, mastered rather easily by the Japanese, were applied directly to novel architectural proposals. The need to shorten construction time in overcrowded Japanese cities encouraged this rapid development.

During this ten-year period, the shadows of things Japanese seemed to disappear—on the surface. If one observes the method of space composition, however, one would understand that this method did not break with the composition of traditional Japanese architecture at all. Modern architecture aimed at destroying stationary space within the traditions of Western architecture, which was conceived on the basis of enclosed, three-dimensional volumes. To accomplish this, a new model was created. This model, probably accidentally, turned out to be similar to that for traditional Japanese architecture, which had always pursued two-dimensional space composition. For this reason, Japanese architects, who unconsciously followed the Japanese model, began to understand modern architecture for the first time. Modern architecture, with a basis similar to the traditional Japanese model, was thus naturally reflected in the majority of contemporary Japanese architecture.

In the 1970s, advocates of critical trends incorporating solid geometry as their main feature distanced themselves from the formal aspects of Japanese space construction. A preference for abstract geometry, the enclosure of space with walls that did not use a post-and-beam structure, the breaking down of architectural form into a more conceptualized composition, and many other radical intentions began to appear. But again significant Japanese themes—the increased sense of materials, the emphasis on shadows, the absence of colors, and the reintroduction of silent spaces as voids—surfaced as well. Furthermore, since the beginning of the 1980s, several of these *Japanesque* patterns of traditional place-making have been consciously advocated.

Thus, while contemporary Japanese architecture appeared to pursue a roughly common course with the modern architecture of Western Europe after the 1960s, the undercurrent of feelings, serving as *basso ostinato*, in Japanese works has been different, suggesting that things Japanese, although with a changing emphasis, have come to life again.

Contemporary Japanese architects always distinguish between a main melody and *basso ostinato* and consider their own position accordingly. If one theme could summarize their common interests with regard to contemporary architecture, the concern for a conscious and purposeful discussion of the relationship between these two aspects of their architecture would almost be sufficient.

Contemporary Japanese architecture implicitly or explicitly reveals a considerable reliance on local traditions that have been critically reevaluated but retained nevertheless. That this basis is visible to a lesser—almost undetectable—degree in some structures can be attributed to Japan's defeat in the war and the consequent third opening of Japan's ports. These events again turned the tide against things Japanese; incorporating traditional concepts into Japanese architecture was viewed as rightist and regressive, and there was a conscious tendency to eliminate these forms. Whether recognizable Japanese concepts appear or do not appear, however, wiping them away is merely impossible. This should be kept in mind while reading this book, to understand the architectural trends discussed.

Strangely enough, in Japan the few books that have been written on contemporary Japanese architecture do not examine the overall picture. Since Japanese critics and historians are deluged with an overwhelming number of facts right before their eyes, they seem to find it difficult to distance themselves from these facts—a case of once again not seeing the forest for the trees. Botond Bognar's study of contemporary Japanese architecture clearly analyzes the conditions after the third opening of Japan's ports, with the advantage of looking at them from the outside. Perhaps we can say that he is the very first author who is able to view the entire spectrum of contemporary Japanese architecture over the past forty years. I think that he has, in each of his assessments, hit the mark with regard to the intentions and achievements of the many colorful architects discussed. I would like to emphasize again that these achievements stem from the recurring mediation between modernization and tradition in Japan. This is the one and only way to understand, without exoticism and mystification, contemporary architecture in a peculiar but great country, Japan.

ARATA ISOZAKI

Introduction

In recent years Japanese architecture has begun to assume an increasingly significant role in the development of contemporary architecture in general. This is no doubt due to the fact that, although Japanese modernization commenced little more than a century ago, the nation has been able to raise its industrial and economic production to levels comparable to those of the most highly developed capitalist and socialist countries. As a result of this "Japanese miracle," Japanese development has, in many respects, surpassed that of many other countries. Moreover, this tendency seems to continue at an astonishing pace despite the overall consequences of the energy crisis of 1974, so that Japan, with its extraordinary capacity to adapt to changing conditions, is without doubt the most future-oriented society in the world today.

The dialogue between East and West in Japan started in 1868 after some 230 years of isolation.[1] Until then, the Western world and Japan knew very little about each other, and even after the opening the dialogue was subject to an unequal exchange of information. Despite the hardly more than one hundred years of modernization, Japan today knows more about Western culture and technology than vice versa, and this imbalance clearly extends to the field of architecture. Other than a working knowledge of Japanese architectural

Japanese names in this book are written according to the generally accepted English rule: family name follows the given name. If, however, the person lived before the Meiji Restoration (1868), the name is given in the still-customary Japanese way: family name followed by given name.

history, we know little about Japan's complex social and cultural background. This makes it difficult for us to understand fully the present architectural evolution, which is to a large degree derived from tradition.[2]

Modern architecture and traditional Japanese architecture display certain similarities in form, functional flexibility, and in methods of construction. Modern architects have long since taken note of this fact, but beyond the external, formal, and thus largely superficial affinity, the spiritual or symbolic content of Japanese "space," the multivalent character of traditional Japanese architecture, and its concept of *genius loci* have been remarked on by only a few and even then little understood. In other words, the enthusiasm of the West for things Japanese was never impelled, to cite Francastel, by the desire to attain the state of mind that inspired these works in the first place. The Japanese idea of Japanese architecture has thus remained foreign to us; the scheme we have employed to grasp the significance of the architecture has nothing to do with the Japanese mentality.[3] The Japanese mental set manifests important characteristics that still affect the relative development of Japanese and Western architectural cultures. The manifest differences in approach become more and more evident the further they are traced back in time; so the idea that any significant resemblance between traditional Japanese and modern Western architectures exists has to be categorically rejected.

During its long history, Japanese culture has been shaped extensively by several foreign cultures. Among them the ancient Chinese and the modern Western are by far the most significant; both have had a strong impact on the character of Japan, including its art and architecture. Despite these strong influences, however, Japan did not become converted into a province of China or much later into a cultural satellite of Europe or America, as many are inclined to believe. The confrontation between new and old has never appeared to the

Japanese as a one-sided choice between "either-or" but rather as a feasible compromise between "both-and." Indeed, as Arata Isozaki has noted, in Japan "nothing really goes away."[4] New elements of knowledge, ideas, or concepts have always found their ways and places within the old patterns; that is to say, they have served as inspiration and have been assimilated by the previous value systems. In this way the Japanese spiritual heritage has survived and is alive and operative today, even if this is not always evident to superficial Western eyes and to the numerous short-term visitors who pass through the country on the conveyor belt of a package tour. The surface conceals something else, or as the Japanese themselves say—in the words of George Mikes, who quoted them—"the *outward* acceptance of Western customs helps perhaps to preserve our *internal* values. . . . Today westernization is our only chance of remaining Japanese (italics in original).[5]

With the intensity and vitality of its pervading traditions, Japan remains without doubt second to none among the industrialized nations. This paradox—a prompt eagerness to assimilate the new combined with a strong adherence to traditions—has various and complex sources. Japan is an island country, a geographical fact that has always played an important role in its life and development. The surrounding ocean is a natural boundary, one that in the past, during the epoch of exploration by small and primitive ships, formed the prime barrier to communication. As a result, the flow of information between Japan and other continental countries was hardly spontaneous. For the same reason, Japan was never subject to foreign invasion; until the latter half of the last century it had never been at war with other nations.[6]

This geographical isolation allowed Japan the possibility for a conscious, selective, and controlled relationship with other cultures, a relationship never imposed on her by force. The country was closed to foreigners in 1639 and remained, in effect, iso-lated from the rest of the world for as long as the military succession of the Tokugawa Shogunate considered this politically beneficial: throughout the Edo Period, from 1603 to 1868. Over two and a half centuries of seclusion not only deepened the unique Japanese way of thinking and feeling, thereby reinforcing the integrity of its culture, but also preserved these traditions undisturbed until the middle of the nineteenth century.

With the opening of Japan's gates to the world, a totally new civilization was imported into the nation; one that started to change the character of its architecture as well. The Japanese, eager to learn everything, applied and eventually mastered the new construction methods and techniques. At first, they imitated the foreign styles that accompanied the importation of methods and techniques. Then, consciously or unconsciously they supplemented them step by step with their own artistic concepts and way of life—that is to say, with their traditions.

Although the close encounter with Western civilization and the subsequent process of assimilation gave rise to certain problems, conflicts, and contradictions over the years, the rebuilding of Japan after the Second World War saw the emergence by about the early 1950s, of an "independent," self-reliant group of architects who started to evolve a recognizably modern Japanese architecture that soon became known as the "new Japan style."[7]

The end of the war concluded one of the most complex and most difficult periods in the architecture of contemporary Japan. The country emerged with a "new" and democratic society that now freely embraced the concepts and goals of international modernism. Yet the developing self-consciousness of the new society demanded more than just an international architecture. It sought symbols of identity as well. Therefore, after a brief period of an almost unanimous acceptance and devotion to a characteristically nonsymbolic functional modern architecture, the Japanese began to show a positive attitude toward their own tradition. Kenzo Tange and many of his contemporaries "tried to achieve a dialectical synthesis between the Japanese tradition and the 'tradition of the new.' "[8] Thus much of the "new Japan style" was conceived in reinterpreted traditional forms and in Le Corbusier's reinforced concrete architecture of *beton brut.*

Interestingly enough, this somewhat critical stance toward modern architecture was bolstered by the unprecedented industrial and economic boom of the 1960s, an industrialization that had always constituted the very basis of modernism. The numerous large-scale and utopian proposals of the Metabolists thus depended on a strong belief in a limitless technology readily available in Japan by that time. The technologically oriented and too often mechanistic architecture and urbanism, however, eventually proved to be inadequate to establish a valid public realm. The 1970 Osaka World Expo, the grandiose showcase of Japan's miraculous economic progress and that of the Metabolist movement linked to it, turned out to be the closing gesture of Metabolism itself, signaling also the final bankruptcy of the positivist ideology of modernism in Japan.

The decline of modernist ideology ran parallel with the evolution of postindustrial mass societies, which, since the 1970s, has been further accelerated by the still-continuing worldwide energy crisis. The resulting tendency toward mass consumption—and so a demand for increased information—provided the impetus for the unchecked proliferation in various regions of the world of populist mass cultures, a sentimental vernacular and nostalgic historicism in architecture. In opposition to these tendencies to mediocrity, however, a new architectural awareness is on the rise; in Japan, it was first referred to as Post-Metabolism, and lately as "A New Wave of Japanese Architecture."[9] In its various individual expressions the new awareness rejects not only the technological phantasmagoria of Metabolism and by extension the reductive rationale of a dogmatic and universal modernism, but also the equally rootless and value-free norms of consumerist populism. Often taking a critical attitude toward both of them, these still-developing intentions aim at redefining and recreating a profound sense of place with and within architecture. This sense, previously neglected for the most part, is correctly assumed to be rooted in the particular cultural heritage, the qualities of a specific locality, and the urban conditions of Japan.

Accordingly, history is not regarded as something disconnected from the present and the future, nor is it necessary or possible *pro forma* to return to it, though this often was and still is attempted. In Kazuo Shinohara's words, "tradition can be the starting point for creativity, but it must not be the point to which it returns."[10] In this sense, the generation of the New Wave is in the self-conscious process of retaining or reestablishing what may be called a subtle link with the past; at the same time it continues to draw from Japan's present conditions and also from sources outside of its own cultural sphere a pattern that has always characterized the essence, dialectics, and vigor of Japanese culture. After the bankruptcy of Modernism, these new directions—what Kenneth Frampton has termed Critical Regionalism—"recognize that no living tradition remains available to modern man other than the subtle procedures of synthetic contradiction."[11]

The renewed recognition of this traditional possibility suggests that Japanese architecture now has enough qualities and potential to exert a positive influence on the Western world, and that it is now time for the West to assimilate the Japanese example and change its attitude from the one Aldo van Eyck characterized when he wrote " 'Western civilization' habitually identifies itself with civilization as such on the pontifical assumption that what is not like it, is a deviation, less 'advanced,' 'primitive' or at best, exotically interesting—at a safe distance."[12]

It remains to be seen whether the West, in order to find its own alternative to the current crisis, can or is willing to accept the challenge of Japanese sensitivity and flexibility. Whatever the outcome, the Japanese are certainly going to play an important role in shaping the character of architecture during the years to come.

NOTES

1. With the exception of a small commercial outpost on Dejima Island in Nagasaki harbor, open to a handful of Chinese, Korean, and Dutch traders, Japan was closed to the outside world from 1639 until 1853. The arrival of Commodore Perry with his fleet in that year forced Japan to reopen her gates and eventually to resume relations with the West.

2. When it comes to information, Japan clearly imports much more than it exports. According to recent statistics, Japan publishes about twelve times more material about Western countries than these countries about Japan. (Quoted in Minoru Takeyama, "Japan's Architectural Schizophrenia," *San Francisco Bay Architects' Review*, No. 25 [Summer 1982], p. 11).

3. Francastel is quoted by André Corboz in his introductory essay, "Modern Architecture and Japanese Tradition," in Tomoya Masuda, *Living Architecture: Japanese* (New York: Grosset & Dunlap, 1970), p. 5.

4. Arata Isozaki, as quoted by Kenneth Frampton in the keynote address to the ACSA annual national conference, Vancouver, B.C., Canada; March 17, 1985.

5. George Mikes, *The Land of the Rising Yen* (Middlesex, England: Penguin Books, 1970), p. 34.

6. The only exception was an attempt by the Mongolian armada to attack the southern part of Japan during the Kamakura period (1185–1333) in 1281. However, the Mongolian fleet while crossing the sea was wrecked by a sudden hurricane. This historical event is the origin of the word *kamikaze* ("divine wind").

7. Robin Boyd, *New Directions in Japanese Architecture* (New York: Braziller, 1968), pp. 31, 34.

8. Hajime Yatsuka, "Architecture in the Urban Desert: A Critical Introduction to Japanese Architecture After Modernism," *Oppositions*, No. 23 (Winter 1981), p. 3.

9. The term "Post-Metabolism" was coined by the editors Kazuhiro Ishii and Hiroyuki Suzuki, as the title of a special issue of *The Japan Architect* (October-November 1977), p. 9. "A New Wave of Japanese Architecture" appeared as the title of an exhibition that toured the United States at the end of 1978 and early in 1979. A catalog was published by the Institute for Architecture and Urban Studies, New York, 1978.

10. Kazuo Shinohara, "A Theory of Residential Architecture," *The Japan Architect* (April 1964); also in "The Savage Machine as an Exercise," *The Japan Architect* (March 1979), p. 46.

11. Kenneth Frampton, "Prospects for a Critical Regionalism," *Perspecta: The Yale Architectural Journal* 20 (1983), p. 147. The term "critical regionalism," however, was first coined by Alex Tzonis and Liliane Lefaivre in "The Grid and the Pathway: An Introduction to the Work of Dimitris and Susana Antonakakis," in *Architecture in Greece* 15 (1981), p. 178. It is meant to distinguish this regionalism from a sentimental regionalism with which it is often mistakenly associated.

12. Aldo van Eyck, "The Interior of Time," in C. Jencks and G. Baird, eds., *Meaning in Architecture* (New York: Braziller, 1970), p. 71.

1. First Impressions

Despite its steady increase, the curiosity of the West about things Japanese is seldom accompanied by an interest in the authentic Japanese environment in which these things have been conceived and without which they cannot be correctly understood. Thus our knowledge of Japan is necessarily fragmented and out of context, still relegating this Oriental culture to the realm of the exotic. "Deprived of its original ground, the exotic item is only permitted a single function, that of titillation," which can successfully prevent the average Westerner and visitor to Japan from developing a realistic picture about the Japanese world.[1] The media and various tourist organizations more often than not exploit and further reinforce this tendency by images carefully created to cater to tourists. As Chris Faw-cett observed, "people coming . . . from the West usually have such a strong preconception of what they are in for, during the customarily short period of their stay, that preconception is not modified in any way, but becomes also their ultimate perception."[2]

To obtain a genuine picture, a more profound understanding of Japan, is by no means an easy task for anyone, not even for those more determined to do so who also have the opportunity to stay longer in the country. One of the most difficult things for a Westerner to cope with in Japan is the actual reality of the physical environment. This is made all the more true since the first encounter with Japan invariably takes place in the city, and frequently the encounter does not go beyond the limits of such metropolitan areas as Tokyo, Osaka, and the like. Against all expectations, the quality and extent of the urban scape are so overwhelming that it is practically impossible to experience aspects traditionally associated with Japan without referring to the "covering veil" of the contemporary city.

Tokyo is exemplary of Japanese cities and towns where, for the foreigner at least, everything is surprising, strange, and confusing. Thus the initial image that strikes the visitor is one of an apparent chaos and disorder (1). The density and infinite variety of sights, forms, colors, and materials, in addition to the constant crowd of vehicles and

Illustrations are numbered sequentially throughout the book. They are designated by figures in parentheses.

17

1. Shibuya Station Square in Tokyo. The Japanese urban space arouses feelings of chaos and apparent disorder in the Westerner.

people, add up to turbulent visual and sensory overload. On the other hand, contrasting with the few high-rise buildings, the flood of tiny and "shabby" wooden or concrete structures still gives the impression of Tokyo as the world's largest village instead of a metropolis.

Beyond the few main roads or avenues, the crowded rows of small buildings generate an irregular network of incredibly narrow streets without sidewalks, some impassable even to the small Japanese cars. These streets are further jammed by a mass of electric poles, transformers, and cables crisscrossing overhead, sometimes to the extent that the sky as well as most buildings are rendered invisible, thereby turning the whole urban scene into a visually and physically impenetrable labyrinth (2). In this jungle there are no clear differentiations, no exact boundaries, and no sense of a focal center. Such incomprehensibility is augmented by a thick forest of billboards, neon signs, supergraphics, posters, and other advertisements—complemented by the countless traffic lights—that cover practically the entire city. Such pageantry is all the more apparent in the evening when everything is lit, when the skin of the city pulsates with flashing forms, colors, and inscriptions; a stupefying "electrographic city" compared to which the lights of Las Vegas look like poorly designed, pale imitations (3).[3]

Above all, the most extraordinary feature for the Western eye is the radical and compact coexistence, a mixture of perfectly organized and totally disordered elements of the supermodern with the old, of the streamlined with the shabby, the beautiful with the ugly, the big with the small. Without actually seeing and experiencing it, this thick, heterogeneous mass is beyond imagination (4). Only superlatives can appropriately describe the ever-present contradictions. Despite its size, Tokyo has one of the most convenient public transportation systems in the world, consisting of fast trains and subways. At the same time its surface traffic is very congested and the city very polluted;

yet, paradoxically enough, it boasts the cleanest households of any megalopolis. The radically eclectic cityscape is in direct contrast with the well-ordered, strictly protected, rational, and more or less spacious appearance of the existing cities in Europe and the United States.

Apart from the cramped manmade environment, one is always confronted by the perpetual throngs of people, for Japan is an overcrowded country where more than 110 million people live in a territory not much larger than the state of California.[4] In addition, the entire elongated island chain is covered by high mountains, volcanoes, and lakes, leaving only about 20 percent of the total area available for human settlements, agriculture, and industry. Therefore, the traveler riding from Tokyo to Osaka or farther west on the fabulous Hikari of the Shinkansen line—the fastest superexpress train in the world—witnesses a continuous network of unparalleled urbanization. During the three-hour (350-mile) ride—the Japanese prefer to express distances in terms of time—the train hardly ever travels outside the built-up areas, thereby making it difficult to know when one has left Tokyo or reached Osaka. For one's orientation the station names are the only sure markers. This area, stretching along the Inland Sea from Tokyo down to Fukuoka in Kyushu, may consequently with justice be called a megalopolis. It is characteristic of this megalopolis that Yokohama, Nagoya, Osaka, Hiroshima, and Fukuoka do not differ much in character from Tokyo. They all feature a similarly disordered cityscape, an equally crowded, flat, horizontal setting with the same high density of population.

Since the average Japanese home is extremely small, it is hardly a place to entertain guests or meet others. Hence social life takes place elsewhere: in pubs, bars, coffeeshops, small restaurants, or just on the street. The quiet residential areas and the numerous compounds that house traditional buildings such as temples, shrines, and the like are

2.

2. Typical streetscape in Shinjuku, Tokyo. Streets are narrow and crisscrossed by electric wires, sometimes beyond number, even in the centers of the cities.

3. The Dotombori district of Osaka by night. With dusk falling, Tokyo, Osaka, and the rest undergo a metamorphosis and turn into pulsating electrographic cities enveloped almost completely in neon.

4. Cityscape in Tokyo. Cities display the most varied contradictions; old and new, big and small, busy and quiet, attractive and ugly are juxtaposed in an extremely cramped setting and an *ad hoc* fashion.

constantly interwoven by sinuous and labyrinthine commercial and amusement areas. Some of these, like the famous Ginza or Shinjuku, Shibuya, Roppongi, Akasaka in Tokyo or the Namba, Nipponbashi areas in Osaka, are in fact nothing less than "small" towns within the huge metropolises. Unlike similar areas in the West, these districts, sometimes reminiscent of Disneyland, serve as organic parts of everyday urban life. Nearly everything here suggests a world of fairy tales or fantasy lands, a jungle of extraordinary and fanciful images; restaurants, drink bars, sushi bars, bath houses, game and pachinko (Japanese pinball) parlors, boutiques, shops, cabarets, moviehouses, tea ceremony rooms, tiny love hotels and motels (some of which are dressed up as enchanted palaces or castles)—all these are mixed with the everyday commercial symbols of the Western world including Kentucky Fried Chicken, McDonald's, Dunkin' Donuts. This creates an urban environment that by virtue of the consistently heterogeneous quality of its elements becomes homogeneous and where every built urban element is destined to constitute its own context.

With nightfall, while being jostled, pulled, and tossed around, the pedestrian feels as if he or she has been transformed into a participant in a dreamlike play, complete with continuously changing visual and acoustical effects, all of which add up to an experience difficult to imagine. Michael Franklin Ross calls this phenomenon "movable . . . or instant city."[5] Mobility, changeability, or volatility is definitely another important feature of the Japanese townscape, leading to an impression that all the elements and components are only provisional. Here everything is relative; nothing is immutable.

Further proof of this lies in the fact that renovation or restoration of contemporary structures is not a general practice in Japan, even with the more prominent buildings, a fact clearly visible in some of the photographs presented in this book. The Japanese would rather change the entire skin or surface, as has been done with Takeyama's Niban-kan Building in Shinjuku, which has been covered over with a completely new pop-art design several times since its completion in 1970 (314).

But all these are still symptoms, the surface only, as revealed through the first and cursory glances at the Japanese environment. This environment at all events has a very special quality. According to the architect Charles Moore, Japan is a mirror wherein "each Western visitor sees something of himself."[6] Nevertheless, if the Westerner wants to understand Japan and the Japanese, he will have to look beyond the surface of the mirror into the cultural, social, and behavioral heritage.

NOTES

1. Chris Fawcett, *The New Japanese House* (New York: Harper & Row, 1980), p. 9.
2. Ibid., p. 26.
3. Michael Franklin Ross, "Futurism: Electrographic City," *Architecture and Urbanism* (June 1976), p. 18.
4. The total area of Japan, together with the numerous small islands, is about 370,000 square kilometers.
5. Michael Franklin Ross, *Beyond Metabolism: The New Japanese Architecture* (New York: McGraw-Hill, 1978), p. 192.
6. Charles Moore, "Impressions of Japanese Architecture," *The Japan Architect* (February 1978), p. 5.

2. Cultural Traditions

Traditionally Japanese culture evolved from and is deeply rooted in the intense, uniquely intimate relationship of the Japanese to nature, which itself reveals basic differences between Eastern and Western mentalities. The Westerner tends to have a superior-inferior relationship with nature, while the Oriental thinks of himself as a coordinate, equivalent to and identifying with nature. Modern Western culture, along with its predecessors, the ancient Egyptian, Greek, and Roman cultures, openly declares its intention of conquering nature. By contrast, the Oriental wants to live in harmony with it. In other words, the traditional Japanese attitude is characterized by a strong impulse to merge with, rather than to overcome, nature.

The Western mind, ultimately of Greek origin, is characterized by the achievements of rationalism leading to logic and scientific systematization, a clarity of thought reflected throughout the centuries even in Western art. Because of this predominantly analytical mode of thinking, life and the universe have been divided into several different spheres, compartmentalized with a separate name (*logos*) for each particular discipline. Dividing the world like this into sectors for the study of reality seems to have entailed a certain loss in the Western capacity for perceiving the complexity of life.

In contrast, Oriental cultures, including the Japanese, display a synthetic mode of thinking and approach the phenomena of the universe in their mutable totality and multiplicity. This complex view is represented by an Oriental sensibility that emphasizes not the absolute nature of God and the eternal conflict between the universe and victorious Man, but on the relative character of all existence, bringing man into unity with the world in which he lives.

Shintoism, Buddhism

Japanese cultural patterns are largely determined by two major elements: Shintoism and Buddhism. Shintoism dates back to prehistoric times, while Buddhism was not introduced into the country until the sixth century A.D. Shinto, meaning precisely the "way of gods" or "divine way," is not a religion in the strict sense of the term. Rather, it is a form of Oriental animism and Japanese mythology. Shintoists believe that spirits dwell in practically every phenomenon of nature, including such living and nonliving things as the sun, stars, mountains, trees, stones, wind, and echo, as well as in a particular locality.

This divine spiritual essence recognized in everything is indicated by the Japanese word *kami*.[1] Each "god" is personalized, but not in an anthropomorphic way as in Greek mythology; this perhaps explains why Shinto practically has not contributed to the visual or fine arts. There are myriads of *kami*, which makes Shintoism a pantheistic and polytheistic religion from a Western point of view. Thus, the innumerable shrines that dot the landscape all enshrine a different deity, each a more or less specialist *kami* to whom the Japanese pay homage for particular protections and blessings, often in a large variety of rituals, ceremonies, and festivals (*matsuri*).

As Jean Herbert noted, "the attitude of the shintoist to his religion is emphatically nonintellectual."[2] There is hardly any metaphysics, and there is no clear distinction between good and evil deities. Nor is there a distinction between what we call material and spiritual. As a religion of practicality, original Shintoism is common sense or, as Takeo Nakajima put it, it is "a feeling . . . of values found in daily life, rooted in Japan's climate and natural conditions. It is a practical view of the world, without any quality of absolutism, built around the . . . ideas of respect for nature and natural features, and the belief in a divine response to prayer in this world."[3] It also appeals to an inborn sense of duty and responsibility, a spontaneous love on the part of man for his surroundings that is closely akin to his family relationships—and also it appeals, as Herbert pointed out, "to a large extent, to an aesthetic sensibility."[4] Thus, it might well be said that Shinto

is the worship of nature and its varied beauty (5). Accordingly, it is an insistence "on the maintenance and furthering of harmony between all men, nature and the god heads, respectful consideration for everything that exists, a cult of ancestors, a feeling of security . . . and assurance in a world all of one's own kin, and also a spontaneous behavior fitting to a society in which the individual was only a link in the unending chains of time and space."[5] Therefore, Shinto, like many other Oriental religions, does not have creed, dogma, or a code of ethics.

The word *kami* literally means "above," "higher," "superior," or the top of the hierarchy, and by no means "transcendental." Each family, smaller or larger communities, and, further, the whole of Japan has its appointed *kami* as a protector or an ultimate ancestor. This shows that in Shinto there is no clear distinction between man and God. Man is not the creation of the gods but, in a sense, the direct biological descendant of them. When a Japanese dies, he is promoted up the ladder of hierarchy by becoming a member of the larger familial *kami*. It is in this respect that the Emperor of Japan, representing the whole nation, has the highest living position, since the Imperial Family is believed to have its divine origins in Amaterasu, the Sun Goddess of Japan.[6]

The first written record of Shinto mythology, the *Kojiki* ("Records of Ancient Matters") of A.D. 712, describes the history of Japan and the Imperial Family's divine origins.[7] Thus, even if on a mythical basis, it can be regarded as Japan's first history book. It, too, does not contain ethical teachings or norms, neither does it offer directions for good behavior or avoidance of sin. Important features of Shintoism are, however, clearly perceived in it. First, human beings are naturally good and should follow their natural impulses; second, the cult of worship of ancestral spirits and the need for respect of one's ancient forebears are spelled out.

Observance of the hierarchy as later inspired

5. Landscape north of Kyoto, with the garden of the Shugakuin Imperial Villa (1659). The Japanese landscape is abundant in natural beauty that impresses one with its gentleness and human scale.

6. The image of Amida Buddha by sculptor Jocho in the Byodo-in Temple, Uji City near Kyoto (gilded wood, ten feet high; 1053). The introduction of Buddhism from China in the sixth century produced radical changes in just about every aspect of Japanese life and culture.

by Confucianism resulted in a highly structured and complex social system; beyond the relation to the gods, relations between people of different position or, as the Japanese say, "proper station," was also determined. To quote Ruth Benedict, "the Japanese, more than any sovereign nation, have been conditioned to a world where the smallest details of conduct are mapped and status is assigned."[8] Yet it is interesting to note that, while the positions and classes in this hierarchy were clearly set, men taking these positions were not strictly bound to them. They could often change their status and climb up the ladder—a significant difference between this and the Hindu caste system. Evidently, higher positions have more privileges, but "those who exercise these privileges act as trustees rather than as arbitrary autocrats."[9] In other words, in Japan Confucianism works for ethics, while Shintoism and Buddhism for religion.

The introduction of Chinese culture during the Asuka Period (A.D. 552–710) brought about a significant change in Japan. At that time China already had a well-organized state machinery, to say nothing of a highly developed artistic and religious culture constituting a virtually infinite source from which Japan was able to profit for several hundred years. For her leading role in influencing the cultures of the Far East, China could well be compared to the ancient Greek culture that set the direction and standard for intellectual life in Europe and, later, for that of the whole Western world. The vehicle for the transmission of Chinese culture was Buddhism, imbued with the philosophies of Taoism, Universalism, and Confucianism. Buddhism became the fundamental element of transformation in Japanese culture, starting from the sixth century A.D.

The origin of Buddhism dates back much earlier than Christianity. Its founder, the first Buddha, was born in India in the middle of the sixth century B.C. Gautama Siddhartha (or Shakyamuni) was the first man to reach that state of enlightenment called Buddhahood (6). After his death, Gautama's teachings quickly spread outside India across Southeast and East Asia. Buddhism arrived in China by way of the famed silk route in the first century A.D. and was to dominate the country shortly thereafter. Then, from China through the Korean peninsula, Buddhism found its way to Japan. Spreading throughout the continent, Buddhism gradually altered its character as new sects developed en route. The state in which it finally arrived in Japan was simpler and clearer than its original form; it was the so-called northern, or Mahayana, Buddhism.[10] Even so, the Japanese—as with everything else—modified it further, and shaped it according to their national character and mentality.

The basis of Buddhism, in contrast to Christianity, is enlightenment achieved through learning and cognition, not faith. The way to salvation is found through eschewing rituals and, further, even the world itself. The ultimate goal is not eternal life, but nirvana, the domain of nothingness, or the Great Void. It is a state of absence in which the complete cessation of psychic complexes—desire, hatred, attachment—is reached, and in which all feelings, passions, conceptions, all endeavors, and finally the whole of consciousness come to an end; or, as Dale Saunders writes, "it is a state of a person reposing on himself, withdrawn from the stress and movement of phenomena."[11] Nirvana is negative existence.

According to Buddhist teachings, existence is eternal suffering. In order to eliminate suffering, existence or, better, the chain of existence eventually has to be suppressed. Self is illusory; without *absolute* existence; everything is only the temporary coexistence of its composing elements and subject, therefore, to decomposition. In other words, everything in this world goes through a succession of various forms of existence, in which each new form of existence, good or bad, is kindled by the previous one while perpetuating itself in the same manner—like the flame that keeps burning regardless of changes in fuel. This chain of cause and effect is therefore a self-maintaining perpetual process, the cycle of which can be broken only through the exercise of knowledge or by disciplining the self in deep meditation. While turning the human senses inward, meditation aims at the final equilibrium or tranquility that is nirvana, the only permanent state toward which Buddhist conduct leads.

"The Great Void, being a metaphysical concept, is a uniform quiescence in which all change and transformation is stilled."[12] Void thus is not a nothingness conceived in negative terms; it is not a nihilistic concept. Neither affirmation nor negation, it is as well both the affirmation and negation of things; in it, being and nonbeing are the same. In this sense, meditation is the state of consciousness in which the ultimate and "essential oneness of all things, of Self with the universe, achieves realization."[13] This way "Buddha *replaced* the soul by the theory of a mind-continuum, by a series of psychical states rigorously conditioned as to their nature by the casual law governing them."[14] Thus Buddhism came to regard human emotions, feelings, imaginings, perceptions, and intuitions as equal constituents of the existing reality and the world. By teaching the sameness of the essences of nature, man, and Buddha, Buddhism transcended a purely intellectual relationship among them.

Regarding the universe as a never ending flow of phenomena, as a perpetual but cyclical motion with a possible end in nirvana, Buddhism contains two doctrines important to us. The first states that everything that exists is constantly changing, constantly in transition. The second holds that, in the cycle of continuous rebirth, there is always a third state, an intermediate existence between two different identities or states. It is simultaneously both the old and new forms of existence and yet neither. This third state shows that the old and the new are interchangeable, so that the concept of permanency has no significance, just as the idea of perfection loses its absolute character, since there can always be something new that is more "perfect."

In this sense Buddhism became one of the pioneers of relativity and, as Zen Buddhism, perhaps even of phenomenology. For related reasons, Buddhism recognizes and accepts any kind of culture, civilization, and even religion as a meaningful step toward a more "perfect" one. What we encounter in Buddhism is one of the sources of the unique multivalent character of the Japanese culture. Indeed, the coexistence of Buddhism and Shintoism is an example of Buddhist-inspired multivalence.

There is no doubt that Buddhism represented a much more sophisticated and developed metaphysical and philosophical system than Shintoism. Accordingly, educated Japanese aristocrats not only initiated and promoted Buddhism, but they were also the first to practice it.[15] The Japanese commoner could grasp only the more superficial ideas, mainly those regarding change and the transitoriness of everything that exists.

Shintoism did not fade away with the emergence of Buddhism, however. It was retained and practiced, so that the two developed simultaneously without any real conflict between them.[16] The initial peaceful coexistence then turned into a gradual process of mutual influence to the extent that each adapted several elements from the other. Shinto deities were regarded as manifestations of Buddha, while Buddha became one of the Shinto gods. The emphasis in Buddhist teachings shifted to "man in the phenomenal world in search of a transcendental realm. Thus in Japan, Buddhism too became a religion that affirmed the phenomenal world," while Japanese culture in general came to identify "absoluteness" with the real phenomena of mundane human existence.[17] Because of this religious parallelism—that is, the coexistence of Shintoism and Buddhism—the Japanese follow both at the same time without the slightest hesitation.[18]

Western culture and civilization and Christianity were introduced into Japan in the nineteenth century in much the same way as Chinese culture and Buddhism had been introduced 1,400 years before.[19] Going beyond mere tolerance, Japan accepted many of the foreign ideas and assimilated them willingly. China had never in her history wanted to force her civilization and culture on other peoples or nations. Thus Japan remained free to select from Chinese and other foreign cultures exactly those features that corresponded to the innate mentality of the society, assimilating some while rejecting others. Because Japan cultivated this attitude of critical choice, Japanese culture has always been able to retain its own unique and exclusive characteristics, which at the same time became inclusive of the imported and synthesized foreign elements as well.

Art and Aesthetics

"In Japan," writes Jack Seward, "feelings outrank logic. Scorning reason and satisfying emotion, the Japanese cherish sensitivity more than intelligence. They prefer to deal with things intuitively rather than rationally."[20] Therefore they can be approached and understood best in a related manner, through their art or, better yet, through the spirit of their art. As an extension of nature herself, Japanese art seeks a perpetually renewed identity with nature. The Japanese react to any change in nature—topographical, climatical, seasonal, and so on—very sensitively; the response to nature's minor and major manifestations is their art.

Visitors to the country are usually astonished to find how intensively a sense of aesthetics links the Japanese to practically everything in their lives. It seems that the cult of beauty and art as forms of knowledge ranks above religion. Nearly everyone in the society, from early childhood through late adulthood, is absorbed by the same enthusiasm for artistic and aesthetic values. Again, this results in an interesting duality; Japanese art is simultaneously heterogeneous and homogeneous—heterogeneous as an outcome of the influence of various cultures, but homogeneous in that its spirit pervades the whole society. Indeed, the Japanese are perhaps the most homogeneous people and culture in the world.

When the Japanese artist creates, he seeks to harmonize with nature and natural materials rather than simply to command them. The result of his art is intended to be the revelation of natural intentions and spirit instead of the display of his own personal struggle. His relationship with the material is reciprocal; he learns from it just as he inscribes and shapes it with the movements of his hands and the sensitive irregularities of these movements. However, it is this very sensitivity that makes his works poetic and natural.

As a result of this naturalness, there is a point where beauty and ugliness merge. We cannot speak about ugliness when it comes to nature; therefore beauty cannot be spoken of either. Not subject to evaluation, nature itself stands as the criterion for judgment. Therefore, a Japanese approaching art tries to see how far and how deeply the artist has interpreted the inner character or order of nature. Between beauty and ugliness, where the two overlap in a state of being that is at once different from and identical with both, the aesthetics of nature is born. This perception, rooted in Shintoist and Buddhist teleology, is instinctively nondichotomous and so also nondialectical, as opposed to the strict dualism of Plato and Aristotle.

Moreover, to the Japanese, nature is never separate from human perception, insofar as perception always affects the world observed. The essence of nature is colored by human involvement, even if this involvement stems only from memory and imagination. It might even be said that nature as such comes into being through human artistic abilities—abilities to feel, ponder, discuss, write about, and interact in various other ways with nature.

These actions are always, necessarily, interpretive. Yet they are not mere participation of man with nature. There is no dichotomy between man and nature; rather, they mutually imply each other. We are constituted by nature as much as it is constituted by us. There is no "pure" nature—or pure anything, for that matter—for the Japanese. The dualism of identity and difference between man and nature is dissolved; they are both identical and different at the same time.

This first characteristic of Japanese art—its instinctive, natural nondialectic, unfettered by the logic of a true-false dichotomy—is enhanced by another characteristic: the importance of time in Japanese aesthetics. For the Japanese, "art is the child of time." While time plays a dynamic role in the West as well, Western art aims at eternity, the artist attempting to grasp perceived moments as perfect and consummate. The Japanese artist, in contrast, attempts to depict and express the eternally flowing and relative character of time, as well as the circumstantial significance of a temporary situation. In Tomoya Masuda's words, he is interested in "delicate earthly changes rather than in heavenly permanency."[21] Perhaps the Japanese are the only people who see beauty and harmony in aging, in transition, or in impermanence and appreciate these aesthetically.

The process of change attracts them more, and they find it more beautiful than perfection. Their concepts of beauty and harmony tend to be dynamic rather than static.[22] This could explain why the Japanese avoid symmetry in just about every aspect of life. Instead, they strive for asymmetry; against the singularity of symmetry, asymmetry provides an endless array of variations that are always in harmony with time. For similar reasons, odd numbers dominate in many of their arts, and in everyday things as well. Thus there is no symmetry or centricity in the typical mature Japanese artist's work, or when there is it occurs partially, being consistently overruled by the asymmetry of the whole com-

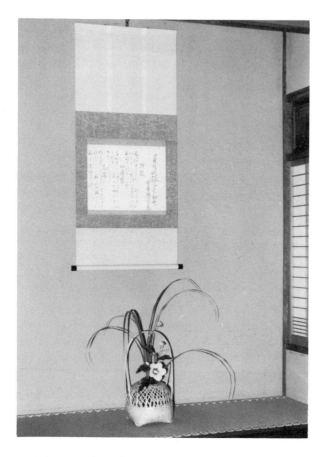

7. Ikebana and scroll in the decorative alcove, the *tokonoma*.

8. *Bugaku*, the dance of aristocrats in the Imperial court during the Heian period (794–1185).

position. The composition is always a momentary equilibrium in a complex of relationships.

A deeper investigation of Japanese art and aesthetics would reveal other distinctive features, particularly as viewed in contrast with their Western counterparts. Monumentality is largely missing from Japanese art and architecture. Once again the explanation is found in how the Japanese relate themselves to nature. Since their approach does not assert man's superiority over the universe or aim at the triumph of eternity over time, they have never created anything supernatural, nor for that matter do they expect anything to be everlasting. Their art above all is the art of the petites; or, as Alfred East puts it: "Japanese art is great in small things, but small in great things."[23] It is for this very reason that they are able to reach such depths in existence.

In reaching for this depth through "little things," the Japanese have been able to create an extremely refined and subtle system of codes, signs, and symbols almost completely unknown to Westerners. One of the most beautiful and delicate examples of this is the flower arrangement, or *ikebana,* that evolves as a creation of "time" and also in the spirit of "here and now."[24] The tea ceremony (*chanoyu*), woodblock printing, genre pictures (*ukiyoe*), scroll painting (*emakimono, kakemono*), monochrome ink painting (*sumie*), the ancient forms of music and dance practiced by the aristocrats (*gagaku* and *bugaku*), the *Noh* drama, the *Bunraku* puppet theater—these and other typical arts may all be cited here as representatives of the Japanese symbolic way of thinking, according to which anything fully pronounced impoverishes reality by freezing the process of change and abridging the multiformity or variety of perceived phenomena (7, 8). The Japanese believe—and this might well be the substance of their art and aesthetic symbolism—that the implicit can express more than the explicit. Therefore they suggest, rather than directly declare or assert, while their art implies but does not confirm. Thus, in the Japanese traditions of aesthetics and symbolism, less—if properly suggested—represents most certainly more.[25] "Less" here is not the reduction or elimination of symbolic intentions and content, but the condensation or compression of phenomena perceived and their gathered meanings. The same spirit characterizes Japanese behavior and manner of speech and can be sensed in the traditional *haiku* poems.[26]

The Japanese painter says that the spot left empty on the paper accumulates more meaning and has more to say than the area marked with the brush. This "emptiness," void, inner space, or *ma*—known from Buddhist philosophy—is therefore not empty at all. It is the "natural distance between two or more things existing in continuity" or "the natural pause or interval between two or more phenomena occurring continuously," like the sense of a moment in the passing of time.[27] By both separating and linking them together, *ma* becomes the common essence of all the parts, from which everything springs and to which everything is related. This would also explain why a Japanese is able to visualize, perceive, and eventually receive more from an artistic work than is actually depicted. The idea of void and simplicity was developed to its extreme by Zen Buddhist monks, many of whom, like Shuko (d. 1502), Sen-no-Rikyu (1521–1591), and Kobori Enshu (1579–1647), were famous artists and philosophers. It was further elaborated in Zen aesthetics, which left a strong mark on nearly all Japanese art; an influence evident in such terms as *wabi* (humble, subdued or quiet taste), *sabi* (elegant simplicity, patina, antique look), *shibui* (incompleteness, quiet, sober taste), and *yugen* (unexplainable, mystery, occult, profundity, subtlety), and the like.[28]

Since this kind of art is more suggestive or ambiguous than directly expressive, it necessitates a two-way communication, one that calls for something more than passive reception. The person who experiences Japanese art must actively participate in the artwork, basing his participation on his own world of imagination and fantasy. The Japanese tend toward a preference for imagination over fact and, indeed, for them poetic imagination and fantasy have always been the most important forms of learning and knowledge. This artistic communication nevertheless both presumes and is based on the homogeneous system of codes already mentioned; it depends on a culture shared by the society (9).[29]

Although it is inspired by nature, Japanese art nonetheless cannot be classified as naturalistic or realistic; indeed, it is more abstract than is generally believed. This is reflected in the descriptive arts, where the rules of verisimilitude, of perspective in form and color and the effects of light and shade are disregarded. In fact, very often the lack of perspective means a multiplicity of it, that is a multiplicity of vanishing points as if the painting or print was the composition of loosely related parts or visually "independent" smaller pictures. Also, it is not uncommon that actually the reversal of perspective appears, with the viewer as a van-

ishing point, thereby necessarily involving the perceiver more in the process of interpretation and so, making him or her an integral part of, or participant in, the depicted scene. Japanese art, despite all its concrete qualities—or perhaps because of them—therefore also displays an abstract approach to nature, in which both the abstract and concrete are forged as an inseparable unity.

In general, the Japanese have always been more interested in their natural environment—thus in the domain of immediate experience—than in the conceptual and transcendental. In this way they shape the rhythms of their daily life and their patterns of behavior. Consequently, Japanese art and aesthetics have always been preoccupied with issues of existence rather than essence, where the symptom of existence is the potency of the thing (*mono*) in the state of change. As Tomoya Masuda explains, "the sensitivity to every symptom of change is the sensitivity to the potency or the vector of being. . . . If being is vectorial, that is to say, symbolic, then sensitivity may be concerned not only with sensation, but also with emotion . . ."[30] This aes-

9. Calligraphy from the Nanzen-ji Temple, Kyoto.

thetic sensitivity is referred to in Japanese as *mono no aware*.[31] Since its conception and ontology are rooted in an implicit phenomenology, Japanese art can be properly understood and appreciated if approached phenomenologically.

Architectural Traditions

An investigation of Japanese architecture reveals comparable features through which the Japanese have enriched not only their own culture but also world architecture.

Important architectural monuments can be found throughout the country, and the memory of the past lingers everywhere without exception. There are, however, some regions where the number of old monuments is exceptionally large and where the traditional atmosphere is particularly strong. They are usually the ancient capitals, such as Nara (710–794) and Kyoto (794–1868), or governmental headquarters like Kamakura (1185–1333), but the same feeling can be sensed in such settlements as Takayama, Kurashiki, Matsumoto, Himeji, Hirosaki, and many others.

Traditional architecture first and immediately impresses one with its homogeneity. Every single building displays some similarities with every other, so that they may all look alike at first glance. This is due to an identical attitude toward architecture and the manmade environment generally, rather than to the identity of buildings per se. Despite the similarity of certain forms and patterns or similarity in construction methods, a large variety is revealed in details, elements, and their relation to one another and to the entire architectural composition.

In accord with their traditionally close relationship to nature, the Japanese purpose was not to build anything in conflict with it. Their shelters were developed to harmonize with the geographical, topographical, and climatic conditions of the natural environment, and with the local "spirits," the *kami*. In this last respect, the structures invariably comply with the principles of orientation, or geomancy, known as *kaso*, which is of Chinese origin. Architecture was not only a framework for life but in effect also the Japanese way of life. The protective role of Japanese buildings tended to be more subdued compared to the defensive function of Western counterparts. In many cases, this role was reduced to a minimum.

Just like a tree, a building traditionally had to be an organic part of nature. Architecture was absorbed into the surrounding landscape, with a sensible continuity between them. The unity of the two is well illustrated in Japanese painting, in graphics, and in woodblock prints, where buildings never appear by themselves; architecture alone is never the subject of descriptive art. This may be verified by a visit to one of the countless traditional compounds. For instance, on a walk in the gardens of the famous Kinkaku-ji (1397), the Ginkaku-ji temples (1483), the Katsura (1647), or the Shugakuin Imperial Villas (1659), the smaller and bigger pavilions are hardly noticeable, since they are modestly concealed behind bushes, trees, and hillocks (10). Another good example of this integration is the setting of the Itsukushima Shrine (c. 811; in its present form, 1167 and 1241), which faces out over the bay of Miyajima Island not far from Hiroshima. In high tide the entire group of buildings and the *torii* gate—symbol in all Shinto shrines—appear to be floating on the water in front of the hills, which are often clad in bluish mist (11).[32] Inspired by the fascinating harmony of the sight, the Japanese refer to it as one of their three most famous *natural* beauties.[33]

Since wood was virtually the only building

10–11. Traditional Japanese architecture was conceived to be in the closest harmony with nature.

10. The Chitose-bashi Pavilion in the garden of Shugakuin Imperial Villa in Kyoto (1659; the bridge pavilion, early 19th c.).

11. The buildings and the *torii* gate of the Itsuku-shima Shinto Shrine (c. 811; 1167, 1241) were built over the sea at the entrance of Miyajima Island Bay, to create one of Japan's scenic beauties.

material, traditional Japanese architecture is essentially of wooden frame construction; its typical buildings are characterized by small size and an overall horizontal character. On the whole the Japanese had little use for largeness or enormous height nor did they entertain the idea that architecture should overwhelm one. Thus even the exceptional Izumo shrine (sixth c., 1248, 1744) and the Todai-ji temple (752, 1199, 1709) are diminutive compared to the celebrated historical monuments in other architectural cultures, and the relatively high pagodas are consistently and strongly attenuated by the horizontal lines of several overhanging roofs (12, 17, and 20).

Buildings in Japan likewise never had the everlasting character of the colossal Egyptian pyramids, Greek temples, or the formidable Gothic cathedrals, neither in the materials used nor in the spirit in which they were conceived. Nitschke notes that "Japan shows few attempts to build monuments for eternity, to outwit time by the seeming durability of certain materials."[34] Wood is subject to the ravages of time and aging far more than stone; its exclusive use—consistent with an affinity and love for nature—also indicates a definite lack of concern for permanence.

More practically, wooden constructions ventilate better than masonry structures and suit the extremely humid Japanese summer climate; they are also more resistant to earthquakes. They particularly suit local conditions in that ill-fated wooden structures can be rebuilt with greater ease and speed after inevitable natural disasters like typhoons and earthquakes and their consequent fires. Through the artistic skills and techniques of carpenters, the cult of wood developed into the Japanese "culture of wood," as Professor Kiyoshi Seike calls it (13, 14).[35]

Thus, although Japan is equally blessed with both wood and stone of good quality, the importance of stone as a building material has always been minimal. Its use is limited largely to foundations and podiums in architecture and to decorative or other elements in landscaping and garden design. Even in medieval castles, only the bases and ramparts were built of stone, while the structures themselves, though sometimes heavily plastered, were made completely of wood; because of

12. Todai-ji Temple in Nara, the largest wooden structure in the world (752, 1709).

13–14. Traditional architecture was solely of wood. Japanese carpenters mastered structural techniques and decorative details and brought them to the level of art.

this they look like graceful palaces rather than mighty fortresses (15, 16).

As in the religion, we are able to distinguish between Shinto and Buddhist traditional architectures.[36] Shinto clearly is the earlier; the first shrines appeared sometime in the Kofun (or Tumuli) Period (A.D. 250–552), well before the introduction of Buddhism. These shrines were straightforward in design and built according to the simplest structural methods. They represent the prototypical forms of contemporary houses and palaces and thus, in a sense, embody the archetype of the original "primitive hut." The roof, uncurving, is of thatch. The floor is raised and supported by wooden posts dug directly into the ground. The wooden structural elements are not painted but are left in their natural state or only polished. This type of structure may be regarded as the Japanese style before Buddhism. The oldest and most beautiful examples of this architectural style are the famous Izumo (*taisha-zukuri*) and Ise shrines (*shinmei-zukuri*) (17).

The Ise Shrine is dedicated to Amaterasu Omikami, Sun Goddess, and thus symbolizes the origin of Japan and the Imperial Dynasty.[37] Starting in the seventh century, it was completely rebuilt at certain intervals like most of the Shinto shrines. Today it is the only shrine in which the very interesting tradition of reconstruction every twenty years is regularly observed.[38] Even the most recent form of the shrine, however, probably closely resembles the original ancient structure (3rd–5th century), because each rebuilding has attempted to retain the previous design as much as possible (18).

Although these shrines, too, are built of wood (Japanese cypress, or *hinoki*), they cannot be destroyed by aging within the comparatively short period between rebuildings. The reason behind each rebuilding is symbolic rather than practical. This custom is the continuation of the archaic ritual of returning to mythic origins, of the cosmogonic attempt to renew time "by reinstituting the conditions which were in the beginning." Such procedures

13. Detail of the bracketing system at the Chion-in Temple in Kyoto (1619).

14. Detail of the Kusakabe House (1881) in Takayama.

15–16. With their wooden structure (except for the stone base) and graceful appearance, castles are palaces rather than fortresses.

15. Matsumoto Castle (1581–1640).

16. Himeji Castle (1610).

form an important part of Shinto purification rituals as well. In addition, as Joseph Rykwert reminds us, "the Japanese example suggests an identity between the house (shrine) and the land. So the rite not only renews time for the occupant of the house (shrine) but for all those who inhabit the land which the hut (shrine) represents."[39] At the same time, within the ritual of renewing time, structure, or dwelling for the enshrined deity, the Japanese attitude toward permanent things is also expressed. "What the Japanese wanted to preserve," according to Ota Hirotaro, "were not the things themselves, but the forms that carried the spirit. The Japanese observed that things were, after all, but a means of expressing the spirit and that things themselves could not be permanently preserved."[40] Hence the details and the forms of structural elements are charged with strong symbolic content through a system of codes that set the pattern for shrines to be built later.

The Ise compound—both *naiku* and *gekku*—comprises other smaller edifices besides the main sanctuary (*shoden*) (19).[41] These are surrounded by four rows of fences (*tamasaki*) of various sizes and styles at varying distances from one another, each with a gate on the north and south sides. These fences create a clear hierarchy; as one passes through them, they suggest a feeling of increased distance between the world of gods and ours. As an early symbol of purity, both the *naiku* and *gekku*—similar to early Buddhist monasteries—are laid out along a geometric order, and strict axial symmetry pervades every structure and element as well.[42] This initial early ordering principle of the Japanese later on showed not only various permutations but also significant deviations, which eventually led to the gradual dissolution of the rigid geometric order.

Other symbolic features of the buildings here include the two pairs of fork-type finials (*chigi*) at the end of the ridges, which denote either the male or female deity enshrined, according to the direction of cut at the end of the beams.[43] The ten wooden logs (*katsuogi*) placed across the ridge can be found only in shrine architecture. The two poles (*munamochi-bashira*) in front of the gables that support the ridge are likewise characteristic and structurally interesting. The most significant element, however,

17. The Izumo Shrine is one of the oldest and largest buildings in Japan (6th c.).

18. The Ise Shrine (Naiku compound; 5th c.), possibly the oldest shrine in Japan, has come to symbolize the origin of Japan and the Imperial Family from Amaterasu Omikami, the sun goddess. It is the only one that today preserves the Shinto practice of rebuilding shrines at regular intervals. (Photograph courtesy of the Japanese Consul General, Los Angeles, California.)

19. Layout of the Ise-jingu Shinto Shrine inner, or *naiku*, compound. The complex of several small edifices surrounded by four rows of fences with gates is rebuilt alternately on the two bordering sites once every twenty years. The last rebuilding, the sixtieth, took place in 1974.

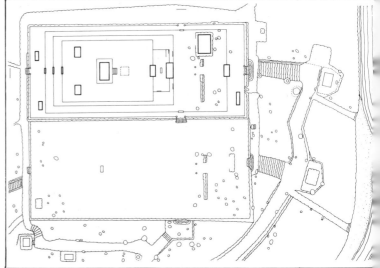

20–24. The most famous early Buddhist monastery, the Horyu-ji was built near Nara under the patronage of Prince Shotoku in A.D. 607. Some of its buildings, such as the main hall (*kondo*), are original structures and are considered to be the oldest existing buildings in Japan.

20. Detail of the pagoda roofs.

21. Main Hall and the
pagoda.

22. Lecture hall.

23. Bell tower.

24. Yumedono, Prince Shotoku's memorial chapel.

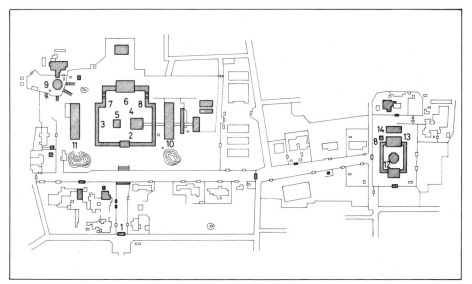

25. Layout of the west and east compounds of the Horyu-ji. 1. South main gate (*nandaimon*). 2. Middle gate (*chumon*). 3. Surrounding corridors (*kairo*). 4. Main Hall (*kondo*). 5. Five-storied pagoda. 6. Lecture hall (*kodo*). 7. Sutra repository (*kyoro*). 8. Belfry (*shoro*). 9. West round hall (*Saiendo*). 10. Shoryoin chapel. 11. West quarters and *Sangyo-in* chapel. 12. *Yumedono*. 13. Portrait hall (*Edono*) and relic hall (*Shariden*). 14. Lecture hall (*Dempodo*).

26. Layout of a mountain type of temple compound, the Kyomizu-dera in Kyoto (1634).

has no structural function at all. It is the Heart or Heavenly August Taboo Pillar (*shin-no-mi-hashira*) that is sunk in the earth beneath the floor of the main building (*shoden*) and covered by a miniature hut. The deity enshrined was believed to dwell in this main sanctuary; being intangible, invisible, and therefore incapable of pictorial representation, the deity was symbolized by a mirror for purity, a jewel for knowledge, and a sword for authority. Thus the Ise Shrine stands as a huge symbolic object rather than a building with interior space, and as such its exterior space-organizing role increases in importance. Shrine buildings, starting with the Ise, are in effect not meant to be spaces to enter but rather remote places to approach and arrive at.

The influence of Buddhist architecture and religion, started in the latter part of the sixth century, led primarily to the importation of Chinese temple architecture, with the first structures designed by Chinese monks who also supervised their construction. In addition, Buddhism brought with it a whole series of new trends that resulted in considerable changes in Japan. Since Buddhist temples were freely accessible to everyone at all times, their architecture introduced new building types. In the typical temple compound the principal buildings are the main hall (*kondo*) and the pagoda (*to*).[44] These are surrounded by covered corridors (*kairo*) connecting with the main gate (*chumon*) in the south. Usually joined to this rectangular system are the lecture hall (*kodo*), the treasury of sutras (*kyoro*), and a bell tower (*shoro*); (20–24). In some cases these might be complemented by an office, the monks' dormitory or residence, and a couple of storage buildings (*kura*), all of which are enclosed by a system of outer walls with another principal gate to the south (*nan-daimon*) (25). Yet along with the development of Buddhist monasteries in remote mountain retreats a process of "Japanization" also began in the Heian Period (794–1185), expressed in an arrangement of the buildings that showed several deviations from the originally symmetrical pattern.

Unlike the original Shinto shrines raised on wooden pilotis, the Buddhist wooden buildings were invariably erected on sturdy stone bases. The roof, covered with glazed roof tiles, shows the typical protruding and curved forms supported by an intricate system of wooden brackets (13). The building itself was painted and adorned both inside and out.

Later on, however, the original Shinto and Buddhist building modes as well as their respective building rituals started to influence each other. The fusion was already evident by the eighth century, when several Shinto shrines were built with curved roofs and were painted. As a result of the assimilation, the original Chinese style became increasingly Japanese, hence more gentle and mild. Buddhist temples built were in many cases provided with raised wooden floors and gently curving cypress-shingled roofs. In addition, Buddhists conducted ceremonies (*Jishu-shin*) to seek the protection of the site's spirit in practically every temple they built, and that spirit was necessarily a *kami*.[45] In the layout of the temples, asymmetry arose to overcome the strict symmetry of Chinese and early Japanese compositions, resulting in another general feature of traditional Japanese architectural compounds: lack of dominant straight axes, generating a pattern of constantly shifting axes (26). The Hoyu-ji in Nara (607), the most renowned of the early Buddhist monasteries in Japan, is already asymmetrical in composition. In contrast to previously built Asuka-dera (588) and Shintenno-ji (593), here the main hall and the pagoda were placed not behind but beside each other—clearly a bold deviation from the traditional Chinese pattern.

Similarly, the contemporary residential architecture of the aristocrats, the *shinden-zukuri*, also changed. The originally strictly symmetrical group of buildings arranged around a main hall (*shinden*) and connected to it by covered corridors became less symmetrical and somewhat less formal by the end of the Heian Period.[46] No sample of the original *shinden* style survives from that age. Some impression of the appearance of this style can be derived however from the present complex of the Old Imperial Palace in Kyoto, especially from its main ceremonial hall, the Shishinden, even though the entire compound has been rebuilt several times (794, 1790, 1855). Equally revealing are the small Phoenix Hall of Byodo-in in Uji (1053); and the more recent Heian Shrine (1895) in Kyoto (27–29).

After a period of stagnation, around the end of the twelfth century, Chinese influence once again became important with the trend of Zen Buddhism that soon gained popularity in Japan. The *shoin* type of house developed slowly during this architectural period. This was typically the residence of a warlord, landowner, or Buddhist monk. This type of residence later became more informal as it was influenced by the rustic tea pavilion, and it is now regarded as the prototypical Japanese house (*sukiya-zukuri*). The *shoin* is characterized by a raised floor area covered with *tatami* (rush matting), a small writing desk (*tsuke-shoin*) built-in as a wide windowsill, a system of staggered shelves (*chigaidana*), an alcove (*tokonoma*) in the main rooms, light sliding wall panels (*shoji, fusuma*) in modular arrangement, and above all the expressly asymmetrical and often diagonally staggered (*suji-chigai*) floor plan of the whole complex. The Momoyama Period (1568–1603) followig the Muromachi (1333–1568) witnessed the further development of this house type (30), as well as the birth of such other notable building types as tea houses (*chaya*), urban dwellings of merchants (*machiya* and *nagaya*), castles, and the mausoleum-type shrines that reached the climax of their development in the subsequent Edo Period (1603–1868).

Shoin architecture, originally decorated like the Kinkaku-ji (1397) and Ginkaku-ji (1483) temples or the Nijo palace (1603), resorted to less and less

27–29. The first important residential architecture that carried Chinese features was the *shinden-zukuri* favored by the aristocrats. With the paucity of original structures as prototypes, only a few buildings today are reminiscent of this style.

27. The pebbled courtyard in front of the Shishinden.

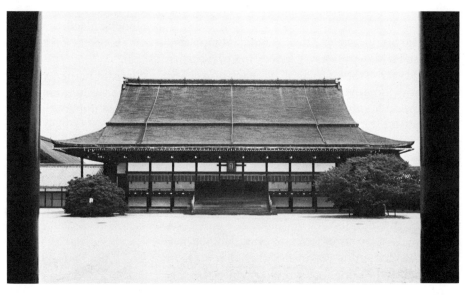

28. Shishinden, the main ceremonial hall of the Old Imperial Palace in Kyoto (794–1855).

29. The Phoenix pavilion of the Bodo-in Temple in Uji City, Kyoto (1053).

ornamentation by around the beginning of the seventeenth century because of the influence of Zen Buddhist philosophy and art theories.[47] Paralleling a more decorative style in shrine architecture, this tendency bore the fruit of an interesting duality of style during the coming century, and stretched to its extremes in such buildings as the tea ceremony room (*chashitsu*) that appeared in humble cottages, and the mausoleums.

Elements inside the tea rooms were reduced to the minimum. Such elements included the 4.5-*tatami*-sized (approx. 9 × 9 feet) floor, the fire pit (*ro*), a pillar (*naka-bashira*), a wooden panel (*naka-ita*) in the middle of the space, and a special low guest entrance (*nijiri-guchi*).[48] The designers of these pavilions and surrounding tea gardens were Zen Buddhist monks, like the famous Sen-no-Rikyu or Kobori Enshu. They abandoned all decoration except for a calligraphic scroll on the wall, the *ikebana*, and a small incense holder (*senko-date*) set in the *tokonoma*. Decoration was abandoned in order to enhance meditation, the spiritual joy of the tea ceremony (*chanoyu*), which involved all human senses. The tea ceremony ultimately became a technique of detachment from the rush of daily activities, most especially for the warriors, or *samurai*. Such spiritual pursuit of austerity was converted gradually into an aesthetic trend. In order to allow one to experience and absorb the tranquility of an elegant simplicity (*wabi*) mellowed with age (*sabi*), all building materials were allowed to remain in their natural state and form. Beyond the harmony

30. Later, residential architecture was increasingly influenced by Japanese aesthetic standards and Zen Buddhism, as in this early example of the evolving *shoin-zukuri* style, the Ginkaku-ji Pavilion in Kyoto (1483).

of the applied rustic materials, the beauty of the interior lay in the abstract and expressly graphic composition of the small asymmetrical spaces revealed through simple surfaces and dominant lines (31).

On the other hand, the early seventeenth century also produced the richly adorned mausoleum architecture typified in the Toshogu Shrine (1636) built in Nikko for the famous shogun Tokugawa Ieyasu (1542–1616). This monument of the so-called Japanese Baroque is a paragon of the traditional decorative architecture (32). On the whole, however, ornamentation in traditional architecture played a more limited role than it did in this mausoleum. The idea of luscious decoration on buildings

31. Detail of the Shokin-tei tea pavilion in the garden of Katsura Imperial Villa (early 17th c.). Zen Buddhist monks, designers of the tea pavilions, eschewed all decoration except for a wall scroll and the *ikebana* in the alcove.

32. The turn of the seventeenth century brought not only the extremely austere tea pavilions, but also the richly adorned mausoleum architecture. The best example of the latter is the Toshogu Shrine in Nikko (1636) dedicated to the famous shogun Tokugawa Ieyasu. Detail of the Yomei-mon gate.

was often based on the taste of the Chinese aristocracy, especially in the extravagance of the Momoyama Period, but the effect of this influence had always been kept in check by the Japanese and blended in a delicate way with their "abstract," ascetic taste. Contrary to the widely accepted belief, however, decorative and nondecorative trends have in actuality always coexisted in traditional architecture and, more often than not, have formed a symbiotic relationship. The most delicate examples of architectural decoration are in the painted walls, screens, and ceilings, the wood carvings in temples such as the Nishi Hongan-ji (17th c.) in Kyoto and the Onjo-ji (1600) in Otsu, and in palaces such as the Nijo-jo (1603), the Old Imperial Palace (*Gosho*), and the Katsura Villa (1647) in Kyoto.

Finally, one more question deserves attention in the history of Japanese architecture, the problem of styles. In art and architecture, styles have always been the direct expression of certain ages and places in close relation to scientific, technological, and socioideological developments. This is true in Japan as well, but with an important reservation. Throughout the centuries-long history of the Japanese, only slight changes—if any—have been observed in their fundamental world concept, in their attitude to nature as guided by Shintoism and Buddhism, and in their social structure. As is not true in Western Europe, science and technology in Japan for the most part displayed no remarkable progress or revolutionary leaps forward. The basic approach to art and architecture also remained unchanged until the impact of Western civilization. As a result, a European type of stylistic sequence failed to evolve.

Wood, as almost the sole building material, predetermined the kinds of construction methods to be used along with the types of structures to be built. So in discussing styles in traditional Japanese architecture, one would not necessarily refer to new systems of the primary or supporting structures; least of all would there be any reference to

new solutions for achieving spans of increasing dimension, as in the stone architecture of the West. The traditional Japanese construction method has to a great extent been the *post and lintel* system, thereby excluding vault and dome completely.[49] Stylistic change thus manifested itself in variations in structural details, accompanied by alterations in proportion, appearance, form, decoration, and most of all, in new aesthetic principles of composition that imbued architectural space with increasingly subtle symbolic meanings.

The Japanese House and Its Space Concept

Concepts of space have always played a very important role in Western architectural history and were to become a key point in the evolution of Modernism. Space was looked upon as something concrete, although infinitely extensive, having an existence independent of the physical entity of objects or even of its own fixed boundary. Space had the definite quality of being a "container" and so was always subject to rational, even scientific approaches and treated according to the rules of mathematics, geometry, perspective, and so on.[50]

This notion of space has never occurred in Japanese history and so the Japanese developed no theory of space. Spatial construction in traditional Japanese architecture seems to be only a leftover or neglected entity. In line with Shinto belief, space was seen as "universal," rooted in nature, and thus to be represented by the land rather than by buildings.[51] It was always induced and limited by the spiritual quality of natural or environmental phenomena—by hills, rocks, trees, water, and so on. Therefore, it had no separate existence as a spatial entity. Rather it had a symbolic character as the meaning of the constituent forms, combining varied natural formations with other, "artificial" things. In brief, it was the experiential quality of place. Architecture as well was regarded as an organic part of nature and thus could not imply a different spatiality.

This instinctive understanding or intuition brought the Japanese close to the philosopher Martin Heidegger's conclusion that "Spaces receive their being from location and not from 'space.' "[52] With the spirit of space rooted in the forms that compose it, in conjunction with other perceptual qualities of the place, the physical or material permanence of buildings in Japan—in contrast to the case in the West—was not considered something indispensably important; shrines, temples, imperial palaces, and even capitals were often relocated or completely rebuilt. The concept of *genius loci* acquired an additional relative character.

According to the ancient belief, the strongest spirituality (*kami*) was attributed to the least perceivable natural locations, remote and misty mountains, thick forests, various small islands of rocks and cliffs impenetrable to the eye and unapproachable physically; in architecture, the dimmest, innermost, and least visible places (33). The spatial interpretation of this perception understands space not as homogeneous but heterogeneous, with increasing density around places where it would be the least spatial in the traditional Western sense—

33. The "Wedded Rocks" near Futamigaura, Ise peninsula. A cluster of straw ropes (*shimenawa*), indicative of sacred places or shrines, ties together a pair of rocks in the sea, which symbolize Japan's mythological ancestral couple, Izanami and Izanagi.

that is, where space, as in a "black hole" or darkness (*yami*), converges to zero.[53] "Thus space was perceived as identical with the events or phenomena occurring in it; that is, space was recognized only in relation to time flow," writes Arata Isozaki.[54] With this, the most ambiguous concepts of *oku* and *ma* were born, as opposed to the positive and absolute notions of *center* and *space* respectively; they are basic to a quasiphenomenological approach to and understanding of space in Japanese architecture.[55]

The spatial quality of traditional Japanese architecture is best represented by the typical Japanese house, the *shoin* and the later *sukiya*-type residential architecture. Kyoto offers the most outstanding examples, with such famous complexes as the Nijo Palace (1603) and the Shugakuin (1659) and Katsura (1620–1647) Imperial villas. The extremely refined and complex composition of the Katsura Villa became a prototype that inspired numerous modern Japanese architects, among them Sutemi Horiguchi, Kenzo Tange, Kisho Kurokawa, Arata Isozaki, and such foreign architects as Bruno Taut and Walter Gropius, the former even reviving in Japan itself interest in the architecture of *shoin* (34–37).

The spatial layout of the typical *shoin* or *sukiya* complex started with the vicinity, the landscape being converted into the surrounding garden. The role of the garden in Japan is so important that to describe the house without it is virtually impossible. As *katei*—one of the words for family and home or household—suggests, the unity of house (*ka*) and garden (*tei*) in Japanese understanding has existed since prehistoric times. The garden appears on the margin of nature as macrocosm and at the limit of the house as microcosm, establishing a continuity between the two. Thus no matter how small or large, the garden represents or symbolizes the totality of existence. It speaks of nature or the universe, but it does so without the rules of geometry and symmetry. Thus there are no formal or ornamental gardens in anything like the Western sense.

However, in garden design as in other Japanese arts including architecture, formal, semiformal, and informal (*shin-gyo-so*) compositions can be distinguished. The gradation from formal to informal is deeply rooted in the Japanese consciousness. It involves a "progressive reduction in the number of elements used and a greater ease and subtlety in their arrangement"; thus in the *shin* landscapes all elements are distinct and clearly revealed, while in the *so* gardens the elements are more irregular and "suggestive both of a latent force and a sense of unrestrained ease."[56] Very often this gradation from formal to informal runs parallel with a gradation from public to private.

The art of garden design in Japan evolved through the centuries. Its origins can be traced back to the empty courtyards of ancient Shinto shrines surrounded by rows of fences, such as the one of Ise. This graveled court (*yuniwa*) was retained in the Chinese-influenced *shinden* gardens (27), but it was complemented by another with plants and water. A pond or a small brook created the so-called river-style of garden, as in some miniature landscapes of the Nara and Heian periods (29). The main types of garden were clearly developed by the end of the Muromachi Period (1333–1573), although landscape garden design reached its peak in the Edo Period (1603–1868).

Landscape or stroll gardens (*kaiyu-shiki niwa*) are intended to reveal the beauty of nature in its "reality" and original form. These gardens are sometimes so "natural" that it is hard to believe they have been artificially created (38). They are never laid out along fixed geometrical patterns and can never be seen or grasped from any one point. Their actual dimensions elude the visual perception, remaining always hidden, and thus the gardens seem to be larger than they actually are. Their compositional harmony unfolds with "alternating turns" (*oremagari*) as one moves through them.

34–37. Kyoto offers the finest examples of the *shoin* type of residential and palace architecture that eventually came to be known as "the Japanese house" (*sukiya-zukuri*).

34. Nijo-jo Palace (1603).

36–37. Katsura Imperial Villa (1620–1647).

35. Shugakuin Imperial Villa (1659).

38. Garden of the Katsura Imperial Villa in Kyoto (1620–1647). The house was always built in organic unity with its surrounding garden. The stroll or landscape garden, though manmade in every element, reconstructs nature in its original form.

39. Rock garden of the Ryoan-ji Temple in Kyoto (c. 1499). The other main type of garden also recalls nature or the universe, but in a highly symbolic way. These dry or rock gardens accompanying mainly Zen Buddhist temples could also be regarded as abstract compositions.

A stroll in them reveals a sequence of vistas gradually emerging as an endless set of layers. The smaller focal points alternately "hide and reveal" (*miegakure*) in a "discontinuous continuity," cumulatively adding up to an image of the whole and a "feeling of spatiality" (*sumichigai*) in the union of memory and imagination. Any attempt to discover and eventually understand their mutable totality and complexity of meaning demands active participation both physically and mentally. The elements are carefully selected and arranged—a small pond with some islands containing plants, trees, bushes, even moss, and a number of tiny bridges; followed by rocks, stone lanterns, and intricately placed stepping stones along winding paths or in the water that control the attention; then small pavilions and tea houses. Through such an intricate sequence, the garden not only follows or reflects upon seasonal changes but also gains some cosmic dimension, a certain mystic quality or "sophisticated order," as Günter Nitschke described it.[57]

At the other extreme, there are the symbolic or rock gardens, which evolved through the artistic activities of Zen Buddhist monks who worked mainly in Kyoto and Kamakura during the Muromachi Period. Rock gardens accompany only Zen Buddhist temples and monasteries and represent nature in a way basically different from the secular stroll gardens. The elements in the small and extremely simplified composition of the rock gardens, stones and rocks of a highly symbolic character, are reduced to the minimum. The term "dry gardens" could hardly be more appropriate, since even water is represented in the form of raked gravel.

These gardens are usually separated from "real" nature by walls. They are actually looked upon as abstract landscape pictures (*kare-sansui*) or as three-dimensional sculptures. Their composition can be interpreted in different ways and on several levels. They are not meant to be entered or walked in; the viewer absorbs the sight, and, by means of intuition or rather meditation, identifies himself with the garden's symbolic reality and, by extension, the whole universe. As Nitschke notes, "Here we are concerned with the void which is not of rational or analytical conception, but an existential experience of one's whole being."[58] In fact, these gardens were laid out as vehicles for attaining Buddhahood. The garden of the Ryoan-ji temple (c. 1499) could stand as the epitome of these "gardens of absence" and also as the acme of symbolic art in Japan (39).

The intimate relationship between nature and architecture is first of all apparent in the almost complete blending of the house into the garden and the landscape. The building is not the major focal point in the composition but only an element in it. The path or paths approaching the house are usually diagonal, and the house is seen only gradually. Walking toward the group of pavilions in the garden of the Katsura Villa, for example, one at first catches only a glimpse of the softly and gracefully arched roofs. From afar, it would even seem as if the whole building consisted of nothing other than the large overhanging roofs and the deep shadows they cast on the portions beneath (40). The details become visible as one proceeds;

40. On the approach to the Katsura Villa, the first thing that catches the eye is a system of large overhanging roofs shading the house beneath.

41. Interior detail of the Katsura Villa. Inside, the house features "empty" yet elegantly simple and airy spaces.

only gradually one becomes aware of the elevated floor, the surrounding porch or veranda, the light paper-covered walls, and the post-and-beam structure. Entering the house, the visitor is greeted and charmed by the airy and simple elegance of the inner spaces. Everything is clear and clean and, moreover, appears to be empty (41).

As with related building types, the basic structure of the house is a wooden skeleton, in which the principal elements are the columns erected mainly on stone bases and the connecting horizontal beams. Generally, the roof over this skeleton is covered by thatch, shingle, or tiles. Since the roof has always been regarded as a symbolic link between nature and man and between heaven and earth, its size, proportions, and form are very important and also contribute considerably to the outer appearance and beauty of the building as well as to the quality of spaces inside. In fact, as reflected in the Chinese ideographs, the roof more than anything else symbolizes the concept of shelter or architecture for the Japanese.[59] Even the sequence of construction emphasizes the roof's significance. The house was built from the highest level down. The roof and its covering were prepared first; the raised floor elements, the modular *tatami* flooring, and the panels and screens comprising the outer and inner walls were installed only after the roof's completion.

The elevated floor, whether covered by *tatami,* a thick mat of rice straw, or by polished wooden boards, is regarded as a piece of furniture; as such, it is necessary to remove the shoes when it is walked upon. If there is *tatami,* which signifies a place of purity as well, even the slippers customarily worn at home are removed. With the *tatami* serving both as bed and as sitting surface, the traditional Japanese house has little need for furniture in the Western sense. What there is for furniture is mostly built in, like the closet (*oshi-ire*) between two rooms, the shelf system (*chigaidana*), and the alcove (*tokonoma*) (7). Since most of the walls are mobile, any freestanding piece is placed in the middle of the space—for example, the small, low tables around which people sit on cushions.[60] Ascribable to this old custom of sitting practically on the floor, the ceiling is rather low, which adds to the overall horizontal character of the building. Despite this, however, distribution of the light through the paper screens and the natural color scheme keep the floor better lit than the fixed walls and ceiling, which remain dark. In effect, the very spatiality and beauty of Japanese interiors are closely associated with darkness (*yami*), the variations and mysterious quality of shadows. This perception of space is in sharp contrast to Western understanding of space as light. In Japanese architecture, shadows and darkness cast by the extensive roof provide depth and evoke the spirit of the house and building. Jun'ichiro Tanizaki, in his novel *In Praise of Shadows*, explains that, in fact, the essence of the whole Japanese culture can be interpreted as derivative of the Japanese poetic appreciation of darkness and invisible depth.[61]

The *tatami* contributed to the character and layout of interior spaces in other ways as well. Besides the fact that it is elastic and ventilates naturally, it serves as the common denominator in the whole design. Everything in the house, from material to texture and color, harmonizes with the *tatami*. It is also the basis of the modular system. Its size has evolved from the human activities of sitting and sleeping and is about 3 by 6 feet.[62] The dimensions of major components in the house are closely related to the size of the *tatami*, which generally guide not only the dimension of the span between columns but also the typical vertical and horizontal dimensions of such elements as the *tokonoma* (3 x 6 ft.), bath (6 x 6 ft.), toilet (3 x 4.5 or 6 ft.), veranda (3, 4, 5, or 6 ft. wide), corridor (3 or 4.5 ft. wide), sliding screens (3 x 6 ft.), and others. The size of the premises is given by the number of *tatami*, usually: 3, 4.5, 6, 8, 10, 12, and so on which also provides a convenient way of estimating the size of a house or apartment.

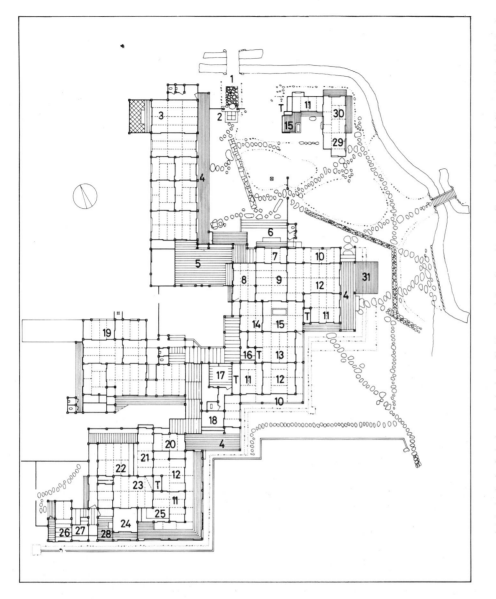

42. The concept of *oku* and *ma* as reflected in the floor plan of the Shoin complex and the Gepparo tea pavilion of the Katsura Imperial Villa. 1. Small bridge. 2. Inner gate. 3. Inner entry hall. 4. Veranda(*engawa*). 5. Old kitchen. 6. Entrance. 7. Place for the arrival of the Imperial coach (*mikoshi yose*). 8. *Shozen-no-ma*. 9. *Yari-no-ma*. 10. Veranda with *tatami*. 11. First room (*ichi-no-ma*). 12. Second room (*ni-no-ma*). 13. Third room (*san-no-ma*). 14. Guards' room (*tsumesho*). 15. Sunken hearth (*irori*). 16. Shelves (*tana*). 17. Women's bath. 18. Storage of musical instruments (*gakki-no-ma*). 19. Old offices. 20. Kitchen (*daidokoro*). 21. Pantry (*mizuya*). 22. Cloakroom. 23. Imperial bedroom (*oyoru-no-ma*). 24. Dressing room. 25. Shinto altar (*kami-dano*). 26. Bathroom. 27. Sink. 28. Lavatory. 29. Anteroom. 30. Middle room (*naka-no-ma*). 31. Moon-viewing platform. T. Alcove (*tokonoma*).

The modular system of the house developed in close relation with standardization (*kiwari*), creating the conditions for prefabrication and mass production. All the vital elements could be produced in advance and in large quantities, themselves becoming interchangeable in an open system.[63]

In accordance with the multiple use of the *tatami* floor, a number of places in the house also became multifunctional. These *tatami* rooms could be used equally for the various activities of daily life, an implicit denial of functionalism. Even today in a traditional Japanese home, the few pieces of mobile furniture can be rearranged so a room can work as a living, study, or dining space in the daytime and as a bedroom at night. After storing away the furniture in a storage room or, tradi-tionally, store cabin (*kura*), the Japanese takes the folded sleeping mat (*shiki-buton*) out of the closet every night and prepares his "bed," usually in the middle of the room. In the morning the space is rearranged again for different purposes as necessary.[64] As a result of this multiplicity, these rooms are usually not named by function; rather the names indicate their location in the house or their relation to other things. There are, for example, first room (*ichinoma*), second room (*ninoma*), middle room (*nakanoma*), innermost or rear room (*okunoma*), and so on. Of course there are other rooms whose arrangement remains constant most of the time, like the kitchen (*daidokoro*), which is usually placed in conjunction with related areas (entrance, dining room), and the bathroom (*ofuro*)—a place dedicated as much to spiritual as to physical needs (42).

In a similar manner, despite a small Buddhist (*Butsu-dan*) and Shinto (*kami-dana*) altar in most homes, there is no clear distinction between spaces of spiritual purity and of ordinary use, between "sacred and profane" (*sei* and *zoku*). The display of certain symbolic elements and the performance of some religious rituals or ceremonies can transform a space into a sacred place, but only temporarily. On some festive occasions, like a wedding ceremony, a golden folding screen (*byobu*) is set up behind the newly married couple to create a sanctified space. When death occurs in the house, an ordinary folding screen is put around the deceased, but it is placed upside down. For the celebration of New Year, the whole house is converted into a sacred space by hanging *shimenawa*—rice straw cord with strips of white paper, the Shinto symbol of the sacred—over the entrance. After the event, the cord or the screens are folded up and put away. The space thus reverts to the profane everyday use.[65]

Among all the elements in the building, walls have the most complex role, being directly responsible for the special quality of Japanese architectural spaces. In the first place, since the load of the entire roof construction is carried on slim posts, the walls never have supporting functions.[66] In the second place, most of them are made of delicate wooden latticework covered by rice paper and are not fixed but mobile. Therefore columns rather than walls generate the feeling of spatiality; they gather more space than the walls could contain.

While Westerners surrounded themselves with heavy brick or stone walls to serve as exact demarcations between the inner and outer worlds, the Japanese built soft enclosures made of wooden frames with light sliding partitions. The entire system of light wall panels also provides for doors and windows, allowing the interior to open up completely toward the exterior, thereby creating a direct and genuine continuity between these spaces. The boundary between the two is almost invisible, while the picture perceivable through the large opening—since it has depth too—is three dimensional rather than two (43, 44). The house is not only well ventilated and naturally climatized against the muggy Japanese summer, but all these features also permit intense communication between outer and inner spaces. To reinforce the close correspondence, interior decorative elements—scrolls, *ikebana,* paintings, and so on—are also regularly changed to make the space respond to the occasion, whether these be seasons, weather, or others, as these are reflected in the garden and the surrounding landscape. In other words, a Japanese inside his house still lives in the middle of nature.[67]

There exists, however, a transitional zone, where exterior and interior interpenetrate and overlap. This in-between space is represented by the porch or anteroom (*genkan*), but more so by the veranda (*engawa*) around the building and under the eaves. The veranda is slightly lower than the inner *tatami* floor. Along the inner side of the veranda there is always a system of sliding screens (*shoji*) covered by translucent paper, which is followed closely by a system of sliding wooden shutters (*amado*) that provides protection against rain. At the outer edge of the veranda various screening devices are occasionally applied, such as the *sudare,* a blind of bamboo strips knotted together and partially or fully rolled down from under the eaves. More often than not the *amado* is erected together with yet another system of *shoji* panels along this outer edge of the veranda, thus enclosing the space from the outside as well. The space of the *engawa* (*en* means "in between") functions according to the way it is looked upon or how the sliding walls along its sides are opened or closed. It can form a part of either the interior or the exterior. When all of the walls are open, the *en* space belongs to both or neither, in this way approximating in architecture the equivalent of the artistic concept of *ma* (35, 37, 43).

43–44. Because of the mobility of the walls, exterior space penetrates the interior, and the picture perceivable through the large openings is of three dimensions rather than two.

43. Detail of the Katsura Villa.

44. Interior of Nanzen-ji Temple in Kyoto.

45. Interior of the Yoshijima House in Takayama (1881). The theoretical core of the multilayered space-structure of the house is the *oku*, a geometrically undefinable innermost point where the exterior with its beautifully filtered light converges to zero.

Inside the house, aside from the *amado* and *shoji,* there are other thin wall systems layering the space in a multiple way. In this sequence of walls, an outer space always seems to envelope another one inside. Most of these inner walls are also mobile, like the sliding screens (*fusuma*) or the portable folding (*biyo-bu*) screens. With their opening and/or removal, any layer of the space ("room") can be easily joined either to an outer or an inner space or, similarly, to any other surrounding volume. There is thus the capacity to create smaller and bigger spaces at will. Not only the veranda but also any element of the inner space of the house can act as an in-between or *en* space. This vague physical definition of space also corresponds directly with the aforementioned multifunctional nature of rooms in the house.

With this flexibility of the multilayered space, the exterior penetrates into the interior step by step, resulting in a centripetal space structure. Such a unique non-Western pattern, where spaces wrap around one another in variable configurations, always suggests an innermost core or *oku*. It is nevertheless only a theoretical or, rather, a psychological point and in a sense an invisible, unattainable zone, where space together with the beautifully filtered light converges to zero. By virtue of this concept of *oku*—signifying innermost, extending far back, deep, least accessible—the Japanese have always been able to give an illusion of depth to spatial compositions, regardless of their actual, usually small or shallow, dimensions (45).

The ambiguous character of the spatial disposition is also reflected in the lack of a definite, clear geometrical hierarchy. There are no appointed axes and—because the concept of *oku* does not indicate the idea of an absolute geometrical center—there are no centrally arranged organizations, either (42). But just as there is a gradation among formal, semiformal, and informal spaces, there is also a very refined system of hierarchy among the spaces inside and out. Thus the notion of *oku*, like many

others that denote spatial relationships, also implies a value judgment. This hierarchy is also represented by the relative elevation of the floor. The higher the level of the floor, the more inside that particular space is perceived to be and the higher in esteem it is held. This is also shown by the way the house is entered, vertically rather than horizontally: outside path, steps up to the *engawa* or *genkan*, followed by the wooden decking, and finally the *tatami* rooms, which are raised slightly higher again. A visitor on the lower level of the *genkan* or anteroom is not regarded as inside the house even if the area, as in all modern homes too, is behind the entrance door (384). To enter means to remove one's shoes and step *up*. Thus to invite one in, the host asks the guest to *agatte kudasai*, please step up, equivalent to the Western idea of stepping in. In the traditional and contemporary home alike only the *tokonoma* is higher than the *tatami* floor. In the Imperial residences the seats of the Emperor or the most important official were the highest ones, but they were still covered with *tatami*. Only the extra elevation marked the seat out as a special space called *jodan*, within the spatial continuity.

The concepts of *oku* and *ma* show that space did not exist *a priori* or as an independent constituent, but was the function of the actual, pluralistic experience and so was also deeply rooted in the sense of intangible qualities, or the spirit of the elusive events and various phenomena occurring there. Having no spatial quality, space was not created and perceived as a three-dimensional entity. This explains why to the Western eye Japanese architectural and urban spaces often appear two-dimensional or frontal. As a matter of fact, the multiple readings of the Japanese ideogram *ma*, meaning interval in both space and time, indirectly refer to this two-dimensional or planar origin of space. When in different compounds the same ideogram is also read as *ken*, denoting the unit of measurement between two columns, or the room size measured in *tatami* length (1 *ken* or 6 *shaku* =

the length of one *tatami*).[68] Consequently, *ken* can be interpreted to mean area as well. Even *okoshiezu,* the old method of architectural representation used extensively in the Edo Period (1603–1868), seems to point to the conception of space as primarily the juxtaposition of various planes. In this method, as Isozaki writes, "all of the surfaces of the space are analyzed as if they were floor plans. The theory is that the person examining them will mentally raise the drawings or the walls to their position in the completed rooms and in this way imagine the way the space will look."[69] Since visual information and representation remain in the realm of two-dimensionality, space and the environment cannot be decoded in the Western way: primarily along the perspective rules of rationalized and objective sight. In Japan, space has to be interpreted and understood through a significant reliance on all the senses, which, beyond the function of eyes and mind, involve the multidimensional capabilities of the human body, as well as intuition, emotion, and memory so much that they determine or perhaps even "create" the space itself. Jorge M. Ferreras, writing about the uniquely complex "frontal perception" of the Japanese, correctly argues: "We only see 'what we want to see' or what our cultural patterns will let us see; . . . there are culturally reinforced if not culturally determined ways of perceiving space."[70]

Architectural space in Japan then becomes a leftover matter, and yet this void is never really empty let alone vacuous, since, as in the descriptive arts, it is the common essence generated by and surrounding all elements and "happenings" within. Hence the history of Japanese architecture is permeated by a spatial logic, really nothing more than a hidden system, a capacity for aesthetically evaluating the "nonexistent."

The ambiguous quality of this sophisticated order as represented by the basic concepts of *oku* and *ma* is by no means limited to imperfectly compartmentalized architectural volumes. It also applies as much to the carefully layered places and vistas of the gardens and to the texture of urban spaces, just as it does to the "void" pauses in the descriptive or performing arts and poetry. It is present in just about every aspect of Japanese life, including human relations and verbal communication, with special regard to *haragei,* the art of nonlinear, nonassertive or nonpersuasive, and so, nondialectical mode of discourse. The "general vagueness of the interface . . . is felt by Westerners when, in talking, the Japanese smile profusely, while their actual intent . . . cannot be divined," notes Koji Yagi, but he explains that "for a people with a certain degree of common basic sensibility within a defined area, there is the . . . assurance that somewhere along the line things will be understood without clearly stating them in black and white."[71]

Urban Traditions

In Japan the urban environment, the cityscape, is among the topics most frequently discussed by architects, city officials, and the public alike; not to mention the foreign visitors who experience this topsy-turvy world for the first time, in which everything is in a mixed-up state of "disorder." The Japanese city has the unique character of being ugly and depressing as well as charming and lively at the same time. Foreigners either love it or hate it, depending on what they expect a city to be. For many, including the architect Charles Moore, this environment means "the most voracious and . . . most splendid eclectic urges on this planet."[72] No matter how it is evaluated, this obviously polymorphous and polysemantic urban milieu, having evolved all through Japanese history, inevitably forms the inclusive framework of the nation's recent architecture. For this reason it is necessary to mention a few more points about Japanese urban traditions.

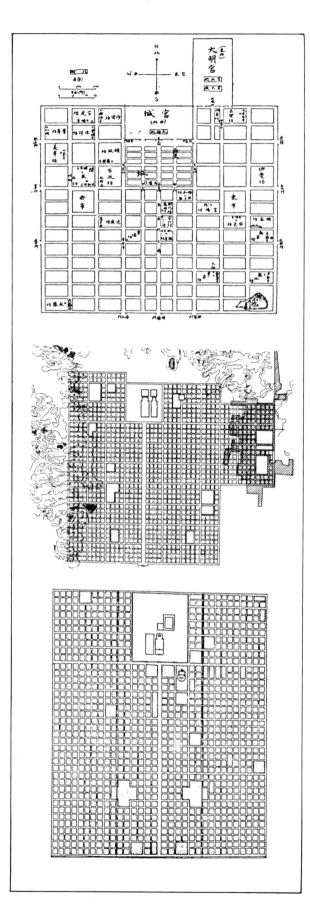

46. Layout of the ancient capitals: Chang'an in China, and Nara (Heijo-kyo) and Kyoto (Heian-kyo) in Japan.

Until about the seventh century, the location of the capital—the seat of the Emperor—changed with each successive reign. The reason lies most probably in the traditional Shinto purification rituals and in the belief that a place where death had occurred was unclean. But with the growing population, the increasing Chinese influence, and with the resulting new centralized government, the need for a permanent capital became evident. The layout of the first planned Japanese cities—Nara, originally Heijo-kyo (710–794), and Kyoto, originally Heian-kyo (794–1868)—reflected basically the town-planning theories of the contemporary T'ang Dynasty of China (618–907). Both cities were patterned after the new and famous Chinese capital, Chang'an (46).

The Chinese city corresponded with the Hindu and esoteric Buddhist cosmic order and world concept. In these, the sky or heaven was regarded as round and the earth rectangular, with its four sides representing the cardinal points of the compass; the realm of in-between was assigned to man. This cosmic order, *ten-chi-jin* in Japanese, complied with the three spheres of existence—the celestial, the atmospheric, and the inferior—and was symbolized by magic cosmograms or mandalas. Patterned after the orders found in mandalas, the city mediated between and represented the essential unity of macrocosmic and microcosmic or human orders.

The site of the city also had to satisfy the Chinese belief in the four-god system, according to which Seryu of the river had to live in the east, Suzaku of the plain in the south, Byakko of the road in the west, and Gembu of the mountain in the north. Rooted in religious considerations, the same orientation was crucial in the most important buildings, like temple precincts, as well. The resulting rectangular city complex then was formed by a system of parallel streets intersecting at right angles in the directions of north-south and east-west. Main thoroughfares were wider than others, especially the one running from the south main gate to the Imperial Palace in the "upper" or northern part. In this way the city was bisected into a western (sa-kyo) and an eastern (u-kyo) section, wherein the plots for residences were allocated hierarchically. In addition, according to the ancient Yin-Yang philosophy, Chinese cities were surrounded by continuous walls. These corresponded to the skin of the human body (*Yin*), the network of streets to the blood vessels (*Yang*).[73] In this symmetrical structure, temples, governmental and other administrative buildings had strictly defined locations. Unlike Greek or Roman examples, these communal facilities were not centrally located around an *agora* or *forum* but arranged along the streets at intervals in a linear pattern.

A layout similar to the Chinese characterized both Kyoto and Nara, although Japanese cities showed some features entirely different from the Chinese prototype and from historical Western city types as well. The western section of both cities never really developed as the eastern ones did, thus, for example, Nara City today occupies only the northeastern region of the originally planned site. As a consequence of Kyoto's rebuildings after fires and wars, the inflexible orthogonal and symmetrical model was gradually transformed into an asymmetrical urban fabric better corresponding to topographical conditions, with the streets slowly forming a random and haphazard network. Today the spatial organization of Kyoto constitutes a mixed

47. The east part of Kyoto as seen from Kyoto Tower.

48. Cityscape in Kyoto around the Nishi-Hongan-ji Temple. Layered spaces and roofs in a long series appear to be superimposed on one another in reversed perspective, creating a vast visual ambiguity.

49. The small lane of Pontocho in Kyoto. The jungle of narrow streets and lanes in densely built, visually impenetrable districts evokes a feeling of depth, suggesting a mystic quality to the spaces behind.

50. The pattern of streets in a Tokyo uptown district suggests the notion of *oku*. The area is surrounded by major roads with secondary roads branching out from them; minor roads were added later. (Drawing courtesy of Fumihiko Maki.)

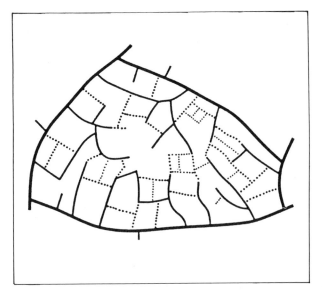

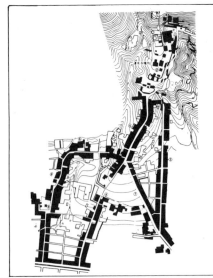

51. The variety of approaches to the Kyomizu Temple in Kyoto.

52. A street leading to the temple in the Kyomizu-zaka district.

system in which an irregular street pattern is superimposed on the ancient grid. In other cities that developed later, as did Tokyo (originally Edo), the grid pattern never evolved, leaving the leading role solely to an irregular texture.

A further difference between the Japanese and Chinese cities, but especially between Japanese and Western cities, is that cities in Japan never had well-defined centers marked by important buildings. They never had towers either since *kamis* were believed to reside not in the heavens above but in the invisible and indefinite depth. Town squares, or *piazzas*, have no tradition and were missing from the townscapes until the modern age. One reason is sociopolitical: the Japanese had no city-states, thus no general assemblies, meetings, city councils. Another reason is more important, since it lies in the unique conception of space manifested in the idea of *oku*. Like the traditional horizontally laid out house, which had no central space inside and was wrapped around only by a vague, almost invisible boundary or several "envelopes," Japanese cities had neither real vertical dimension nor any exact borders, thus no city walls. With no defensive purpose either, cities without such enclosing walls remained open and flexible.[74]

Westerners have always organized their existential spaces around exact centers and surrounded them by fixed boundaries: solid building and city walls. Within them, they created a visual order, an easily intelligible organization or small inner world, as opposed to the disordered, hostile, and unknown outer world. These centers became points of departure from which Westerners were to discover and conquer nature, the infinite universe. Following the same pattern, Western spatial structure is primarily centrifugal in character. In a Japanese city, however, space—represented by the land and nature—moves centripetally from outside in, thus making land overlap with the settlements (47). To date, many large cities in Japan still preserve several small agricultural units within themselves

around the peripheries, sometimes even close to their nominal centers.

While cities have no real spaces and centers, they represent the concept of *ma* and incorporate an endless array of "folded" spaces or *oku*. Right beside modern high-rise buildings there exists a jungle of narrow streets, densely built districts with spatial creases impenetrable to the eye that not only create a feeling of depth but also suggest some mystic quality of the spaces behind and invite discovery. Yet if we try to lift the veils wrapping them in endlessly juxtaposed layers, surprisingly the mystic quality together with the *oku* elude and become "empty" (48, 49). The Japanese city is created, perceived, and understood as an additive texture of its parts or places and thus is denoted by the external distribution of signs and symbols rather than by the physical entity of its objects and enclosures. As typified by Tokyo, it "has neither the structural clarity of European cities built in stone nor the geometric form of grid-planned American cities (50). Instead, it has grown up in a pleat-like, irregular way around a number of nuclei."[75] Because of their different perception and understanding, this notion of urban environment is largely inaccessible to Westerners.

Spaces that are easy to grasp at one glance from certain well-constructed points put the observer in a position superior to his environment. The clear perception of spatial organization and linear or angular perspective, the Renaissance discovery of which was the expression of Western Man as the ruler of this world, cannot exist along the zig-zagging or curving and densely layered roads of Japan. A predominant reliance on visual perception, as in the West, tends to objectify and to instill feelings of mastery over the environment, since the eye sets everything at a distance and establishes and maintains order. In the Japanese built environment, only fragments signified by scattered signs and symbols are encountered. These fail to provide an objective perspective of a definite

53. Innumerable stone votive lanterns line the long paths approaching the Kasuga shrine in Nara.

54. The path leading to the Fushimi-Inari shrine in Kyoto is marked by an endless series of Shinto *torii* gates.

55. The annual *Gion matsuri* is one of the largest festivals in Kyoto.

56–57. Streetscape in the Gion Corner district, Kyoto, and interior of the famous Yoshijima House in Takayama (1881). Streets and street architecture are the most important elements in the Japanese urban structure, where town houses are built in unbroken rows (*machiya* and *nagaya*).

overall spatial pattern. The interwoven fabric of gardens, of architectural and urban spaces, unfolds itself in a more subtle way. Totality as such is never presented visually and in the state of perfection; rather, it is something that the whole human consciousness has to sense and ultimately to understand in its constantly changing sometimes opposing aspects. The more aspects of the phenomena we are able to discover or create, the closer we get to our understanding of it.

As Roland Barthes wrote, the Japanese "city can be known only by an activity of an ethnographic kind: you must orient yourself in it not by book, by address, but by walking, by sight, by habit, by experience; here every discovery is intense and fragile; it can be repeated or recovered only by the memory of the trace it has left in you."[76] This relationship between man and (spatial) reality thus is more phenomenological than objective, based more on the functions of intuition, imagination, and memory, as well as active physical involvement, than dependent simply on vision. Like buildings and gardens, cities too grew piecemeal, in an additive and sequential way, always from the parts toward the whole. The emphasis is on the intimate relationship among the parts, while the whole remains an elusive matter to be conjured up in the imagination of the perceiver.

With this kind of spatial experience, the route, the approach, is as important as the arrival, if not more so. Most Shinto shrines—similar to the mountain type of Buddhist temples—are built outside the cities deep among hills (okumiya), and have long procession paths (sando) that start at the edge of the town (51, 52). These paths, as those around the Kasuga Taisha (early 8th c.) in Nara, the Kompira-san (5th-6th c.) in Kotohira, or the Fushimi-Inari Jinja (founded 711) in Kyoto are often lined with symbols: stone votive lanterns, plaques, gates, and so on. They are full of curves, steps, and small hidden places always hinting toward another one (53, 54). Yet after all the thrill of the approach, the inner sanctuary and its interior with the sacred images still remain hidden: these spaces were not meant to be entered physically, only mentally, spiritually or symbolically. In a Shinto complex there is no real climax or absolute destination. Every node of the paths signifies both a partial arrival and also a point of departure, layering the space in a conspicuous manner. The universal validity of the conception and perception of the environment and space itself as a discontinuous continuity is also well illustrated by the woodblock print (ukiyoe) series of Ando Hiroshige (1797–1858). In one, the famous pilgrimage road between Tokyo (Edo) and Osaka along the seacoast is depicted as a sequence of "Fifty three stages of Tokaido" (1833).[77]

As the kaleidoscopic but open system of the cities evolved and developed, streets have always played a very significant, unique role. Without city centers, squares, or piazzas, the city street became the forum, the place of action and social intercourse, and also took over other public functions. However not even the street exists as an independent urban formation. Consistent with the Japanese understanding of place as ambiguous, the street has come to be regarded as an en space, as an area both the extension of and overlapping with the residential or other quarters along the street's sides. It frequently functions as a living space and a place of common activities as well, where its spatiality is dependent on the current "happening." Among the most spectacular examples of such spatial definition through event occurs during the large number of seasonal festivals all over Japan—like the Aoi-, Gion-, and Jidai-matsuri in Kyoto. These are all processional, never static. The street space gains a new quality for a certain period of time; it is transformed into a special place by way of a "temporary activity" (55).[78] Strange though it may seem to the foreigner, as a leftover or buffer zone between various domains, the street has no name. Instead, districts, wards, and the like are given code numbers or names. Japanese mailing addresses still comply with this scheme. Among the overall examples of the unique Japanese urbanism, probably the most beautiful ones are the webs of those small, narrow streets formed by town houses (*machiya* and *nagaya*) in unbroken rows, such as those in Kyoto and Takayama (56, 57).

As an in-between space like the *engawa* in the house, the street transforms itself into a medium of communication. In fact, this living information channel becomes the most dynamic space in the city. Nowhere else in the world is this more true of streets than in Japan. In certain cases, the street itself is nothing more than diversified forms of information. In the example of shopping street or arcade (*shotengai*) often covered by an extensive glass roof, individual buildings seem to vanish behind open display areas, signs, supergraphics, and advertisements. The information charge, along with the size and form of the street space, then changes constantly according to the functions of the individual cells. This phenomenon renders vague the clear distinction between building and city, interior and exterior, private and public, turning such street

architecture into the most ambiguous urban formation, which further enhances the traditionally multivalent character of Japanese architecture and urbanism (58).

Notes

1. *Kami* in Japanese actually means "spirit," but in English it is often translated as "god" or "goddess."
2. Jean Herbert, *Shinto: At the Fountain-head of Japan* (London: Allen and Unwin, 1967), p. 33.
3. Takeo Nakajima, "Spatial Composition of the Shrine," *Japan: Climate, Space and Concept—Process Architecture No. 25* (1981), p. 103.
4. Herbert, op. cit., 2, p. 33.
5. Ibid., p. 43.
6. In their Shinto mythology, the Japanese consider themselves and the ancestors of the Imperial Family as descendants of Amaterasu, the Sun Goddess. *Nippon*, the name of Japan in Japanese, refers to this (*ni* = sun, *hon* or *pon* = origin). And it is a fact that Japan in its history, as opposed to China for example, has had only one Imperial Dynasty. Thus Hirohito, the present Emperor, is regarded as the 124th sovereign descended in an unbroken line from Jimmu (660–585 B.C.).
7. *Kojiki* covers an era ranging from Japan's prehistoric mythical creation until about A.D. 500 and provides

58. Shotengai in Osaka. The most ambiguous urban formation is the omnipresent small shopping street (*shotengai*), where distinctions between interior and exterior, building and city are rendered vague.

as well additional data about the Imperial Family for the next century and a quarter. *Kojiki* preceded *Nihon Shoki* (Chronicles of Japan) of A.D. 720; the latter is a much longer work and besides mythology contains a fairly reliable history of the sixth and seventh centuries.

8. Ruth Benedict, *The Chrysanthemum and The Sword* (Tokyo: Tuttle, 1954), p. 70.

9. Ibid., p. 54.

10. There are two main branches of Buddhism. The first is *Mahayana* (Greater Vehicle), according to which everybody can attain Buddhahood, that is, can have a place in the vehicle. This branch spread in the north, in China, Korea, Japan, and so on. The second is *Hinayana* (Lesser Vehicle), where Buddhahood is the reward of only a selected few. This grew primarily in the south, in Ceylon and Siam (Thailand, Burma, Cambodia, Laos).

11. E. Dale Saunders, *Buddhism in Japan* (Tokyo: Tuttle, 1972), p. 66.

12. Günter Nitschke, " 'MA': The Japanese Sense of Place," *Architectural Design* (March 1966), p. 154.

13. E. D. Saunders, op. cit., 11, p. 67.

14. T. R. V. Murti, *The Central Philosophy of Buddhism* (London: Allen and Unwin, 1955), p. 32.

15. One of the most prominent figures of the Asuka Period (552–710), the time of the introduction of Buddhism, was Prince Shotoku (574–622), who started and best promoted the relationship with China and the importation of Buddhism. The construction of the first Buddhist temples is attributed to him. The most famous of all is the Horyu-ji (607) built near Nara, where a memorial shrine, the Yumedono, was later erected in his honor.

16. Prince Shotoku himself did not see any contradiction between the two, saying that Shinto was the religion of the past and Buddhism the religion of the future.

17. Mitsukuni Yoshida, "The Ethos of Japanese Life," in Mitsukuni Yoshida, Ikko Tanaka, and Tsune Sesoko, eds., *The Compact Culture* (Hiroshima: Toyo Kogyo, 1982), p. 11. Chikao Fujisawa points out, "few people are aware of the undeniable fact that Zen Buddhism was able to reach the culminating point of its development under the overwhelming influence of Shintoism, which constitutes permanently the kernel of the Japanese existential thought pattern." (*Zen and Shinto* [New York: Philosophical Library, 1959], p. 92).

18. Considering, however, the implemented elements of Taoism and Confucianism, this attitude toward religions could also be correctly called religious pluralism. Yet, surprisingly, the Japanese are not really religious, or at least not according to Christian notions. While the lives of most Japanese are intertwined with religious observances, the majority, according to Edwin O. Reischauer, "some 70 to 80 percent [,] even though carried on the rolls of one or more religious bodies, do not consider themselves believers in any religion" (*The Japanese* [Cambridge, MA: Harvard University Press, 1977], p. 224).

19. The first Christian priest who landed in Kagoshima, south Japan, was the Jesuit Saint Francis Xavier in 1549, but the influence of the first missionaries remained limited throughout the centuries. Under the Tokugawa Shogunate, Christianity was suppressed for political reasons. Japan has been open to this "new" religion from the middle of the nineteenth century however, Christianity is not dominant in Japan. Today it has approximately 800,000 followers—far less than one percent of the total population.

20. Jack Seward, *The Japanese* (Tokyo: Lotus Press, 1977), p. 194.

21. Tomoya Masuda, *Living Architecture: Japanese* (New York: Grosset and Dunlap, 1970), p. 9.

22. As Günter Nitschke pointed out, the distinction between "dynamic" and "static" should be understood not as a judgment of the aesthetics of a composition, but as an evaluation of its adaptability to change, that is, of its relation to time or life itself. (Nitschke, op. cit., 12, p. 151.)

23. Alfred East, quoted by Basil Hall Chamberlain, *Japanese Things* (Tokyo: Tuttle, 1971), p. 53.

24. The English equivalent of *ikebana* is "flower arrangement"; however, the original Japanese meaning refers to the birth of the flower or to bringing life to the flower, and also capturing it alive. It has an intense poetic quality as well, making it the medium of a refined communication between nature and man and, further, between man and man.

25. This idea seems to coincide with Mies van der Rohe's principle "less is more," but for Mies "less" also meant *absolutum,* the final truth, while for the Japanese it means the relative character and mutability of everything existing.

26. *Haiku,* a traditional form of poetry, is composed of only seventeen syllables, with poetic images arranged in a sequential and very compact but impressive way. According to Dr. R. H. Blyth, "A *haiku* is the expression of a temporary enlightenment, in which we see into the life of things." (Quoted in D. T. Suzuki, *Zen and Japanese Culture* [Princeton, N.J.: Princeton University Press, 1973], p. 228.) Since the Japanese language does not specify a subject, the *haiku*'s time is also conspicuously nonspecific. Roland Barthes characterizes this poetry as being "articulated around a metaphysics without subject and without god," corresponding in

this way "to the Buddhist *Mu,* to the Zen *satori,* which is not at all the illuminative descent of God, but 'awakening to the fact,' apprehension of the thing as event and not as substance" (*Empire of Signs,* trans. Richard Howard [New York: Hill and Wang, 1982], p. 78). For further details on Zen, see also note 28. The most famous *haiku* poet was Matsuo Basho (1644–1694) who wrote the following poem, among many others:

> Scent of Chrysanthemums
> And in Nara
> All the many ancient Buddhas.

27. The meanings of *ma* as explained by Iwanami's *Dictionary of Ancient Times,* Tokyo.

28. *Zen* means "silent meditation." Meditation and self-discipline, sometimes to the point of self-denial, are ways to enlightenment (*satori*), the momentary insight into the ultimate oneness of all things or the Great Void that contains the I and everything else. But Zen also teaches the importance of active participation in everyday affairs, as opposed to the withdrawal from the world into mysticism advocated by other Buddhist schools. The involvement in daily activities acknowledges the concreteness of the world through a reflective attitude, the reflection upon the self in a particular situation, and, as such, it is basically the direct, intuitive grasping of the transitorial nature and relative truth of life deeply hidden in the nature of things, in the nature of being. Since the perception of this inner "truth" transcends any mental process or construct—which is outlined in the Zen doctrine of No-Mind (*mushin*)—*satori* cannot be achieved by means of intellectual conceptualization, logic, or rational analysis; it can be expressed, if at all, only in paradoxical forms. In such awareness the Zen mind temporarily experiences the simultaneous existence, or rather the unity, of the physical and metaphysical, the material and the spiritual, the concrete and the abstract in every phenomenon of life, wherein, of course, there is also no dichotomy between analysis and synthesis, between part and whole, between temporality and eternity. With its attention focused on the nature of being/nonbeing Zen can be regarded as perhaps the pioneer of an early Existential philosophy. Yet because no distinction is made between the subject and the object, the subjectivism of most Existentialist schools is absent from Zen. Participation in Zen is a special experience. Participation in Western metaphysics is generally synonymous with the generation and unilateral affirmation of self. In Zen, however, the participant aims to achieve the realization of the oneness of everything. Just when the participant fully realizes itself in this process, it ultimately becomes a part of it. Experiencing this plural "void" (*Sunyata*) occurs when subject and object, being and nonbeing, are the same; that is, when being is both affirmed and negated. In this primordial condition, the center of being is nonexistent, or ambiguous and so temporary and illusory at best, while the very notion of meaning is meaningless. Because it is not logocentric, Zen has avoided all the pitfalls of Western philosophy centered around the primacy of the self and the presence of an absolute truth behind all existence. The philosophy of Zen approaches that of certain branches of contemporary phenomenology, and is even closer to post-structuralist thought. In their life-style and their aesthetics, Zen Buddhist monks favored simplicity and poverty. For further details see D. T. Suzuki, *Zen Buddhism* op. cit., 26.

29. One immediate example of this two-way communication is in the writing of Chinese characters (*kanji*), which is also taught as one of the bases of artistic education. In this form it is called *shodo* (calligraphy). *Kanji* essentially have preserved the symbolic character of Chinese writing and its origin in Chinese painting, as opposed to the Roman alphabet, which has been reduced to a small number of neutral signs or letters. In fact, many Zen-Buddhist paintings were elaborated upon with a written text within the same frame, both inscribed with the same brush. Thus, a certain continuity exists between the writing and the painting, often making it difficult to determine where one ends and the other begins. (With the borrowing of *kanji* parallel with the introduction of Buddhism, Japan adopted her entire system of writing from China. These characters were later somewhat simplified and limited in number—there are approximately 2,000 today—and were complemented with two systems of syllabary writings: *hiragana* and *kata-kana.* Japanese writing today is a mixture of the three systems. Despite borrowing Chinese writing, Japanese language differs basically from Chinese.)

30. Tomoya Masuda, op. cit., 21, p. 9.

31. *Mono no aware,* often translated as the "sadness of things," actually connotes a dialogue with nature, the Japanese sensitivity to the world.

32. Both the form (there are several variations) and the name of the *torii* gates refer to their symbolic or Shinto mythological origin, the perches (*i*) for birds (*tori*). As Jean Herbert explains, "they commemorate the help which some birds gave to the Gods when by their singing they so much intrigued the Sun-goddess Amaterasu-o-mi-kami, that she came out of the cave to which she had retired. And it is probably not wrong to imagine that in its original significance the torii . . . was a magical, protective device." (Herbert, op. cit., 2, p. 95.)

33. The other two famous natural sites are Amanohashidate, along the shore northwest of Kyoto, and Matsushima, at Sendai in the Tohoku district.

34. Günter Nitschke, "Shime: Binding/Unbinding," *Architectural Design* (December 1974), p. 748.

35. Kiyoshi Seike, "A Culture of Wood," *Japan: Climate, Space and Concept—Process Architecture No. 25* (1981), p. 17.

36. In Japanese, Shinto shrines are indicated by the words *jinja, jingu, omiya,* while Buddhist temples by *otera, -dera, -ji, -in.*

37. The Ise Grand Shrine compound has actually two precincts, of which only the inner one or *naiku* (c. 3rd century A.D.) is dedicated to Amaterasu-o-mi-kami, the other outer one or *gekku* (A.D. 478) to Toyouke-no-okami, grain-god.

38. Besides the *naiku* and *gekku* precincts in Ise, the fourteen subsidiary shrines are also rebuilt. Since 1609 the interval between rebuildings has been twenty years, with one exception of twenty four years after 1929. Prior to 1609 it varied slightly. According to Yasutada Watanabe, the first reconstruction took place in A.D. 690 and was repeated irregularly at eighteen, nineteen, twenty, and twenty one years until 1462, when—due to extensive civil warfare—there was an interval of 123 years. The reconstruction after 1585 was twenty four years later, in 1609. (Yasutada Watanabe, *Shinto Art: Ise and Izumo Shrines* [New York: 1974], p. 128.)

39. Joseph Rykwert, *On Adam's House in Paradise* (Cambridge, MA: The MIT Press, 1981), p. 182. For further reference see Mircea Eliade, *The Myth of the Eternal Return* (Princeton, NJ: Princeton University Press, 1954, 1974).

40. Ota Hirotaro, ed., *Japanese Architecture and Gardens* (Tokyo: Kokusai Bunka Shinkokai, 1972), p. 38.

41. See note 37.

42. Yet, as Nitschke pointed out, the early Japanese man was already aware that "it would appear irrelevant to the gods if he, impure and imperfect as he was, succeeded in producing purity and perfection. So . . . he introduced a visual statement of his human limitations: he moved the first gate slightly off the axis. This act had nothing to do with aesthetics." (Nitschke, op. cit., 12, p. 120.)

43. These finials in the case of Ise shrine Naiku compound, where Amaterasu the Sun Goddess is enshrined, is cut horizontally, while in Izumo shrine, the sanctuary of Okuni-nushi no Mikoto, the god of farming, fishing, medicine, and so on, the finials are cut vertically.

44. The Japanese wooden pagoda is derivative of the Indian stupa and as such represents a place for Buddha relics. Later, this function of the pagoda changed, and it came to symbolize, with its size, height, and exquisite design, the importance of the temple. Pagodas are known to have several "stories," indicated by the overhanging roofs. The number of roofs is always odd, three, five, seven, and so on. The quadratic plan and structural arrangement of the pagoda, similar to the layout of the whole temple compound, followed the form of *mandalas,* the maps of the cosmos in esoteric Buddhism.

45. In some cases the fusion between Shinto and Buddhist trends was so extensive that it was debated whether the compound was Buddhist or Shintoist. In the case of Kotohira (or Kompira) it has been decided only fairly recently that it should be considered a Shinto shrine whatever it may have been in the past. (Herbert, op. cit., 2, p. 56.)

46. Beyond the overall symmetry of the compound, the *shinden* type of residence was also characterized by large unified spaces in the buildings, by the lack of both built-in *tatami* floors and sliding wall panels. In their place were polished wooden flooring, fixed or horizontally hinged wooden exterior wall panels, and folding mobile partitions. Columns were cylindrical rather than rectangular.

47. Both Kinkaku-ji, Ginkaku-ji, and the Byodo-in Phoenix Hall, in addition to several other Buddhist temples, were originally private residences or summer retreats. They were converted into religious buildings in accordance with the last wills of their aristocrat owners, Ashikaga Yoshimitsu, Ashikaga Yoshimasa, and Fujiwara Yorimichi respectively.

48. The size of the tea room varied, however. For example, Sen-no-Rikyu famous for his 4.5 *tatami* tea rooms, which in fact were first devised by Takeno Jo-o (1502–55)—designed several three- and even two-*tatami* tea rooms. The *nijiri-guchi* is a low (approximately 28-inch high by 24-inch wide) sliding wooden door through which guests enter the tea house on their knees and onto the elevated *tatami* floor inside. The small size of this entrance symbolizes equality and peace; crawling through it, the person leaves his rank and status behind.

49. The Azekura-zukuri, where the walls—like those of the Shosoin in Nara—were built of horizontal wooden logs, is an exception. Also, it is interesting to note that traditional Japanese wooden structures excluded diagonal bracings employed widely in the West as the means of structural stability.

50. Christian Norberg-Schulz in his book *Existence, Space and Architecture* (London: Praeger, 1971) describes very precisely how far Western conceptions of space were and in many respects still are rooted in the different though rational interpretations of the ancient Greek and later European philosophers. Leucippos, for ex-

ample, "considered space a reality, though it had no bodily existence." Plato, Euclid, and Descartes relied on elaborate geometries as the science of space, and even Kant "regarded space as a basic *a priori* category of human understanding different from and independent of matter" (pp. 9–10). Change has come with Einstein's theory of relativity; only very recently has space come to be regarded not as a physical entity but as the field of perception. This can be seen particularly in the works of such phenomenological philosophers as Martin Heidegger, Gaston Bachelard, Maurice Merleau-Ponty, and so on.

51. Very often spaces where *kami* were summoned and believed to be descending into (*himorogi*) were marked off on the ground only by a pebbly surface surrounded by a rope (*shimenawa*) stretched around four poles in a rectangular pattern.

52. Martin Heidegger, "Building Dwelling Thinking" in *Poetry, Language, Thought,* trans. Albert Hofstadter (New York: Harper Colophon Books, 1971), p. 154.

53. The Japanese believed that spirits (*kami*) lived in a world of darkness, and thus the feeling of space became associated with the appreciation of things hidden in darkness and shadows. This appreciation is expressed in Jun' ichiro Tanizaki's short novel *In Praise of Shadows* (Tokyo: Tuttle, 1984).

54. Arata Isozaki, "Space-Time in Japan—MA" In *MA: Space-Time in Japan,* catalog for the exhibit "MAN transFORMS" in the Cooper-Hewitt Museum during the Japan Today Festival (New York: 1978), p. 13, also *The Japan Architect* (February 1979), p. 70.

55. Parts of this chapter appeared also in Botond Bognar, "Typology of Space-Constructions in Contemporary Japanese Architecture," *Japan: Climate, Space and Concept—Process Architecture No. 25* (1981), p. 135.

56. Nitschke, op. cit., 12, pp. 147–148.

57. Ibid., p. 131.

58. Ibid., p. 154.

59. As Koji Yagi points out, in contrast to ancient Egyptian hieroglyphs of houses and buildings, which indicate the importance of the walls in construction, Chinese ideograms, used also in Japanese writing, emphasize the key role of the roof in architecture. Koji Yagi, *A Japanese Touch for Your Home* (Tokyo: Kodansha International, 1982), p. 6.

60. The custom of sitting on cushions on the *tatami* floor still exists in Japan. Even in the most modern homes, at least one room is arranged in the traditional way with *tatami* floor, sliding screens (*fusuma*), and so on.

61. Op. cit., 53.

62. The size of one *tatami* is regarded as the minimum area to sleep on; one-half of that size is the minimum space for sitting. Thus, contrary to such Western misinterpretations as those of Bruno Taut: this size—like other related dimensions in the house—is not the result of an analytical derivation from the "perfect" proportions and symmetry of the human body as in Leonardo da Vinci's "normal man's scheme" or Le Corbusier's Modulor concept (Ching-yu Chang, "Japanese Spatial Conception," *The Japan Architect* [April 1984], p. 67). Originally, during the Heian Period, there were no fixed-*tatami* floors in Shinden-zukuri residences and palaces, only polished wooden ones. *Tatami* was a thin rush mat carried with the person and rolled out on the board floor for sitting. It was only later, with the development of the *Shoin-zukuri* residence, that the *tatami* became thicker (1.8 and 2.5 inches) and was used as a permanent fixed floor cover in rooms of special significance. *Tatami* has always been highly regarded, and rooms with this floor are slightly higher in elevation. Among the several standard *tatami* sizes three are most commonly used. Traditionally, in the Kansai area (Osaka and Kyoto and vicinity), the length of the *tatami* depended on the distance in between the columns. Thus: 12.6 shaku ÷ 2 = 6.3 shaku (191 cm.) (1 shaku is the traditional unit of measurement in Japan and equals 30.3 cm.) while the width was half of the length, 3.15 shaku = 95.5 cm. Therefore the *kyoma tatami* has a size of 95.5 × 191 cm. Around Nagoya, the distance between the columns was smaller, only 12 shaku. Thus, the size of *chukyoma* is 91 × 182 cm. This way of deriving the basic module (*tatami* size) from the length of the span between posts also characterized the *sukiya-zukuri* style in general. In the Kanto area (Tokyo and vicinity), the size of the *tatami* is determined by the dimensions between the centers of the columns, which is 12 shaku (364 cm.). After deducting the dimension of the column (12 × 12 cm.), the rest is further divided by two (364 − 12 = 352 ÷ 2 = 176). Hence, length of the *edoma* (or *inakama*) is 176 cm., while the width, complying with the other dimension between the column centers is 87.0 cm. (9 shaku or 273 cm. − 12 cm.) ÷ 3 = 87.0 cm. This kind of modular derivation, based on the length of the span between posts, measured from the center of each post, was followed mainly in the *Shoin-zukuri* style of traditional architecture. These *tatamis* of three different sizes are used today everywhere in the country. The most popular is the smallest, the *edoma*. (This information was kindly furnished to me by the staff of Design System Co. Ltd., Tokyo.)

63. About the role of *tatami* in the modular system of Japanese architecture, see Hirotaro Ota, ed., *Japanese Architecture and Gardens* (Tokyo and New York: Ko-

kusai Bunka Shinko-kai, 1972), pp. 43–44, and Koji Yagi, *A Japanese Touch for Your Home* (Tokyo and New York: Kodansha International, 1982), pp. 42–46. Arata Isozaki, in his essay "Katsura: The Ambiguity of Its Space," points out that the *kiwari*, or modular system, of the *shoin*-type architecture was eventually relaxed in the development of *sukiya*-type residences, which became the "free-style" architecture of the common people (unpublished manuscript, pp. 33, 34).

64. If the residence is large enough, however, customarily certain rooms are appointed as sleeping spaces, eating spaces, and so on. But every *tatami* room can be used easily, just as they are, for various purposes.

65. Before a house or any building is constructed, prescribed rituals are performed to make the site sacred. According to Shinto purification rituals, first the sacred rope (*shimenawa*) is stretched around, then a temporary altar is set up within. During a short ceremony the Shinto priest petitions the spirit of earth for the successful completion and good fortune of the building. The deity thus becomes a guardian of the house, protecting it and its occupants.

66. See note 49.

67. The typical house is constructed primarily to mitigate the discomfort of the rainy season, summer, and the typhoon season. Spring and autumn, the most pleasant seasons, cause no problem. As for winter, the traditional Japanese attitude is that the human body can endure the discomfort caused by the cold.

68. See note 62.

69. Arata Isozaki, op. cit., 54, p. 33.

70. Jorge M. Ferreras, "Frontal Perception in Architectural Space," *Japan: Climate, Space and Concept—Process Architecture No. 25* (1981), p. 62.

71. Koji Yagi, "Climate and the Japanese Way of Life," *Japan: Climate, Space and Concept—Process Architecture No. 25* (1981), p. 30. Michihiro Matsumoto outlines this very special art of communication as follows: "What argument is to Westerners, *haragei* is to Japanese. The former is verbal boxing, wherein strategy is what counts. . . . Japanese *haragei* practitioners listen more attentively to the pauses between the words and gestures. One doesn't need the art of persuasion that underlies Western communication practices to be a successful communicator in Japanese society. In fact, *haragei* performers are verbally inadequate in front of others, and by no means logical, coherent, or articulate, because they give *ma* full play. . . . There is in Japan no historical evidence of great public orators like those known in the West"(Michihiro Matsumoto, *Haragei* [Tokyo: Kodansha International, 1984], pp. 32, 40).

72. Charles Moore, op. cit., chapter 1, 6.

73. Isozaki in his "Nine Quotation Sources" (JA [October-November 1977], p. 20.) describes this ancient Chinese philosophy as "A diagram of the universe in which change gives birth to change, opposition gives birth to opposition, and all of this results in an indefinite transmigration. The Yin and Yang philosophy interprets the world of nature as a nondialectic process of revolution in which cavity, or void, not the *logos* of the West, is the central element." The two opposing forces, Yin and Yang, exist in everything. They perpetually interact with and control each other, providing the basis for existence. The Yin element represents the female element, negativity, melancholy, depth, secrecy, darkness, and odd numbers; it also symbolizes the skin of the human body and other surrounding boundaries such as city walls, fences, the outer walls of the house, and the like. The Yang element represents the male element, positivity, heaven, the sun, the heights, movement, daytime, and even numbers; it also symbolizes blood circulation in the human body and such other interiors as street organizations in the city or living and moving inner spaces. For further details, see Simon F. Gale, "Orientation," *Japan: Climate, Space and Concept—Process Architecture No. 25* (1981), pp. 37–39.

74. Townsmen or commoners were not involved in the wars among feudal landlords; wars were fought by the warrior class (*samurai*). Thus a defensive role was assigned to castles only, but even in this case, it was limited.

75. Kazuhiro Ishii, "The Intellectual and Today's Urban Hopelessness," *The Japan Architect* (May 1980), p. 5.

76. Roland Barthes, *Empire of Signs*, trans. Richard Howard (New York: Hill and Wang, 1982), p. 36.

77. It should be noted that the whole Japanese way of life has evolved along such a "natural" rhythm, as described by the concepts of *hare* and *ke*. While *hare* refers to what might be called the nodes in one's life, special occasions and events that are recognized formally and socially, *ke* indicates the periods between *hare* events. *Hare* events, such as birth, graduation, marriage, promotion, and so on, are widely celebrated, after which life returns to the calm and peaceful flow of time. It might be said that *hare* occasions are the various checkpoints in a person's journey through life. For further details see M. Yoshida, op. cit., 17, p. 11.

78. Nitschke, describing its role in detail, refers to the city street during these special festivals or "linear 'happenings,' " as "temporary activity space." (Nitschke, op. cit., 12, p. 128.)
The word *matsuri* originally referred to Shinto religious rituals, though today it has a wider range of meaning.

While most of these annual festivals have retained their traditional form and significance, some have been adapted to modern times. As special events they are regarded as *hare* occasions in one's own life or that of the community.

59. The Kaichi Primary School in Matsumoto city exemplifies the way Western styles influenced provincial architecture in the early Meiji Period. Traditional master carpenter and architect of the building Kiyoshige Tateishi adopted Western plan and style but used Japanese techniques borrowed from "godown" architecture (an Asian type of storehouse or department store) on the exterior walls and used traditional wooden techniques in the structural system (1876, K. Tateishi).

60. Parliament Building (Tokyo; 1936). With the introduction of Western architecture, the Japanese started building with new materials, new technology, and in a new spirit.

61. Kabuki Theater in Ginza, Tokyo (1924, S. Okada). The age of assimiliation of Western culture was pregnant with contradiction, resulting sometimes in rather anachronistic buildings.

3. Modern Japanese Architecture

Introduction of Western Architecture

With Emperor Meiji's rise to power in 1868, Japan opened her gates once more to the rest of the world after more than 200 years of isolation. A new relationship with the West became possible in just about every area. Yet it was clear that if Japan wanted to become an equal partner and ultimately a member of Western society, she had to keep abreast of the West's social, political, industrial, and commercial development. Japan lagged behind in many fields, especially science and technology; adopting elements of the new civilization and culture was now a matter of survival. She had to accomplish this within a very short period of time.

The thirst for new ideas and things Western was clearly manifested in the most diversified fields of culture and art, with architecture in a foremost position. Invitations were extended to Western architectural theoreticians and technical experts to come to Japan; their main task—besides practical work—was to teach. They included the Englishman Joshiah Conder, the Frenchman C. de Boinville, the Italian C.V. Capelletti, and the German Hermann Ende. Conder (1852–1920), certainly the most prominent among them, worked and taught in Tokyo for more than four decades beginning in 1877. Indeed, he did more to advance and modernize Japanese architecture than any other foreigner, for which he is loved and admired even today. Conder designed a large number of prestigious buildings, among them the Imperial Household Museum (1882), the Rokumeikan (1883), the Nikolai Cathedral (1891), the Mitsubishi Building No. 1 (1894) in Tokyo, and many residences in Tokyo, Nagoya, Osaka, Kobe, and so on, primarily for members of the wealthy upper class. Understandably they were all patterned after the contemporary European Eclectic styles. Conder was as important a teacher as he was an architect; he raised the first generation of Western-type architects, who graduated from Tokyo Industrial College in 1879.[1]

After only a brief time, these young architects

took over the various design and teaching functions. Kingo Tatsuno (1854–1919), one of the leading figures of this group, was also the first to go abroad. He went to England after graduation to study and gain further experience. Upon his return to Japan, he subsequently became a professor in the Imperial University Building Engineering Department.[2] After Conder retired, Tatsuno and his fellow Japanese teachers assumed full responsibility for educating the new generations of architects. Tatsuno is credited with founding the Japanese Institute of Architects (JIA) in 1886, where he served as president from 1898 until 1918, and for opening the first private design office in 1903.[3] Besides Tatsuno, Otokuma Katayama (1853–1917) and Yorinaka Tsumagi (1859–1916) should be mentioned as the most important and influential architects of the Meiji Period (1868–1912).

The first period of Western architecture in Japan was marked by the activities of foreign architects and the feverish learning of the Japanese. A great number of these young Japanese traveled and worked abroad; their sense of purpose—to make good use of the foreign knowledge at home—was deeply instilled in their hearts. Their basic assumption, however, as Teijiro Muramatsu points out, was not to import the foreign spirit but rather the new materials and techniques of the West. Their attitude was succinctly expressed in their slogan, "Japanese spirit and Western knowledge" (*Wakonyosai*).[4] The construction methods and building technologies long applied in the West were to be transplanted to Japanese soil. The architectural use of steel, reinforced concrete, brick, and glass was novel to the Japanese. Inevitably the application of these new methods and materials in Japan was accompanied by the contemporary European architectural style. Despite the honest intention of many architects to continue a "Japanese spirit," imitations (59) and even replicas of Neoclassical and Eclectic architecture began mushrooming in Japanese cities. They drew increasing criticism from

other architects and the public alike.

Carpenters (*daiku*), the masters of traditional techniques in wood, first constructed these buildings. The skilled hands adopted the new construction methods of the heterogeneous Western architecture surprisingly fast and with no great difficulty. These very same carpenter dynasties later founded several of today's biggest construction companies. Truly complex in nature, these dynasties had—and as construction companies still have—quite a special character. Before modernization, carpenters were jacks of all trades, structural engineers as well as architects. The new companies have carried on the tradition of total building activity, from architectural design through production, research, engineering, and the construction work itself. Among the most often heard names are Takenaka Komuten, the Shimizu Construction Company, Ohbayashi Gumi, Taisei Corporation, and the Kajima Corporation. These are sometimes referred to as the Big Five. The modernization of the building industry has seen the consolidation of power in the hands of this group. Today it controls more than one-third of all construction in Japan. Big Five designs are frequently prize winners in national competitions. In addition, these companies regularly turn out large-scale and prominent projects, which will be discussed in later chapters.

The four decades commencing at the turn of the century were one of the most difficult, most complex periods in the history of Japanese architecture. It was a time of confusion, overflowing with contradictions and clashes among several opposing theories and trends, a period that was slowly paving the way for the new Japanese architecture that emerged after the Second World War. The first trend, pursuing the newly acquired technology and engineering, blindly copied the forms of Western buildings. The parliament building constructed in Tokyo is an example. In 1908 the government dispatched an official delegation to several European countries; on their return they presented proposals for the building based on what they had learned abroad. This was met with resistance from another group that had formed around Kingo Tatsuno and Chuta Ito (1867–1954). They wanted a "Japanese Style" combined with Western technology; yet they had no idea what such a style should look like. A fruitless debate resulted in the postponement of construction for several years. Whatever its drawbacks, the structure finally built in 1936 reflects an overall technical skill in prewar Japanese architecture (60).

Engineering-oriented architects gained significant momentum after the great 1923 Kanto earthquake; it destroyed most of Tokyo, including many of the new buildings. Only those built with reinforced concrete or with steel escaped largely undamaged. This marked the beginning of a general emphasis on these structural methods and their widespread acceptance. With increasing self-confidence, the architect-engineers began to opine "architecture is not an art." Engineers ruled the architectural world during this period.

The deepening worldwide economic depression of the 1930s reached Japan soon after this, to be followed by a rapid militarization and the subsequent aggression in Asia. The developing political situation, one leading to fascism, created conditions conducive to the growth of a new architectural ideology. Led by the architect-theoretician Chuta Ito, this trend resulted in an extremely nationalistic architecture. The designs were characterized by an emphasis or better, an overemphasis on their Asian qualities. Invitations for competitions required that entries follow "a Japanese style founded in Oriental taste."[5] This extreme academicism produced many reinforced-concrete buildings that resembled wooden houses. With their heavy, tiled roofs they looked more than anachronistic and contradictory. Shin'ichiro Okada can be cited as a prominent representative of this trend, called the Imperial Roof Style (*teikan yoshiki*) (61).

The first architectural movement that was highly critical of—and broke radically with—the ruling trends of Eclecticism and academic thinking is linked to the activities of the so-called Secession Group. The group, as suggested by its name, came under the particular influence of Viennese Secessionism and European Art Nouveau as well. The original six members were all 1920 graduates of Tokyo Imperial University.[6] Though they worked together as a group only until 1928, their liberating effect on contemporary Japanese architecture was most significant. With its rather Expressionistic interpretation of Secession, Mamoru Yamada's Tokyo Central Telegraph Office (1924) well exemplifies their work in the early 1920s.

In many respects the introduction and beginning of modern architecture can also be attributed to the group. Several of its members, like Bunzo Yamaguchi (1902–1978), Chikatada Kurata (b. 1895), and Mamoru Yamada (1894–1966), were soon moving beyond Secessionism and Expressionism to turn to a more rational design based on logic and functionalism. Later, Sutemi Horiguchi (b. 1895), Kikuchi Ishimoto (1894–1963), and others became flagbearers of Modernism. Yamaguchi became known through his design for the Dental Specialist College (1933), one of the first Japanese buildings in the International Style. Yamada worked for the Ministry of Communications, where a small but talented group was coming together to implement the latest achievements of contemporary European architecture. Apart from Yamada, Tetsuro Yoshida (1894–1956) was a leading figure in the group. He designed many buildings; the Central Post Offices in both Tokyo (1934) and Osaka (1939) are his best works from that period (62).

In 1916 Frank Lloyd Wright came to Japan to design and build the new Imperial Hotel (1922).[7] He set up an office in Tokyo that he often visited while commuting between Japan and America. Interestingly, Wright's influence on the development of modern Japanese architecture, apart from drawing the attention of the Japanese to their own traditions in the midst of wholesale Westernization, was rather limited. His long-time disciple Arata Endo (1889–1951) continued to design in Wright's style and produced some noteworthy buildings like the Koshien Hotel (1930). But beyond Endo, few architects were inclined to follow Wright's path.[8] This is true even of Antonin Raymond (1888–1976), a Czech-born American architect who in 1919 worked as Wright's chief assistant in Tokyo.

Raymond broke with Wright a year later, well before the Imperial Hotel was completed, but decided to stay in Japan and establish his own design practice in Tokyo. In the difficult period that followed, Raymond was able to throw off Wright's influence and develop a new philosophic basis for his architecture. As Michael Czaja pointed out, this was "the functional approach to style" that Raymond followed ever after.[9] His intentions thus coincided well with those of the International Style, yet Raymond was able to achieve a somewhat Japanese interpretation of this style in many of his works. The change in his approach was signaled by the completion just after the 1923 Kanto earthquake of his own House in Reinanzaka in Tokyo.

With this, Raymond became the foremost representative of a straightforward modern architecture and, as such, he was one of the most influential designers in Japan for years to come. His role in Japanese architecture can be likened to that of Conder's a few decades earlier. His office turned out numerous significant projects and produced a number of prominent architects, among them Kunio Maekawa and Junzo Sakakura, and furniture designer George Nakashima; they all later opened their own offices. Maekawa worked with Raymond for five years, from 1930 to 1935. Important Raymond projects of this time included the Rising Sun Petroleum Company Office Building (1926) in Yokohama, the Tokyo Golf Club (1930) in Saitama Prefecture, Houses for the Akaboshi family (1932 and 1933), and many others. The Yokohama office building not only shows the strong influence of the Viennese architect Otto Wagner, but also—as Kenneth Frampton points out—seems to be influential in recent Japanese architectural intentions.[10]

In addition to Raymond, Bruno Taut, a refugee from Nazi Germany, was invited by the Japan International Architectural Association to come to Japan in 1933. Before finally settling in Turkey, he lived in Tokyo for several years and toured the country extensively. His critical writings reinforced the modern trends in Japan, while drawing worldwide attention to such historical monuments as the Ise Shrine and the Katsura Imperial Villa. Yet, beyond recognizing their greatness, along a somewhat biased, modernist view, he saw them only as simple and logical constructions, achievements of a purist and functional-rationalist attitude. As such, for Taut they were designs that coincided with the similar intentions of the Modern Movement. Like many other modern Western and Japanese architects later on, Taut considered these buildings the direct predecessor of modern Japanese architecture. In so doing, he not only failed to recognize the ambiguity of spaces, but also dismissed or neglected the existence of ornamentation, the "brilliant, gorgeous, sometimes gaudy elements of style which went into the design work" of Katsura. Katsura, in fact, "is a complex mixture, bound up with a literary geneology, architectural styles (*shoin, sukiya*, etc.), political sentiments, and the relations between all of these," as Isozaki pointed out.[11] The same failure to understand caused Taut to reject completely the exquisitely but extensively decorated Toshogu Shrine in Nikko, which he labeled as "fake" shogun style.

At the same time that foreign architects were active in Japan, many young Japanese architects went abroad to study in various schools and receive first-hand experience in the offices of famous modern architects. By this time Walter Gropius and Le Corbusier were idolized in Japan. Both Bunzo Yamaguchi and Chikatada Kurata went to study

62. The Osaka Central Post Office Building (1939, T. Yoshida). At first the contemporary modern architecture of Europe influenced only a small group of young architects who, in governmental service, were responsible for several educational and other public buildings.

in the Bauhaus and worked with Gropius. Tetsuro Yoshida also studied in Germany. Takamasa Yoshizaka (1917–1981), Junzo Sakakura, and Kunio Maekawa all worked for Le Corbusier at various times. Some of these architects slowly began to claim an international reputation. Sakakura's Japanese Pavilion at the 1937 International Exposition in Paris, for example, won the Grand Prix and high praise from Sigfried Giedion.

In the same year, Togo Murano (1891–1984) completed his Ube Public Hall (1937). With its curving brick facade and characteristic volumes, the building represented a line in early modern Japanese architecture that ran parallel to the development of the more radical International Style. Throughout his career Murano interpreted Modernist intentions in his own and sometimes rather expressive way. Both the Morigo Building (1932) in Tokyo and the Sogo Department Store (1935) in Osaka are early but good examples of his approach. Until his recent death, Murano continued to make significant contributions to contemporary Japanese architecture (63).

The Japan International Architectural Association (Nihon Kokusai Kenchiku Kai) was founded in 1929 in obvious response to Gropius's demand for an "International Architecture." While promoting internationalism in its program, the association did not reject a "genuine localism," which more often than not was tantamount to "establishing their theory on a basis of nationalism." Critical of this attitude, the outstanding theoretician Yukichi Kono wrote in a 1930 essay called "A Suggestion for International Architecure": "We should aim at creating an architecture which can be applied universally by reexamining Japanese traditional architecture from the standpoint of modern architecture."[12] He also warned of the prevailing sociopolitical setup in Japan, which hindered the development of modernization and internationalization in architecture.

It was in the spirit of this nationalism that

63. The Sogo Department Store in Osaka is one of Togo Murano's early contributions to the development of Japanese modern architecture (1935).

Maekawa's (b. 1905) entries in many architectural competitions were rejected.[13] Maekawa's designs were consistently based on advanced technology, industrialization, and rationalization. In this respect he was much ahead of his time in Japan. As the best-known representative of international modern architecture, he was frequently criticized in official circles because his works were not in harmony with the "Asian-Japanese style." Maekawa answered these charges by saying, "You request something Japanese. But this modern architecture is as Japanese as the battleships of the Imperial Navy of which you are proud."[14] Nevertheless, increasing militarization and the tight grip of the government's demagogic ideology and nationalist politics were radically to suppress the advanced thinking and intentions of young artists and architects. By the mid-1930s the Japanese modern architectural movement collapsed.

With the end of the Second World War, the first chapter in the history of modern Japan and the first period of her new architecture were brought to a close. This first period marked the time for learning and for seeking ways and means of renewal. Thus it is difficult to speak about it in terms of an independent architecture. It was a time of transition and seething change rather than of accomplished and exalted synthesis. Change was to come after the war with the end of reconstruction work and the rebirth of Japan as a democratic society and an economic power on the world scene.

International Trends

The Second World War left Japanese cities in ruins, with many leveled to the ground; the great extent of the devastation was partly because cities were built almost completely of wood. A total of 4,200,000 homes were destroyed, a figure corresponding to a quarter of all the homes at that time. Air raids, shellings, and fires damaged 119 cities; 28 more than 70 percent destroyed and 10 more than 80–90 percent destroyed, including Hiroshima and Nagasaki.

Millions of people were without shelter. Reconstruction work, immense and urgent, became imperative, yet systematic rebuilding was hampered by the lack of a well-elaborated government city planning policy. When such programs were prepared, there was still a delay in implementing concrete measures. Because of this delay, during the first two years after the war families were pressed to begin rebuilding their homes on their own in a fashion described as "self-construction." The clearing away of debris composed of ash and wood did not take long, so the work could start almost immediately and without much difficulty. Homes were rebuilt on their previous lots, which also meant that most cities would retain their original prewar structure. Nagoya and Hiroshima were the only exceptions, where newly devised plans for rebuilding could be more or less executed. Other cities, including Tokyo, employed self-construction and were thereby denied the chance for up-to-date city planning. These cities suffer even today from such ailments as traffic congestion, lack of greenery and parks, and so on.

Reconstruction work naturally became the main order of the day for the architects. The large number of urgent tasks meant that quantity won over quality. The great demand for residential buildings could be met by new prefabricated systems. Several systems were developed and tested in actual use. The first successful one was Maekawa's PREMOS System of prefabricated family homes, which used wood as its main building material. But with the basic industries still incapacitated, manufacturing proved to be sluggish and more expensive than the traditional on-site building methods. PREMOS was thus shortlived despite the good and up-to-date ideas. Later systems based on steel, glass, and plastic were somewhat more successful, since they could take advantage of recovering industrial production. Kiyoshi Ikebe's (1920–1979) serially produced houses, marked only with numbers like SH-1, SH-2, SH-3, or Makoto Matsuzawa's Minimum House were conceived in the spirit of pure economy.

Although no outstanding buildings can be cited during the first five years after the war, the period proved to be useful for architects, especially for the young generation, in elaborating and clarifying their theories for the years to follow. The ideas of international modern architecture gained ground and won wide acceptance, a breakthrough that caused no problems and encountered no resistance this time.

The reason for this success lies, first of all, in the situation created by war's end. The work of reconstruction assigned more or less the same tasks to architects all over the world. In order to identify and discuss these common tasks, the dialog among architects from different countries was resumed with renewed vitality. CIAM held its first meeting after the war in Bridgewater, England, in 1947 and the second in Bergamo, Italy, in 1949.[15] The topics naturally focused on the "Rehabilitation of Europe" and the "Continuity in Homes," respectively, as well as on the duties of architects in relation to the work. The problems of developing new cities and new community centers, "The Heart of the City," was the main issue of the eighth congress in London in 1951. The Japanese participated for the first time with the presence of Maekawa, Tange, and Yoshizaka. Tange took the opportunity to introduce his plan for the reconstruction of Hiroshima. As a consequence of the increasingly active participation of Japanese architects in the work of the international forum, more ideas of the Modern Movement were imported into Japan.

The task of establishing new building-material industries and the industrialization of architecture in general were the same in America, Europe, and Japan. The growing amount of work and simultaneous pressing labor shortage made the introduction of a wide range of industrialized methods and prefabrication necessary. Strict rationalization and careful analysis of economic factors were obviously no less necessary. The scrupulous intention of meeting the demands of function further emphasized the traditions of functionalism in the Modern Movement. Such concerns influenced the early development of new buildings at the beginning of the 1950s.

The first in Japan was designed by Antonin Raymond.[16] His Readers' Digest Building (1951) exemplifies the American and European architecture of that time. It has a simple T-shape ground plan, steel and ferroconcrete skeleton structure, rough concrete surfaces, steel and glass elevations, and total air conditioning. The same year saw the completion of the Modern Art Museum (1951) in Kamakura, which was in fact the first modern building designed by a Japanese after the war. Junzo Sakakura (1904–1969), a disciple of Le Corbusier, implemented his master's ideas, but his own way of setting this asbestos panel-clad museum into the historical surroundings and the landscape made the finished building undeniably Japanese (64).[17]

With the increasingly urgent demand for more public buildings, architects of the third generation assumed leading roles. Kenzo Tange, Kunio Maekawa, Junzo Sakakura, and others, although graduates of several years before, began their real careers only after the war. Designs in demand included office buildings, railway stations, factories, and the like. Sakakura finished another project in 1951, the Japanese-French Institute in Tokyo. In the following year, the new Kyoto Railway Station, designed by the Department of National Railways, was ready, which in an extended form serves as the main building of the recent complex. Living up to his reputation as the most notable representative of the International Style, Maekawa in

64. The early postwar years brought about genuine modern Japanese architecture. The Modern Art Museum in Kamakura clearly shows the Corbusian vocabulary, yet its setting is unmistakably Japanese (1951, annex 1966, J. Sakakura).

1953 designed the first completely prefabricated public building, the Nippon Sogo Bank. Its system includes a welded steel-frame structure, large glass surfaces in aluminum frames in the main elevation, and concrete wall panels on the sides.

The application of industrialized methods and the strictly functional approach are clearly visible in the projects of Kenzo Tange (b. 1913) as well. Both the Haramachi Factory of the Tosho Printing Company (1954) near Numazu and the City Hall in Shimizu (1955) were built purely of steel and glass. The former is characterized by its large spaces with no intermediary supports, while the latter bears the typical office building arrangement pioneered in the West by Mies van der Rohe. The birth of these buildings closely coincides with the mushrooming of huge and dull boxes of steel and glass skyscrapers all around America, Europe, and other countries, reaching their climax in such buildings as the Lake Shore Drive Apartments in Chicago (1951), United Nations Headquarters (1950) and Lever House (1952) in New York, and the Crown Hall and other edifices of the Illinois Institute of Technology in Chicago (1955).

The Tokyo Metropolitan Government Office (1957), also by Tange, was conceived in a spirit consistent with his two earlier works mentioned above, but this building incorporated additional, new features (65). The supporting skeleton is made of reinforced concrete—a better protection against earthquakes. Moreover, the elevations do not follow the solution of simple glass surfaces; Tange applied a special balcony-type system of *bris-soleil* very similar in effect to the light- and shade-controlling roof and veranda of the traditional houses. The historical reference is even stronger in the open mezzanine floor, where a broad flight of stairs leads pedestrians directly to the entrance under the pilotis. Tange admits that the prototype here was the Old Imperial Palace in Kyoto (27–28).

Revival of Traditional Architecture

Most cities were rebuilt in the traditional way after the war. In Tokyo, some 80 percent of the buildings—mostly houses, even today—are of wood. As has been pointed out, these buildings were erected by the citizens themselves or with carpenters' minimum help, to replace their lost homes as fast as possible. They were the direct carryover in method, material, and style from their long-existing traditional architecture. Though smaller, with very little comfort, and inferior in quality, they provided

shelter similar to what they had known before.

As the situation consolidated, industry and the economy improved to the point where people could afford bigger homes designed by architects. The types covered a wide range—the Westernized International Style at one end and the strictly traditional at the other. It was through the very activities of the new generation of architects, most of whom at first totally rejected the application of traditional elements, that the two extremes were gradually brought together in a highly successful way. The revival of the traditional style made its debut in Japan's residential architecture. Large houses of concrete or steel that provided Western-style comfort in a rational and functional way were

65. Tokyo Metropolitan Government Office (1957, K. Tange). In the first period following World War II, the theories and practice of the Modern Movement exerted the strongest influence on Japanese architecture.

built with *tatami* rooms, sliding screens, and wooden details—all reminders of the historical forms. It was at this point that Kiyoshi Seike (b. 1918) established his reputation with his residential architecture, a reputation that endures to this day. Based on concrete wall structures, both of his two early designs, the residences for Professor Mori (1951) and Professor Saito (1952), made use of the formal elements of the old *shinden-zukuri* houses (66). Then in 1953, Kenzo Tange designed as his own house another ferroconcrete version of the *shinden-zukuri;* unlike Seike's, this house—as a prelude to his Hiroshima project—is elevated on pilotis.

Kenzo Tange's genius was manifested in his role as leader of the vanguard of those architects who, apart from introducing the ideas of contemporary international modern architecture, blended traditional Japanese formal elements into the more important public buildings. By recognizing the significance of the trend, Tange commenced a new phase in postwar Japanese architecture. The first step was the Hiroshima Peace Park with the Atomic Memorial Museum (1955). The museum, a milestone in itself, became the first world-famous building of Japan's modern era (67).

Tange won the commission through a nationwide competition held in 1949. Since it required several buildings on a broader scale than customary for him, buildings to be placed in the context of the entire memorial park and the city as well, the Peace Park project gave Tange his first opportunity to delve into issues of urban design. The complex was laid out along a straight axis, with the museum in front as the symbolic gate to the whole, a pattern also found in Shinto compounds. At first glance, the building suggests two associations. On the one hand, the sturdy reinforced concrete structure, the unfinished rough surfaces, and the simple form creating an impressive image, all bring Le Corbusier's architecture to mind. On the other hand, the proportions of the building, the horizontal volume on pilotis, undeniably refer to the ancient Ise Shrine, but more so to the Shosoin (752), the building of the Imperial Treasury in Nara dating back some 1,000 years. The symbolism here is even more complex. While the Ise Shrine and the Shosoin symbolize the origin and the ancient spirit of Japan respectively, the Hiroshima Peace Museum has become the symbol of the birth of a new Japan and a new Japanese architecture.

The museum also marks the beginning of the extensive use of ferroconcrete structures. This—beyond the influence of Le Corbusier and Gropius—is traceable to the features and the advantages provided by such structures in the Japanese circumstance. Ferroconcrete structures can be almost freely fashioned into any shape. The typical post-and-beam system, not to mention the more dissolved softer forms and shell structures, can all be constructed with equal ease. These structures are highly resistant to seismic movements—a quality of basic importance in Japan—and are undamaged by fire, which accompanies most earthquakes. Such features have contributed to making the use of ferroconcrete all the more imperative. Indeed, Japanese architects went so far as to declare "Concrete is ours." In this spirit, the numerous and distinctive concrete buildings gave birth to what Robin Boyd called the "New Japan Style."[18]

The revival of traditional forms might be better understood in the larger international context of that time. The end of the 1950s saw an increased interest in national and local architectures all around the world. One reason is that countries crushed and ruined during the Second World War had managed to restore their economies, industries, and social structures by then. Economic prosperity was followed by the strengthening of national self-consciousness in every area, including art and architecture. The thesis—"Only that art can be truly international that is basically national"—became generally accepted. It was at about this time when such things as, say, modern Mexican or Finnish

66. The Saito House in Tokyo (1952, K. Seike). The revival of traditional design elements first appeared in residential architecture. (Photo courtesy of Kiyoshi Seike.)

67. The Atomic Memorial Museum in Hiroshima (1955, K. Tange). Early examples of independent modern architecture, the "Japan style," were designed and built by Kenzo Tange. These buildings of unfinished concrete were conceived in the spirit of the new brutalism, but nonetheless incorporated several formal and structural references to traditional architecture.

68. The Kagawa Prefectural Government Office Building in Takamatsu is one of the most successful modern ferroconcrete versions of the traditional wooden post-and-beam architecture (1958, K. Tange).

69–70. In other buildings, Tange exploited the graphically strong surfaces of old wooden houses in the clearcut geometric pattern emerging from prefabricated concrete elevation panels.

69. Kurashiki City Hall (1960).

70. Detail of the multi-story lobby in the city hall.

71. Kyoto Hall (1960, K. Maekawa). Maekawa's style is also characterized by heavy horizontal forms, ferroconcrete post-and-beam structures, stretched-out balconies, but above all, by the protruding and dominant arched cornices.

architecture based on their respective traditions began to unfold on a larger scale. The use of local traditions once again became conspicuous in Japan too. However, the bases of the trend differed greatly from those during the days of prewar propaganda campaigns, when twisted ideology had led to an architecture that rigidly emulated the historical forms.

Several essays dealing with the reevaluation of architectural traditions were published. In 1960 and in 1962, Kenzo Tange wrote volume-thick dissertations in which, through the examples of the Katsura Imperial Villa and the Ise Shrine, he delved into the "tradition and creation in Japanese architecture" and the "prototype of Japanese architecture," respectively.[19] He pointed out the differences between two periods of Japanese history: the Jomon culture (8000 B.C.-300 B.C.) and the Yayoi culture (300 B.C.-A.D. 300). Tange compared the former to Greek Dionysian art, the latter to Apollonian. The vitality, strength, and in many cases even the brutality of Jomon art were based on the creativity of the commoners. On the other hand, the Yayoi tradition originated from the subtle, elegant, and abstract taste of the aristocracy. Tange regarded the creative power of Japanese architecture as the struggle between the two traditions. Curiously enough, however, his works at that time reflected the greater influence of the Jomon culture.

His buildings were mainly city halls and cultural centers. Such structures were comparatively new to Japan, since the real demand for them was triggered only by the quick postwar economic and social development. In 1951 a government program was enacted for their construction, and so within a period of five years—1957 to 1962—a great number of them were built. They include the new Takamatsu city hall (1958).

This city hall, the Kagawa Prefectural Government Office, is a successful modern ferroconcrete version of traditional Japanese wooden architecture. The eight-story high block is surrounded on each floor by a cantilevered balcony-type shade system with prefabricated parapet elements (68). The whole design with its articulate detailing closely resembles the construction method used in a multistory pagoda (20, 21). The simple two-winged complex is complemented by a charming Japanese-style garden around a small pond, accessible from the street by passing through the pilotis under the lower block.

The Kurashiki City Hall (1960), on the other hand, appears to be a huge ferroconcrete rendition of the old azekura-zukuri type of storehouse with its interlocking wooden log structure. The look of the robust prefabricated panels and the structural details on the elevation leave little doubt about this. In the clearcut geometric design, the only curvilinear element is the massive entrance canopy, which subtly hints at the gracefully curved forms of Shinto torii gates. Yet the canopy itself is too small to soften the strong and rather aggressive appearance of the building (69, 70). A similar vocabulary appears in another example of Tange's work built the same year; the Osaka Offices of the Dentsu Advertising Company (1960). The effect here is less aggressive, but also less interesting. This period in Tange's career came to an end in 1962 with the construction of the Nichinan Cultural Center in South Japan, which displays to the uttermost the brutal character of the Jomon culture that Tange had written about in his book.

Along with the traditional forms expressed in these buildings, the strong influence of Corbusier is also beyond dispute. This influence is more evident in Kunio Maekawa's and Junzo Sakakura's designs, both of them having worked in Corbusier's Paris office for several years before the war. When their master himself came to Tokyo to design the National Museum of Western Arts (1959) in Ueno Park, his three disciples worked with him and participated in the development of the working plans.[20] The building is far from being one of Corbusier's more successful works, but reflecting as it does the flow of many of his ideas, the museum directly lured and motivated Japanese architects.

Around the early 1960s both Maekawa and Sakakura recognized the significance of traditional elements and began to incorporate them in their designs. Maekawa's first steps toward this direction were in two buildings, the Kyoto Hall (1960) and the famous Tokyo Metropolitan Festival Hall (1961), which is right beside Corbusier's museum. These two buildings are cultural centers and thus exhibit many similarities in both functional and formal solutions. The sturdy ferroconcrete post-and-beam structures, the long-stretching balconies, the protruding arched cornices, and the massive horizontal volumes all speak of an evolving "Maekawa style" (71).

Junzo Sakakura with his Kure City Hall (1962) proceeded a step further. In the same building complex he employed two different structural and formal solutions. The high-rise office block follows the clear and simple post-and-beam construction method best represented by Tange's Takamatsu City Hall. The cultural center and auditorium block have softer circular and spiral wall structures, with other indirect references both to some traditional Japanese architectural forms and also to Corbusier's Chapel in Ronchamp. The juxtaposition of these two gives a special character to the City Hall, where Corbusier's high modernism is complemented by the Japanese sense of nature. Particularly attractive is the manner in which the curving volumes, covered by bluish-green glazed mosaic tiles, harmonize with the gentleness of the hilly landscape around the city (72, 73).

In breaking loose from rigid forms and applying more flexible ones, Kiyoshi Seike took the road first trod by Murano, Maekawa, and Sakakura (74). He designed the Ohara Ikebana School and Art Museum (1962) in Kobe with sinuously undulating concrete roofs, brown hollowed-brick facades, and rough granite masonry in the sustaining base walls that bring ancient castle architecture to mind. Just as Sakakura's Kure City Hall does, this building deviates significantly from the previous modern ones, thus foreshadowing Tange's designs for the 1964 Olympic Games in Tokyo (75).

The new formalist trend naturally grew out of the notion of locale, simultaneously implying some criticism of the rational architecture of steel and glass, or concrete "boxes." In 1955 Corbusier built the Notre Dame du Haut Chapel in Ronchamp, which was followed by Saarinen's designs for the Chapel at the Massachusetts Institute of Technology (1955) and the TWA Terminal Building at Kennedy Airport, New York (1956–62), and Jörn Utzon's Sydney Opera House (1957–73). The slow yet gradual abandonment of strict and sterile geometric forms by more and more architects signaled as well the beginning of a break from the previously dominating narrow functionalism. The so far near-unanimous use of steel, glass, and concrete yielded in some cases to a more differentiated application, complemented by a greater use of such materials as brick, wood, stone, plastic, and so on. The resulting buildings appeared less abstract and more varied. Nevertheless this emerging trend was still nascent and thus, except for a few works, architecture generally remained univalent, reduced to elementary and homogeneous forms—pure systems with meanings assumed to be self-explanatory and clear. With the structural elements, which is to say the construction system itself as ornament, the sculptural quality of the buildings became predominant.

Tange's subsequent designs reflected an evident deviation from the rigid functionalism of the Modern Movement. His buildings from around the late 1950s revealed a growing richness in function represented by the differentiated types of spaces, and finally reached maturity in the best of his symbolic architecture a few years later. He called this methodology the "typification of functions."[21] Necessarily, the question of how to organize the typified functional elements into an organic whole arose. The answer seemed to point toward communication

72–73. The Kure City Hall complex is the combination of two different structures with different forms. The softly curving forms and the colorful glazed tile finishing of the auditorium represent the first step toward a more Expressionist architecture in Japan (1962, J. Sakakura).

74. The expressive forms and details of the World Peace Memorial Cathedral in Hiroshima are representative of Murano's interpretation of Modernism (1953, T. Murano).

spaces as connecting media. The first signs of this methodology—though in elementary form—were already present in his previous designs, like those of the various city halls. For example, the large multistory entrance hall of the Kurashiki City Hall hints at this (70). But the "typification of functions" takes concrete shape in such world-famous buildings as the National Gymnasium for the Tokyo Olympics and St. Mary's Cathedral, both completed in 1964.

The two buildings of the Tokyo Sports complex provided the opportunity to combine these separated architectural spaces. Tange found the solution in turning the two main entrances toward each other. Between them, he arranged the elevated walkway as the communication space, in a manner resembling street architecture; this design approach becomes more evident in Tange's later Structuralist architecture. The complex's remaining service functions are accommodated under this elevated platform or plaza.

The structure of the suspended roofs is identical in the two buildings, representing with its unique tensile cable solution the very highly industrialized background of Japanese architecture. The impressive forms of the stadium emanate from the shapes of these roofs (76, 77). Their soft arches—reminiscent of the forms observed in traditional architecture—incline close to the ground, allowing the buildings to remain within human scale despite their huge size. As a matter of fact, the forms of the whole complex are generated in every way only by arches, giving the impression of merry-go-rounds in a revolving motion. This feeling of motion is also implicit in the ground-plan, drawn up by the combination of three hyperbolic lines, as if to symbolize one of the crests of Japan, the *mitsutomoe* (78). Something similar occurs in the cathedral. Here the eight hyperbolic paraboloid concrete shells, the roofs and the walls of the building, are constructed so that their upper edges form the enclosed pattern of the cross, also indicated by the stripes of roof windows. Thus the symbolic charges of both build-

75. Ohara Ikebana School and Art Museum in Kobe (1962, K. Seike). In the early 1960s, more curvilinear forms, more natural and varied materials, and more personal and local features appear in the buildings in accordance with the deliberate attempt to break away from the rigid "boxes" of the Modern Movement's International Style.

76–77. The delicately
shaped suspension
structures of the Olympic
Sports Stadiums in Tokyo
express both the forms of
traditional roofs and the
highly developed
industrial background of
Japanese architecture
(1964, K. Tange).

ings are carried and transmitted on different levels, making their expression all the richer in meaning (79–81).

As the climax and closing accord of a period, numerous other buildings were conceived in Japan in the spirit of the expressive new and traditional forms. Kunio Maekawa, Kiyoshi Seike, Junzo Sakakura, Kenji Imai, and Togo Murano head the long list of architects whose careers were flourishing. In addition, during the period of 1959–1960 a new group of young architects made their debut. Overwhelming both in their formalism and expressive appearance, the buildings of this so-called Metabolist group marked the first indication of a new approach and starting point that only in the years to follow unfolded entirely. Kiyonori Kikutake built the Shimane Prefectural Museum in Matsue as early as 1959, then Fumihiko Maki the Nagoya University Toyota Memorial Auditorium in 1960, but this period can still be regarded as their years of learning.

Reviewing the architectural scene from the 1950s to the 1960s, a period of hardly more than ten years, it is apparent that Kenzo Tange had the leading role. Therefore, it was not mere coincidence that the new modern Japanese architecture, having just received worldwide attention, was associated with his name. His fame was due to his being the Japanese architect who most successfully combined modern and traditional features in his works. Yet the execution of this combination included its own contradictions and difficulties. In fact, the influence of traditional architecture even in Tange's widely acclaimed early works does not go beyond the level of forms and details. In several cases, as in the Kurashiki City Hall, "Tange has lapsed into the very regionalism he condemned ('the decorative use of traditional elements') simply because he has applied past forms without (as he insists) 'challenging' them."[22] From this point of view, the architecture of Tange and his generation until about the early 1960s was a high-level introduction of ideas from international modern architecture rather than a true reevaluation and expression of the Japanese traditions in their complexity and multivalence. Consequently, with the fall of the Modern Movement, these architects could not avert the crisis, and a need for change arose.

78. The floor plans of the Olympic Stadiums reveal a combination of three dominant hyperbolic lines similar to those found in one of the crests of Japan, the *mitsutomoe*.

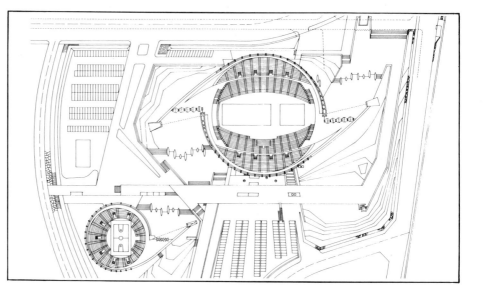

79–81. Eight hyperbolic-paraboloid concrete shells covered by corrugated alu-plates serve simultaneously as roofs and walls. They were designed in the shape of a cross for St. Mary's Cathedral in Tokyo (1964, K. Tange).

81. Site plan. 1. Cathedral. 2. Bell tower. 3. Offices. 4, 5. Seminary.

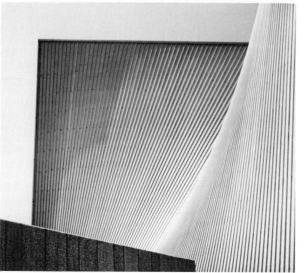

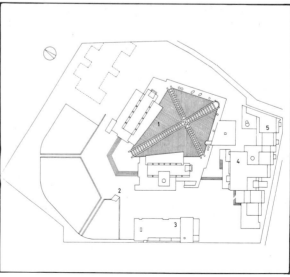

Failure of the Modern Movement

Around the middle of the 1950s there were already clear signs that the Modern Movement, represented and led by CIAM, was in rapid decline. At the tenth Congress in 1956, in Dobrovnik, Jerzy Soltan, ex-chairman of the Harvard University architecture department, stated the reasons in his address: "the vital force that Modern Architecture won in a battle was already lost."[23] The voice of criticism had, in fact, been present earlier; at the previous meeting at Aix-en-Provence in 1953, a group of younger architects, in response to the CIAM VIII report, flatly rejected many of the prevalent dogmatic principles and rigid, abstract conclusions. This group, apart from Soltan, included Alison and Peter Smithson, Aldo van Eyck, Jacob Bakema, Georges Candilis, Shadrah Woods, and several others.[24] Because it became active in the preparation and organization of the Tenth Congress, the group was commonly called Team 10 thereafter. In Dubrovnik, the split between Team 10 and the older guard, the rest of CIAM, further deepened, making it evident that the unity of the movement and of CIAM itself was not possible to maintain any longer. Three years later, in 1959 in Otterlo, Holland, the dissolution of CIAM was officially announced, whereby the more pluralistic intentions of the new generation played the dominant role at the consecutive meetings of Team 10.

Thus, despite its many early positive achievements, the Modern Movement failed. The reasons underlying this failure are complex. Perhaps none of them is as important as the reductionist functionalism that characterized the movement from the very beginning, wherein functionalism was based on an overwhelmingly rationalistic interpretation of both architecture and urbanism and, by extension, on a simplistic understanding of their relationship to the individual and society. Nevertheless, the movement started out with a strong commitment to humanistic and social goals by putting man in the center of its activities. Yet, within the functionalist methodology, "man in general" more often than not did not mean actual people; there was little or no differentiation made among the variety of social, political, or cultural groups. With the overall generalization, human needs and social activities were given short shrift and understood as a collection of some elementary physical, material, or mechanistic functions that in turn became the determining principles in design.

In order to achieve functional and productive efficiency, the movement, epitomized by the so-called International Style, developed a strong, almost sole reliance on technology and constructivism.[25] Its activity was thus permeated with the fetishes of industrialization and standardization, and with the scientific order and aesthetics of the new god, the smoothly working, sleek, idealized Machine. Parallel with the intentions of meeting almost exclusively the material needs of society or rather as a consequence of them, there was a systematic reduction of meaning, that is to say the progressive elimination of symbolic and poetic intentions and content. Design, while becoming increasingly preoccupied with the instrumentality of means, was being gradually turned into a mere tool of problem solving. With utility and function assigned primary importance, the experiential and aesthetic qualities of architecture were considered, if at all, as the logical outcome of the correct and optimal functional and structural arrangements.

Thus the extremely purist language—in fact, a scientific prose—spoke only about how clearly and rationally the building had been constructed. If the program and the structural solution had been selected well and they corresponded properly with each other, "beauty" and "meaning" were assured. "What the new functionalism came to be taught in the Bauhaus and other schools, the aim of 'expressing the function,' was considered to be the working method by which spaces could be organized into highly articulated masses."[26] Architecture, with buildings turning into sterile industrial objects, became the expression only of its fabrication—production and applied technology—and of its operation as "machine." Later on, however, the technological model as a working method and architectural expression ended up largely as superficial stylistic preference and empty formalism.

Obviously, meaning was intended to be singular and clear. Eero Saarinen, for example, like most modern architects, wanted to design his buildings and their spaces so transparently that their purpose and meaning would be unquestionable or self-evident to everyone at once. Commenting on his CBS Building in New York, he said: "When you look at this building, you will know exactly what is going on. It is a very direct and simple statement."[27] With his design he aimed at an "ultimate and absolute reality" that does not know human compromise and that is also basically at odds with the fundamentally ambiguous nature of human reality.

In a like manner, CIAM arbitrarily overemphasized the differences between our "machine age" and previous ages, as if man in order to enter into the twentieth century had to relinquish the basic human properties largely unchanged through the centuries. To quote Aldo van Eyck: "Modern architects have been harping continually on what is different in our time to such an extent that even they have lost touch with what is not different, with what is essentially the same."[28] For the same reasons, they not only disregarded the variety of existing cultures with their own particular traditions but, with functional formulas believed to be universally applicable, also wanted to do away with this variety. Consequently, historical categories and history itself as rich storehouses of human experience were categorically rejected. Past became taboo

and, with a deepening split, its continuity with and within the present and the future was severed.

Behind this attitude one may recognize the profoundly rational, dualistic traditions of Cartesian thought and the whole Western culture, which have always been characterized by the sharp distinction between man and his world, or man versus the world. Like the self-confident Renaissance man who believed in and sought a universe controlled and controllable by a homogeneous numerical and dimensional order, modern architects presumed that architecture, architectural space, and, further, even societies could be comprehended and controlled by a simplistic functional model, the instrumentality of the machine. But, as opposed to the Renaissance belief in the mythical and divine origin of order and thought, a belief maintained implicitly until the end of the eighteenth century, the modern world after the Enlightenment, particularly in the twentieth century, was rapidly being turned into the more deterministic order of rational and scientific certainty. The power of reason was accepted as the only form of knowledge and the only way to action. It became the tool in the process of mere utilitarian production, control, and also exploitation. Therefore, it required a great deal of naive optimism and idealism for the pioneers of the Modern Movement to believe that an architecture largely limited to rational considerations and prescriptive rules of technological intentionality would bring solutions to the human environment and even to social evils while offering salvation to mankind. Thus, as Jane Jacobs wrote: "Le Corbusier was planning not only a physical environment. He was planning for a social Utopia too."[29] Aldo van Eyck was more to the point in arguing: "The dilemma of the modern movement in architecture is that it missed the boat by sidestepping the philosophical implications of what came to light around the turn of the century and since, through the astounding intelligence, artistry, and perseverance of a small number of artists and scientists in every media and field. What they discovered, unfortunately, hardly penetrated the minds of architects. . . . CIAM was simply not interested. . . . The magical appeal of technology, industrial production, systems, applied art and science (not art and science) cast a long shadow—clogging the mind."[30]

The failure of the Modern Movement, however, was not solely the result of the single-mindedness of a handful of modern architects. It was also the outcome and manifest sign of the crisis of modern man in general—that is, the whole modernist project with its modes of production and consumption rooted in positivist thought and instrumental sciences.[31] Outside of a growing number of philosophers, anthropologists, and other thinkers, Aldo van Eyck was one of those very few architects who fully realized the fact of this failure.[32] Van Eyck's profound interest in anthropology and thorough knowledge of non-Western cultures so often labeled "primitive" enabled him to remain consistently and sharply critical of both the narrow exclusivist stance of rational and positivistic Western thought and its direct reflection in the increasingly alienating abstraction of modern architecture.

In spite of the fact that in its architectural intentions the Modern Movement deeply concerned itself with pressing social issues, its rationally derived city planning theories and practices were not only expressly "antiurban" but also disastrous. The univalent, "complete" individual architectural units, characterized by their self-sufficient, oftentimes sculptural beauty and the functional concept of developing the design unilaterally "from inside out," resulted in serious, far-reaching problems on the urban scene. Modernist city planning theories were almost exclusively based on the conclusions of the 1933 CIAM Athens Charter. Guided by this ultimately destructive document, modern architects and city planners were ready to reduce urban life and the city into five separate functions, splitting their interwoven fabric into living, working, recreation, transportation, and historic areas.

The aim was the effective "Functional City." Yet, as Reyner Banham said of the document, the "persuasive generality which gives the Athens Charter its air of universal applicability conceals a very narrow conception of both architecture and town planning and committed CIAM unequivocally to: (a) rigid functional zoning of city plans, with green belt between the areas reserved to the different functions, and (b) a single type of urban housing, expressed in the words of the Charter as 'high, widely-spaced apartment blocks' . . . [which] effectively paralyzed research into other forms of housing."[33]

The following decades then witnessed the planning and construction of "new towns" all over the modern world that included ample sunshine and light, huge open parks for the residents, spacious industrial parks, smoothly running vehicular and pedestrian traffic free of congestion; but the cohesive force, the urban spirit, was missing; the residents could not find themselves. First the rigid system of residential neighborhood units and superblocks failed, resulting in the rapid decline of these areas; later on this process in many cases resulted in the "death of the city" itself.[34] Examples from England, Sweden, the United States, and even from Brazil, such as Harlow New Town, Wällingby, the outskirts of Boston or St. Louis, and Brasilia, stand witness to this.

These new urban conceptions and their architectural designs apparently deliberately rejected every possible continuity with the heritage of traditional urban formations and references to the cultural patterns of living. Assuming some responsibility for the failures, the English city planner Jack Lynn wrote in 1962: "In our zeal to erase the evils arising out of lack of proper water supply, sanitation and ventilation, we had torn down streets of houses which, despite their sanitary shortcomings, harboured a social structure of friendliness and mutual aid. We had thrown the baby out with the bath water."[35]

In the third phase of its activity, after the Second World War, there were signs that CIAM was becoming aware of the inadequacies of many of its theories and ideologies. As early as 1943 Sigfried Giedion and José Luis Sert had written about the need for an architecture expressing social and community life, the necessity of symbols of a "new monumentality," that is, of "spaces of public appearance."[36] But, as Kenneth Frampton noted, "despite their now manifest concern for the specific qualities of place, the old guard of CIAM gave no indication that they were capable of apprising the complexities of the post-war urban predicament realistically."[37]

In many respects this statement applies to the next generation of modern architects as well. Beyond these timely criticisms and more appropriate intentions, in their actual works very few members of Team 10 were able to transcend the central dilemma of CIAM. The majority, while trying to distance themselves from the prevailing functionalism, ended up in increasingly formalistic manipulations that even at their best generally missed, as they still do today, the fundamental issue of reconciliation among architecture, the manmade environment, and the essentially ambiguous reality of the human condition. Architecture, just as much as contemporary man and society at large, seems still largely incapable of coming to terms with the significance of "place," unable to derive the meaning of human existence.

Notes

1. This first generation of Western-style Japanese architects was comprised of four graduates: Kingo Tatsuno, Otokuma Katayama, Tatsuzo Sone, and Shichijiro Sadate.
2. In 1885 what had been the Tokyo Industrial College came to form the basis of the Engineering College of Tokyo Imperial University, which offered architecture education. Eventually this university became today's Tokyo University.
3. At the time of its founding, JIA was called the Builders' Association (*Zokagakkai*) and had only twenty-six members. At that time anyone in the construction industry could be a member.
4. Teijiro Muramatsu, "The Course of Modern Architecture," *The Japan Architect* (June 1965), p. 45.
5. Noboru Kawazoe, *Contemporary Japanese Architecture* (Tokyo Kokusai Bunka Shinkokai, 1965), p. 19.
6. The members were Kikuchi Ishimoto (1894–1963), Sutemi Horiguchi (b. 1895), Mayumi Takizawa (b. 1896), Shigeru Yada (1896–1958), Mamoru Yamada (1894–1966), and Kei'ichi Morita (b. 1895). Later Bunzo Yamaguchi (1902–1978) and Chikatada Kurata (b. 1895) joined the group.
7. Wright's Imperial Hotel was demolished in 1963 to make way for the hotel that presently occupies its site. The central section of Wright's hotel was relocated and rebuilt in 1976 in Meiji-mura, an open-air architecture museum north of Nagoya.
8. Hiro Sasaki, "The Development of Modern Architecture in Japan," *The Japan Architect* (June 1965), p. 67.
9. E. Michael Czaja, "Antonin Raymond, Artist and Dreamer," *Architectural Association Journal*, Vol. 78, No. 864 (August 1962), p. 61.
10. Kenneth Frampton, "The Japanese New Wave," in *A New Wave of Japanese Architecture: Catalogue 10* (New York: The Institute for Architecture and Urban Studies, 1978), pp. 8–9.
11. Arata Isozaki in a recent essay analyzes the various interpretations of Katsura by such modernist architects as Bruno Taut, Sutemi Horiguchi, and Kenzo Tange. He also gives his own "reading" of the complexity of the whole design and points out the essential ambiguity of its spaces in both the garden and the villa itself. The whole complex was built in several stages, incorporating the activities and influences of many people. This resulted in a "multivalent and non-homogeneous design." (A. Isozaki, "Katsura: The Ambiguity of Its Space," John D. Lamb, trans. [Forthcoming].)
12. Yukichi Kono, quoted by Kawazoe, op. cit., 5.
13. One such much publicized competition was in 1931 for the design of the Ueno National Museum (formerly the Ueno Imperial Household Museum) in Tokyo. It was eventually built in 1937 from Hitoshi Watanabe's first-prize entry, with heavy Japanese forms molded in reinforced concrete and large tiled roofs (Imperial Roof Style).
14. Kunio Maekawa, quoted by Noboru Kawazoe, op. cit., 5, p. 32.
15. Since CIAM (Congrès Internationaux d'Architecture Moderne) was founded in 1928, the Bridgewater and the Bergamo congresses were the sixth and seventh congresses respectively.

16. In 1938, with the political situation rapidly worsening, Raymond left Japan and returned to America. He closed his Tokyo office in 1941 and reopened it after the war, in 1948.

17. The museum was built within the compound of the famous Tsurugaoka Hachiman Shrine of Kamakura.

18. Robin Boyd, op. cit., Introduction 6, pp. 28, 31, 34.

19. Walter Gropius, Kenzo Tange, and Yasuhiro Ishimoto, *Katsura: Tradition and Creation in Japanese Architecture* (New Haven: Yale University Press, 1960), Kenzo Tange, and Noboru Kawazoe, *Ise: Prototype of Japanese Architecture* (Cambridge, Massachusetts: MIT Press, 1962).

20. The third architect was Takamasa Yoshizaka (1917–1981).

21. Kenzo Tange, "Development of Design Concept and Methodology," *The Japan Architect* (August-September 1976), p. 11.

22. Charles Jencks, *Modern Movements in Architecture* (New York: Doubleday, 1973), p. 323.

23. Jerzy Soltan, quoted by Kenzo Tange, "My Experiences," *Space Design* (January 1980), p. 186.

24. Alison Smithson, ed., *Team 10 Primer* (Cambridge, Massachusetts: MIT Press, 1974), p. 2. Until about 1962, members of Team 10 included Jacob B. Bakema and Aldo van Eyck (Holland); George Candilis (France); Alison and Peter Smithson (England); Shadrach Woods (U.S.A.); Giancarlo de Carlo (Italy); F. Coderch (Spain); Charles Pologni (Hungary); Jerzy Soltan (Poland); Stefan Wewerka (Germany); and Ralph Erskine (Sweden).

25. Henry-Russel Hitchcock and Philip Johnson, *The International Style* (New York: The Norton Library, 1932, 1966).

26. Robert Maxwell, "The Venturi Effect," *Architectural Monographs 1: Venturi and Rauch* (London: Academy Editions, 1978), pp. 8–13.

27. Eero Saarinen, quoted in George Baird, "La Dimension Amoureuse," C. Jencks and G. Baird, eds., *Meaning in Architecture* (New York: Braziller, 1970), p. 85.

28. Aldo van Eyck, op. cit., 24, p. 22.

29. Jane Jacobs, *The Death and Life of Great American Cities* (New York: Vintage Books, 1961), p. 22.

30. Aldo van Eyck, "What Is and Isn't Architecture: A propos of Rats, Posts and Other Pests (RPP)," *Lotus International*, Vol. 28 (1981), p. 17.

31. For further details see Edmund Husserl, *The Crisis of European Sciences and Transcendental Phenomenology* (Evanston, Illinois: Northwestern University Press, 1960) and Alberto Perez-Gomez, *Architecture and the Crisis of Modern Science* (Cambridge, Massachusetts: MIT Press, 1983).

32. Among such philosophers can be mentioned the phenomenologists Edmund Husserl, Martin Heidegger, Maurice Merleau-Ponty, the existentialist Jean Paul Sartre, and the structuralists Claude Levi-Strauss and Jean Piaget.

33. Reyner Banham, quoted in Kenneth Frampton, *Modern Architecture: A Critical History* (New York: Oxford University Press, 1980), p. 270.

34. Jane Jacobs, op. cit., 29.

35. Jack Lynn, "Park Hill Redevelopment, Sheffield." *RIBA Journal* (December 1962).

36. Sigfried Giedion, José Luis Sert, and Fernand Lèger in their 1943 manifesto wrote: "The people want buildings that represent their social and community life to give more functional fulfillment. They want their aspiration for monumentality, joy, pride and excitement to be satisfied." Quoted in K. Frampton, op. cit., 33, p. 271.

37. Ibid., p. 271.

4. New Directions in the 1960s:
Early Departures from Modern Architecture

The crisis, a general vagueness in both theory and practice, that followed the fall of the Modern Movement all over the world did not bypass Japan, for she had by that time maintained a close relationship with international Western architecture for several decades. However, the crisis there was not as critical as in Europe or America, since modern Japanese architecture had early discovered its own traditions and—though often only on a formalistic level—relied on them considerably. But in Japan, too, there was an obvious need for change. This was manifested both in the shifting direction of the older generation, made up of Tange and his contemporaries, and in the early works of a new generation of architects, which as a matter of course represented a new approach to and understanding of architecture.

On the international scene, changing direction was not as peaceful and smooth a process as in Japan. Architects reorganizing their strategies and ways of thinking and changing their attitudes were much more polemic and vocal. Smaller and larger groups were formed one after the other. First Team 10 had an influential role and, since its members were active designers, they were able to put their new theories into practice almost immediately. Team 10 was soon followed by Archigram, Super-studio, and Archizoom, to mention but a few groups. In most cases these groups exhausted themselves in the elaboration of new theories. Admittedly—as with Archigram and Super-studio—new design conceptions were created either only for the sake of theory or were simply not feasible. Their impact was indirect but significant in stretching the limits of architecture and the architects' awareness of them.

Two important theoretical works were published almost at the same time, Robert Venturi's *Complexity and Contradiction in Architecture* and Aldo Rossi's *Architecture of the City.*[1] Although each came to quite a different conclusion, both were strongly critical of modern architecture. Their influence is undeniable in the development of the American populist and European neorationalist trends, but these surfaced almost a decade later in the mid-1970s. In the early 1960s, there were still only a few works and architects to try, much less to accomplish, new complexities in architecture. Among the examples, should be mentioned buildings by Aldo van Eyck, Herman Hertzberger, Giancarlo de Carlo, James Sterling, Robert Venturi, Louis Kahn, Hans Hollein, and Charles Moore.

The situation in Japan was both similar and somewhat different. First, fewer theoretical publications appeared and more works were built. The social and cultural background presented a nearly ideal atmosphere for the notion of change—a concept well known from Japanese traditions—to be realized in new forms again. Thus Japan is characterized by the activities of an increasing number of prominent architects who, upon reflecting on the new ideas from the West and on their own reevaluated past, come up with more and more buildings that so far could not be realized elsewhere. Though he somewhat exaggerated, Charles Jencks made a point when he said: "It seems Japan is the only live architectural culture in the world where modern architects of exceptional talent are accepted on a large scale."[2]

The 1960s witnessed the most interesting, most dynamic, and fastest-developing period in the history of Japanese architecture. The period coincided with a boom in Japan's industrial, economic, and cultural life thus far unprecedented not only in the history of Japan but also of other countries. In the course of approximately ten years Japan overwhelmingly scraped away the damage inflicted by the war to become the world's third industrial power.[3] Naturally this progress influenced the nation's architecture, too. With almost unlimited industrial and financial investment, many new technologies were experimented with and numerous large-scale projects and complexes built—and most of them with various megastructures; without such industrial and financial back-up none of this would have been possible. The process was pervaded by the keen and receptive spirit of testing and applying everything new, a spirit that—beside the respect for tradition—has always characterized the Japanese.

In this bold age of experiments, many ever-growing trends evolved, Structuralism and Metabolism to start. Already by the mid-1970s, the process of differentiation and enrichment resulted in a rather complex state, in which a general picture of Japanese architecture could be derived only from the variety of, and differences—at times, contradictions—within, the intentions of individual architects and smaller or larger teams. However, within these various trends there were, as there still are, several common points of intersection at which these trends frequently overlap. Along with their general interest in semiotic research that was developing in such disciplines as linguistics, literary theory, and art criticism for example, Structuralism became an important part of Metabolism and, with a different emphasis, also of Contextualism. In turn, the Contextual approach influenced Isozaki's evolving Symbolism and is also present in Kurokawa's recent Metabolism. A certain Mannerism is very explicitly traceable in Isozaki's works and implicitly in Maki's and others', while a definite Symbolism is always expressed in most of the intentions that individually emphasize a certain aspect of the complexity in the "language of architecture" and lately in "architecture as text."[4] Therefore, making strict distinctions among the different directions is often a mistake. Nevertheless perhaps the most suitable way to discuss Japanese architecture of the 1960s is on the basis of its multifarious and simultaneously existing trends.

Criticism of Functionalism

As the functionalist Modern Movement failed, its design methods, based on the fetish of simple and single functions, were gradually abandoned. The denial of functionalism is by no means a new phenomenon in Japan, since her traditional architecture maintained a similar attitude throughout the centuries. The new tendency to criticize narrow functionalism, it may be said, has gained general validity; even if many architects enrich their design theories and methodologies with Structuralism, Metabolism, Contextualism, information theories, semiotics, and so on, their starting point remains in the complexity of functions, or "multifunctionalism." This first meant the introduction of flexible multipurpose spaces, then the more complex communication spaces and the multipurpose buildings and building complexes. Several of these complexes are so rich in function that they can hardly be called a "building" in the traditional sense of the word—like hotel building, office building, residential building, department store, or railway station, but rather a small city. Along with the commercialization of architecture a new type of creation has appeared that is not only a shell to accommodate a host of displays or shows inside but also a "skin" to show off outwardly. The building itself has become a huge advertisement or information-transmitting device in which the unusual forms, the supergraphics produced or amplified by flashing neon lights and even multistory "electrographic" kinetic images, catch the eye and implant themselves in the subconscious.

One of the first of these show buildings was built in Tokyo as early as 1963. The San-ai Dream Center (Nikken Sekkei Co.) on the Ginza intersection promises something extra, inviting one into a dreamland by its very name (82). The cylindrical glass tower is a display building for the Mitsubishi Trust; the greater part of it is occupied by showrooms and only a small portion by offices. The center is a kind of prototype for such structures as the Sony buildings by Yoshinobu Ashihara in Tokyo (1966) and in Osaka (1976) by Kurokawa (141–143). In all of these buildings, the main purpose is to provide information both inside and out. The upper part of the San-ai Building, for example, which amounts to about one-third of its height, incorporates a surface designed for constantly changing, flickering neon lights that also include the emblem of the trust. Moreover, through its glass surfaces the building communicates the various functions taking place inside both day and night. The tower has also become the symbol of this famous Tokyo business district.

Office buildings too have started to make way for several different functions, like shopping arcades, catering services, restaurants, and cafeterias. An early example of such a complex is the Palaceside Building (1966, Nikken Sekkei Co.) in Tokyo. Here the upper floors are occupied by the offices of the Mainichi Newspaper and other businesses and the six basement levels by heavy printing machinery. The floors between feature numerous shops, boutiques, coffeeshops, even a supermarket; these are arranged on the two entrance levels (83).

Some, like the Shinjuku High-rise Buildings, are even more complex in function (84).[5] Almost all the skyscrapers in this rapidly developing urban subcenter are small cities within the city. Their common feature, reflecting the recent trend of corporate urbanism, is uppermost and ground floors designed for public use as well. On the top there are restaurants, bars, clubs, game centers, and so on. The lower entrance levels are converted into plazas complete with sunken parks, cafeterias, exhibition halls, and the like. The lowermost, underground stories serve as garages and offer such sports facilities as indoor swimming pools and bowling alleys.

The enrichment of function is also very conspicuous in department stores. Most are built in conjunction with railway or subway stations and bus terminals. Thus usually the lower and underground levels are traffic junctions, while the upper ones are commercial centers. However, traffic lines quite often penetrate the buildings at upper levels as well, as in the Odakyu Department Store (1967) in Shinjuku, which is part of Tokyo's busiest traffic junction. The whole complex, complemented by the connecting double-level station square, belongs

83. The Palaceside Building in Tokyo is a prototype of the multipurpose building in Japan. On its two entrance levels there is a large array of commercial facilities, while the levels above and below the entrance contain the offices and printing machinery of Mainichi Newspapers (1966, Nikken Sekkei Company, Ltd.).

82. Built at an intersection of the famous Ginza in Tokyo, the San-Ai Dream Center was designed with the explicit purpose of communicating information. The upper third of the glass cylinder is of vibrating neon lights (1963, Nikken Sikkei Company, Ltd.).

84. With the development of the Shinjuku subcenter in Tokyo, a new generation of high-rise buildings started mushrooming in the area. Each of the more than fifty-story skyscrapers provides a large variety of functions and a number of public plazas as part of the corporate urbanism.

85. Department stores in Japan are very often run by railroad companies and built together with large train stations. The Odakyu Department Store Building in Shinjuku accommodates Tokyo's busiest traffic junction with the connecting double level Station Square (1967, J. Sakakura).

86. The "Selcy" Leisure Center in Senri New Town near Osaka is a small city in itself, arranged around a central plaza and mall (1972, Fujita General Contractors).

among Junzo Sakakura's remarkable works (85).

Department stores have gradually been transformed from mere commercial facilities into special recreation centers. Fully in accord with the interest of the consumer society, the wide sales rooms have been converted into showrooms too, allowing customers and visitors alike to stroll along, window-shoppers taking a closer look at the new products, freely collecting more personal experience and information, all of course to encourage some eventual purchase. To serve customers better, there are other facilities as exhibition halls, display areas, playgrounds, movie theaters, and a wide selection of restaurants, coffeeshops, and bars. There are travel bureaus, airlines, and ticketing offices as well. As a result of this complexity of function, department stores number among the buildings being transformed into urban forums, information and communication centers where people may enjoy a constantly bustling life and, though artificially induced, a feeling of urban milieu.

This complexity characterizes the "Selcy" Leisure Center in Senri New Town near Osaka (1972, Fujita General Contractors). The building—a small city again—is arranged around a shopping mall and arcades, with a system of terraces and linking bridges between them for pedestrians. The rapid train connecting the center with Osaka comes in to its terminal on the fourth level under the building; the different floors are reached by either escalator or elevator. Pedestrians and automobile commuters have access to the building on several other levels. The complex contains practically everything that a city center is supposed to have, from a shopping center to outdoor swimming pools. Yet, the focal point of the whole project remains the outdoor central plaza, a "communication space" that could at the same time stand for a small, intimate urban square; the plaza also distinguishes the center from its Western counterpart, the more hermetically enclosed and artificially conditioned American shopping mall (86).

The names of the growing number of multipurpose buildings more often than not contain references to some kind of "center" or "plaza," terms originally attributed to appropriate formations in the city. More simply put, these types of buildings, just emerging, are intended to be not only the sum total of certain basic functions; they also suggest something more, based on the idea of center or plaza. This is especially true with hotels today, even if their original names often remain unchanged. They accommodate so many different events—cultural, commercial, political, social—and offer such a wide range of services that the original function of providing lodging is at times almost secondary. This can be observed, for example, even in the exterior of the Hakata Miyako Hotel in Fukuoka (1972, Nikken Sekkei Co.). The rooms are designed along the two sides, clearly distinguishable by their forms and colors. Between these two sections a system of large spaces evolves almost without intermediary support. This allows the free arrangement of communal spaces found here (87).

In the Nakano Sun Plaza (1973, Nikken Sekkei Co.), a youth center in Tokyo, functions other than those of the included hotel are just as important, if not even more important (88, 89). The unusual triangular shape of the building follows the interior arrangement and safety considerations. The uppermost floors contain the hotel rooms; these floors would be occupied by the least number of people, a consideration in the event of an emergency evacuation. Downward, the building presents an array of facilities—conference rooms, restaurants and banquet rooms, educational facilities, a huge multipurpose theater and concert hall; and in the basement a swimming pool and bowling alleys—all attended by larger numbers of people than those that stay in the hotel section (90). The vertical service facilities—staircases and elevators—are grouped along the windowless two sides, while windows and roof terraces, one of them with a rock garden, are found only on the other two facades. The slanting transparent roof structure of the entrance hall provides an interesting transitional space between the building and the square in front of it.

The Nikken Sekkei Design Company, a huge organization comparable to the American SOM, designs mainly public buildings, some with conspicuously odd shapes indeed. Among them, probably the most striking is the PL Tower (1969) in Tondabayashi, an unusual amusement center near Osaka owned by a new Buddhist sect called Perfect Liberty. The building also serves as their head temple (91).

Structuralism

Nineteen-sixty signaled an important turning point in the course of modern Japanese architecture. With the ailing Modern Movement as background, plans for the forthcoming World Design Conference to be held in Tokyo urged Japanese architects to search for new directions. Organized for the first time by Japan, the design conference was an occasion of prestige and great stimulation even in the course of its preparation. The primary task was the elaboration of proper theories and methods. This work embarked on two paths that nevertheless were connected to each other in many ways. One led toward the formation and activity of the Metabolists, while the other led toward Kenzo Tange and his team's proposal for the reconstruction of Tokyo. By this time, Tange had abandoned the simplistic functional approach and had started with a fresh attitude.

"The interpretation of architecture must go beyond the functional to deal with more general concepts. Gradually inner and outer functions, private and social spaces, human scale and mass-human scale, began to play parts in our methodologies of design," Tange himself wrote later.[6]

In the course of seeking more complexity with his typification of different functions, he came to the conclusion that in both a building and city, some functions change fast while others do so slowly or not at all. In trying to rely on and express these qualities by proper relationships among architectural spaces, the problem of how to organize the typified functional space units into a homogeneous system still remained. Tange and his team found their organizing principle in Structuralism.

The theory of Structuralism has its roots in linguistics, in the pioneer works of Ferdinand de Saussure, Roman Jacobson, Roland Barthes, and others. It was developed further by French anthropologist Claude Lévi-Strauss and Swiss psychologist Jean Piaget.[7] Later it gained ground in philosophy, history, sociology, human behavior, and literary theory. The structure of human languages, as Saussure pointed out, consists of the grammatical or code system (langue), which forms the language's backbone, and the basic rules and channels of speaking (parole), which convey the endless variations of messages. As the product of a conscious act, the message or information constantly changes in content, while by contrast the "unconscious" element is relatively fixed in the patterns of grammar. Structuralist theory postulates in a like manner that, as Howard Gardner wrote: "There is structure underlying all human behaviors and mental functioning and . . . that this structure can be discovered through orderly analysis, that it has cohesiveness and meaning, and that structures have generality."[8]

Structure in general is a complex yet closed set of relationships in which the elements can be changed or replaced, but in such a way that they remain dependent on—while their meanings are determined by—the whole structural system. In other words, the individual units have meaning only by virtue of their relationship to one another. Structuralism is concerned with the formal structures underlying languages, including the "languages"

87. Hakata Miyako Hotel in Fukuoka (1972, Nikken Sekkei Company, Ltd.). Different in form and color, the exterior shows a clear distinction between the private hotel rooms along the two sides and the public spaces in the middle.

88–89. The triangular shape of the Nakano Sun Plaza, a busy national youth center in Tokyo, follows the circulation determined by the different functions inside (1973, Nikken Sekkei Co., Ltd.).

87.

88.

89.

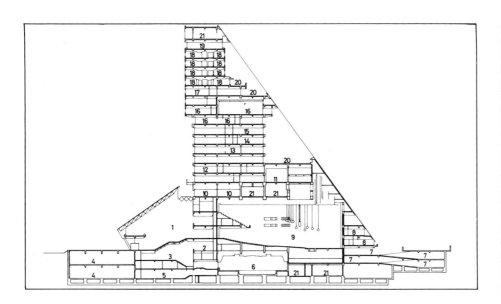

90. As shown by the section of the Nakano Sun Plaza, the less frequented hotel was placed on the upper levels, while the large auditorium and the sports facilities were located on the lower levels.
1. Entrance hall. 2. Hotel lobby. 3. Shops
4. Bowling alleys.
5. Training hall.
6. Swimming pool.
7. Parking. 8. Dressing rooms. 9. Theater and concert hall. 10. Computer room. 11. Audiovisual room. 12. Director.
13. Medical clinic.
14. Classrooms. 15. Multipurpose rooms.
16. Conference rooms.
17. Ballet room. 18. Hotel rooms. 19. Dining hall.
20. Terrace gardens.
21. Mechanical room.

91. A gigantic monster, the unusually shaped 186-meter-high PL Tower in Tondabayashi is the head temple of the new Buddhist sect Perfect Liberty. The tower rules the skies south of Osaka (1969, Nikken Sekkei Co., Ltd.).

of art and other human activities, and not with any manifest meaning or value system the languages may express. Structuralism is the system of signs, which Saussure classified as signified and signifier, a symmetrical unity. In the process of scientifically examining the sign, it is necessarily severed from its referent, that is, from the real or external world, and thus is regarded as constant or synchronic. Consequently, the meaning or value represented by the signs or individual units within the system is taken for granted; Structuralism is unable to accept the reality of specific phenomena, which are always a part of a particular social, ideological realm, within a particular historical context.

Structuralism gives priority to the relations among phenomena and their constancies, and to the systems into which these relations enter, rather than to the nature of phenomena themselves. In other words, there is an emphasis on form, on the primacy of invariable relations over entities. Thus distinctive features of human beliefs, behavior, institutions, and society are regarded as following certain universal laws that are "reflections of the fundamental nature of human thought, and hence, the biological structure of the 'human mind.' "[9] Such a concept, however, is inevitably deterministic and—as in the radical branches of Structuralism—even fatalistic, and implies a mind-body dichotomy that is still fundamentally rooted in the dualistic Cartesian tradition. Emphasizing the primacy of the system, Structuralism minimizes individuality, the intentional realm of the subject, and, in so doing, minimizes humanism as well. In Structuralism, man is "decentered" or dissolved through the determining system itself; the individual is no longer the source of meaning. Thus, in principle, Structuralism and Existentialism are opposite poles. While Structuralism justifiably questions the tyranny of the individual subject in Western metaphysics and bourgeois ideology, it replaces this emphasis with the tyranny of the collective and universal system—that transcends any specific culture—

thereby eventually transforming the structure itself into the subject. In architecture too, Structuralism has systematically repudiated the transcendental or semantic dimension in favor of the formal or syntactic dimension, thereby denying the importance of the historicity of meaning. This denial is the essence of its principal thesis, synchrony.

Parallel with the similar and implicitly Structuralist intentions of Team 10—especially the Dutch group within it led by Aldo van Eyck—Kenzo Tange and the architects working with him were probably among the first to apply this methodology to architectural design.[10] Tange admits the influence of Structuralist ideas during that time by saying: "It is probable that the linguistic concept of structuralism played a part in our thinking, which was directed toward examining the structures in architectural and urban spaces."[11] Following the language analogy, Tange found that the basic structure of spaces with various functions could be the communication channels, along which the space units are able to change in both space and time. This also suggests that the meaning or content of the information borne by these architectural space units is allowed to change as well, while still generated by, and dependent on, the overall structure.

Concerning the methods of structuring architectural language and meaning, Dutch architect Hermann Hertzberger wrote later, in 1963: "We don't have knowledge of everybody's personal images and associations with forms, but we assume that they can be seen as individual interpretations of a collective pattern. This relationship between collective pattern and individual interpretations can perhaps be linked with the relationship between language and speech. . . . What we must look for in place of prototypes, which are collective interpretations of individual living patterns, are prototypes which make individual interpretations of the collective patterns possible; in other words, we must make houses alike in a particular way, such that everyone can bring into being his own interpretation of the collective pattern."[12] In short, here the collective pattern plays the role of basic structuring.

Despite the obvious influence of Dutch Structuralism on Tange and the numerous similarities between that philosophy and Tange's, his interpretation of Structuralism in practice is based on what may be called a cybernetic model and thus differs significantly from the more pluralistic and conciliatory Dutch version derived from cultural anthropology.[13]

KENZO TANGE

Kenzo Tange elaborated his new Structuralist architectural and urban design theory in *A Plan for Tokyo—1960* together with his URTEC team, which then included Sachio Otani, Kisho Kurokawa, and Arata Isozaki, among others. The subtitle of the project, *Toward a Structural Reorganization,* stated Tange's intention very clearly. As the basis of the reconstruction he proposed a three-dimensional communication system structuring the whole urban fabric, old and new alike. Along a double yet interconnected main transportation network with the civic axis extending in between, the original city formation that so far had been centripetal was converted into a linear one. The city was to stretch across Tokyo Bay and thus be supported by huge bridges and platforms. Secondary roads and rapid transportation lines branched out from the primary ones as perpendicular substructures connecting the residential units to both the main transportation channels and the civic axis, which included government and office buildings, public facilities, parks, stadiums, and the like.

Since the emphasis was clearly on the consistency of the overall system, all the elements of the new city were conceived in megastructures, including the buildings of the axis and the residential units themselves (92, 93). The enormous concrete shafts containing the vertical communication were at the same time intended to carry the load of the buildings partially or totally. This way the residential blocks, for example, took the form of slightly curving inverted Vs, easily reminiscent of the roof shapes of Buddhist temples. Thus they can be regarded as formal forerunners of the Yoyogi Olympic Stadiums designed and completed somewhat later in 1964, (76, 77). The extensive communication channels fulfilled their role of connecting the various superblocks and the large community spaces—public plazas, shops, parking areas, schools, kindergartens, and the like—under the "roofs," but the linear system of these channels in the overall scheme, with all movement concentrating along the central spine, made them largely impractical for vehicular transportation and traffic. They also remained rather independent from the body of the city.

Tange's intention was to achieve a more liberating human urban environment that the functionalist Modern Movement had attempted before, but the rigidity of the system, the uniformity of its elements, and the structural redundancies resulted instead in a plan even more centralized, absolutist, and authoritarian than its Modernist predecessors. The scheme inevitably lacked human scale and sense of place. Peter Smithson had this to say: "It is ludicrous to think one can hang all these enormous slabs around the place, and hope that the small things below on the ground would have the attractiveness of small scale things on the ground, as they are now, undiminished."[14]

Indeed the Tokyo Plan had little chance of realization, but Tange probably did not even think about that seriously; rather he used it for the purpose of clarifying his new ideas, the new Structural theory and methodology. Therefore it is not surprising that the plan as a prototype provided the point of departure for many projects to follow. The spirit of the age was appropriate for it, and almost every architect, most especially those identified with Metabolist ideas, was busy drawing up his own plans for a futuristic ideal city conceived

92.

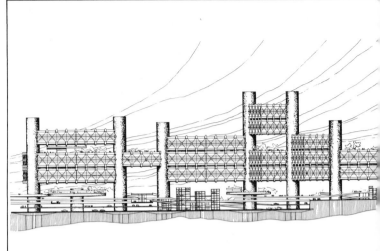

94.

92–93. *Tokyo Plan–
1960—Toward a
Structural Reorganization*
(1960, K. Tange). Tange
and his staff prepared the
first Structuralist urban
vision as the recon-
struction plan for Tokyo.
The linear city, arranged
along an organizing
communications and civic
axis on huge bridge-type
megastructures, was
planned to be built across
Tokyo Bay. (Photographs
courtesy of Kenzo Tange.)

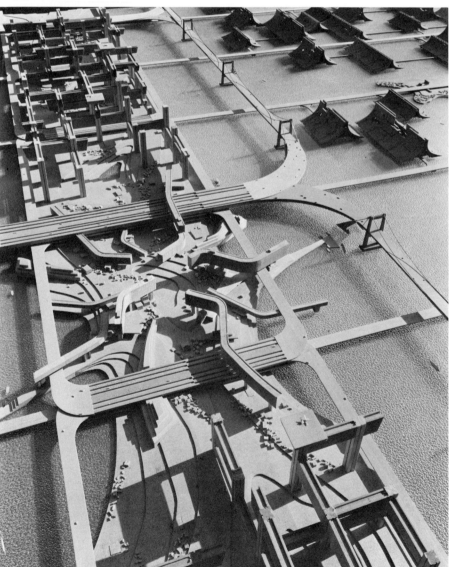

93.

94. Arata Isozaki, then a member of Tange's URTEC Office, designed another yet more poetic Structuralist city prototype, the *City in the Sky* (1962).

in megastructures. Also, architects could be assured that such designs were the safe route to public attention and fame. Tange himself prepared several other Structuralist city plans, like the Tsukiji Plan (1964) for a district in Tokyo. Isozaki too came up with a series of unbuilt urban visions, the City in the Sky, No. 1–4 (1962). Like the civic axis of the Tokyo project, these schemes were based on gigantic vertical communication and service shafts linked together by bridges. But here for the first time these supporting cylindrical shafts were intended as symbolic or poetic recollections of ancient Greek columns, while the configuration of the various blocks evoked the image of traditional Japanese wooden bracketing systems (94). Later on, Structuralist ideas found their way to smaller-scale projects, including concrete buildings, and were executed in large number.

Sachio Otani (b. 1924), a student and later an associate of Tange, designed several complexes in the same spirit. The Kawaracho High-Rise Apartment Dwellings (1974) were built in the form of huge inverted Ys very similar to the ones that appeared in the Tokyo Plan as inverted Vs (95, 96). The two halves of the letter, supported by ferroconcrete frames of enormous size, lean against each other to form what could be called a large community zone or plaza under the buildings. Otani's other famous project, his first in fact, also recalls the traditional roof motif, which is the most successful element in the Tokyo Plan. The slanting structural system of the Kyoto International Conference Hall (1966) thus brings to mind the Ise Shrine with its ornamental fork-type finials *(chigi)*. But seen from the far side of Lake Takaragaike, with the heavy prefabricated concrete elements and volumes made less conspicuous by distance, the building gives the impression of a white pleasure boat floating on the water (97, 98). The conference hall inside is an intricate system of interconnected public and/or communication spaces that at the same time has a convincing dialog with the garden

and the landscape. The basic openness of the whole complex's structural pattern enabled Otani to extend the building rather successfully in 1973.

Though the *Plan for Tokyo—1960* had to remain in blueprint and in the form of an impressive much-publicized model, ten years later Tange had a unique opportunity to realize many of its important ideas in the designs he had been commissioned to prepare and coordinate for the World Exposition in Osaka (Expo 70). His master plan showed an improved Structuralist design methodology that left behind much of the Tokyo plan's inflexibility. Although the manner and the vast scale of the structural solutions were equally pretentious, considering the significance of a world exposition and because of its small size and temporary nature as compared to a permanent city containing everyday human activities, his "showcase" and somewhat heroic attitude were less conspicuous in this project than in the previous one. Altogether, Tange's work at Expo 70 could have been indeed an impressive and successful display of Japan's strong self-confidence and future-oriented attitude if it had not signalled at the same time the end of such an optimistic and positivist attitude in the wake of the shocking economic depression, cultural crisis, and so, the decline of the symbolic realm.

The basis of the master plan was the Symbol Zone, which—apart from the Main Entrance (M. Otaka)—consisted of the Expo Tower (K. Kikutake), the Central Festival Plaza with the Space Frame above it (K. Tange with K. Kamiya), and the Museum of Fine Arts (K. Kawasaki) as the main facilities (99–101). From this zone as the trunk, the communication system structures of Expo 70 branched out: escalators, elevated moving pedestrian walkways in glass tunnels, and several monorail lines (102). The real heart, the physical and symbolic center of the various events and dynamic activities, was the Festival Plaza, a communication and information space covered by a

95. None of the
Structuralist city plans
was built, yet the inherent
ideas influenced numerous
other building projects.
The Kawaracho Apart-
ment Houses with their
huge inverted Y-structure,
recall the form of the
residential units in
Tange's *Tokyo Plan–
1960* (Kawasaki City,
1974, S. Otani).

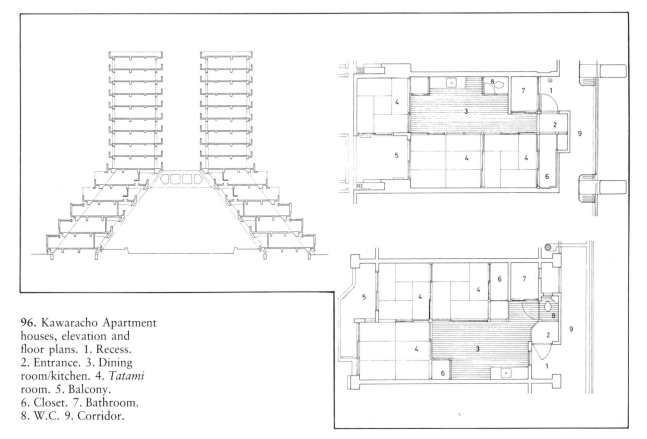

96. Kawaracho Apartment
houses, elevation and
floor plans. 1. Recess.
2. Entrance. 3. Dining
room/kitchen. 4. *Tatami*
room. 5. Balcony.
6. Closet. 7. Bathroom.
8. W.C. 9. Corridor.

97–98. One of the most impressive examples of the Structuralist trend is Otani's Kyoto International Conference Hall. The large complex not only harmonizes beautifully with its natural surroundings but in its dominant structural solution is also reminiscent of traditional architectural forms (1966, 1973, S. Otani).

100.

99–101. The Osaka Expo '70 offered a rare opportunity for Tange to realize partially the Structuralist ideas he had developed earlier in the Tokyo Plan–1960.

101. The Expo Tower, also part of the Symbol Zone, is one of the many contributions of other Metabolist architects. Kikutake designed several geodesic domes as capsules clipped onto the steel structure of the tower (1970, K. Kikutake).

99–100. Tange, as the chief architect, contributed greatly to the conception of the main attraction, the huge steel megastructure of the Space Frame (108 × 292 m) and the Festival Plaza under it (1970, K. Tange).

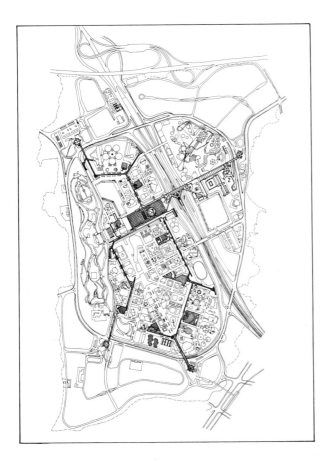

102. The master plan of Expo '70 shows Tange's Structuralist solution with the Symbol Zone as the focal point. Expo's transportation system—monorails, elevated moving pedestrian walkways, and so on—branch out of this center (1970, K. Tange).
1. Main entrance. 2. Expo Tower. 3. Festival Plaza under Space Frame. 4. Museum. 5. Fujii Group Pavilion.

gigantic metal Space Frame. Tange wanted to design a "negative space" here, something like the one naturally created by the clouds in the sky. Accordingly, the frame was covered with translucent pneumatic polyester cushions, 10 meters by 10 meters in size. The active participation of Kurokawa, Kikutake, and Isozaki resulted in Metabolist ideas playing a dominant role in the design of the numerous facilities, among them the first experimental devices—operated by robots cybernetically controlled by means of feedback—to create and manipulate spaces according to the various human activities.

Today, more than fifteen years after the exposition, only the Tower and the Museum remain intact. Because of the huge maintenance costs, in 1978 the impressive Space Frame was demolished, and it seems the whole previous age with it.[15] Tange's other urban projects, in which he attempted further to expand and improve his Structuralist methodology, either have not been realized or have been, but only partly. These include the Skopje City Center (1966), the designs for the Bologna Fiera District Center Project (1971–83), and the master plan for Yerba Buena Center in San Francisco (1969).

Nevertheless, Tange was able to implement his ideas in actual building projects, and so the first real megastructure, the Yamanashi Press and Broadcasting Center, was built in Kofu in 1966. It brought Isozaki's City in the Sky into reality in the form of a three-dimensional communications structure (103, 104).[16] Every vertical connection between spaces in the building is made up of sixteen reinforced concrete cylindrical shafts (105). These shafts, like gigantic columns, support the whole structure in addition to accommodating the stairways, elevators, air conditioning, and some of the sanitary facilities, with all the necessary ducts within themselves. The floors stretching across them like bridges are without any other intermediary support, thus making the spaces of the complex functions—

103–104. The first project built consistently according to Structuralist theory, the Yamanashi Press and Broadcasting Center in Kofu features a three-dimensional "communication" pattern supported solely by the sixteen vertical reinforced concrete shafts. Among them the floors stretch like bridges in a seemingly random pattern, leaving several void spaces in the body of the building (1966, 1975, K. Tange).

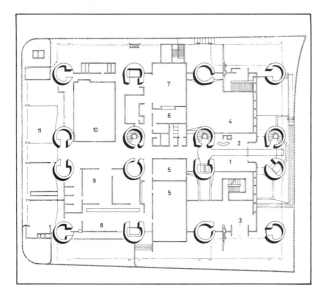

105. First-floor plan of the Yamanashi Communication Center in Kofu (1966, 1975, K. Tange). The shafts as huge columns accommodate all the necessary elevators, staircases, and sanitary facilities by means of the additional ducts within them.
1. Lobby. 2. Information. 3. Rental offices. 4. Open to below. 5. Storage. 6. Kitchen. 7. Service entrance. 8. Storage and office. 9. Print shop. 10. Garage.

106–107. Two other buildings exploit the idea of the Yamanashi Communication Center but on a much smaller scale.

106. With its one cylindrical shaft, the Shizuoka Press and Broadcasting Company Office Building stands like a huge exclamation mark in the eastern part of the famous Ginza, Tokyo (1967, K. Tange).

107. The Kuwait Embassy and Chancery Building in Tokyo was constructed with two concrete shafts, square in section (1970, K. Tange).

TV and radio studios, printing shops, offices and so on—fit together properly, while allowing for alterations if necessary.

Within the arrangement of the functional units in the three-dimensional grid, several "empty" spaces have been designed, like a system of tunnels or cavities in a sponge, that penetrate the total volume deliberately and reveal its structural and spatial quality. These voids—an idea seen also in traditional Japanese aesthetics—give meaning to the whole concept and allow further alteration and expansion of function without upsetting the original structural and aesthetic order. And indeed when the building was enlarged in 1975, its original overall appearance hardly changed. The empty spaces, though decreased in volume and rearranged in form, have remained a dominant feature of the building together with its deliberate unfinished quality. Nevertheless the enormous structure with its inhuman and overpowering presence failed even more than earlier structures to establish any dialog with its environment, and it has remained an isolated body in the intimate urban texture of Kofu.

The cylindrical service shaft system of the Kofu Communication Center soon became a prototype both in Japan and around the world, in most cases losing the essence of the original idea on the way.[17] Tange himself built most of his subsequent projects using this system. He designed the Shizuoka Press and Broadcasting Company's Tokyo office (1967) with only one cylindrical service shaft and the Kuwait Embassy and Chancery Building (1970) with two quadratic shafts, once again completed with the void spaces (106, 107). While both of these buildings can still be regarded as a successful variation on the same concept, his proposal for the University of Oran in Algeria (1972), where the whole extensive complex is laid out with an indiscriminately repetitive and rigid use of the three-dimensional communication system, indicates the end of the road for the development of Tange's Structuralist intentions.

These intentions have turned out to be overly positivistic, revealing the inherent contradiction and inflexibility of the design methodology. One of the problems was the strictly closed character of the communication channels where all circulation and movement within the building were virtually trapped inside. They consequently had very little visual and physical contact with either the interior or exterior spaces. Indeed, these communication channels in most cases ended up as independently developing and rather mechanistic structural systems, on which other elements and spaces were nonetheless highly dependent or sometimes almost eaten up by them. Based on super- or megastructures, Tange's Structuralist methodology became uncompromisingly rigid, unable to reconcile any variety of circumstances. Attempts to improve these contradictory qualities are quite evident in the Shizuoka Press and Broadcasting Center (1970) in Shizuoka and the Sacred Heart International Schools in Tokyo (1968) and in Taipei (1967), among others. A somewhat better understanding of the problems appears in the growing activities of the Metabolists and in the simultaneous emergence of a Contextual approach to design.

The Metabolists

The Metabolist trend, like the previous Modern Movement, started out with a strong commitment to addressing social problems, a commitment, however, based on a different understanding and approach. In the line of modern Japanese architecture, by the end of the 1950s a new avant-garde group was moving on to represent what may be called the fourth generation. Unlike their masters Tange, Maekawa, Sakakura, and the like, who belonged to the third generation after the Meiji

Era, these architects had no practical knowledge of or direct roots in international modern architecture. They were educated after the war, when Japan was in a period of rapid transition toward becoming a leading industrialized nation. Their architecture, reflecting the new social developments, was from the beginning in admitted opposition to CIAM's, which had ended with a stereotyped aesthetics in an established "classical" order. While Tange and his contemporaries had a long and difficult road to a new design attitude, their disciples started from and progressed beyond that hard-won new attitude.

The young Metabolists took another step beyond Tange's Structuralism toward a more flexible design approach and became the avant-garde. Some, like Kurokawa and Maki, were still Tange's students at Tokyo University; some, including Kurokawa, in addition to Isozaki and Otaka, were assistants in his office and participated in the development of A Plan for Tokyo—1960. Later on they left Tange to pursue their own careers and follow independent paths. From then on, the Metabolist trend evolved in parallel with Tange's Structuralism and at the same time incorporated it as a starting point.

Their shared background was the strong economic and industrial development of Japan, inspiring them to interpret architecture in terms of industrialization. Thus the Metabolist urban visions were all conceived in megastructures and with prefabricated mass-produced space units, like leaves on a tree. These capsules were intended to be interchangeable and replaceable in a "plug-in" manner (108).

Metabolist ideas about the city were taking shape when a group of young architects began holding regular meetings in preparation for the 1960 Tokyo World Design Conference. The group included Kiyonori Kikutake, Masato Otaka, Kisho Kurokawa, Fumihiko Maki, industrial designer Kenji Ekuan, and architectural theoretician and critic Noboru Kawazoe. After more than two years of discussion, debate, and theoretical work, their first declaration was introduced during the Tokyo Conference: Metabolism 1960—Proposal for a New Urbanism.

The word metabolism refers to metamorphosis or transformation, a continuous process of change within organisms. The machinelike mechanical model of the Modern Movement was replaced by a biological one in which the parts, like living cells, could come to life, develop, and die out while the whole body—the building, the city, or the entire built environment—went on "living." "We regard human society as a vital process—a continuous development from atom to nebula. The reason that we use the biological word metabolism is that we believe design and technology should be a denotation of human vitality," their declaration read.[18] The statement pointed out two other elements basic to the Metabolist ideology. First, society as a whole, in close relation to architecture and urbanization, was regarded as a living and changing reality, while technology was regarded as the extension of human intentions whereby change—the Metabolist process—was at the same time to be realized and controlled. Second, they not only regarded the quality of change as inherent in society and architecture, but they were also eager to induce this change with their design; thus by extension they also promoted a metabolic consuming mechanism. They said: "The architect's job is not to propose ideal models for society but to devise spatial equipment that the citizens themselves can operate."[19] Their intentions represented a noticeable shift from prevailing modernist master-planning toward system-planning, wherein any given cluster in the city was regarded as self-developing and self-regenerating, while the unity of the whole city in each stage of its growth was maintained at the same time.

The Metabolists expressed the system of complex interrelations in the form of a triangle. It

108. The young Metabolist architects also started out with large-scale urban projects predicated on the idea of change. With his Marine City project, Kikutake preceded even Tange. The huge towers on the sea are based on megastructures filled with industrially prefabricated capsulelike units that were "plugged in" (1958, K. Kikutake; photograph courtesy of Kiyonori Kikutake).

reflects the connections among human, social, and natural metabolisms as well as those systems that make the connections possible.

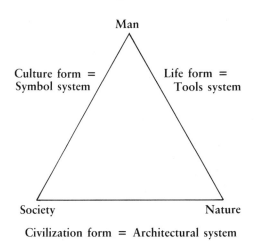

Civilization form = Architectural system

The idea of metabolic cycles of change clearly shows—and not accidentally—the influence of Buddhist philosophy. The young Metabolist architects turned deliberately toward their own architectural traditions in their opposition to the Modern Movement's functional international trend, placing strong emphasis on their national roots in Buddhist culture. "It is impossible to discuss the essence of Japanese architecture, music, drama, painting or literature without referring to Buddhist philosophy," wrote Kurokawa.[20] Thus with their aesthetics of the unfinished image they rediscovered the special in-between architectural and urban spaces, where all the elements are interchangeable. These basic features they decided to reintroduce by means of the latest Western technology—prefabrication, mass production, and the like; the eventual result, however, turned out to be a rather mechanical interpretation of the issues involved.

When they examined the relationships between the Oriental individual, his society, and architecture, the advocates of this new trend pointed out that Japanese society had always had some unique fea- tures, like group spirit, mobility, and, recently, orientation toward mass-society. Mobility, by which a great number of people travel, often change where they live and/or commute daily for several hours back and forth to work, is actually a historical tradition in Japan. For example, over the centuries, the capital or administrative center of the country was moved from place to place several times; large building complexes, too, were often relocated. In addition, there has always been a great variety of pilgrimages throughout the country, and there is a constant yearly migration from one part of the country to the other during certain national festivals.[21] This devotion to moving around prompted the famous *haiku* poet Matsuo Basho to say that traveling was his dwelling.[22] It is therefore no wonder that Japan today has the most advanced mass transportation and communications systems in the world, the former exemplified by the Shinkansen Line with its fabulous computerized superexpress trains.

The members of the Metabolist group worked independently of each other. They developed the original ideas in several directions according to their individual methodologies and the aspect each chose to emphasize. This explains why despite a common starting point reflected in the many similarities in their early buildings, differences gradually began to appear in their architecture. Kurokawa and Kikutake remained the most radical of the group for the longest period of time. Otaka and Maki followed, adding new colors to the Metabolist spectrum. Maki's departure from strict Metabolism became so extensive that he is now referred to as the most important representative of Japanese Contextualism. Isozaki, who never really belonged to the group, pushed his way swiftly and deliberately toward symbolism or rather Mannerism.

The significance of the group and the Metabolist philosophy—besides achievements in individual works—lies distinctly in its influence on other Japanese architects and on foreign architects as well, including probably the English Archigram group. Because of cultural heritage, the ideas the Metabolists newly fashioned were certainly not completely novel to the Japanese. Consequently Metabolism was fairly widely accepted, and its ideas can be found expressed in the approaches of several other contemporary architects. Thus Metabolism was far from limited to the activities of the group members. As a general trend for about ten years, between the early 1960s and 1970s, it manifested itself in many works, including large government projects.

Yet these manifestations as the realization of change remained in most cases only partial at best. Most buildings, including those of the group, were constructed along rather conventional lines inasmuch as they were not designed to be changeable or extendable; even if they were so designed, almost none was actually changed or extended. Beyond expressive and often overwhelmingly heavy forms generated by the extensive use of megastructures, Metabolist practices exhausted themselves by employing mostly prefabricated building components; industrialization heavily dominated Metabolist designs, yet flexibility based on interchangeability remained largely an elusive matter.

Günter Nitschke's criticism seems appropriate: "As long as the actual buildings get heavier, harder, more and more monstrous in scale, as long as architecture is taken as a means of expression of power, be it of oneself or of any kind of vulgar institution, which should be serving not ruling society, the talk of greater flexibility and change-loving structures is just a fuss."[23] Thus much of the Metabolist movement hardly went beyond a much publicized rhetorical avant-gardism.

The first buildings to show signs of the new direction were completed in the beginning of the 1960s; these Metabolist structures bore a resemblance to one another more conspicuous at this time than they did later on. Massive ferroconcrete structures of unfinished surface characterized all the buildings, many of them prefabricated. The master Tange's influence still lingered but the quality of the new and bold spaces had been conceived in the spirit of Metabolism. Fumihiko Maki's design for Nagoya University's Toyota Memorial Auditorium (1960) is probably the first building that reveals a completely new space concept and approach to forms. It was then that Maki started to deal with the theory of group form in connection with city planning, in which positive and negative forms or volumes are equally important in spatial experience. The space under the large roof supported by ferroconcrete pylons—a symbolic gate to the university—is Maki's first attempt to create a transition between exterior and interior. This spatial flow, where outer spaces gradually and unnoticeably turn into inner spaces, and vice versa, forms the basis of his later Contextual approach.

In 1963 two comparatively small buildings very much alike in their design method were completed. The forms of both Maki's Memorial Auditorium of Chiba University and Kikutake's Izumo Shrine Office Building and Treasury symbolize roofs seen in traditional architecture (109, 110). Maki admitted that the image of Shinto shrines formed the background pattern for the design. In both cases the reinforced concrete shafts house the staircases—an influence of Tange's Structuralism. In the Izumo administration building the shafts still act as supports for the two fifty-meter long prestressed concrete roof girders, while in the auditorium they are independent of the supporting structure. These buildings are similar not only in the arrangement of their almost entirely nonpartitioned interior spaces, but also in the direct relationship of the interiors to the exteriors. These features foreshadow Otani's Kyoto International Conference Hall, which was completed three years later (97, 98).

Arata Isozaki also left Tange in 1963 to set up his own atelier. He immediately started his independent career with new and bold projects that transcended his master's in many respects. His

109.

109.

109–112. The early Metabolist buildings were designed with unfinished massive concrete structures and extensive prefabrication and are intended to reflect a new approach to architectural spaces. Several of them deliberately incorporate such traditional architectural forms as the slanting roof motif.

109. Memorial Auditorium of Chiba University (1963, F. Maki).

110. Izumo Shrine Office Building (1963, K. Kikutake).

111. Iwata Girl's High School in Oita (1964, A. Isozaki).

112. Central Lodge of the Yokohama Children's Land (1965, K. Kurokawa).

110.

111.

112.

Iwata Girls' High School (1964) in Oita is arranged around an elevated inner court as communication space. With its rather unusual forms of the cantilevered blocks, the building seems to enclose this space from the top as well. Although quite unlike the manner of Tange's buildings, the design shows some Structuralist features. Here the structural system allows a direct visual connection among the different spaces. A comparison of the Olympic Stadiums in Tokyo from the same year with the Iwata Girls' High School makes clear why Tange called his runaway disciple a rebel (111).

Isozaki's next buildings, which date from the second half of the 1960s, still bore some overtones of Structuralism and Metabolism. However, they also marked the beginning of the road away from these ideas and pointed toward Isozaki's present Mannerism. Kikutake and Kurokawa on the other hand had at that time just introduced their original Metabolist philosophy into practice in an increasing number of completed projects (112).

KIYONORI KIKUTAKE

Kikutake (b. 1928) began his career as a "wonder child." He graduated in architecture from Waseda University in 1950, but even by 1948 he had won third prize in the Hiroshima Catholic Peace Cathedral competition (first prize was not awarded). He opened his own office in Tokyo in 1953. As early as 1958, thus preceding Tange's similar projects, he participated in an exhibition at the Metropolitan Museum of Art in New York, presenting his design for a Marine City. This plan can be regarded as preliminary to the 1960 Metabolist declaration, a sign of the period to come when architects would be restless to draw up imaginary future cities based on changeability. Kikutake surely proved to be the most productive and with his floating cities the most poetic among them. His projects included Tower City (1959), Aquapolis (1960), Ocean City (1961), and so on. They mark the debut of plug-in capsule units (108).

These plans, however—just like the others from this period—were "even more remote and inapplicable to everyday life than the megastructures of Archigram," and so remained on the drawing board and in the pages of magazines.[24] Once more a world exposition helped Kikutake realize his idea, even if on a smaller scale than his original city projects. Tange built his Structuralist city at Osaka Expo '70, ten years after its conception. Kikutake had to wait fifteen years for Ocean Expo '75 in Okinawa; there the huge floating steel construction of Aquapolis was built to his design and remains to serve as a late closing chord to a period of utopian concepts of the city based on Metabolist megastructures (113).

As the leading figure of the Metabolist group, Kikutake elaborated its "new" philosophy: "Architecture is a metabolic process. It is constantly changing in keeping with the life-styles of the people who use it, and there may never be a time when it can be said to be complete."[25] With this fundamental attitude, and influenced by nuclear physicist Mitsuo Taketani's conceptual model of human awareness, Kikutake further developed his architectural design methodology. He called this three-stage model Ka-Kata-Katachi and presented it in the form of the Metabolist triangle. The *ka, kata,* and *katachi* are not only syllables of one word but also independent Japanese words. The three aspects express the dialectics and theoretical basis of Kikutake's work.

Starting in the mid-1960s, Kikutake conceived some excellent buildings in the spirit of this approach. His Izumo Taisha office building was followed by two hotels. The first, the Hotel Tokoen (1964), was a resort hotel at the seaside spa of Yonago in western Japan (114). The building clearly reveals its construction methods: an independent reinforced concrete skeleton structure with rooms like separate boxes within it. This method is both Metabolist and traditional. The special use of pillars is based on one of the old wooden structural sys-

113. A small version of Kikutake's several urban visions intended to be built over the sea was realized at Ocean Expo '75 in Okinawa. As a late achievement, the Aquapolis projects a somewhat anachronistic image in the changed new age (1975, K. Kikutake; photograph courtesy of Kiyonori Kikutake).

114. An independent post-and-beam concrete skeleton with blocks of hotel rooms like bridges among them, as well as the curving lines of the roof, re-create an image known from old Japanese houses. In the Hotel Tokoen in Yonago, Kikutake superbly brings together elements from both the modern Western and traditional domestic architecture (1964, K. Kikutake).

115. The rooms of the Pacific Hotel in Chigasaki were arranged along a spiral corridor rising continuously from the first floor to the top (1966, K. Kikutake).

116. Floor plan of the Pacific Hotel. 1. Lobby in front of elevators. 2. Hotel room. 3. Bathroom. 4. Storage, and service personnel. 5. Spiral corridor. 6. Open to below.

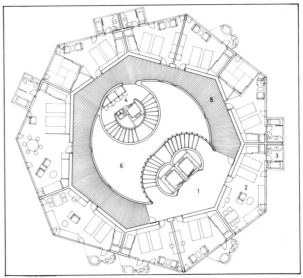

tems, where the main pillars were supported by smaller ones (*nuki*) on the sides. Thus the architectural spaces are determined by these posts and beams as well as by the floor slabs placed over them. The upper block of the fifth and sixth floors is suspended from huge roof beams and is separated from the second and third floors by an "empty" space of roof terraces. Here is another solution that precedes Tange's void zones at the Yamanashi Communication Center in Kofu (1966). The highly flexible inner spaces all contain *tatami* rooms. In addition, the entrance hall and public spaces occupying the somewhat elevated first floor are directly connected to the Japanese garden behind the building. The slightly curving lines of the ferroconcrete roof accentuate the impression of traditional architecture. Such roofs were to become a characteristic motif in Kikutake's later works.

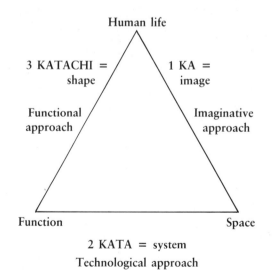

Human life

3 KATACHI = shape

Functional approach

1 KA = image

Imaginative approach

Function

Space

2 KATA = system
Technological approach

The second hotel, the Pacific Hotel at Chigasaki (1966), is located along the seashore some sixty kilometers from Tokyo. The rooms are arranged along a continuous spiral corridor that encloses a multistory space with an open ceiling. This vertical tube accommodates the separate guest and service elevators and the staircases. Kikutake aimed at solving two problems in this project. With the spiral arrangement of spaces he tried to make future vertical expansion possible without altering the overall image. In addition for the first time he designed bathroom units as prefabricated capsules and "plugged" them into the rooms from outside; this allowed their easy replaceability, not unlike some elements in his earlier proposals for floating cities (115, 116).

Kikutake only partially employed prefabricated ready-made units for the elevation of this hotel. Several years later Yoji Watanabe (b. 1923) exploited the idea to its full extent in his design for Sky Building No. 3 (1970) in Tokyo with story-high three-dimensional wall elements. The Sky Building can be regarded as a further step toward Kurokawa's capsule architecture, epitomized best by the Nakagin Capsule Tower. Here Watanabe settled for a conventional supporting skeleton structure made of reinforced concrete and steel elements. The industrially ready-made facade of steel-frame panels—covered by silver-coated metal plates and equipped with the necessary windows, air-conditioning units, and so on—are fixed to this skeleton. Because of the way these large elements are piled up, along with the forms of all the machinery on the roof, the building's appearance suggests a huge battleship (117).

According to Kikutake, the Civic Center in Miyakonojo (1966) was also designed and built with the Metabolist idea of change. This strange-looking building accommodates a huge auditorium with massive fixed ferroconcrete structures. It has a light steel-frame suspension roof that covers the spectators' hall and the potentially extendable stage plus stage loft. Its changeability, however, is rather questionable since the roof is not movable at all; its appearance nevertheless creates a range of metaphors in relation to movement. It is possibly reminiscent of an enormous baby carriage or—in the local context—a Japanese fan. Robin Boyd com-

117. With its specially designed prefabricated wall units and the forms of its machinery rooms on the roof, the Sky Building No. 3 in Tokyo suggests the image of a huge battleship (1970, Y. Watanabe).

118. The odd forms of the Civic Center in Miyakonojo invoke a range of metaphors—camera bellows, baby carriage, Japanese fan—yet none of them seems to be appropriate for the activities inside (1966, K. Kikutake).

119. The simple solid concrete walls are topped with the steel framework of the roof covered by white metal plates around the side, resulting in the unusual exterior of the Hagi Civic Center (Hagi, 1968, K. Kikutake).

120. Inside the Hagi Civic Center, suspended lights create the ceiling under the steel framework.

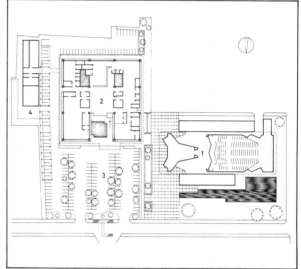

121. Site plan of the Hagi City Center (1968, 1975, K. Kikutake). The civic center and the city hall in close relationship with each other form the center of the small town. 1. Civic center. 2. City hall. 3. Parking and Plaza. 4. Existing building.

122. Under an upper section in the form of a Japanese roof, the Hagi City Hall has a large inner court as semipublic space that connects the interior with the plaza in front (1975, K. Kikutake).

pared it to a bent camera bellows.[26] For a civic center, however, none of these metaphors seems really appropriate (118).

Kikutake started to develop another city center in 1968 with the completion of the Hagi Civic Center and continued in 1974 with the construction of the City Hall. The Hagi Civic Center was designed along principles similar to those followed at the Miyakonojo complex. Here, too, the lower sections were made of reinforced concrete and the upper roof of steel-lattice frames in radial arrangement covered outside by white-coated metal plates. The steel structure of the roof is exposed to the spaces below, the lobby, and large and smaller auditorium. A system of lighting fixtures suspended from this steel structure creates a feeling of a ceiling surface above. The huge expansive roof and, even more, the free-flowing space of the lobby play the organizing role among the separate functional units; as an in-between element, this space connects the building to the urban plaza in front and the City Hall nearby (119–121).

The City Hall in Hagi has a somewhat more flexible arrangement. With the introduction of the inner courtyard, the relationship, which is to say the transition, between exterior and interior is more subtle. Using Metabolist terminology, these semi-public spaces are assigned the role of connectors between public and private areas. This constantly recurring theme in Metabolist works refers to similar qualities of traditional architecture. In addition, Kikutake designed the upper section of the City Hall in the form and color of Japanese roofs. He arranged the different departments, offices, and conference halls within its megastructure of story-high steel-lattice frame trusses, while reserving most of the first floor for large communal spaces (122).

After the early example in his first remarkable work, the Sky House (1959) in Tokyo, the importance of the roof as a dominant element had become evident and by this time reappeared in many of Kikutake's projects. One such project is the Kyoto Community Bank Shugakuin Branch (1971); where the whole design is dominated by the unusual umbrellalike roofs (123, 124). The small building is nothing but four quadratic capsules of 9.6 by 9.6 meters each, individually represented by the roofs, and arranged in the form of a swastika. The swastika refers to the historic environment around the bank in Kyoto: it symbolizes Buddhist temples and monasteries in Japan. The traditional central post (daidoku-bashira) is also recalled in the design, where steel columns organize the space and of course also support the roof. The shape of the four quadratic roof elements is the same twisted hyperbolic-paraboloid surface used earlier on the Hotel Tokoen in Yonago.

The idea of capsules—though never presented in such a provocative manner as in Kurokawa's architecture—has always been one of Kikutake's preoccupations as well. It first appeared somewhere in his early city projects of 1959 and 1960 and continued in use as subsystems in different forms commensurate with the Ka-Kata-Katachi design theory. Capsular elements are present in the Pacific Hotel, the Hotel Tokoen, the Kyoto Bank Building, and, in a new version "à la Tange," in Kikutake's Hinoyama Restaurant (1973) located on a mountaintop in Shimonoseki. Here the functional units, a revolving restaurant and an observation platform above it, are cantilevered from a huge central service shaft in a way similar to Tange's Shizuoka Communication Center in Tokyo (125 and 106).

However, no other project of his is based so clearly on the application of capsules than the Expo Tower (1970) in Osaka. Similar to the unbuilt tower project for the Montreal Expo by Archigram member Peter Cook, Kikutake's tower is built with a megastructure of steel pipes—identical in principle to the megastructure of the Space Frame over the Festival Plaza nearby—with plugged-in multilateral domes as capsules (101).

In keeping with his Metabolist Kata design theory, Kikutake has also been deeply involved in

123–124. The small
building of the Kyoto
Community Bank
Shugakuin Branch is
nothing but four
quadratic "capsules"
represented by their
umbrella-shaped roofs
(1975, K. Kikutake).

125. One huge cylindrical
shaft with cantilevered
platforms, the Hinoyama
Restaurant in Shimo-
noseki overlooks some of
Japan's most beautiful
scenery (1973, K.
Kikutake).

126–128. Kikutake in the "Pasadena Heights" Terrace Houses (1974) reintroduces the traditional Japanese pattern, wherein the veranda (*engawa*) provides the means of communication and circulation. Here the terraces become "urban streets," semipublic spaces for residents and pedestrians (1976, K. Kikutake).

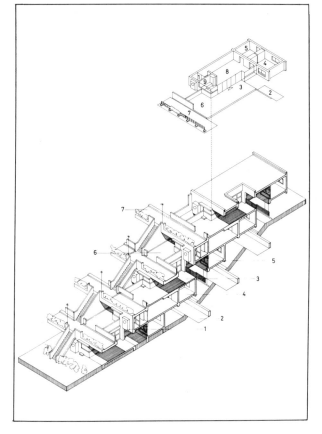

128. Axonometric section of the "Pasadena Heights" Terrace Houses (1974, K. Kikutake). 1. Bathroom unit. 2. Corridor under building. 3. Inner courtyard. 4. Bedroom #1. 5. Bedroom #2.

6. Front garden.
7. Walkway on terrace.
8. Living room.
9. Kitchenette.

the problems of group dwellings or mass housing from the very beginning of his career. This was the core of numerous city plans and of the Tonogaya Apartment Houses (1956), and led to the elaboration of the Kata-Housing System in the early 1970s. In this series of projects, he introduced several Metabolist systems with megastructures—treelike, slablike, towerlike, tiered, continuous, netlike, and layered Kata mass housing.

Kikutake believes that the key issue in mass housing is a collective way of living in contrast to individual family life.[27] Therefore residential architecture should provide the conditions for the evolution of community life beyond the primary functions of living. The Metabolists saw these conditions in the in-between or semipublic zones where a feedback relationship between architectural space and human or social behavior could evolve.

The first kind of Kata housing, the Pasadena Heights (1974), was realized as a system of terrace houses among the hills near Mishima City (126, 127). The design deviates from the usual pattern of such complexes in several respects. First of all, though the terraces follow the slopes of the hill, they do not "land" on them but are raised on ferroconcrete pilotis. This solution permits a second rear access to the apartments from the walkways under the building, while the main approach is provided from the long, curving system of terraces. The most exposed, attractive, and sunniest part of every level becomes a communication space or an "urban street," already known from traditional architecture as engawa (128).

The joining open or covered gardens—even more, the apartments themselves—show some features of multifunctionality. The bathroom is a "traditional" Kikutake solution; its exterior wall is a prefabricated unit—including some of the facilities and installations—made of plastic panels on aluminum frames. The first floor of the complex accommodates more community spaces, such as game rooms, reception halls, the administration office, a children's library, and the laundry and drying rooms. But without doubt the most arresting feature of the Pasadena Heights is the interpretation and design of the terraces as a sort of amphitheater viewing the endless stage with its breathtaking scenery.

KISHO KUROKAWA

With his strong commitment to capsule architecture, Kisho Kurokawa (b. 1934) became the most celebrated Metabolist. By the mid-1970s, along with Isozaki, he was one of the most prominent and influential architects in Japan. His membership and positions in various private and governmental organizations were numerous; his popularity could be compared only to a leading pop star. Though probably no longer true, some years ago he was regarded as the third most popular personality in Japan, following the Emperor and Prime Minister Tanaka.

Kurokawa, only twenty-six years old when the Metabolist declaration appeared in 1960, was the youngest member of the original group. He graduated with his degree in architecture from Kyoto University in 1957 and obtained his master's and doctor's degrees at Tokyo University under Kenzo Tange. While at the university he worked in Tange's URTEC office and participated actively in the elaboration of A Plan for Tokyo—1960. His devotion to city planning had earlier brought Kurokawa into close contact with Kikutake, in 1958. During the years that followed they worked together on the theory that later became known as Metabolism.

As his contribution to the first declaration, Kurokawa drew up his own futuristic plans for an Agricultural City (1960), Space City (1960), and, the next year, the famous Helix City (129). In his design philosophy he relied more than anyone else in the group on modern technology and the Buddhist tradition. His architecture, like his personality, is a unique and sometimes contradictory mixture of Western and Oriental, futuristic and

129. Kurokawa's early futuristic plan for a Helix City, an "entrance ticket" to the Metabolist group (1961, K. Kurokawa; photograph courtesy of Kisho Kurokawa).

130. Drive-in at Otome Pass (1968, K. Kurokawa). One single capsule unit, the restaurant block is placed within an overwhelming structural system.

130.

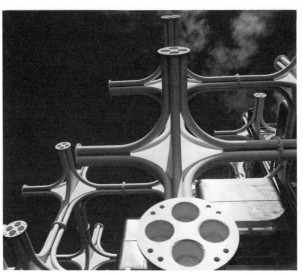

129.   131.

131–132. Expo '70 in Osaka served as a testing ground for the Metabolists. Kurokawa built his first real capsule buildings here.

131. Takara Beautilion Pavilion (1970; photograph courtesy of Kisho Kurokawa).

132. The experimental Capsule House suspended in the space frame of the Theme Pavilion (1970).

132.

traditional. To elaborate on his ideas, he wrote several books, most of which are available only in Japanese: *Metabolism '60, Prefabrication and Metabolism* (1960), *House in the Future-Metabolism* (1964), *Urban Design* (1965), *Action Architecture* (1967), *Homo Movense* (1969), *The Concept of Metabolism* (1972), and *Metabolism in Architecture* (1977).

In 1962 Kurokawa left Tange's office and set up his own in Tokyo. From that time on he has played a role of growing significance in Japanese architecture. His preoccupation with capsules and megastructures started in the late 1950s at the very beginning of his career, but it took him a few years to realize these Metabolist ideas and even then he did not succeed every time. Too often the nature or the size of the project was just not appropriate for such solutions, which thus appeared rather forced. One example is the Odakyu Drive-in (1969), a small roadside restaurant in the Hakone Mountains. Kurokawa placed the boxlike unit of the restaurant within an independent steel-pipe space frame that also supported the tent structure over the open-air beer garden on the rooftop. The overwhelming structural system was further emphasized by the joints of the frame, conspicuously fashioned to suggest further extension or easy disassembly (130).

This restaurant was only a forerunner of the numerous and more genuine capsule projects designed and built in the following years. The real opportunity for Kurokawa to introduce his new architecture on a larger scale came with Expo '70 in Osaka. He participated in the preparatory work along with other Metabolist architects by designing two pavilions, the Toshiba IHI and the Takara Beautilion, as well as the experimental Capsule House suspended in the huge space frame of the Theme Pavilion (131, 132). The pavilions were based on prefabricated three-dimensional steel frameworks as independent and open structural systems, with various capsule units in them. In the

Capsule House every function was encapsulated and the individual units joined to a central living space.

Kurokawa also attempted to transplant the highly industrialized prefabricated systems and the idea of capsules into ferroconcrete structures. Thus the Sakura Civic Center (1971) features concrete boxes made of hollow floor slabs and panels supported by steel-pipe columns (133). The achievement here is at best only partially successful. It is even more questionable in the Seibu Sports Plaza (1973) in Tokyo, which is one huge concrete capsule, or as Kurokawa calls it, a Big Box. To convince the skeptics of its Metabolist qualities, the building incorporates some smaller prefabricated capsules: the toilet and stairway units are attached to its side, and the main elevation features a multistory supergraphic that constantly changes image by means of a revolving mechanism.

By the early 1970s the spirit of Metabolism permeated the Japanese architectural scene rather extensively; Kurokawa, Kikutake, and their colleagues were certainly not alone in pursuing the new philosophy and methodology. A small and quite unusual building designed by the Pendacon Institute in Tokyo, the Meguro Gakuen Kindergarten (1973) also reveals the Metabolist influence in its spaces and aesthetics (134). The pillars in this entirely ferroconcrete building are grouped in fours, accommodating the staircases and the lavatory facilities within each of them. The functional units, however, formed as large capsules among the service and communication facilities, are separated only by differences of floor level or by glass walls, allowing a free and continuous flow of space all around. On the other hand, their exterior forms create a varied, playful, and ad hoc image with symbols remarkably suited to the children's world.

The most consistent and successful application of capsule architecture is without doubt found in the Nakagin Capsule Building (1972) in Tokyo. This tower has become one of Kurokawa's most

133–134. The capsule idea has also been implemented in prefabricated reinforced-concrete structures.

133. Sakura Civic Center (1971, K. Kurokawa).

134. Containing a series of interconnected spaces in a rationally ordered structural system, the Meguro Gakuen Kindergarten in Tokyo displays a facade with playful forms appropriate to the world of children (1973, Pendacon Institute).

134.

133.

135–137. The epitome of capsule architecture as well as of the whole Metabolist movement, the Nakagin Capsule Tower in Tokyo accommodates, like leaves on a tree, 144 small studio units clipped onto two vertical shafts, creating an image both futuristic and traditional (1972, K. Kurokawa).

135.

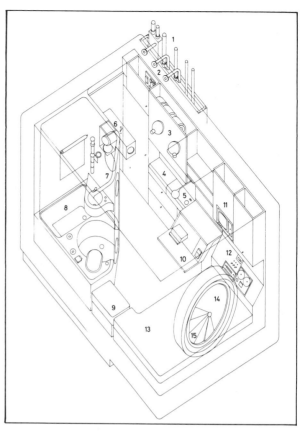

136.

138. Axonometric drawing of a capsule unit on the Nakagin Tower (1972, K. Kurokawa). The industrially prefabricated, ready-made living capsules in a minimal space provide all the necessary facilities and comfort for one single person. 1. Mechanical shaft. 2. Flexible joints. 3. Air conditioner. 4. Kitchen sink. 5. Desk lamp. 6. Ventilation fan. 7. Shower. 8. Bathtub. 9. Stool. 10. Calculator, typewriter. 11. Television set. 12. Stereo. 13. Bed. 14. Window. 15. Blind.

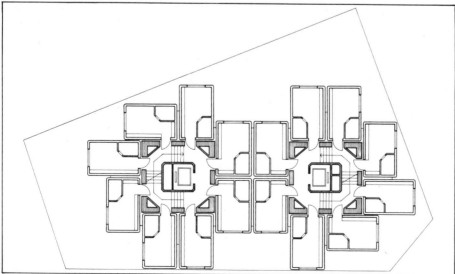

137. General floor plan of the Nakagin Capsule Tower.

notable buildings and of the whole Metabolist movement as well (135–137). Through the application of capsules, Kurokawa intended to restore human identity *(jiga)*, which, with the evolution of the mass-oriented society, had begun to fade rapidly. The minimal architectural space was meant to guarantee the basic living conditions and freedom of the individual in society. It was to express and represent as well as to protect the person, while assuring his necessary and controllable relationship to society. Yet with their identical exteriors and limited variety of interiors, these mass-produced units have done little to reduce human anonymity.

The capsule, like the version known from space technology, is a high-quality ready-made industrial product equipped with a large variety of installations in a small space (138). Its highly mechanized and standardized connections to the "docking" structure make the unit easily interchangeable and the whole system flexible. When, by means of four bolts, the capsule unit is clipped on, its facilities and equipment are simultaneously and simply plugged into the vertical and central utilities system: electricity, water, drainage, and so on.

The Nakagin Building consists of 144 studios in capsules made of welded steel frames covered with galvanized rib-reinforced steel panels—identical to the structure and size of shipping containers. They are stacked on two ferroconcrete communications and service shafts. Consequently the appearance of the building depends on how many units are used and in what way they are piled up. Kurokawa refers to this unfinished look as the "aesthetics of time," the aesthetics of Metabolism. Indeed, this look implies an ambivalent system of metaphors, which changes according to the culture it is interpreted from. Kurokawa speaks of a stock of Japanese "bird cages"; to Michael Franklin Ross it resembles "ancient wood bracketing systems"; Charles Jencks describes the building as "superimposed washing machines" because of the round plexiglas windows.[28] These images clearly reveal the mixed or in-between East and West character of the building.

The same is evident in Kurokawa's own Capsule House 'K' (1972) at Karuizawa, which he designed with only four of the units he had invented for the Nakagin Tower. Since the size of these capsules (2.4 x 3.8 m) corresponds to the dimensions of a 4.5-*tatami* tea ceremony room with the additional alcove *(tokonoma)* and storage, Kurokawa arranged one for himself in the style of Kobori Enshu, once again bringing the traditional and the modern together (139).[29]

The Kibogaoka Youth Castle near Otsu City was built in 1972, the same year the Nakagin Building was completed (140). As living quarters, the designer, Tatsuhiko Nakajima, employed capsules similar to the ones Kurokawa used in Tokyo. The castle, part of an extensive recreational and cultural park, proves, however, to be even more complex in function than Kurokawa's building. The fifty-four prefabricated units, which are fastened to the cylindrical reinforced concrete service shaft at six levels, contain single and double bedrooms and separate lavatory facilities. Spaces for community functions are lined along a multilevel streetlike inner plaza that Nakajima calls the City Tube.

Capsule architecture has not remained the domain of individual architects. Kurokawa, Otaka, and Kikutake acted as technical consultants for several construction and manufacturing companies. As a result, large trusts such as Sekisui Chemical, Nippon Steel, and Mitsui Zosen started producing prefabricated capsule homes along with their principal line of activities. Sekisui developed a system called Sekisui Haim that made use of a large number of plastic installations and finish. The interior of the bathroom unit is for example one homogeneous box incorporating the tub, basin, lavatory, walls, and so on. Mitsui Zosen, one of the biggest shipbuilding companies, ventured into steel box house units by applying the technology used in ship construction. A separate production line was introduced in their Chiba shipyard to mass produce these ready-made three-dimensional units, which were then assembled at the building site.

Kurokawa's capsule architecture reaches its most refined "high-tech" quality in the Sony Tower Building completed in 1976. The building stands like an exclamation mark in Shinsaibashi, one of the busiest commercial and amusement districts in Osaka, becoming both an advertisement for Sony Corporation and a landmark for the whole area (141–143). Kurokawa calls the tower an "information tree," referring both to its purpose of displaying a wide range of Sony audiovisual products and to his own design methodology.[30] In this electronics show building, the circulation and flow of visitors—a form of communication in itself—was a decisive factor in the design. The communication channels here—escalators and elevator shafts—contrast with, for example, Tange's Communication Center in Kofu; they are open and exposed both to the interior and, through the glass walls, to the exterior as well. Consequently the movement of people can be followed easily from outside, especially when the building is illuminated in the evening; what is even more exciting, people in the building can have a glimpse of the bustling city life below as they move up or down inside the glass-walled capsules of elevators and escalators. Thus there is a relationship between the activities within and without (144).

Several three-dimensional capsules—known from the Nakagin Tower—are lined up vertically on this information tree. Here, however, these small boxes are wrapped in stainless steel plates put together with the utmost precision. Their appearance in conjunction with the bare copper or painted ducts and the pipes and fittings exposed both in the interior and exterior are mixed with colorful and popular details, signs, and supergraphics that foretell the aesthetics of an age to follow. This building, with its sleek, sublime appearance and its subtle symbolism, is not only the last representative of Kurokawa's orthodox Metabolist philosophy but is at the same time also the beginning of a more complex and mature architectural approach best represented by his more recent National Ethnological Museum, also in Osaka, or the Saitama Prefectural Museum in Urawa City (262–269). The Sony Tower could therefore be regarded as transitional, or, to use Kurokawa's term, an "in-between" building, linking two periods of his architecture.

MASATO OTAKA

The oldest member of the Metabolist group, Otaka (b. 1923) was thirty-seven at the time of the Metabolist declaration of 1960. Like Kikutake and Kurokawa, he was also involved in the design problems of architectural and urban spaces as constantly developing or changing entities. In 1960 Otaka was co-author with Fumihiko Maki of a proposal for the Shinjuku Terminal Project and a study on group form. With its conclusion, which resembled the Metabolist theses at several points, the study became a chapter in the declaration. With this as background, we can see that Otaka's architecture shows an interesting transition between that of his master Maekawa and of the Metabolist ideas, complemented as well by elements of Maki's Contextualism.

One of his earliest buildings, the Chiba Prefectural Cultural Center (1967), was still designed à la Maekawa, but the next—the Chiba Prefectural Central Library (1968) nearby—is already a prototype of the post-and-beam architecture that followed, based extensively on prefabrication and other industrial methods. This design method unfolds itself completely in the Tochigi Prefectural Conference Hall (1969) in Utsunomiya, which is clearly one of his most mature works. Together with Sachio Otani's Kyoto Conference Hall, it is regarded as one of the best and most successful prefabricated ferroconcrete buildings in Japan (145).

139. Floor plan of the Capsule House "K" (1972, K. Kurokawa). Kurokawa used four capsules, identical to those of the Nakagin Tower, in his own summer house at Karuizawa.

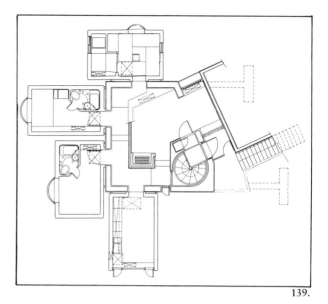

139.

140.

140. Built in the same year as Kurokawa's Nakagin Capsule Tower, the Kibogaoka Youth Castle, with capsules arranged around a cylindrical vertical shaft, was also conceived in the spirit of Metabolism (1972, T. Nakajima).

141–143. Elegantly elaborated sleek details, shiny stainless steel capsules, supergraphics, and vividly colored interiors make the Sony Tower Building in Osaka a refined mixture of high-tech and pop. Referring to its function as show-room and its role as a commercial trademark or symbol both for the Sony Corporation and the district in which it was built, Kurokawa calls the tower an "information tree" (1976, K. Kurokawa).

141.

142.

143.

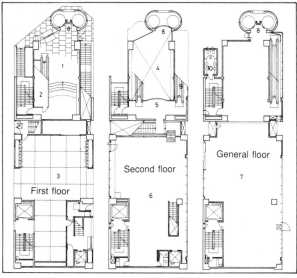

144. Floor plans of the Sony Tower (1976, K. Kurokawa). 1. Lobby. 2. Storage. 3. Parking. 4. Open to below. 5. Gallery. 6. Banking. 7. Exhibition. 8. Elevators. 9. Escalator. 10. Washroom.

145. Metabolist Masato Otaka's preoccupation with special structural solutions is evident in most of his buildings. The Tochigi Prefectural Conference Hall in Utsunomiya is a clever combination of an in-situ as well as a prefabricated reinforced-concrete system (1969, M. Otaka).

146. The multistory entrance hall of Tochigi Prefectural Conference Hall.

147–148. The Motomachi and Chojuen High-rise Apartment Houses in Hiroshima follow the curving line of the Otagawa River in a zigzag pattern. The buildings decrease in height as they approach Hiroshima Castle and the surrounding park (1973, M. Otaka; photograph [147] courtesy of Masato Otaka).

149. Floor plans of the apartment units in the Motomachi and the Chojuen Apartment Houses, Hiroshima (1973, M. Otaka). The skeleton structure of the high-rise blocks is double in nature. The primary steel frame is accompanied by a secondary reinforced-concrete one. Reflecting this solution, there are also two types of apartments.

(*top*) 1. Elevator lobby. 2. Garbage disposal. 3. Corridor. 4. A-type apartment. (*bottom*) 1. Corridor. 2. Staircase. 3. Entrance. 4. Dining/kitchen. 5. *Tatami* room. 6. Balcony. 7. Storage. 8. Bathroom. 9. W.C. 10. Garbage.

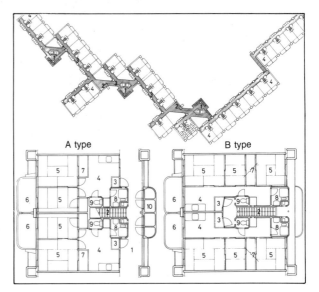

Otaka's conference hall is a clever combination of two different structural systems. The assembly hall, the core of the complex, made of in-situ reinforced concrete, is enclosed by the office wings on its three sides, built of fully prefabricated structural elements. The backbone of these wings is a primary structure of two huge main beams that span some ten meters above ground level and are supported by eight massive pillars in each wing. This primary system in turn supports a secondary one, the interlocking precast post-and-beam frame structure of the second and third levels. All these prefabricated elements are exposed to the exterior, recalling the forms of traditional wooden structures. Beyond the well-balanced appearance of the building, the design of the interior spaces is also remarkable. The focal point of the spatial arrangement is the multistory entrance hall and the public zone around the assembly hall, both lit by rooflights (146).

Otaka proved with his next significant work that even large-scale housing projects based fully on industrialized prefabricated systems need not be monotonous, dismal, and desolate. Construction of the Motomachi and Chojuen High-rise Apartments, to house fifteen thousand people, started in 1968 and was concluded in 1973. The two housing complexes are organic extensions of each other, since both were designed along the east bank of the Otagawa River near Hiroshima Castle (147, 148). The blocks of houses, raised on pilotis to accommodate additional parking under them, are laid out like folding screens in a zigzag pattern, enclosing areas for parks, playgrounds, and such community facilities as kindergartens, schools, clubhouses, shops, public baths, and so on. The shopping center has been sunk below ground level, allowing the green park to extend farther along on its roof. In a similar way, the top of each building is formed as large continuous roof-gardens and other public spaces.

To correspond better with the surrounding urban scape—the more intimate scale of low-profile residential districts and the Hiroshima Castle—the height of the different buildings decreases from twenty to eight stories. This Contextual approach, like Maki's in his Osaka Prefectural Sports Center (158–160), takes into consideration the varying scales within the city. The main elevations face south, consistent with the typical orientation of Japanese houses and apartment complexes, while the apartment units look southeast or southwest, the corridors always on the opposite side.

The structural system of the buildings is again double in nature. The main supporting skeleton is of steel with pillars arranged along the intersections of a module net of 9.9 by 9.9 meters. The main girders connect with them only at every other floor. In this way one three-dimensional space unit of the skeleton accommodates two apartments in both vertical and horizontal directions. This primary structure in itself is capable of supporting all the vertical load as well as resisting all the horizontal forces acting upon the buildings. The secondary structures, the pillars, beams, and the floors of the four enclosed apartments, are made of prefabricated ferroconcrete elements and connect with the steel skeleton constructed first.

The same two-story structural arrangement is followed by the communications system of the houses. Corridors are designed only for every other story and elevators accordingly stop at these floors. Nevertheless the layout of a four-apartment unit is such that the upper two have access from the corridor by means of a small flight of stairs. Since the staircases and elevators join only at every second level, there are always spacious and sunny areas at the landings, which, double in height, were meant to provide some common meeting place for the tenants (149). Unlike the totally prefabricated system of the apartment blocks, the service towers are of in-situ reinforced concrete, their unique forms making the overall look of the buildings even more varied.

With the success of experiments by individual

architects and private companies, government agencies too started to employ Metabolist ideas extensively. The Ashiyahama High-rise Apartment Houses were designed and built with maximum industrialized technology and production. Built near Kobe in 1979, this large low-cost housing project was based on the first-prize-winning entry in a competition sponsored by the Japan Housing Corporation in 1973. It was a team effort by the Ashiyahama City Council, the Shinnippon Steel Company, the Takenaka Construction Company, and the Matsushita Electric Company (ASTM). The buildings range from fourteen to twenty-nine floors and are supported by huge steel megastructures produced by the steel company. The prefabricated apartment units are grouped in these independent skeletons so that every four levels of apartments are followed by an open area as a community zone. As a new urban formation, the Ashiyahama housing complex, which includes numerous service facilities, is surprisingly impressive compared to most of the previously completed large residential projects in Japan (150).

Contextualism

The term for this "rediscovered" architectural approach comes once again from linguistics. The word *context* means the inner relations of the spoken or written language according to which the meaning of an individual word or sentence is interpreted in the whole paragraph or text. Thus a certain word or sentence in different contexts may have different meanings. In a broader sense, however, context points to the dialectic interrelationship among various elements, more precisely between "parts" and the "whole."

This analogy is the second between verbal and architectural languages that more and more architects came to recognize. But while Structuralism in architecture has made use of the construction, the very fabric of the language *(langue)*, Contex-

150. In the Ashiyahama High-rise Apartment Houses, a government project, the maximum degree of industrial prefabrication has been used. The huge blocks were constructed with steel megastructures in which apartment units are situated like boxes on store shelves (1973–1979, ASTM under the directorship of Takenaka Construction Company).

tualism has delved into the meanings of "sentences and speech" *(parole)* in order to transmit "correct" messages and thus to promote architectural and urban integrity. In practice, it means the semiotic examination of the different relationships between man and architecture, between the building and its vicinity in the city, and between architecture and its cultural background, which are all, in one way or another, variations or interpretations of the part and the whole relationship. According to Contextualist theory, an architectural complex can be understood—or rather the meaning of new architectural spaces can be derived—only after a careful examination of the nature of these complex relationships.

This slowly developing design theory and practice is again in sharp contrast with the methodology of orthodox Modern Architecture, which started with the smallest architectural element, the room, followed by the house or the building with its inner functions. The modern city was understood as a loose sum total of these independent functional units. The connecting medium, an internal linkage, was missing physically, perceptually, and culturally. To quote David Wild, "The major weakness in the Modern Movement was the total disregard for context, in the urbanistic sense."[31] According to the contextual understanding, the various parts of the built environment could retain their individuality, though at the same time they are meant to create—sometimes in several ways—a larger unit new in quality.

It can safely be said of Japanese architecture that it is the history of a most complex network of relationships among man, architecture, and the physical and cultural environment; every single building can be read and understood with this context in mind. It is well represented by the Japanese preference for incessantly progressing from the particular to the general, that is to say, from the more immediate and concrete parts or elements to the largely elusive whole, affording thereby the "open" yet intimate character of their traditional architecture together with the relative or multivalent character of the built urban spaces and forms. Commenting on the same issue, Heather Willson Cass wrote: "Indeed, for philosophical as well as applied precedents, a more earnest study of Japanese art, architecture, and letters would seem to be in order for anyone trying to create a more coherent body of theory of the welter of words currently associated with the contextual approach to design."[32]

One of the most prominent recent representatives of this "new" approach in Japan is Fumihiko Maki. His Contextual architecture today, however, does not remain unchallenged by others, such as Kurokawa recently, Isozaki, and especially a large number of young New Wave architects, who also show an increased interest in and sensitivity toward many aspects of this approach to design. In several cases this New Wave group has extended the limits of Contextualism toward, in post-Structuralist terminology, "intertextualism," which involves far more than just the formalistic fit/nonfit implications of Contextualism. Most of the earlier examples, including Maki's first buildings, seem to reflect a more simplistic understanding and mechanical interpretation of the inherent issues and as such represent only the initial steps toward a more complex Contextual Japanese architecture.

FUMIHIKO MAKI

Born in Tokyo in 1928, Fumihiko Maki started his architectural studies at Tokyo University under Kenzo Tange. He graduated in 1952 and enrolled in the Cranbrook Academy of Arts in the United States, where he received his first master's degree in 1953. The next year he acquired another master's from Harvard University, where he studied with Jose Luis Sert. After working for Skidmore, Owings and Merrill for a short while, he joined Sert–Jackson and Associates. During his two years with Sert–

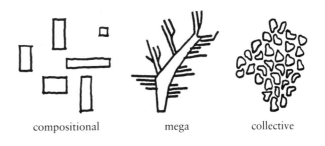

compositional mega collective

Jackson he participated in several large projects, including the American Embassy in Baghdad. In 1956 he accepted a teaching position at Washington University in St. Louis, where he worked mainly in the theory of city planning. He later taught this subject at Harvard University, serving as associate professor until 1966. In 1958 he concluded a field trip in Asia and Europe as a fellow of the Graham Foundation. In the course of this trip he examined the development and structural order of several historical cities in the countries visited. Upon his return to Tokyo in 1965 he established his own office, where he has been working ever since.

Problems of urban design drew him into close contact with the Metabolists. In 1960, together with Masato Otaka, he wrote an essay entitled "Toward Group Form," which became a part of the declaration called *Metabolism—1960*. He delved into the forms and fabric of the city and how these develop in context and in relation to group form. Later, Maki extended this thesis with *Investigations in Collective Form*, which constituted the basis of his succeeding Contextualist approach and preceded Venturi's theory of "complexity and contradiction" and Giurgola's theory of "partial vision," which consider similar topics and reach similar conclusions.[33]

With his long professional experience abroad, Maki is among those Japanese architects who most consistently assimilate both the Japanese and Western attitudes, bridging in a convincing way the differences between the object-oriented traditions of the West and the evolution-oriented traditions of Japan. He wrote in 1970: "The ultimate aim of architecture is to create spaces to serve mankind, and in order to achieve this, the architect must understand human activities from the standpoints of history, ecology, and action circumstances. He must also know the relationship existing between human activities and architectural spaces and processes by means of which these relationships develop."[34]

Exploring the relationship between components and the whole in urban design, Maki distinguished among three basic morphological types: compositional form, mega form, and group or collective form.

In compositional form the individual elements are the most independent; the links—if any—among them are minimal. Yet their configuration—following a functionally optimal diagram and the mechanistic rules of a usually two-dimensional geometry—is the most deterministic. This formal and organizational pattern characterizes the master-planning concepts of the orthodox Modern Movement. The Rockefeller Center in New York, the Illinois Institute of Technology (IIT) campus in Chicago, and the cities of Chandigar and Brasilia are good examples of this kind of design. In mega form, the links among the elements constitute a system with the inherent possibility of self-development or change. The various architectural and urban spaces join to the connectors so that they become highly dependent on the overall system and become in themselves of secondary significance. This pattern of master system is analogous, for example, to the basic features of Tange's Structuralism as seen in his Tokyo Plan-1960 or to Kurokawa's numerous town-planning projects. In the last type of form the elements are clustered along group structures with collective forms in such a way that the elements do not depend on an a priori system but themselves generate it; in turn this connecting system necessitates and promotes the development of the elements. In other words, the relationship between the elements and the system is reciprocal both in design and in operation. This is the pattern of old villages and towns, the prototypical urban residences, particularly in traditional Japanese cities and among houses characterized by their additive, aggregate forms and ambiguous spatial organization based on the concepts of *ma* and *oku*.

With his postulation of collective form, Maki's

understanding of urban organisms, apart from their direct affinity with traditional Japanese patterns, came surprisingly close to those of his friend Aldo van Eyck. He too maintained that the vitality and human significance of the built environment lie necessarily in the ambiguous relationship of the environmental elements, which he called "kaleidoscopic" with a "labyrinthian clarity."[35] Obviously such an understanding of the built environment is fundamentally at odds with the forced separation between architectural and urban designs. Maki spoke of elements that "invoke" a system. To accomplish this, design should aim not only at controlling but, more, at permitting spontaneous connections between human beings and spaces. Space should generate activities, while activities define space. This intimate relationship between the two is an interaction, a continuous chain of feedbacks, a qualitative two-way communication.

A person feels at home in his environment under two related conditions: if he is able to interpret and appropriate it as his own and by so doing create and find identity; and if he is able to perceive and relate to his location within its larger context, which is to say, to orient himself by actively participating in the environment. In other words, the built urban environment has to make the person feel that he is "somebody living somewhere."[36] It is therefore important to realize, as Nicholas Habraken pointed out, that "possession is inextricably connected with action. To possess something we have to . . . make it part of ourselves, and it is therefore necessary to reach out for it. To possess something we have to take it in our hand, touch it, test it, put our stamp on it. Something becomes our possession because we make a sign on it, because we give it our name, or defile it, because it shows traces of our existence."[37] Thus the city has to provide places for creative participation or interaction, and those places as interrelated parts are able to suggest their broader relationships with gradually larger units or domains and, finally, the whole, which is by no means a finished, complete entity.

To create such places, however, the architect not only has to record the physical facts of the environment, but should also understand its human associations; that is, how this environment "lives" with or within people who use and experience it—how much it may mean to them. He should be able to anticipate, imagine, and suggest the significance that a new architectural element might generate within its physical and cultural context. Accordingly, Maki distinguishes between two aspects of the human environment: the first is a "primary landscape," the physical reality and relationships of the elements, which respond to how people can live in their environment; the second is an "imaginary landscape," which exists in the human understanding and awareness from where it acts on the physical reality and provides information on how people would like or intend to live in that environment.

With his more sensitive interpretation of the man-environment relationship that finds real affirmation in the phenomenal world, there is no doubt that Maki has gone far ahead of the more formalistic and technological interpretations of Metabolism. Because he is convinced that "spatial design must become a fountainhead of spontaneous, rich human events," he attributes great importance to public places and urban plazas or, as he calls them, "city corridors and city rooms," which can best serve as catalysts in generating interaction and communication.[38] To achieve this, Maki, contrary to other Metabolist architects, does not rely on futuristic high technology, space-age techniques, and pretentious special structures. Industrialized methods like prefabrication are only tools for him, not the goal itself. No megastructures or capsules characterize his architecture. Already conspicuous in such early urban designs as Maki's Shinjuku Redevelopment Project (1960), the Golgi Structures (1965), and buildings such as the auditoriums of

Nagoya (1960) and Chiba (1963) Universities (109) is a deeper interest in the nature and metamorphosis of architectural and urban spaces wherein, for example, "exterior spaces . . . first serve as the generators of the interior space, and become eventually the interior space themselves."[39]

His ideas developed further in such projects as the Rissho University Kumagaya Campus (1968), where the plaza among the glass-wall buildings becomes an organic part of the interiors that surround it, and later, in 1970, the Senri Chuo Building in Osaka not far from the site of Expo '70 (151). The interior spaces of this last building, a city hall and civic center, are arranged to refer to the greater environment, the surrounding double-level urban plaza. The upper entrance hall with large glass surfaces and three entrances on different sides forms a part of the exterior, the urban vicinity. Furthermore, there is direct access from this space to a three-story community space on the mezzanine floor in the center of the building. This multipurpose city room includes the freestanding shafts of the staircases and elevators grouped in the middle. These shafts are then linked to the surrounding sections by bridges, from where the whole space is clearly visible. The movement of the people on these different levels can also be followed visually from the lobby, cafeteria, exhibition rooms, and other facilities on the mezzanine level.

From the early 1970s Maki became more obviously involved in organizing individual parts—themselves complete units—into one "easy whole."[40] He has found the connecting media in multipurpose communication spaces in both the exterior and interior. He divides the program into basic functional elements that remain comparable to or suggest the whole; and then he puts them together again through a system of these intermediary spaces, so that the resulting building points toward complex urban formations.

Maki often quotes Aldo van Eyck, who said that "a house must be like a small city if it's to

be a real house—a city like a large house if it's to be a real city."[41] In the Kato Gakuen Elementary School this rediscovered idea is represented by the arrangement of the classrooms in groups separated as well as connected by several open inner courts and a system of interwoven multipurpose community spaces. Classrooms can also be opened up and enlarged by means of sliding partitions (152). The ambiguity of the relationship between the component units and the whole—in addition to the usual urban quality of Maki's buildings—suggests another kind of complex human habitat as well, that of an ocean liner. Maki designed the rooftop of the school as the deck of the "ship," adding fun and broadened experience to the lives of the children.

Contextual design with increased attention to various relationships between new and existing elements developed slowly in modern Japanese architecture, with a definite emphasis at the beginning on the physical aspects of these relationships. The Yamaguchi Municipal Center by the Nikken Sekkei Company (1977) and the Yamaguchi Prefectural Library by Azusa Kito (1973) exemplify this gradual evolution rather well. In the municipal center complex the different elements are linked together by an inner urban plaza directly accessible from the street through the pilotis under the lower wings. The height of these wings matches the scale of the surrounding streets, while on the other side of the plaza the block of auditorium and cultural center strikes out with the heavy solid concrete walls of the towering stage loft. The huge glass surfaces of the lobby at the same time create direct visual contact with the plaza and with the surrounding streets as well (153–155).

The library, located not far from the municipal center, reveals more organic features. Kito had to accommodate various functions within the building. He grouped them in individual architectural spaces in a way similar to Maki's so that they retain their independence yet comprise an organic whole that

151. The first sign of
Maki's early deviation
from Metabolist ideas is
already represented by his
buildings of the late
1960s. He became more
interested in the problems
of architectural spaces
than in the technological
approach. The Senri
Chuo Building near
Osaka was designed with
a multistory community
space connected directly
to the surrounding urban
plaza (1970, F. Maki).

also becomes a successful urban element in the surrounding texture of the city. The two-story central hall, which contains the library's open stacks and a reading room as well, is linked to the entrance hall within the same space and to the small park and plaza around the building through the three entrances. With its intricate relationships to other parts of both the interior and the exterior, this space turns into the most important place within the building; it is also a vital part of the city center's urban environment. This example reflects today's tendency for libraries, like other structures, to become increasingly multifunctional (156, 157).

As Maki very consciously distanced himself further from Metabolist ideology in the years that followed, his architecture underwent a slow but definite metamorphosis. Heavy reinforced concrete structures with *beton-brut* aesthetics were giving way to a more refined appearance, better elaborated details, and a more intricate, richer spatial quality. Though concrete remained an important material for him, other materials like steel, glass, glass block, glazed tile, and so on, have added variety to the Contextual design methodology. In both the Osaka Prefectural Sports Center (1972) and the Tsukuba University Central Building (1974) Maki extensively employed various steel structures that contributed to the overall effect he wanted to achieve.

The individual and separate large spaces—the gymnasium, swimming pool, training hall, and administration section of the Osaka Sports Center in the suburb of Takaishi are brought together along a double-level streetlike circulation space. This long central "urban corridor" accommodates the entrance hall, the lobby, a coffeeshop, and a restaurant on the gallery, creating a physical and visual link between the different spaces inside as well as between the exterior and interior. Separating/connecting inner courts in the form of roof gardens and terraces over the first floor appear here again.

Maki also responded to the confrontation between two different urban formations around the

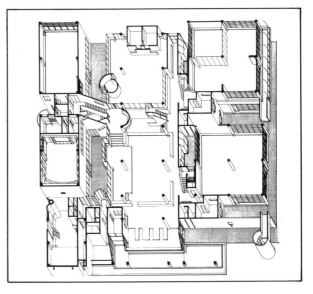

152. Axonometric
drawing of the Kato
Gakuen Elementary
School (Numazu, 1972,
F. Maki). Different
functional parts of the
building are organized
and connected by flexible
multipurpose spaces and
separated by small inner
courts.

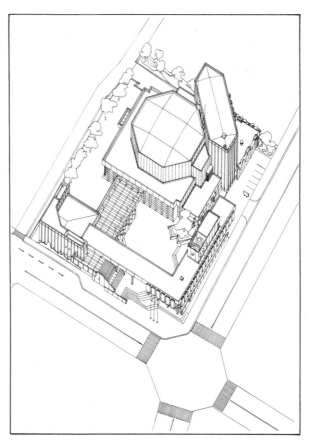

153–155. The auditorium of the Yamaguchi Municipal Center is accessible through an inner plaza surrounded by low-profile wings on pilotis (Yamaguchi, 1971, Nikken Sekkei Co., Ltd.).

155. Axonometric drawing of the Yamaguchi Municipal Center.

156. With its arrangement, three entrances, and an open passage, a section of the first floor of the Yamaguchi Prefectural Library becomes an organic part of the surrounding urban plaza and the focal point of the whole spatial design (Yamaguchi, 1973, A. Kito).

157. First-floor plan of the Yamaguchi Prefectural Library. 1. Main entrance. 2. Entrance. 3. Reading room with open stacks. 4. Braille seminar room. 5. Braille library. 6. Lobby. 7. Lecture hall. 8. Stage. 9. Teaching material. 10. Storage. 11. Director. 12. Print shop. 13. Copy room. 14. Office. 15. Stacks. 16. Dressing room. 17. Service entrance.

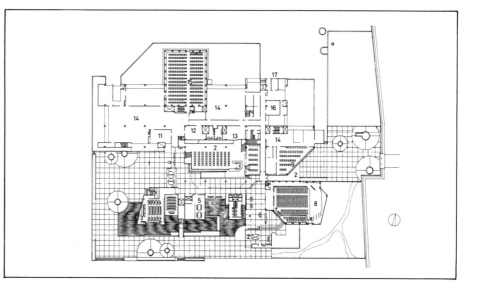

building: traditional residential in the immediate vicinity and vast-scale industrial across the canal. He attempted to reconcile these sharp differences on two levels. First, he designed the sections that face the old wooden houses to be lower and smaller in scale, while allowing the opposite front toward the port and oil refineries to step up into monumental volume. The second level of attempted reconciliation is symbolic, wherein Maki employed ambiguous structural forms and colors. The dark-colored roof structure—prefabricated on the site—made up of arched steel girders supported by huge tubular steel ridges and columns, and the light translucent walls imply the architectural vocabulary of residential and industrial districts (158–161).

The University Central Building was designed to accommodate the main facilities of the new campus, some hundred kilometers north of Tokyo, named after the Tsukuba mountains nearby. The classrooms, studios, laboratories, and administrative offices of the physical education and art departments are clustered in four independent groups linked by a system of multistory and multipurpose spaces that cut across the whole building in both directions. At their intersection, a large open hall, a "city room" (in Maki's terminology) comes into being as the focal point of the complex. It houses the free-standing main staircase that connects to the galleries around the hall by means of bridges in a manner similar to the Senri Chuo Building (162, 163).

This central space becomes the starting point of the vertical and horizontal communication. However, unlike the city room in the Chuo building, which was actually a closed space, here the central space is completely open on the first floor, where the entrance hall crosses the building like a tunnel. This solution provides a passage, a direct physical and visual continuation of the elevated walkway—the main approach to the building—toward the large green park of the campus behind, turning the whole building into the symbolic gate to the university (164).

The construction method of the central building recalls Maki's previous work, the Osaka sports center, which was also prefabricated on the site. The university building had to be completed as soon as possible; as a result the whole complex with the exception of the basement was built and assembled out of a prefabricated steel skeleton, steel floor panels, and light aluminum-framed partitions. Nevertheless, the most appealing feature here is not the structural solution but the handling of the expressly massive, volumetric forms defined by the vibrating texture of the large translucent exterior surfaces. Since the entire outer skin of this extensive building is made of glass-block curtain walls, the overall image suggested is indeed close to "a small glassy mountain."[42] Commenting on his design, Maki explained that as opposed to the oftentimes superfluous structural acrobatism of Modern architecture with cantilevered forms, he wanted to create the feeling of timeless stability brought about by mountains or the Egyptian pyramids.[43]

The same intention with stable configurations of forms is also present in his more recent works, like the Okinawa Aquarium (1975) or the small and simple building of the Iwasaki Museum (1979). In these cases Maki had admittedly been inspired by the "silhouette of (the) medieval town with the highest building in the center" expressing the collective nature of this urban formation.[44] The Tsukuba University Central Building has an additional direct reference to the 1932 Maison de Verre in Paris (Chareau and Bijvoet), where glass block had been applied extensively for the first time, and which Maki had visited earlier in his career.

Growing concern in the 1970s about the existing natural or urban environment resulted in several buildings that incorporate design principles as well as more specific features similar to Maki's Contextual approach. Although in a way different from the Tsukuba University Central Building, glass plays an important role also for Kiyoshi Kawasaki

158.

159.

158–161. In the Osaka Prefectural Sports Center in Takaishi, Maki's main concern was to create a transition between a low-profile residential and a large-scale industrial development. This Contextual approach is seen in the size, form, and color scheme of the different sections, and it is also found in the careful structural solution (1972, F. Maki).

160. Interior of the lobby. The several functional parts of the building are composed into a complete whole by means of a connecting streetlike communication space.

161. The first-floor plan. 1. Entrance hall. 2. Main gymnasium. 3. Swimming pool. 4. Subgymnasium. 5. Courtyard. 6. Office. 7. Lobby. 8. Storage. 9. Machine room. 10. Women's locker room. 11. Men's locker room. 12. Rental shoes corner. 13. Machine room. 14. Meeting room.

(b. 1932) in his investigation of the interrelationships between different architectural and environmental elements. He designed the Tochigi Prefectural Museum of Fine Arts (1972) in Utsunomiya so that the main attraction in the total composition is created by the contrasting characters of the highly geometrical, abstract prism of the administration tower and a group of trees nearby. The conflict between artificial and natural is mitigated by the mirror-glass surfaces of this multistory block reflecting back the image of the trees together with everything around, thus dematerializing and dissolving the high volume into its environment and the blue sky. Viewed from the surrounding low-profile exhibition halls and the stepped open-air sculpture garden, they are at the same time mirrored in the small pool, thus underlining the ongoing dialog among the various elements of the composition and its orchestration. Within this museum—a carefully arranged stage set, in fact—the architectural elements and their background are turned into art objects on exhibit (165).

Niigata and Kurashiki are cities quite different in character and located far away from each other. The only feature in common is their location near the sea. This proximity became a decisive factor in the designs of Shin'ichi Okada (b. 1928) from the early 1970s for a medical facility in each city. The Nippon Dental College, Niigata Campus, was built in several phases between 1971 and 1975, and the Kurashiki City Hospital in 1973. Both of them respond to the environment with an architecture that features extensive solid walls—barely pierced by windows—clad in dark brick tiles. Instead of windows, Okada employs skylights with sloping glass surfaces and glass-box "porches" in front of the elevations. This solution minimizes the hazards of long winters, especially severe in Niigata along the shores of the Japan Sea, when the snow and cold wind leave white sea-salt deposits that attack even the best metals. The closed units

162–163. Maki designed the Central Building of the Tsukuba University with a translucent skin made entirely of glass-block panels. This "glassy mountain" also has a large interior multistory community space connected directly to the exterior by wide, tunnel-like gates (Tsukuba, 1974, F. Maki).

164. Elevation and the plan of the second level of the Tsukuba University Central Building (1974, F. Maki). The huge complex—as almost always with Maki's buildings—is "disassembled" to its component functional units and put together again with connecting intermediary spaces, creating the impression of a small city. 1. Entranceway. 2. Central hall. 3. Lobby. 4. Classrooms. 5. Laboratory. 6. Lounge. 7. Seminar rooms. 8. Office. 9. Faculty rooms. 10. Lecture hall. 11. Bridge. 12. Terrace.

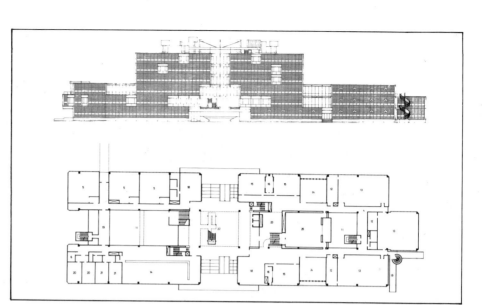

165. In Kawasaki's design the whole composition of the Tochigi Prefectural Museum of Fine Arts in Utsunomiya becomes an art object on exhibit (1972, K. Kawasaki).

166–168. Because of severe winter weather, the Nippon Dental College in Niigata was designed with brick-clad solid walls and skylights (1971, 1975, S. Okada).

166. To capture precious sunshine, several glass cages extend the lobbies and study lounges in front of the elevation.

167. Skylights of the clinic building.

168. The longitudinal entrance hall between two buildings was also shaped to capture the sunlight. Entering its space, one is puzzled to feel both inside and outside of the building at the same time.

169–170. The Kurashiki
Ivy Square Hotel was
built by remodeling an
old textile factory that
had been built in the
nineteenth century. With
the reinstated traditional
atmosphere, the building
blends remarkably with
the mellow old town
(1974, S. Urabe).

171. Following the new
Eclectic trend, Urabe has
achieved a less than
convincing result in his
latest work, the New
Kurashiki City Hall
(1980, S. Urabe).

of the different faculty and auditorium buildings turn their backs on this unfriendly environment, while the glass structures of the lobby and study lounges in front of the classrooms let in as much sunshine as possible. Particularly attractive is the architectural solution of the long entrance hall under a V-shaped glass roof suspended between two separate buildings. This hall, as in several Metabolist designs, becomes an in-between space. What makes it exciting is the ambiguous feeling—also experienced in the glass-roofed Japanese shopping streets, the *shotengai*—that makes one ponder whether he is inside *the* building or still outside of *them* (166–168).

The issue of inside-outside relationship in the urban context inevitably leads to the question of what defines—or how to define—the boundaries between the buildings and the city. In addition to the physical aspects of the building–city context, every architect also has to cope in one way or another with how the additional element is to respond to the existing environment—that is, what the relationship between the new and the old is going to be. This becomes a primary challenge to architects working in such places as Kurashiki, a city with a traditional urban milieu. The design of Shizutaro Urabe (b. 1909) for the Kurashiki Ivy Square (1974) provides a surprisingly simple and attractive solution to this difficult problem. For the new hotel he remodeled an existing textile factory dating back to the nineteenth century, restoring its historical mood and thus least disrupting the atmosphere of this mellow old town. The building is a system of two-story pavilions arranged to surround two spacious inner courts, one of which is free from vehicular traffic. Open to the general public, these courts are transformed into genuine piazzas and become links between the hotel and the city (169, 170).

A native of Kurashiki, Urabe has contributed significantly to the preservation of the city. Over the past two decades he has built several complexes in the spirit of local traditions; among these complexes are the Ohara Art Museum Annex (1961), the Kurashiki International Hotel (1963), and the Kurashiki Civic Center (1972). His latest work, however, the Kurashiki New City Hall (1980), displays a more questionable eclectic style. It combines elements of various historical and modern European, American, and Japanese architectures sometimes in a rather exaggerated fashion that results in a less successful overall response to everything around (171).

With their two complexes in Tokyo, the "From 1st" Building by Kazumasa Yamashita (b. 1937) and the Hillside Terrace Apartments by Fumihiko Maki, the designers have approached the problem of boundary with a new understanding that here creates genuine urban environments and inviting architectural places of human scale. The redefinition of the buildings as small cities or as cities in the city has brought about a spatial arrangement wherein the positive volumes are consistently perforated by an intricately interconnected system of negative spaces. In other words, both buildings have virtually acquired the porous quality of a sponge.

Located on a street corner, the "From 1st" Building creates a connection between the two streets that border the site. The connecting media are formed inside by an open-air double-deck plaza extending in different directions that eventually joins the street. Lined with various shops, boutiques, snack bars, cafés, Japanese tea shops, and so on, the open passages, outdoor corridors, and bridges on several levels, together with the stairways and elevators, provide a three-dimensional communications network all through the exteriors and interiors. A look in any direction from here will always catch a glimpse either of the busy streets or the open sky (172–175).

On the upper levels, Yamashita created a series of small offices and design studios that have something to surprise the visitor. They are actually arranged as apartments and furnished as residences. With the exception of bedrooms, all other home comforts are provided. Commenting on this obvious extension of the basic functions of the workplace, Yamashita wrote: "Of course offices are places for work. But as long as they are spaces for human beings, they must not lack individuality, drama, and psychological comfort. . . . If this is true, there is no reason why offices should not partake of the nature of the residence. On the contrary, it is preferable that they be residential and not factory-like"[45] (176).

Though they were completed in the same year, 1976, Maki's Hillside Terrace Apartments as an implementation of his concept of mutually interdependent collective forms goes back several years earlier than Yamashita's somewhat similar intentions seen in the "From 1st" Building. The apartments were designed and built in three phases, 1969, 1973, and 1976. The whole complex stretches in between the edge of an important metropolitan road and a wooded part that includes old shrine buildings. The complex, then, is in the collision zone or crossfire of two urban environments, one busy and the other quiet. In his sensitive solution to this dilemma, Maki allows both environments to penetrate into the small inner courts of the buildings through the various perforations of the surfaces and volumes, while filtering and taming them. This way these semipublic plazas, surrounded by a host of small shops and restaurants, manage to retain their identity and privacy while establishing a connection with one another and with their surrounding environment. The brief partial vistas of both street and park as visual reminders of previous and potential experiences spin a delicate web that ensures a physical and perceptual discontinuous continuity and thus ensures as well the mutual agreement between the two opposing urban elements. At the same time, the buildings are still capable of evoking the image of solid street facades, a kind of street architecture. This combined and interrelating environment is what Maki calls "low profile informal urban design" (177–179).[46]

It is revealing to follow the manner in which Maki responded to the problem of context in each of the three different phases of the work. When the project started, the street was relatively friendly and quiet, so the first buildings had more glass surfaces and openings facing it. The increasing traffic, noise, and pollution of the following years prompted Maki to react more defensively to the growing hostility of the urban environment by orienting the second and third phases more toward the atriums, the courts inside, and the green park behind (180).

In this process, interestingly, new features and aspects appear or become more conspicuous and more elaborate in Maki's architecture, a development that altogether may be called an increased concern for cultural context. To quote him, "I believe there is an important design agent to be found in experience, both cultural and physiological."[47] This notion goes back to the beginning of the evolution of his Contextual approach to design and can be found in his spatial compositions; they have always indicated a certain affinity with various aspects of the traditional architecture, including the intricate and gradual transition between spaces of different quality. Thus the Japanese concepts of space layering and *oku* have become important features of Maki's buildings, presenting as of now a rich variety and refined application.

His National Aquarium for the 1975 Marine Expo in Okinawa was designed to use on-site prefabricated reinforced concrete structural elements of simple curving forms. The basically two-dimensional concrete arches create extensive shadowy arcades on several levels around the huge enclosed aquariums to tame the hot tropical sunshine of the island. In addition, they layer the space that leads from the exterior into the interior. The spatial complexity is based on various combinations of one basic element. They are applied alone or in

172–175. Yamashita's "From 1st" Building in Tokyo (1976) is indeed a small city within a city. Arranged around an inner multilevel court or plaza, the building features a wide range of informally arranged commercial facilities—cafés, boutiques, and other shops— in addition to the small offices on the upper levels.

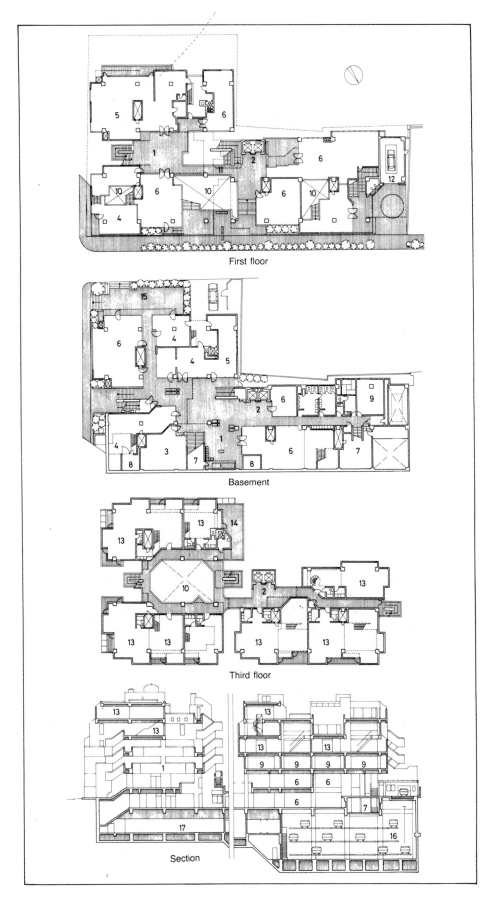

175. Floor plans and sections. 1. Double-level plaza. 2. Elevators. 3. Beauty salon. 4. Café. 5. Restaurant. 6. Shops. 7. Storage. 8. Ventilation plant. 9. Office. 10. Open to below. 11. Bridge. 12. Car elevator. 13. Office/design studio. 14. Terrace. 15. Plaza. 16. Parking. 17. Athletic club.

First floor

Basement

Third floor

Section

176. Floor plans of a double-level design studio. The small studios of the "From 1st" Building were designed with practically all the comforts and functions of an apartment.

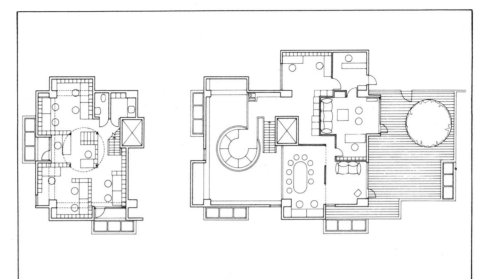

177.

177–180. The Hillside Terrace Apartments in Tokyo retain the impression of a solid street facade; yet, by means of interpenetrating semipublic spaces, the building can act as a connecting link between the busy street and the quiet old park behind it (Phase I, 1969; Phase II, 1973; Phase III, 1976; F. Maki).

179.

178.

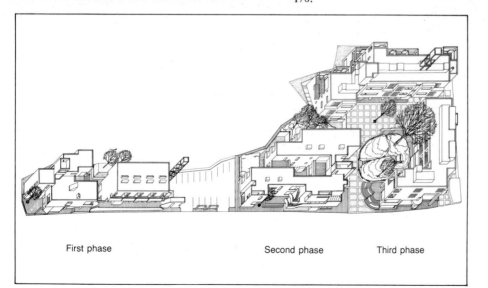

First phase

Second phase   Third phase

180. Axonometric
drawing of the whole
complex.

pairs, forming the semicircular arches, a motif then repeated horizontally and vertically. These arches thus lend elementary strength to the composition not unlike the way arches are used in Louis Kahn's Dacca project in Bangladesh (181).

Besides the skillful technique of space layering in the third phase of the Hillside Terrace Apartments, Maki introduced there a sensitive and subtle symbolism. The last addition appropriately complements the previous buildings—which had so far been among his most remarkable works—by retaining the "intimate concern for the living spaces of a single or of a few human beings," yet at the same time departs from them in many respects.[48] In contrast to the first two phases, the third is more delicate and refined in its setting, in its formal and spatial composition, and in the handling of surfaces and details. In short, Maki had taken another step away from his previously strong rational attitude.

In designing the third phase of the apartments, Maki considered the small Shinto shrine that crowns a tiny hillock as among the most important existing conditions at the site. With the new buildings placed in a U shape, Maki integrated the sacred object into the total spatial composition by assigning it the role of the center; more precisely, he meant it to stand for the concept of *oku*. This invisible core is so heavily surrounded by trees and bushes that it is really impossible to see through them. The carefully arranged spaces and surfaces of the buildings wrap around this hillock and the tiny shrine on it. Particularly interesting is the manner in which Maki opened up one of the blocks toward the inner court. He cut the corner along a 45-degree angle, providing better visual contact with the mound and the spaces behind yet retaining the corner in the form of the structural skeleton or of a false facade. This almost Mannerist treatment of the surfaces based on the delicate balance of voids and solids—best represented elsewhere by Charles Moore's somewhat similar scenographic architecture—is certainly new with Maki (182–184).

The buildings of this last phase are entirely covered by square beige tiles, recalling the color of the clay walls around Buddhist monasteries. Yet there are strong associations with Baroque designs, particularly with Bernini's S. Andrea Quirinale, in

181. The National Aquarium at the Okinawa Ocean Expo '75 with its semicircular arched walls—similar to Louis Kahn's Dacca project—layers the space beautifully from exterior to interior while gradually taming the island's tropical sunshine (1975, F. Maki).

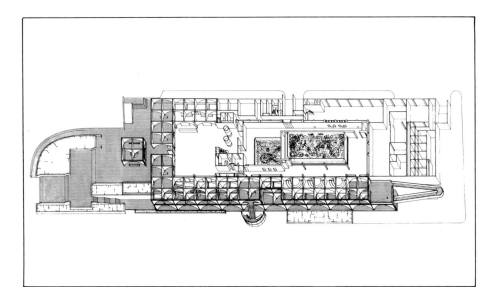

182–183. Fumihiko Maki's recent shift toward a more sensitive, pluralistic approach has resulted in increased attention to the cultural context of his architecture, here represented in Phase III of the Hillside Terrace Apartments in Tokyo (1976).

184. Axonometric drawing of Phase III of the Hillside Terrace Apartments in Tokyo (1976, F. Maki). With carefully layered spaces wrapping around a tiny old Shinto shrine, Maki reintroduces the ancient Japanese spatial concept, the *oku*.

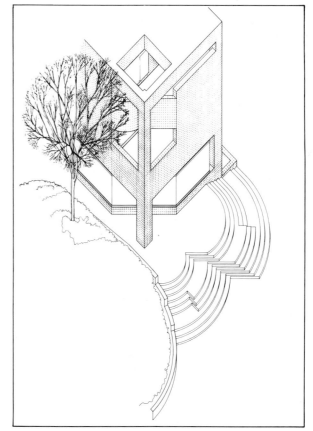

the curvilinear forms of the impressive entranceway and the undulating surfaces of the balcony on the third floor, not to mention the large circular exterior stairway. At the same time, these shapes echo the round and soft forms of the hillock in the court as well. Maki's recent shift toward a more pluralistic approach is obviously based on "a relaxed, but thorough, new look at the historical, rhetorical and visual meanings of architecture," and "a renewal of age-old interest in the beauty of details, materials, and light, color, and compositional elements."[49] These further complement his basic intention of "reflecting on the nature of the immediate environment, or"—as he explains—"what I assume is its nature, and the inner landscape of the collective consciousness of a culture, which define for me the context for architecture. This may be a distinctly Japanese approach and quite different from the European form of Contextualism, although the architectural vocabulary used in my projects is similarly modern."[50]

These are the qualities in his works that make Maki one of the most prominent contributors to the recently unfolding New Wave in Japanese architecture.

Symbolism and Mannerism

Symbolism is surely not a new feature in Japanese art and architecture. The concepts of *ma, en, oku, shibui, wabi, sabi,* and so on, in the nation's traditional philosophy of art and aesthetics and in its whole culture have made it clear that the Japanese appreciate the implicit more than the explicit and communicate in an indirect rather than direct way. Commenting on the most important of these ambiguous concepts for a recent New York exhibition, "MA: Space-Time in Japan," Isozaki wrote: "*Ma* divides the world . . . *ma* is the structural unit for living space . . . *ma* is the way of sensing the moment of movement . . . *ma* is a place where life is lived. . . . *MA* can't be defined by words. It is not logical. It's a feeling."[51]

The indirect dialog between artist/architect and connoisseur/user, based on a long series of mutually refined symbols, inevitably makes the one experiencing art and architecture also a participant in the course of their creation. Therefore, just as silence is not dumb, neither is space empty in Japan. Space gains its quality depending on the things, events, or phenomena that it helps define, among which it establishes relationships and, in turn, by which it is also evoked. Spaces and their different interpretations are of basic significance in Japan's recent architectural trends as well. Among these trends the symbolic approach is held in high esteem; its presence is perceivable in various intensities in the works of practically every architect previously discussed. Nevertheless it is so important in Arata Isozaki's evolving Mannerism that it is in this form that it certainly deserves particular attention and further explication.

ARATA ISOZAKI

Arata Isozaki (b. 1931) is unique in current Japanese architecture. With his active career of more than two decades, his consistent devotion to Symbolist design, his mature talent and brilliant technique, his works represent most of the architectural directions today, and he is thus looked upon appropriately as the father of the Japanese New Wave, which he both influenced and has also been greatly influenced by. He has rightfully achieved international fame as well.

Isozaki started as a disciple of Kenzo Tange in the late 1950s and early 1960s. As an associate in Tange's URTEC office, he collaborated on several large-scale urban projects such as Tokyo Plan-1960.

Although he was not a member of the group, he sympathized strongly with Metabolist ideas and, with some futuristic new city projects of his own, he contributed significantly to the spirit of the age.[52]

Yet even these early architectural attempts display expressly Mannerist features. His Cities in the Sky (1962) were conceived as a metaphor of ruined classical columns and were meant to reflect as well the wooden bracketing systems of traditional Japanese architecture, here blown up to enormous size (94). Since he left Tange's studio and set up his own atelier in 1963, Isozaki's commitment to a Mannerist-Symbolist architectural approach has crystalized further.

His first buildings were designed and built by exploiting the expressive qualities of heavy, even brutal, unfinished concrete structures. In this sense they appear now more "real" than his recent more elegant and refined works that, as Koji Taki put it, suggest sometimes a "world in a mirror."[53] Despite the extensive use of rough concrete, Isozaki's first significant building, the Oita Prefectural Library (1966) already showed that the direction he was to pursue had deviated sharply from the one rep-

185–186. The rough, unfinished concrete structures recall the architecture of the Metabolists, but the unusual spatial composition of Isozaki's first famous work, the Oita Prefectural Library, is new. Form and function, exterior and interior, clearly contradict each other (1966, A. Isozaki).

187–188. One of Isozaki's earliest works, the first phase of the Oita Medical Hall already presents his Mannerist design approach and, with its "flying tube," also foreshadows the concept of the City in the Sky. Isozaki says the initial image in the conception was of stratocumulus clouds (First phase, 1960; Second phase addition, 1972; A. Isozaki).

resented by Kikutake, Kurokawa, and Otani, not to mention Tange (185, 186).

Still unsettled and hesitant at several points, the bold forms and spaces of the library display most of the features of the method he called at that time "process design." The exterior of the building, with its robust solid blocks, differs from the interior that is by contrast somewhat friendlier, softer, and richer in color. The same characterizes his other two buildings from this period, the Oita Medical Hall (1960; annex 1972) and the Fukuoka Sogo Bank Oita Branch Building (1967). Preceding his 1962 City in the Sky proposals, it was the medical hall that first featured the column and beam as the basic formal elements of the project; yet it does so in a rather distorted fashion. The horizontally constructed hollowed-out oval volume in the first phase of the building is an early representation of the tube in the air or "flying tube" motif that was to characterize Isozaki's architecture in the future (187, 188). The rectangular yet still unusual exterior of the bank building covers an equally unusual interior that is arranged along a 45-degree diagonal geometry.

Though Isozaki's shift away from the Metabolist approach was evident in these buildings, it was in his designs for the Fukuoka Sogo Bank Home Offices (1971) that he broke most consistently with Metabolism. He selected and brought together a great range of multifarious elements in this building, and thus his Mannerist architecture reached a new, more mature stage. The unusual combination of forms, colors, and materials that makes up the bank's uniquely powerful image reveals the influence

of another old master, Tange's arch rival Sei'ichi Shirai (189–192). The blade-shaped high-rise block of management offices not only seems to cut apart the lower sections of computer rooms and banking offices, but also appears to differ from them in every aspect of design. The simple and solid form of the high-rise block, for example, is covered by rough red Indian sandstone, while the highly irregular and futuristic shapes of the lower sections feature curving glass and polished granite and metal surfaces. This kind of disparateness also manifests itself in the realm of unrelated smaller details: windows, entrances, huge horizontal square tubes closed with the metal structures of ventilation outlets, the enormous cylindrical supports that are again exaggerated and distorted metaphors of columns, and so on.

189–192. A collection of radically juxtaposed elements and exaggerated forms, materials, and colors, the Fukuoka Sogo Bank Home Office Building stands as an unusual landmark at the Hakata Station Square in Fukuoka (1971, Arata Isozaki).

192. Detail of the lobby.

The interior of the bank just as much as the exterior is a conglomeration of contradictory motifs, images, and spaces including high-tech, pop, ordinary, and historical. Yet the building does not appear to be disordered or chaotic. The Australian architect Jennifer Taylor described the bank as one wherein "the general is combined with the particular, and put into conflict with each other. In the building . . . each section has its own individual character which is discordant with, yet ordered by the imposed discipline of the whole."[54] This observation holds true for Isozaki's whole architectural philosophy and methodology.

Yet Isozaki's architectural approach to a large extent is focused on the construction of spaces with abstract, symbolic qualities. He wrote: "Today humanity has been atomized, made anonymous and rendered abstract," and so, "it is scarcely surprising that the architecture designed for the anonymous human beings should be abstract and standardized."[55] To achieve this, along with his newly rediscovered Mannerism, Isozaki has turned to the use of a sometimes overwhelming Cartesian geometry with the simplest Platonic solids: the cube and the cylinder and their projections, the square,

and the circle. The different operations—amplification, slicing, projection, transformation, and so on—applied to these geometrical elements then constitute almost without exception the underlying conceptual skeleton of his buildings spatial organization, forming also their tectonic deep structure. This can best be seen in the Gumma Prefectural Museum (1974). The building is composed of a set of giant cubes arranged so as to set up a three-dimensional skeleton (199).

Isozaki's buildings can be classified into two types: those based on formal manipulations of the cube and those in which the cylinder plays the primary role. Starting from the early 1970s, this polarization was already clearly evident in his works. It was introduced in the designs for small branch offices of the Fukuoka Sogo Bank, and later it appeared in such well-known large projects as the Gumma Prefectural Museum (1974), the Kitakyushu Municipal Art Museum (1974), the Kitakyushu Municipal Central Library (1975), and the Fujimi Country Club (1974). Isozaki employed the same formal approach in his few designs for private houses as well. In his most recent works, however, he attempts the combination of the two types, at times with rather convincing results. Thus the Kamioka Town Hall (1978) and the Oita Audiovisual Center (1978) incorporate large cylindrical forms both vertically and horizontally in addition to rectangular elements.

The cubes as basic operative units very often comprise a three-dimensional orthogonal network that is both a background or point of departure in the design and also the representation of what might be called the artificial infinite. The spatial structures of these buildings are generated as integral multiples of the cube so that its projections, an "endless" coverage of squares, appear on all the two-dimensional surfaces, whether solid exterior or interior walls, windows or doors, floors or ceilings, and even built-in furnishings. The result stupefies the visual perception. The often highly

193. The Ropponmatsu Branch Office (Fukuoka, 1971, A. Isozaki). Designing several small branch offices for the Fukuoka Sogo Bank gave Isozaki the opportunity to elaborate his Mannerist methodology further.

194–198. Isozaki's most unreal building, the Gumma Prefectural Art Museum in Takasaki, evokes the elusive image of a "world in a mirror" (1974, A. Isozaki).

195.

196.

197. The huge stepped sculpture in the lobby was designed with a reversed perspective by the sculptor Aiko Miyawaki.

198. The polished marble walls of the main stairway reflect the soft forms and colors, creating an effect similar to the illusory spaces of the Baroque.

199. The unifying concept in the Gumma Museum's spatial composition is a set of giant cubes that constitute the physical and theoretical deep structure of the building as well (1974, A. Isozaki).

200. First-floor plan of the Gumma Art Museum.

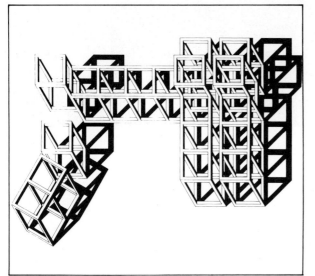

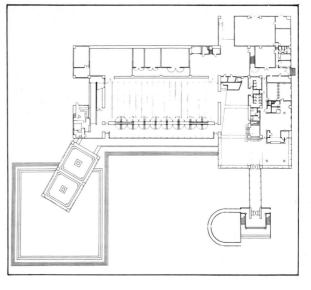

201. Influenced by the projects of Russian Constructivists, the Kitakyushu Municipal Art Museum cantilevers aggressively from one of the hilltops near Kitakyushu (1974, A. Isozaki).

202. Detail of the entrance hall of the Kitakyushu Municipal Art Museum. Highly polished and shiny surfaces render the interiors sleek and cool with an inherent feeling of void.

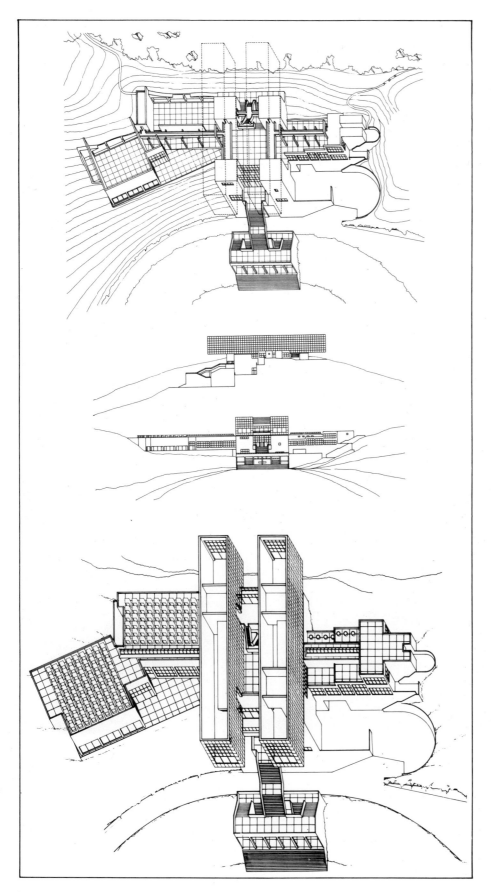

204–206. The simple structural framework of cubes in the Shukosha Building in Fukuoka establishes a region for the aggregation of fragments without interconnection; this includes the semicircular main entrance with eight mirror-doors and the stepped composition of the managerial office designed by Aiko Miyawaki (1975, A. Isozaki).

polished and shiny thin membrane of aluminum, glass, or stone—the "skin" over the deep structure—further boosts this effect. Isozaki explained that "covering the exterior of buildings with endless series of simple uniform units (a process I call amplification) minimizes differences and produces a twilight effect of non-differentiation" (193).[56]

The Gumma Prefectural Art Museum (1974) in Takasaki is probably Isozaki's most "unreal" building. It is composed, as all of his works are, of a series of paradoxes. With the sparkling, high-tech aluminum facades set against the smooth, extensive green park and reflected in the small pool, the museum, like a mirage, turns into an "elusive vision." Yet the exterior is only the beginning of a play based on illusions, since the interiors, too, offer a number of similar effects (194–200). The boldly cantilevered double-barrel structures of the Kitakyushu Municipal Art Museum (1974) and the simple multistory block of the Shukosha Building (1975) are again clear derivatives of the cube, either as a solid form or as a frame, with the all-pervasive orthogonal grid both on the exteriors and in the interiors (201–206).

In contrast, the compositions of the Fujimi Country Club and the Kitakyushu Municipal Central Library were inspired purely by the cylinder. The softly curving vaults, like giant squeezed oil paints on enormous palettes or like huge bent pipes laid on the site, generate images inescapably related to motion. "I seemed to have been fascinated by an operation in which movement arises and its traces are solidified in the air," wrote Isozaki.[57] Indeed both buildings suggest the feeling of some changing, endless forms cut abruptly by a huge saw. It is as if most of the original form, including the "power plant," has been removed, thus bringing the remaining part to an eternal standstill. In other words, with their severely truncated bodies they appear as "accidental" or *ad hoc* portions of dismantled extensive works (207–216).

In no case, however, does Isozaki want to create an absolutely pure and consistently rigid Platonic system that cannot tolerate the slightest deviation. In fact, his purpose is exactly the opposite, "the inversion of Platonism" and the "violation of its cosmic order," or as Hajime Yatsuka observed, "His strategy is not to present the impregnated essence (whether it be formal or conceptual) in its clear and perfect figure, but to 'crack' the 'overwhelming prerogative' 'enemy' (the 'tyrant') that 'powerfully exists, . . . restricts, oppresses, fixes, and becomes the immutable,' [his intention is] to 'ruin its lucidity.' "[58] As the first step toward this goal Isozaki in an insidious manner shifts one of the sections of his buildings out of the overall orthogonal system, thus deliberately breaking the previously chosen rule (200, 203). Among other works of his, the Gumma museum, the Kitakyushu museum, the Social Service Building of the Nippon Electric Glass Company (1980) exhibit this. But nowhere else is it so conspicuous as at the Kamioka Town Hall (1978). The building is designed with two geometric volumes along a broken axis. The motion of shifting the larger block out of the system of the smaller one can be pictured if the circular forms of the low one-story section are looked upon as what they can also suggest, a huge revolving stage forcibly turned at an angle of 22.5 degrees. This image is reinforced by the discovery that the circle is indeed completed on the other side of the building in the form of a curving low brick wall and the paved area between it and the building. Traces of the "impact" are manifested by the "ripped out" and "deformed" section of the entrance hall and the undulating aluminum skin departing the tectonic body of the higher block on the lower rooftop, creating a transitional zone between the aluminum- and the sonte-clad wings that were "crushed" into each other and "interpenetrated" (217–221).

There is also a definite, deliberate inconsistency in Isozaki's application of finishing materials. In many cases the high-tech aluminum panel or stone

207-210. The cylindrical roof of the Fujimi Country Club House, which blends into the natural landscape of the golf course, has been designed as a gigantic questionmark (Oita, 1974, A. Isozaki).

209. Like the surrounding scenery, the freeflowing vaulted interior is soft in both form and color.

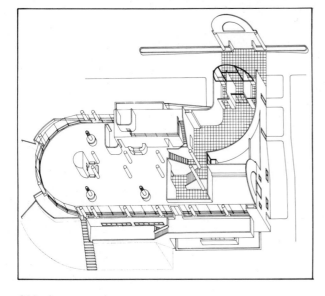

210. Axonometric drawing of the club house.

plate cover falls short of the total exterior or interior surfaces, leaving unfinished some parts of the usually reinforced-concrete tectonic body, thus creating another kind of paradox and the impression of incompleteness, as seen at the Fukuoka Sogo Bank Home Office and its Ropponmatsu Branch Building, or the Gumma Prefectural Art Museum, and so on.

This deviation from perfection or the lack of interest in completed, finished entities may seem to be an arbitrary attitude, but it is not. Deeply rooted as it is in the traditional Japanese aesthetic based on the intuitive appreciation of things incomplete or imperfect, for Isozaki such an attitude is almost natural. Commenting on this mentality, Yuji Aida wrote: "The active affirmation of transience, the way of thinking based on the idea that the essence and beauty of things are to be found precisely in their mutability . . . is the true spirit of Japan."[59]

Nevertheless, if Isozaki's works remained only on the level of such geometric operations, his architecture would most probably be a mere distorted Japanese variation of, say, the International Style, high-tech style, or, at best, Peter Eisenman's Structuralism. On one level it is all of this, but Isozaki

211–216. The two horizontally curved cylindrical wings of the Kitakyushu Municipal Central Library are built with prefabricated ferroconcrete vaults (1974, A. Isozaki).

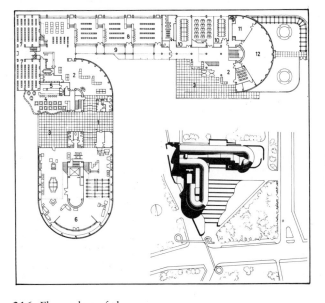

214–215. The reinforcing ribs of the concrete panels, exposed in the interior, generate specific historical references.

216. Floor plan of the entrance level.
1. Entrance. 2. Lounge.
3. Terrace. 4. Restaurant.
5. Kitchen. 6. Exhibition hall. 7. Book stacks.
8. General library.
9. Ramp. 10. Meeting room. 11. Storage.
12. Studio.

217–221. With its image of a huge, shiny UFO just landed in the small mining town, the Kamioka Town Hall strongly contrasts with its urban environment (1978, A. Isozaki).

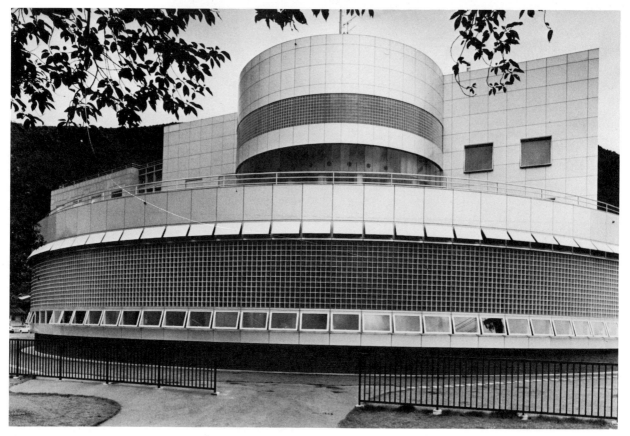

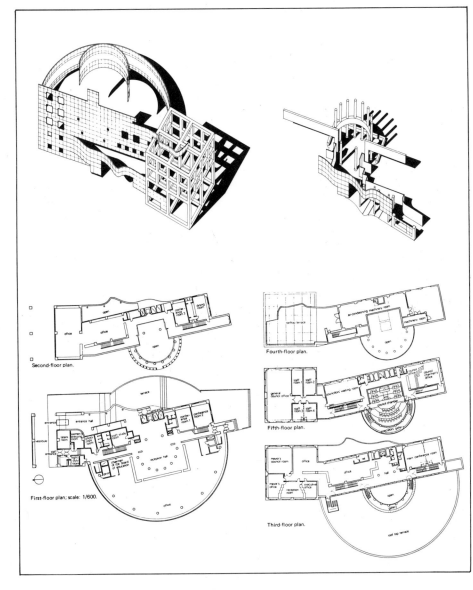

219–220. Entrance elevations with the thin, undulating layers of the false facades departing the tectonic body of the building.

Second-floor plan.

Fourth-floor plan.

First-floor plan; scale: 1/600.

Fifth-floor plan.

Third-floor plan.

221. Plans and axonometric drawing.

goes further than just conceiving a framework architecture. "Architecture is a machine for the production of meaning," he himself has said.[60] It is not difficult to discern in this statement similarities to the theories of Noam Chomsky and the American school of generative linguistics.[61] Isozaki's interpretation, however, also implies that a structural system alone—the grammar, to use the language analogy—is inadequate to create meaning and transmit messages. Architecture can perform this job as "text," that is to say through an appropriate stock of elements, signs or codes, and images, a selected and, in Isozaki's opinion, sufficiently multivalent architectural vocabulary.

But Isozaki is more than reluctant to invent new "words" in order to "communicate," as the Modernists were so apt to do. Instead, he believes that architects today already have a large and rich vocabulary at their disposal to express themselves freely. For him this expressive vocabulary developed and grew throughout history and therefore can equally span different cultures and ages, including, naturally, Modernism as well. Isozaki then selects from among this readily available stock to set up his "sentences" or, as he says, "rhetorics." This selection, however, is rather arbitrary and characterizes Isozaki's idiosyncratic architecture. Among the numerous sources he quotes from, the most important are Marcel Duchamp, Palladio, Lissitsky, and the Russian Constructivists, Piranesi, Ledoux, Boullée, *Alice's Adventures in Wonderland*, the principle of Yin and Yang, and, of course, his trademark, the ubiquitous motif of Marilyn Monroe's figure.

One aspect of his use of these sources should be noted. The quotations he employs never appear as replicas, copies, or as direct references modified or distorted by errors of memory, as can often be seen in the works of the American Neorealists, particularly in the scenographic architecture of Venturi, Stern, and Moore. In Isozaki's Mannerism the quotations are inspiratory types and appear as remote motifs filtered through an invisible opaque screen, that is, abstracted significantly; they become parts of his metaphors to the extent of losing the singularity of their original image and meaning. Therefore, any explanation of his works on the basis of these sources alone is seriously limited. Only with such limitation in mind should the semicircular multistory interior space in his Kamioka Town Hall be understood as reminiscent of Palladio's Teatro Olimpico, for example; or, that the flat and arched elevations of the Fujimi Country Club with their openings again recall a motif of Palladio's, this time the Villa Poiana, here deviating from it greatly at the same time because the corresponding openings have been placed on two different planes and a pair of columns has been left out where they would normally be seen as necessary (207, 221). In a similar way, the vaulted inner spaces of the Kitakyushu library have their admitted model in Boullée's 1780 project for the extension of the National Library in Paris, and the Shukosha Building has some affinity with Adolf Loos's Tzara House of 1927. In the Fukuoka Sogo Bank Home Offices, large horizontal tubular beams like architraves span over short but extremely wide cylindrical columns (189, 190).

Isozaki's historical quotations are complemented by a wide range of elements drawn from a wonderland or distorted reality: illusory effects, visual tricks, changes in scale, reversed perspective, and the like. In one of the rooms of the Fukuoka Sogo Bank Home Offices the walls are decorated with painted shadows of different groups of people, giving the sense of a hidden double light source and of an imaginary center to the room. This is seen again in the large dining hall of the Nippon Electric Glass Company Social Service Building, where the capitals of the columns appear as painted shadows "projected" onto the ceiling from a hidden central spot; the paintings consequently can be perceived as capitals only from that one point.

The Shukosha building features a semicircular

entrance with eight mirror-glass doors along the concave surface, only two of which are real, the rest fake (205). For the large lobby of the Gumma museum, Isozaki's wife, the sculptor Aiko Miyawaki, designed a large stepped platform composition that accommodates the elevator, among other things, and thus builds the concept of enclosure of one architectural space within another. The idea is repeated in a like manner in the Shukosha building, where the stairstepped "sculpture"—the image reminiscent of the traditional built-in uneven shelf system (*chigaidana*)—conceals the management offices. In the museum this composition's forms were generated according to the rules of reversed perspective, as if in attempt to execute one of the incredible visions of the Dutch artist Maurits Escher. These stepped forms, just like Escher's infinite stairways, do not lead anywhere. Yet this is not all. The real main stairway in the museum is also misleading. This solemn staircase, with its quality of pompous yet illusive Baroque space, ironically does not lead to the main exhibition halls at all but to the rather cramped anteroom of a small display area and of an even smaller lecture room (197, 198, 206).

In three recent projects, the Kamioka Town Hall, the Hakubi Kimono School (1980), and the N.E.G. Company Social Service Building, Isozaki has extensively employed glass block, the newly rediscovered "Japanese" building material, as complete walls or elevations. Glass-block surfaces have a translucent quality that renders ambiguous both to the exterior and interior the events taking place behind them, and filters daylight in a way similar to the paper-covered sliding screens (*fusuma, shoji*) in traditional wooden buildings (218, 222, 226, and also 45).

The numerous visual ambiguities of Isozaki's buildings create a quality in which real and unreal are blended deliberately, often resulting in surreal images. This takes a new and, disappointingly, somewhat trivial form in the Kimono School. Here,

in addition to the play with mirror-reflected spaces, the lobby presents several unexpected "events" in the form of the "half-finished" yet already "crumbling" columns and the cast-metal kimonos "spontaneously thrown" onto the handrail of the gallery. The metamorphosis of the columns may symbolize motionless or singular time, since their lifespan from beginning to end is compressed into one simultaneous moment. Beyond the physical connection, these columns could create a symbolic transition too between the dark, highly polished reflective floor and the light-gray matte walls and ceiling, while altogether the space suggests a transition from one reality to another beyond it. Yet the sense of this reality beyond is not as convincing as in Isozaki's other buildings (223).

A similar approach to interior space is obvious in one of the upper rooms. The vertical surfaces between the orthogonal structural skeleton are openings toward the exterior by virtue of their being glass-block walls or because they are simply painted to resemble infinite blue skies with scattered white clouds. In other words, the boundary or transition between inner and outer worlds gains meaning according to the mode of representing the exterior. Here, with the conceptual grid of the glass block and with the perceptual pop supergraphics, an abstract and a representational mode are brought together to generate ambiguity and illusion again.

Pop elements, colors, supergraphics, or lettered signs are by no means foreign to Isozaki's architecture in general; in most cases their application is more successful than in the Kimono school. His Tokyo Branch of the Fukuoka Sogo Bank (1971), for example, is modestly concealed behind the story-high stylized inscription of "Home Office" as its elevation. Isozaki explained that "when a facade or plan is prepared from transformations or deformations of letters, multilevel meaning comes into being" (224).[62] The N.E.G. Company Social Service Building offers another prominent example;

222. The Mannerism of Isozaki's new building for the Hakubi Kimono School in Tokyo encompasses Sant' Elia's futuristic images for the Cittá Nuova and Hans Hollein's elusive and sublime architecture, yet with a less convincing result (1980, A. Isozaki).

223. Detail of the entrance hall of the Hakubi Kimono School.

224. Elevation of the Fukuoka Sogo Bank Tokyo Branch Office, made up of a story-high sign that reads "home bank" (1971, A. Isozaki).

225–226. With its particular materials, structural elements, and color scheme, the Social Service Building of the Nihon Electric Glass Company fits appropriately into its industrial environment (Otsu City, 1980, A. Isozaki).

227–228. Because of suspension structure, the forms and overall image of the West-Japan General Exhibition Center refer to both the nearby industrial port and the sea (Kitakyushu, 1977, A. Isozaki).

here all the solid exterior walls are made of pre-fabricated colored panels covering the whole building with brown and ochre horizontal stripes. Pop in this pervasive form is a new feature in Isozaki's work, providing a quality that allows the building to respond appropriately to its context. While the applied glass refers directly to the products of the glass factory, the stripes relate properly to the industrial environment where, for safety reasons, projecting edges and surfaces are treated in a similar way. Furthermore, in front of the elevations Isozaki conspicuously exposes the steel-bar braces, the structural means of the building's stability, a feature that again can be correctly associated with industrial architecture (225, 226).

A comparable sort of symbolism, namely the conscious reliance on the significant qualities of certain selected structural solutions, can be observed partly or completely in several of his earlier projects as well. This implies that Isozaki is interested in some special structural, technological, or industrial solutions as far as they have something more to express than their role as supports or can refer to more than their method of fabrication. His main concern is how far they are able to *generate* meanings. Therefore it is clear that for him structures are tools (means to an end) rather than the goal itself, as in Modernism. Writing of Isozaki's architecture, Kazuhiro Ishii correctly noted that "we must follow a path different from both the people who overemphasize and people who underemphasize structure."[63]

Yet the symbolic images Isozaki creates this way can vary in intention from a maximum correspondence with the character of the context, through neutrality, toward a total disparity from it. With the intention of achieving maximum correspondence between image and context, he designed the West Japan Exhibition Center in Kitakyushu in 1977, followed by the N.E.G. Social Service Building in 1980. In the Exhibition Center Isozaki tried to find and build as many analogies as possible between the building and its physical environment—the surrounding industrial port—by employing a multiple system of codes. The pylons and cables of the suspension structure match the forms of the port installations and also create metaphors of bridges and ships that, by extension, refer to the presence of the sea (227, 228).

With the sensitive treatment and introduction of light into the large halls through their glass walls and skylights, Isozaki wanted not only to symbolize the sea in another more delicate way but also to suggest ambiguous, indefinite spaces inside. A shallow pool in the enclosed courtyard was to reflect sunshine onto the wide ceilings and, as the shiny, glittering surfaces appeared overhead, to generate a feeling of being under water. This was done to create a metaphor relating to the sea through the idea of water itself; yet Isozaki admitted that he had not been completely successful in achieving the effect.

The vault as a structural system in the Fujimi Country Club and the Kitakyushu Library resulted in two sharply different symbolic images in the interiors. At the club the structure is a homogeneous ferroconcrete shell with smooth surfaces and, like everything else, painted a light pastel. Since the cylindrical columns supporting the huge vaults are placed outside the continuous all-around glass walls, they do not really belong to the interior, making the whole roof—an enormous question mark in actual form—appear to float over the softly lit spaces and the softly undulating surrounding scenery (207–210). On the other hand, the vaults of the library are a system of prefabricated curved and ribbed reinforced concrete panels; since the ribs are visible inside, they enhance the sense of the sturdiness and heaviness of the structure covering the enclosed spaces below. Where the vaults are constructed along longitudinal axes, they evoke the image of Romanesque interiors; where constructed along semicircles, with the ribs branching out from the center, they evoke the image of Gothic interiors (214–216). To reinforce this second association, Isozaki designed in one of the flat end walls a large circular "rose window," here with the motif of a Buddhist mandala.

While the horizontally laid out cylindrical forms blend with the natural landscape of the Fujimi Country Club and with the green park around the Kitakyushu Library, these forms remain more or less indifferent to the built environment, as seen at the Audiovisual Center in Oita (229). Other projects by Isozaki assert an expressly aggressive appearance. The stepped structural skeleton and huge slanting glass roof over the entrance and the lobby of the Hakubi Kimono School, for example, flash a futuristic vision not quite unlike the ones conceived by Sant'Elia in his 1914 drawings for a Citta Nuova (222). Another building of this kind is the Kitakyushu Art Museum, where the boldly cantilevered double box-beam structures are reminiscent not only of its prototype, the "Cloud Props Project" (1924) by the Russian Constructivist Lissitsky, but probably also of a fortress with gun barrels at the ready, poised to attack the town and its spreading suburbs below (201).

The best example of this anti-urban attitude in Isozaki's architecture, however, remains the Kamioka Town Hall, which was designed for a small mining town located among beautiful mountains. Instead of finding ways and means to blend the new into the existing, Isozaki—as he put it—"decided to generate a sense of disharmony [a quality obviously present in all of his works] that borders on the dangerous."[64] The building evokes the image of a shiny metal spaceship from another planet come to take over the helpless settlement. With this almost inhuman character Isozaki wanted to create a strong identity, a shock to the ordinary and thus unchallenging environment (217).

This building, perhaps more than any other by Isozaki, reflects best the way in which his deliberate Mannerism works. Typically he brings together two basic and at the same time seemingly opposite concepts and strategies to achieve his intention of both demolishing and generating meaning in architecture. The first demolition or "deconstruction" is dramatized by his use of "meaningless" abstract geometry. The overall yet consistently ruptured and violated Cartesian orthogonal framework, having lost its ability to act as a common reference, is devoid of an inner substance or center. In fact, it has an assigned role of paralyzing the automated mechanisms of our visual perception together with their routine associations or readings; that is, it neutralizes our taken-for-granted preconceptions. It defamiliarizes architecture to deprive its spaces of everyday meanings and, often, of mass-produced and therefore consumable images. "The user of such 'intellectual' architecture is finding less and less that is familiar—entrances that he can't find, glass that he can't see through, columns that don't support anything, walls denuded of their familiar references," as Jonathan Gale wrote.[65]

But what happens to the seemingly numerous and oftentimes discordantly multifarious quotations and other elements in Isozaki's buildings? The answer lies in his method of juxtaposition and the collages that result from it, which are similar to the process of "*bricolage*" first proposed by Claude Lévi-Strauss, then redefined by Jacques Derrida and employed extensively by Marcel Duchamp in his art.[66] In place of the practical, utilitarian meaning intended to converge toward zero, new metaphysical meanings are suggested.[67] With Isozaki, the person experiencing or "reading" his architecture is not meant to be left in a benumbed state but is given the chance to collect himself again—and in several new ways. And this might be the second concept and strategy, the one that generates meaning rather than demolishes it, the key intention behind all these intricate operations: to generate a new feeling of existence. But how the individual meets this challenge is up to him; after completing the project, the architect has not much to do with that. Isozaki has no ambition to monopolize the rules of the game. He packs his buildings, the rational and neutral frameworks, with a series of paradoxical elements and lets everyone play or struggle with the quotations and metaphors as if they were pieces of a multiple or "infinite" puzzle, to construct whatever image one would like to perceive or is able to put together according to his own knowledge, sensitivity, intelligence, memories, previous experiences, imagination, not to mention his present involvement. This means that for different people there can be different meanings on different levels. Isozaki's buildings lack a definite discourse or easily discernible story because "it is the breaking up of the story that is intended here," as he himself has said.[68] Even if there existed within the architect's imagination an original image that controlled the design process, the final work is open to various reinterpretations. Thus it is possible that the original image, if it makes no echo or creates no response, remains only in the architect's memory. With Isozaki, it is not the building itself that is meant to change in space and time, but the image and meaning generated in human awareness by the varying qualities of interaction between person and environment.

The whole process might be better understood if we recall the childhood experience of enthusiastically watching the different, changing forms created by clouds in the sky. The more meanings the child can discover or project, the greater his joy. In a like manner, Isozaki's architecture brings back the discoveries of our own childhood, of the pleasures of continuously self-creating play. This elusive or suspended reality in his works explains why he does "not regard architectural space as existing in itself, but as coming into being the moment human beings enter that space."[69] As a result of this human involvement, the self simultaneously is transformed, and it too gains a multidimensional or fictive quality. "Self-creation" in Isozaki's architecture becomes an endless process in which the final product is perpetually postponed.

Therefore Isozaki's concept of "manner" is somewhat different from the original Italian concept of *maniera*. As Hajime Yatsuka correctly pointed out: "While *maniera* indicated a particularly personal mode of expression, as in 'maniera di Michelangelo,' Isozaki's 'manner' was understood to be a transpersonal concept, something similar to the concept of 'autoécriture' as developed by the Surrealists or to the idea of the 'procedé' as developed by the French novelist and dramatist Raymond Roussel, a precursor of the Surrealists and Dadaists. In this sense, Isozaki's 'formalism' is not intended to remain on the level of 'formgiving.' Rather, for him, form is something not to be invented but to be manipulated, thus removing the architect from his previous formgiving function as demiurge."[70]

While the intentions of Isozaki and, by extension, those of the young Japanese existentialist architects can be compared at some points to Aldo Rossi's typology, which represents Italian Neorationalist trends, they also differ from it significantly. In Rossi's work, the final image is intended to be strictly controlled; it is abstracted from the existing historical urbanscape through a rational decomposition of the city into its basic "urban facts" to the extent that the minimal forms of these facts will not carry any special meaning. These facts then are put together again to reconstruct something that might be called common denominators or prototypes of the physical and formal elements of the city, and that are supposed to elude meaningful interpretation. Rossi's works, in other words, as a self-evident analogical architecture, are derivatives in every case of the orders of European urban traditions transmitted on an explicitly surrealistic level.

In contrast to Rossi, Isozaki avoids relating his architecture to the city and remains indifferent or in many cases—as in the Kitakyushu museum and Kamioka town hall—adopts a strongly negative attitude toward it. For him a city is not an art object. In any event, to propose an urban integration reminiscent of the one put forward by the European Contextualists would be an absolutely futile endeavor in the cramped, chaotic, and volatile contemporary Japanese urban conditions. This line of understanding that is also "utterly opposed to the 'cataclysmic purity' of Corbusian urbanism" (to quote Bruce Goodwin) has been adopted and pushed to the extreme by the Japanese Hermeticists Tadao Ando, Hiromi Fujii, Monta Mozuna, Hiroshi Hara,

Takefumi Aida, Toyo Ito, Itsuko Hasegawa, and others.[71]

Just as Isozaki's Mannerism differs from European Contextualism—even if it incorporates at times some elements of Rossi's work, like the long ramp to the main entrance of the Oita Audio Visual Center (230–231)—it also differs from the American scenographic architecture. This particular American tradition, reflected in the works of many contemporary Post-modern architects such as Moore, Venturi, Stern, Graves, and so on, offers a more populist approach with some ready-made images. These images, in a take-it-easy manner, end up in romantic dreams (or stories?) wherein everything is beautiful (or "ordinary"?) and that too often offer nothing more than the shallow entertainment of Disneyland kitsch, something Moore admires so much and that works well in the cultural atmosphere of America, particularly California. Here the user's participation remains more on the level of sensation, fun, or thrill and thus is rather effortless.

To underline this difference between Isozaki and the Americans, the Kamioka Town Hall has to be mentioned again. In this building Isozaki employed the idea of independent surface, "superficiality," for the first time, in the form of an undulating false elevation. A small portion of the aluminum skin on the roof departs from the tectonic body of the building and creates a visual continuity with the larger block and a transition to the smaller one clad in stone. With its curving surface, it is similar to the sensual "Marilyn Monroe" line of the entrance hall on the first floor. This superficiality thoroughly avoids direct pop interpretation and even risks the possibility of going unnoticed. Like the simple elements in traditional gardens or residences, these thin layers act more to destructure, wrap around, or suggest another aspect of the relative nature of reality—even of emptiness behind and beyond—than to act as the real thing, reality per se.

229–231. The simple and abstract geometric forms—the cube and the cylinder—in the Audio-visual center reveal a neutral, indifferent attitude toward the building's urban context, the city of Oita (1979, A. Isozaki).

The comparison between Isozaki and American Postmodernism points out another feature of Isozaki's architecture: how far it is embedded in Japanese cultural traditions. The Japanese traditionally have greater appreciation for what is only suggested than for what is explicitly stated. This ambiguity, the quality of in-between, the philosophical and aesthetical concept of *ma,* is still an active constituent in most aspects of Japanese life. It is this very quality of emptiness or void that provides the elusive background of Isozaki's quotations, the multifarious elements becoming the connecting media not only among the various human and formal events, motifs, quotations, and metaphors, but also within the underlying framework and the events or happenings within. This is what renders Isozaki's spaces ambiguous or multivalent, with images that are powerful and also metaphysical. He himself pointed out that even if the exteriors of his buildings may resemble some Western solutions, their interiors are unmistakably Japanese.[72] His works fail to provide the observer with meanings of absolute certainty; in Isozaki's words; they are to evoke the feelings or metaphors of "Degree Zero," "Twilight," "Shadow," and "Darkness," among others (198, 202). It is in this sense that, as Yatsuka has pointed out, "in Isozaki's works there is a crucial 'epistemological rupture' from modern architecture," which was ultimately based on the Platonic and Hegelian philosophy of a dualistic world.[73] Isozaki's architecture may be better understood with the help of the fourteenth-century court poet Yoshida Kenko. In his famous *Essays in Idleness,* Yoshida expressed an important feature of the Japanese mentality: "The most precious thing in life is its uncertainty."[74]

With the unique, expressly antiromantic, nonnostalgic, and traditionally nonclassical manner in which his buildings are put together, Isozaki "has consistently challenged both cozy complacency and chaotic urbanism with imagery that is intentionally aggressive and evocative of the sublime," as Bruce

Goodwin wrote incisively.[75] And—I may add—he has done this in a fresh and creative way, approaching what may be called the "phenomenology of architecture."

NOTES

1. Robert Venturi, *Complexity and Contradiction in Architecture* (New York: Museum of Modern Art, 1966). Aldo Rossi, *The Architecture of the City*, trans. Diane Ghirardo and Joan Ockman (Cambridge, MA: MIT Press, 1982).
2. Charles Jencks, "Isozaki's Paradoxical Cube," *The Japan Architect* (March 1976), p. 47.
3. Japan ranks behind only the United States and the Soviet Union in industrial output.
4. The semiotic interpretation of built form often reduces architecture into a visual language only, trying to find a direct relationship between architectural and linguistic means of communication. For further reference see Charles Jencks, *The Language of Post-Modern Architecture* (London: Academy Editions, 1977); and Geoffrey Broadbent, Richard Bunt, and Charles Jencks, eds., *Signs, Symbols and Architecture* (New York: Wiley, 1980). The more recent phenomenological and post-Structuralist understanding of architecture and environment is critical of the semiotic approach.
5. Shinjuku is a Tokyo subcenter where most high-rise buildings are built. Among the first: Keio Plaza Hotel, 1971 (Nihon sei Co., Ltd.); KDD Building, 1972 (Nippon Sogo Architects); Sumitomo Building, 1974 (Nikken Sekkei Co.); and Mitsui Building, 1975 (Mitsui Real Estate Development Co.).
6. Kenzo Tange, "Towards Urban Design," *The Japan Architect* (September 1971), p. 19.
7. Howard Gardner's *The Quest for Mind* (Chicago and London: The University of Chicago Press, 1973) not only describes Structuralism as becoming one of the most important and influential methods of inquiry in this century directly as the result of the pioneer works of Piaget (1896–1980) and Levi-Strauss (b. 1908), he also argues that Noam Chomsky's school of linguistics is bonafide Structuralism, since "he shared the strategic, formalistic, and biological bent of the first generation of structuralist workers" (p. 258); Chomsky then in the 1970s extended this into "the general areas of social science and humanistic scholarship. . . ."
8. Ibid., p. 10.
9. Ibid., p. 13.
10. Other architects whose works contained Structuralist implications are Moshe Safdie, Alvar Aalto, Le Corbusier, Louis Kahn, Herman Hertzberger, and the Metabolist group in Japan. For further details see Arnulf Lüchinger, *Structuralism in Architecture and Urban Planning* (Stuttgart: Karl Krämer Verlag, 1981).
11. Kenzo Tange, "My Experiences," *Space Design* (January 1980), p. 186.
12. Herman Hertzberger, "Polyvalente Form und Personliche Interpretation," *Forum* (July 1967, March 1973); also in Arnulf Lüchinger, "Dutch Structuralism," *Architecture and Urbanism* (March 1977), pp. 58, 59.
13. Tange was invited to participate in the 1959 Otterlo meeting of Team 10, where Aldo van Eyck, the spokesman of the Dutch group Forum, had an important organizing role.
14. Peter Smithson, "Reflections on Kenzo Tange's Tokyo Bay Plan," *Architectural Design* 34 (October 1964), p. 480.
15. The huge concrete tower, in fact a sculpture by Taro Okamoto, symbolizing the rising sun, was saved. From its place on the Festival Plaza, it used to pierce through the gigantic Space Frame above. The tower also retains its original observation deck.
16. Tange's plan was admittedly influenced by the "City in the Sky," which Isozaki prepared in 1962 while working in Tange's URTEC office.
17. Among them the most conspicuous is Kevin Roche and John Dinkeloo's Knights of Columbus Office Building in New Haven, Connecticut (1969).
18. Kisho Kurokawa quotes from *Metabolism 1960—A Proposal for a New Urbanism* in his *Metabolism in Architecture* (Boulder, CO: Westview Press, 1977), p. 27.
19. Ibid., p. 28.
20. Ibid., p. 34.
21. Historically there were neither closed city-states nor warfare among cities. Individuals therefore were not bound to a particular landlord or place, as often was the case with European feudalism. In Japan the people were free to travel and seek opportunities as they were able. The most famous traditional festival is *o-bon*, when practically every Japanese returns to his or her hometown to celebrate a reunion with other family members and, according to their beliefs, with the spirits of their ancestors. *O-bon* is celebrated annually, July 13–16.
22. Matsuo Basho, *A Haiku Journey: Basho's Narrow Road to a Far Province* (Tokyo: Kodansha International, 1980), p. 29; also see Chapter 2, n. 26.
23. Günther Nitschke, "Akira Shibuya: City Center Project," *Architectural Design* (April 1967), p. 216.
24. Kenneth Frampton, op. cit., Chapter 3, 33, p. 282.
25. Kiyonori Kikutake, "Long Road to Better Urban

Dwellings," *The Japan Architect* (June 1975), p. 23.

26. Robin Boyd, op. cit., Introduction, 6, p. 40.

27. Kiyonori Kitutake, op. cit., 25.

28. Michael Franklin Ross, op. cit., Chapter 1, 5, p. 76. Charles Jencks, *The Language of Post-Modern Architecture* (London: Academy Editions, 1977), p. 40.

29. Kobori Enshu (1579–1647) was one of the most famous Zen Buddhist abbot artists. He designed and supervised the construction of several buildings, tea houses, and gardens, including his own often-imitated residence and Zen temple, the Kohoan in the Daitoku-ji monastery, Kyoto.

30. Kisho Kurokawa, "Information Tree," *The Japan Architect* (November 1976), p. 56.

31. David Wild, "Sour Grapes," *Architectural Design* (January 1977), p. 38.

32. Heather Willson Cass, "Architecture as Human Experience," *Architectural Record* (August 1976), p. 80.

33. Robert Venturi, *Complexity and Contradiction in Architecture* (New York: The Museum of Modern Art, 1966). Romaldo Giurgola, "Reflections on Buildings and the City: The Realism of the Partial Vision," *Perspecta: The Yale Architectural Journal* (September–October 1965), p. 108. Fumihiko Maki, *Investigations in Collective Form* (St. Louis: University of Washington, 1964).

34. Fumihiko Maki, "The Theory of Group Form," *The Japan Architect* (February 1970), p. 39.

35. Aldo van Eyck in Alison Smithson, ed., *Team 10 Primer* (Cambridge, Massachusetts: MIT Press, 1974), p. 41.

36. Peter Smithson, quoted in Charles Jencks, op. cit., Chapter 3, 22, p. 302.

37. Nicholas J. Habraken, *Supports: An Alternative to Mass Housing* (London: The Architectural Press, 1961, 1972), p. 12.

38. F. Maki, op. cit., 34, p. 41.

39. Fumihiko Maki is quoted in Ross, op. cit., Chapter 1, 5, p. 32.

40. As opposed to Venturi's "difficult whole," Maki speaks of the complexity of the environment as the "easy whole." (Quoted in Teijiro Muramatsu, "Dialogue Series—Fumihiko Maki," *The Japan Architect* [September 1973], pp. 93–94.)

41. Aldo van Eyck, quoted in Fumihiko Maki, "An Environmental Approach to Architecture," *The Japan Architect* (March 1973), p. 21; also in Aldo van Eyck's contribution to the 1959 Otterlo meeting of Team 10, which reappeared in Alison Smithson, ed., *Team 10 Primer* (Cambridge, Massachusetts: MIT Press, 1974), p. 27. It should be noted, however, that this interpretation of the house-city relationship originates with the Renaissance architect Andrea Palladio who wrote:

"the city is as it were but a great house, and, the contrary, a country house is a little city." (Andrea Palladio, *The Four Books of Architecture* [New York: Dover Publications, Inc., 1965], Second Book, p. 44.)

42. The "glassy mountain," as Maki calls the building, refers both to the image created in relation to the surrounding Tsukuba Mountain, and to the intention of Maki's structural solution. See Ross, op. cit., Chapter 1, 5, p. 120.

43. Fumihiko Maki, in *A New Wave of Japanese Architecture*, Catalogue No. 10 (New York: IAUS, 1978), p. 75.

44. Ibid.

45. Kazumasa Yamashita, "Mixed Method," *The Japan Architect* (October 1976), p. 27.

46. Fumihiko Maki, "At the Beginning of the Last Quarter of the Century," *The Japan Architect* (April 1975), p. 20.

47. Fumihiko Maki, "On the Possibilities of Twilight," *The Japan Architect* (January 1978), p. 4.

48. Ibid., p. 5.

49. Ibid.

50. Maki, op. cit., 43.

51. Isozaki, op. cit., Chapter 2, 54, pp. 12, 14, 15.

52. Though neither Isozaki nor Tange was officially a member of the original 1960 Metabolist Group, they both took part in an exhibition held by the group in Tokyo in 1964. From then on they were regarded as "part-time" Metabolists until the movement slowly came to its end in the early 1970s.

53. Koji Taki, "World in a Mirror," *The Japan Architect* (March 1976), p. 73.

54. Jennifer Taylor, "The Unreal Architecture of Arata Isozaki," *Progressive Architecture* (September 1976), p. 76.

55. Arata Isozaki, quoted in Taylor, op. cit., 54, p. 72.

56. Arata Isozaki, "Nine Metaphors," *The Japan Architect* (October–November 1977), p. 21.

57. Arata Isozaki, "Rhetoric of the Cylinder," *The Japan Architect* (April 1976), p. 61.

58. Hajime Yatsuka, "Textual Strategy and Postmodernism," *Arata Isozaki 1976–1984—Space Design 232* (January 1984), p. 184.

59. Yuji Aida, quoted in Robert Shaplen, "Letter from Tokyo," *The New Yorker* (April 6, 1981), p. 130.

60. Arata Isozaki, "From Manner, to Rhetoric, to . . . ," *The Japan Architect* (April 1976), p. 65.

61. Noam Chomsky, a linguist at Massachusetts Institute of Technology, examined the relationship between language and mind and argued that the human mind has an inborn "built-in" capacity for a unique logic that generates creative formal models (structures)

through which "ordinary language use is permeated by creativeness . . . [and this] may portend the imminence of a meaningful synthesis of the major structural approaches to cognition" (Gardner, op. cit., 38).

62. Isozaki, op. cit., 56, p. 20.
63. Kazuhiro Ishii, "Structural Systems Inspiring Recollections," *The Japan Architect* (March 1978), p. 5.
64. Arata Isozaki, "Kamioka Town Hall," *The Japan Architect* (January 1979), p. 9.
65. Jonathan Gale, "Tadao Ando's Architecture" (unpublished, 1980).
66. Claude Lévi-Strauss, *The Savage Mind* (London: Weidenfeld and Nicolson, 1962, 1966), Introduction p. 16. Jacques Derrida has redefined Lévi-Strauss's notion of *bricolage,* saying it "is not a particular theme but something that eludes particularization. . . . What attracts us most in *bricolage* is that it 'is a clear abnegation of any reference to a certain center, a certain theme, a certain privilege; an absolute beginning' " (Derrida is quoted by Hajime Yatsuka, op. cit., 58, p. 182).
67. In the text, *metaphysical* is used to refer to either Western or Oriental metaphysics, depending on the context. José Ortega y Gasset defines metaphysics as a "radical coming to terms with the fundamental problems of life." If this definition is accepted, then we can also say that metaphysical development—this coming to terms—was based on different intentions and proceeded along different modes in the West and East. (Ortega is cited in Alberto Perez-Gomez, *Architecture and the Crisis of Modern Science* [Cambridge, MA: MIT Press, 1983], p. 329.)
68. Arata Isozaki is quoted in Yatsuka, op. cit., 58. p. 186.
69. Teijiro Muramatsu in a dialog with Arata Isozaki, "Humanity and Architecture," *The Japan Architect* (October 1973), p. 91.
70. Yatsuka, op. cit., Introduction, 8, p. 8.
71. Bruce Goodwin, "Architecture of the Id," *Architecture and Urbanism* (June 1980), p. 122.
72. Isozaki, in a lecture at Los Angeles's Biltmore Hotel, on May 12, 1981. Also, Isozaki, in Aron Betsky, "Interview: Arata Isozaki," *CRIT* (Winter 1983), p. 19.
73. Yatsuka, op. cit., 58.
74. Yoshida Kenko (1283–1350), quoted by H. Paul Varley, *Japanese Culture* (Tokyo: Tuttle, 1973), p. 77. From the Essays in Idleness (Tsurezuregusa).
75. Goodwin, op. cit., 69.

5. Japanese Architecture Today
Pluralism

Despite its several individual features, the course of modern Japanese architecture in the decades following the Second World War showed well-defined similarities with the developments of contemporary international architecture. Along with this parallel movement, new directions emerged while previous ones lost importance or simply faded away, so that Japanese architecture in any given period of time can always appropriately be characterized by a single distinguishing trend. The 1950s, for example, can be described as dominated by the strong influence of high Modernism and its rational Functionalism. The 1960s were similarly ruled by Metabolism and Structuralism as represented by Tange and his followers. Their strong preoccupation with the idea of physical change based on industrialization and an almost space-age technology in architecture coincided again with contemporary Western trends.

Then, beginning in the mid-1970s, increasingly critical attention was paid to the prevailing and somewhat simplistic Structuralist interpretation of meaning in architecture. Contextual and symbolic trends acquired new dimensions and eventually led to a whole new understanding of the significance of the built environment. This resulted in a more sensitive, pluralistic approach to architectural and urban design. Previous investigation into the physical relationships among architectural elements and the environment was gradually complemented by consideration of various aspects of cultural setting or milieu, so that patterns of Japanese Oriental thought and perception began to reappear in many of the new designs. With increasing emphasis on the cultural context, the spectrum of contemporary Japanese architecture has been extended on an almost unlimited scale.

The socioeconomic, ideological, and political developments of the mid-1970s played influential roles in the very important qualitative changes in architecture. These changes came about as Japanese architects attempted to affirm or deny the cultural developments taking place around them. By extension, these developments have created the social conditions and set the cultural trends for the 1980s as well. The worldwide energy crisis and the subsequent sharp decline in industrial and economic development, added to a continuing economic recession, have had a strong impact on many aspects of social life and individual consciousness. The economic crisis has been coupled gradually with another, a crisis in the intellectual and cultural life of the West. Today, Modernism, originally an aspect of counterculture, has become the official culture, and now, in Jürgen Habermas's words, it is "dominant but dead," signalling the ideological bankruptcy of late capitalist societies.[1]

The recent Postmodern trends in art and architecture emerged out of growing discontent with the exclusivist and cataclismic purity and often explicitly single-minded intentions and values of the Modern Movement, which became and has remained insensitive toward most complex human aspirations. With economic stagnation continuing, the slowly rising disillusionment with faith in the infinite potential of industrial and technological progress gained additional momentum. Yet more often than not, this antitechnological, antifunctional sentiment has prompted in the guise of a stylistic avant-gardism an indiscriminate embracing of the marketplace and the imperatives of consumerism.

The search for possible exits from the alienating abstraction and reductionist strategy of Modernism has generally resulted in an even more alienating superficial variety and in the ideologically manipulated yet finally empty rhetoric of largely commercially oriented Postmodern architecture. This reactionary neoconservative movement repudiates not only the faults and mistakes, but also the achievements and originally critical attitude of avant-garde Modernism. Instead it propagates pastiche, pop or pseudohistorical forms, often only as dress over optimized and utilitarian structures that have been engineered strictly according to the dictates of efficient production and operation. As Hal Foster argues, using Habermas's and Frampton's words, "the neoconservatives sever the cultural from the social, then blame the practices of the one (modernism) for the ills of the other (modernization). With cause and effect thus confounded,

'adversary' culture is denounced even as the economic and political status quo is affirmed—indeed, a new 'affirmative' culture is proposed. Accordingly, culture remains a force but largely of social control, a gratuitous image drawn over the face of instrumentality."[2]

This control is exercised in the guise of meeting the various interests and "privatized" needs of individuals in mass societies. Of course, those needs have been artificially created and depoliticized so that contemporary social control could defuse resistance while covering up its profound disinterest in, and even fear of, the whole, the public domain of society which, as a distinguishing larger culture, is rooted in communication and symbolic interaction free of ideological domination, although always politically motivated. The control process inevitably promotes an unprecedented and meaningless fragmentation of peoples in a world already irreconcilably divided into specialized autonomous fields or spheres.

Nevertheless, amid all these events there has emerged another kind of Postmodernism, which is also derived from the critique of the Modernist project of architecture and culture but is equally critical of the "false normativity" of reactionary Postmodernism. The alternative kind of Postmodernism has produced an "architecture of resistance" that will be termed here *Pluralism*.[3] Because of its critical stance toward the Modern Movement, it too reflects upon man in postindustrial societies, who neither believes in the omnipotence of the Machine and technology, nor worships them as the sole sources of his salvation. Pluralism approves man's claim to identity and thus also accepts the differences among individuals and between individual and social existence, as well as the private and public domains. It acknowledges the multiplicity of human experience and in so doing—as opposed both to the culturally destructive universalization and uniformity of the International Style and also to the senseless fragmentation and superficial variety (the illusion of individuality) of the reactionary Postmodernism—favors meaningful and liberating diversification; diversification without mutual exclusion and heterogeneity without deterministic hierarchy. In its best examples it achieves this by aiming at the cultivation and reproduction of sensitively differentiated yet commonly shared value systems within a given culture. In architecture, these value systems are rooted in and represented by the quality and spirit of actual human *places*.

This means that Pluralism can and should resist the temptations of the value-free commodity culture now proliferating, the commercialization and reduction of architecture to the level of a packaging industry. From this point of view, the heated debate between academic Modernists and reactionary Postmodernists is largely irrelevant. Their ideologies appear as antagonistic only on the surface. In fact, they merely represent the two sides of the same false coin. Pluralist intentions have to be critical toward both of them. At the same time, Pluralists must distance themselves from the dictates and competitive but equally reductionist interest of both technological Productivism and superficial Formalism. In short, as Foster wrote, an architecture of resistance "seeks to question rather than exploit cultural codes, to explore rather than conceal social and political affiliations."[4]

With regard to place, Pluralism can be understood as a synthesis of responses sensitive to a wide range of complex issues inherent in architecture and the relation of man to his physical, social, and cultural environment; thus Pluralism also implies that architects have to interpret critically the nature of available circumstances, including various human perceptual faculties that have been largely disregarded thus far. Beyond their visual, formal aspects, these human faculties necessarily involve physical and tactile as well as intuitive responses of people to their environment. There is, therefore, a tendency for actual solutions to become multivalent even within the scope of one architect. These solutions are open to user interpretation and appropriation. Pluralism should mean that architectural and environmental design in general, while attempting to reflect and reveal many often conflicting social and human needs, cannot remain a neutral, mechanical, mass-produced activity reduced to simple, primarily rational, formulas, let alone to the single combined formula of utility and profitability. It should be at least as complex and multifaceted as the richness and essential ambiguity of human reality, a reality accessible through a critical awareness and the realm of "poetics," in Heidegger's sense of the word.[5] Through a poetry of construction, or the creation of places, architectural practice should aim at reestablishing rootedness, the affinity of man with his environment, inasmuch as this is essential for Pluralism to address critically the issues of the quality of human existence and to disclose the eternal "human condition." It seems now increasingly evident that this can be achieved by deriving architecture from a new mode of knowledge, a new way to knowledge—that is to say, by approaching architecture on the basis of an epistemology different from the dualism of traditional Western thought and its form of representation in bourgeois societies.

Pluralism, with varying renditions and qualities, is gaining ground on the recent architectural scene. For this reason, and also because the Japanese continue to incorporate and implement elements from sources other than their own, the plurality of Japanese architecture in this decade can be compared to the diversification of its Western counterpart, if only superficially. More than before, pluralistic trends are postulated within the reevaluated and reintroduced parameters of distinguishing cultural and social patterns deeply rooted in dissimilar traditions. In the spirit of their conception, recent Western and Japanese architectures are radically different. While modern Japanese architecture previously displayed more parallels than disparities with Western trends, in its latest shift it is largely unparalleled and unchallenged by them. This increasing distinctiveness can be attributed above all to a critical inquiry into traditions and gradual redefinition of the Japanese spirit of place, coupled with an Oriental sensitivity toward the spirit and the designers' ability to evoke and transmit the spirit to others.

At the same time, a growing number of Japanese architects, especially among the younger generation, have developed an understanding in which the mediator between architecture and society is the personal *I,* inasmuch as this personal I is rooted in the realm of intersubjectivity. This necessarily makes their individual interpretations more subjective. The number and quality of personal directions are too large and varied to define a single new feature that would serve to introduce, classify, and evaluate these architects. The only characteristic they do share is their distancing themselves from the rigid standards of orthodox Modernism and their reliance instead on traditional value systems, which they develop further. Therefore, what remains for the critic is to map the individual coordinates, tracing the degree and direction of the components in their architecture by which they deviate from Modernism and Metabolism, as well as reactionary Postmodernism.

It is clear to most architects that the age of big dreams, the heroic period of architecture backed by the miraculous economic boom of the 1960s, is over. Not only have the super- or megastructures, the special "acrobatic" structural solutions, disappeared from Japanese architecture, but architects are no longer even tempted to draw up grandiose futuristic urban schemes. "The age in which architects could project a vision and then expect to fit the entire world into it has passed."[6] The failure of these visions—along with the novelty of the great expectations attached to them—has left a strong skepticism toward global solutions in general. Probably the last one of these one-man-created large urban projects, the Aquapolis of the 1975

Okinawa Ocean Expo, best exemplifies this failure. It stands as an anachronistic monument to the age and the idea (113).

Within and Beyond Modernism

With industrially oriented Metabolism declining and the pluralistic consciousness on the rise, the new Japanese architecture has become unprecedentedly diversified. The total range of today's architecture is wider than the large variety of the "New Wave's" latest intentions since it necessarily includes to varying degrees the directions of the older still active generations as well. A review of their recent endeavors from the viewpoint of Pluralism is important, since it provides further information on the background of the New Wave itself.

Most of the older architects started working within the rather rigid norms of the Modern Movement and many have been following them ever since. Others, among them Maekawa and Tange, made significant attempts to depart from rigidity with varying success; but despite promising and sometimes excellent initial steps, these men eventually returned to the older norms. Especially when compared to the very recent works of these architects, the achievements of the young generation appear truly revolutionary. But the connecting line between consecutive generations of architects is not a broken one at all and the new course of Japanese architecture can still be regarded as an evolutionary one.

The link between the opposing directions is multifaceted in character. The most spectacular role was played by those architects who at first started as propagators of Modernism and Metabolism in the early 1960s but gradually and successfully deviated from them by consistently exploring the contextual or symbolic possibilities in architecture. They eventually became forerunners and, like Isozaki, inspirative leaders of today's avant-garde generation. The trend-setting activities of these post-Metabolists are complemented by those architects who from the very beginning have carefully bypassed hard-core Modernism and the subsequent Metabolism and who, with their "idiosyncratic" developments, were always outside the main course of Japanese architecture. Such architects include Sei'ichi Shirai, Shizutaro Urabe, Kazuo Shinohara, and others. Consistent with the spirit of today's changing times, many of these so far largely disregarded individuals have been "rediscovered," their works reevaluated and appreciated even on the international scene. On the other hand, several previously prominent and influential architects have lost their significance and position.

Kenzo Tange is the most conspicuous example of this latter shift. Indeed, what happened to Tange? "He is the most overrated architect of the twentieth century," said one of the foreign critics visiting Japan recently.[7] This may be a hasty remark and it certainly ignores Tange's outstanding achievements and important role in Japan's modern architecture, but it is nevertheless true that Tange's latest buildings and projects suggest he has taken a step backward, with results below the level of his earlier vigorous architecture based on "information spaces." Though he blames the superficiality of Postmodernism—which he nevertheless seems to accept "from time to time"—he also rejects all recent intentions that question Modernism's claim to universality. He says: "Unless [young architects] are able to do orthodox work while from time to time indulging in jokes without being labeled by them, as Philip Johnson does, they will end up in hopeless impasses. . . . If affirmation of reality is Modernism it is consonant with the demands imposed by the information society. And perhaps

seeking ways to express it in architecture is a kind of Modernism."[8]

The skepticism toward large-scale urban projects based on megastructures has resulted in a greatly reduced number of such projects in Japan. Hence most of Tange's design activity is extended on the international scene, especially that of the oil-rich still-developing Arabic countries. In city and city-center projects like the Qatar Government Center (1977-), the Moroccan Capitol and International Congress Hall (1978-), and Yarmouk University in Jordan (1976-), he returned to his rather inflexible and by now exhausted Structuralist solutions. These jaded forms are admittedly conceived in the spirit of the Athens Charter, making no distinction between Japan and other nations.[9] He tried to explain why he "built in any other country the same kind of things [he] would have built in Japan" with a rather questionable argument: "Although the tradition of a nation derives primarily from climate and natural conditions, *space itself is fundamentally international* [italics added]."[10]

His smaller individual building designs also reflect a partial return to the order and aesthetics of the late Modern Movement. In contrast to the Arts Complex for the Minneapolis Society of Fine Arts (1974) in the United States, which is clad entirely in brick tiles, the New Sogetsu Art Center (1977), the Hanae Mori Building (1978), and the Akasaka Prince Hotel (1982), all in Tokyo, are dressed in mirror-glass in a fashion that brings to mind Philip Johnson's uninspiring sleek glass boxes (232–236). The pleasing elements in these buildings are the stairstepped plaza in the first-floor lobby of the Sogetsu Center—in fact an exhibition space and a large sculpture in itself (designed by Isamu Noguchi)—and the pedestrian walkway under the "crystal boxes" of the Hanae Mori Building.

Tange is a serious and as such a respectable architect. But his recent works more than ever exemplify the inadequacy of the Modernists' well-meaning positivist attitude, which falls short in

232–236. Kenzo Tange's
recent buildings display
an increased experi-
mentation with new
materials and forms, but
the results are less
successful than in his
previous powerful
architecture.

232. The brick-covered
buildings of the
Minneapolis Society of
Fine Arts (Minneapolis,
Minnesota, 1974, K.
Tange).

233–234. The mirror-
glass prisms of the new
Sogetsu Art Center in
Tokyo include an
attractive, stepped plaza
designed by the sculptor
Isamu Noguchi (1977, K.
Tange).

234.

235. The headquarters of a famous fashion designer, the Hanae Mori Building is again a combination of reflective glass boxes (Tokyo, 1978, K. Tange).

236. Akasaka Prince Hotel (Tokyo, 1982, K. Tange).

practice and achievement. In a dialog with Tange, Kazuo Shinohara had this to say about Tange's "new" architecture: "You may insist that the difference between your work of that earlier period and the project you are now doing in cities throughout the world is the outcome of a shift from the industrial to the information society, but I think it is a reflection of the differences that have occurred in the development of your own personal design philosophy."[11]

A shift in Maekawa's architecture is also conspicuous, but this shift is more sensitive than Tange's. The strong and characteristically *beton-brut* architecture of the old master has softened noticeably during the last few years. Instead of the usual unfinished concrete surfaces, his buildings now are covered by brick and are less structurally determined. The work marking the start of the new period is a high-rise office tower in Tokyo. The brick tile skin of the Kaijo Building (1974) certainly brings new color into the mushrooming skyscrapers of the city and also reflects well the similar brick architecture of the old Tokyo Station nearby (237, 238). Nevertheless, the underlying design concept, the spatial and functional arrangement of the building itself, remains conventionally Modern and thus the building represents only a partial deviation from his previous standards. His brick buildings continue to appear as a large number of museums in different parts of the country. The Tokyo Municipal Museum of Art (1975), the Kumamoto Prefectural Art Museum (1977), and other more recent museums resemble one another formally and functionally; they also share a common feature of unobtrusiveness, whereby they better respond to their natural environments (239). In his latest work, the Kumamoto Prefectural Concert Hall and Theater (1982), Maekawa tried to combine the advantages of this brick-tile architecture and his earlier reinforced concrete architecture, with mixed results.

As a matter of fact, more often than before, brick finish has become an alternative to the unfinished surfaces of structural concrete in Metabolist architecture. Yamashita's "From 1st" Building and Okada's Nippon Dental College Niigata Campus Buildings are good examples. Though in itself the brick cover never really defines the underlying architectural qualities, it can surely enhance them. This is exactly one of the points Yamashita puts forward in his further experiments with brick. Among the more successful examples is the Hirano Dental Clinic (1973) in Hiratsuka City, where he introduced some pop elements in the form of horizontal stripes made up of bricks of two different colors, juxtaposed with the stairstepped and curved glass surfaces cascading down on three levels (240).

While Yamashita's architectural experiments and the resulting direction of his design assured him acknowledgement as a representative of the avant-garde, Shin'ichi Okada's new buildings show that he has come to terms with both the architectural and political establishment and feels at home there. His large-scale volumetric architecture flashes something bizarre, even brutal, in the designs of the Supreme Court Building (1974; 241–243). In front of the Imperial Palace at one of Tokyo's busiest intersections, the gigantic "stone" blocks covered by rough, gray granite slabs bring to mind the forms of both ancient Egyptian and new-brutalist modern architectures. Okada apparently was strongly influenced by the architectural vocabulary of his masters Paul Rudolph and Louis Kahn while he studied at Yale and worked for Skidmore, Owings and Merrill. The brick architecture of his Niigata Dental College and the spatial solution of the Supreme Court Building also have their origins in Kahn. The large "served" spaces are enclosed by a system of double walls, containing the "serving" spaces, called space walls by Okada (244).

On the other hand his Metropolitan Police Department (1980), only a short distance away, is a much more ordinary modern, largely monotonous, high-rise building that is nevertheless sim-

237–238. The Kaijo Building in Tokyo is the first representative of Maekawa's recent "brick" architecture (1974, K. Maekawa).

239. Kumamoto Prefectural Art Museum (1977, K. Maekawa).

240. In the Hirano Dental Clinic in Hiratsuka, Yamashita juxtaposed brick with metal and glass, and rectangular with curving forms, in a highly successful manner (1973, K. Yamashita).

ilarly enormous in size and heavy in character. What these designs symbolize is rather simple and explicit. The first becomes an expressive monument of the judicial power of the supreme court, while the other denotes the power of the impersonal and monstrous bureaucracy of the police. The Supreme Court Building, despite its overly monumental and rather pretentious design, is an impressive work. Particularly noteworthy is the way Okada manipulated light and shadow effects within the public spaces of the building, not unlike his mentor Kahn. Some of his recent works, like the Okayama Municipal Museum of Oriental Antiquities (1979) and the Middle Eastern Culture Center (1979), carry further the skillful use of light and form to create interiors of special quality. But one is tempted to think that the old brick structure the new Police Department Building has replaced was more attractive. With their enormous size and oppressive image, both of these buildings are closer to modern Metabolist traditions than to the less ostentatious milieu-creating styles of today, let alone to the easy-flowing serenity and human scale of the traditional architecture.

Yet the best examples of Metabolist architecture itself, like the Hotel Tokoen, the Kyoto International Conference Hall, or the Tokyo Olympic Stadiums, showed that even a primarily structure-oriented architecture could retain some distinguished features from the artistic sensitivity of the past. Several of Kiyoshi Seike's latest works continue this successful blending, but as always on a more intimate, human scale. Seike, a longtime residential designer, has presented the Japanese style from the very beginning, and his achievements in this respect are highly regarded. Along with private houses he has designed a few public buildings, and the number of these is seemingly on the rise. The Izu Mito Sea Paradise (1977), a "sea-world" with several pools, aquariums, display and show areas, and the like, most reveals his recent architectural concerns (245).

Seike employed a long, bridge-type steel frame structure that put the emphasis clearly on the technological, but here this preference is not an arbitrary one. In relation to water and the bay, a building suggesting a bridge is certainly appropriate. In addition to this level of meaning—similar to the one Isozaki evoked in the West Japan Exhibition Center at the Kitakyushu port—Seike applied another that creates an undeniably Japanese atmosphere. The simple graphic effect of the color scheme of dark brown and white and the careful integration of the building in its rich natural environment have a strong affinity with traditional examples, with none so well as the small wooden bridge and pavilion in the gardens of the Shugakuin Imperial Villa in Kyoto (10).

If Metabolism was primarily preoccupied with aspects of construction and technology, post-Metabolism shows an increased interest in formal considerations in which forms often become somewhat arbitrary. Interestingly enough, there are several veteran architects among those who take this path. Though Togo Murano (1891–1984) was always an Expressionist rather than a true Modernist, his moving further in the direction of Expressionism is a case in point. A comparison of his Japan In-

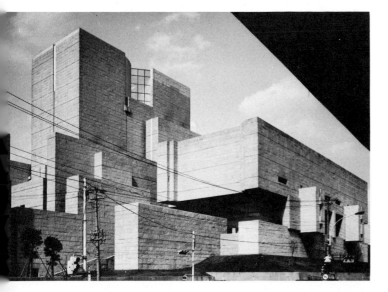

241–244. The volumetric and monumental architecture of the Supreme Court Building expresses the power of the government and state (Tokyo, 1974, S. Okada).

244. Third-floor plan. The spatial arrangement of the building reveals Louis Kahn's influence on Okada's design. 1. Open space of entrance hall. 2. Reception room. 3. Private rooms. 4. Small courtroom. 5. Reading room. 6. Foreign literature. 7. Special study room. 8. Office of civil matters. 9. Office of administrative matters. 10. Judges' rooms. 11. Judges' meeting rooms.

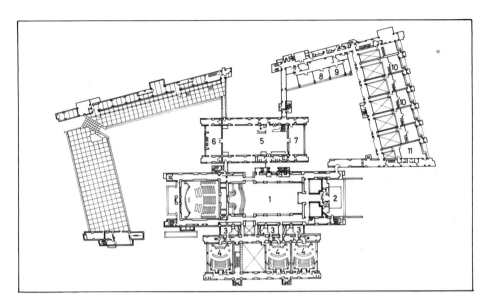

dustrial Bank (1974) to the Chiyoda Life Insurance Company Building (1966) in Tokyo, for example, makes this rather conspicuous. The unusual form of the main elevation of the bank, which resembles the sharp prow of a ship, is puzzling. Surprisingly, the building's machinery and air-conditioning plants were stuffed in here vertically (246). In another project, the Nishiyama Memorial Auditorium in Kobe (1975)—which has its remote origin in the expressive forms of his Takarazuka Catholic Church (1967)—he made an attempt to enhance the unusual effect of the shiny vertical edge by repeating it three times in the triangular design, but with much less success.

Bizarre architecture, which Murano only occasionally flirted with, has as a matter of fact a certain tradition in Japan. But no one was more at home in the world of the bizarre than Sei'ichi Shirai (1905–1983), who presented it from the very beginning of his long career. His Mannerist architecture is a unique mixture of Oriental or even occult and Western mythology, full of suspense and mysticism. He juxtaposed extraordinary forms, materials, and colors to create dramatic effects and surrealist visions. In the Noa Building (1974), a showroom and office tower in Tokyo, a dark oval block covered with extremely smooth blackened bronze plates alternating with slim vertical window towers above a lower section of rusticated red bricks; the image created is that of a temple of some demon cult (247). Since red and black are closely associated with blood and death, the building could also symbolize some past tragedies or the coldness of crypts.

The curving shapes return consistently in Shirai's architecture; they also appear in his Shinwa Bank Home Offices (1975) in Sasebo and the Shibuya Ward Shoto Museum of Art (1981) in Tokyo. In both cases the dominant material on the walls is rough granite masonry, which is contrasted with highly polished marble or stone surfaces and shiny metal elements. Entrances are of superhuman size and significance and, as in the Noa Building, have a chilling, awesome effect. Here their spaces are wrapped in reflecting black and red granite on the first floor, and red brick and white travertine in the basement, accentuated by special lightings. They both foretell a world beyond our familiar reality and even beyond the grave (248).

Indeed, Shirai's architecture has very little in common with a rational approach to design. Experiencing his buildings necessarily involves all the senses. The buildings call forth the deepest emotions. Shirai works very meticulously, taking heed of even the smallest details. This "Germanic precision" is evident in the Shinwa bank. He worked on this significant project for more than ten years and executed it in three phases, the last one—the Computer Center Building—ready in 1975 (249, 250). The work gave him the opportunity to elaborate and refine his method and architectural language; here, as with the Noa Building, the result is the image of a religious center.

The more recent Shoto Museum is both a medieval stone stronghold and a church, with particular references to the Italian or German Baroque (251). The opposing curved lines of the main elevation and of the roof introduce a sequence of

245. With its bridgelike structure, color scheme, and setting, the Izu Mito Sea Paradise becomes an effective recollection of traditional Japanese architecture (Mito, 1977, K. Seike).

246. The polished dark stone surfaces of the Japan Industrial Bank converge in a bizarre manner toward a sharp prowlike edge, its main elevation (Tokyo, 1974, T. Murano).

247. Like the surrealist vision of a cultic temple, the Noa Building towers over a busy intersection in Tokyo (1974, S. Shirai).

"pulsating" interior spaces, a feature reappearing in New Wave works best exemplified by the designs of Shin Takamatsu, Monta Mozuna, and Hiroshi Hara. The passage from the museum's entrance hall continues in a small vaulted tunnel, narrows down here, and, as a tapered tiny bridge, crosses an oval multistory interior courtyard, eventually to lead into the curving gallery of the main exhibition hall. Seen from the exhibition hall, again oval in shape, the gallery resembles some cultic edifice, or rather a huge altar with its back turned to the main approach. The complexity of the dramatically choreographed total experience, however, reaches beyond the ambiguity of Baroque spatial compositions to include strong mystical feelings of supernatural forces, which could make these spaces serve as excellent stages for any Wagnerian opera (252).

Shirai spent a number of years in Heidelberg, Germany, before the war, where he studied philosophy and literature under Karl Jaspers. Upon seeing these buildings of his, one may risk the thought that during those years he was also influenced by such German philosophers as Schopenhauer, Nietzsche, and perhaps by German psychoanalysts as well. Indeed, to analyze Shirai's architecture in more detail requires a considerable amount of psychoanalytic knowledge. Shirai remains one of the most enigmatic figures in Japanese architecture today.

Whether by mere coincidence or as the effect of proximity, the Reiyu-kai Temple (1976) of a new Buddhist sect in Tokyo, only a block away from the Noa Building, displays a similar surrealist deathlike vision. The building was designed by one of the country's largest construction companies, Takenaka Komuten. Though its somewhat modified octahedron form may well incorporate the motif of traditional wooden temple roofs, the total impression is more of a huge black coffin or mortuary (253). But when it comes to bizarre architecture produced by large companies, the Nikken

249–250. The complex of
the Shinwa Bank in
Sasebo resembles a
mysterious shrine of
money worship (1975, S.
Shirai).

251–252. As in the theatrical Baroque designs of Francesco Borromini, a sequence of contrasting, pulsating, and ambiguous spaces in addition to the boldly juxtaposed materials and oval forms constitute the basic concept of the Shibuya Shoto Museum (Tokyo, 1981, S. Shirai).

253. Architecture as an expressive statement of death. The Reiyu-kai Temple in Tokyo is the headquarters of a new Buddhist sect (1976, Takenaka Komuten Co. Ltd.).

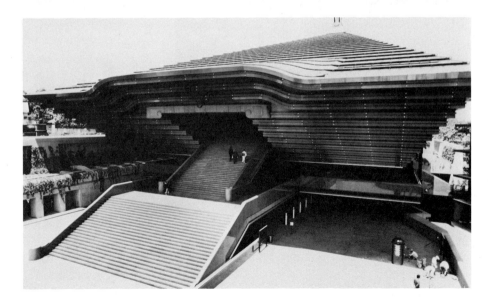

Sekkei Office certainly stands out as the one to have designed the most extreme example of it in the PL Peace Tower (1969) in Tondabayashi (91).

Diversification within the Metabolist movement started several years ago, sometime around the late 1960s. This process, however, was still determined by the scope of the Metabolist ideology and was well within it. Then the mid-1970s witnessed a rapid shift of attention from technology toward architectural meaning and then toward architecture as the art of creating places. To various extents this held true also with the members of the original group. Even the most outspoken theorists, Kikutake and Kurokawa, could not avoid the need for some rearrangement in their strategies, and so their architecture too started showing signs of change.

Kikutake, for example, sums up his philosophy today in one composite word: "eco-equip-tology," to suggest a design oriented to a combination of ecology and equipment. This is a clear continuation of the Metabolist idea, but now a careful use of architectural equipment and technology pays greater respect than before to the human, manmade environment or ecology. In short, he says, "From now on, the following things will be demanded of architecture: expression suiting performance, systematic pursuit of mechanisms conforming to use patterns, investigations into the meanings of artificial environment, and realization of clear images."[12]

His buildings and projects, however, do not fully follow this more flexible philosophy. The Seibu Otsu Shopping Center (1976) is a huge multipurpose community center that accommodates a large number of shops, restaurants, coffeeshops, supermarkets, exhibition halls, a general auditorium, and so on, in addition to the Seibu Department Store. These are lined along a system of stepped balconies, with additional and somewhat over-emphasized emergency stairways at the two sides of the building. The additional circulation line of the exterior stairs and terraces with the interior one add up to a double, or bichannel, pattern, an arrangement that characterized his Pasadena apartments as well (254). Indeed, the two have a rather similar appearance, proving that this building too is primarily Metabolist.

Communities built over the sea continue to be one of Kikutake's strong preoccupations; they show only slight changes in his attitude toward design. Scale has been reduced, and rather than plans for extensive cities the more recent projects are for large individual buildings like the Floating Hotel (1976) for Abu Dhabi or the Floating Luxury Hotel (1977). The project of a floating structure for Hawaii is an ongoing joint venture of Kikutake and Professor John Craven, involving both the Hawaii Department of Marine Programs and the University of Hawaii's Department of Architecture.

Reference to traditional sources has always been a distinctive mark of the Metabolist. Structural, formal, and sometimes even aesthetic solutions within the industrially produced buildings provided links to the past. They appeared together. With Kikutake recently they seem to be separated. His technological structurally determined projects have little in common with the spirit of tradition, while others, like the Tanabe Art Museum (1979) in Matsue or the Shinkoden Reception Office and Museum (1981) at the Izumo Shrine, are based almost solely and literally on traditional architecture (255). As before, the roof plays an important role as a dominant element. Though much less convincingly than his 1960s buildings, these two demonstrate that Hiroshi Watanabe is right when he says: "Kikutake's work is most striking precisely when he has applied Metabolist ideas to conventional programs," that is, to relatively small buildings as opposed to the gigantic and futuristic city or city-scale projects.[13]

Kurokawa's designs of today are significantly different not only from Kikutake's but also from his own earlier work. His "science-fiction fanaticism" has disappeared; even the high-tech look of his latest Metabolist buildings has been changed

254. Stepped terraces, overemphasized outdoor emergency staircases, and the spirit in which it was conceived make the Seibu Otsu Shopping Center representative of the late Metabolist architecture (Otsu, 1976, K. Kikutake).

and tamed, reappearing in the delicate forms and extreme precision of the smallest details and interior installations. The transformation within his Metabolist architecture emerged around the middle of the 1970s. The main feature is the increased attention to cultural context based on certain aspects of Buddhist philosophy expressed in architecture, rather than to the technological aspects. "In-between" spaces, the idea of the "intermediary" is assigned a leading role and elevated to a conceptual level that extends it into the realm of details, materials, and colors. The rigid capsule buildings of the late 1960s and early 1970s have gradually given way to architectural meanings both more refined and meant to be multivalent. Explaining his recent designs, Kurokawa refers to "coexistence," in which certain intermediary regions create neutral or buffer zones among spaces, parts, and even colors of different character.[14]

The Wagi City Hall (1975) and the Fukuoka Bank Home Offices (1975) are first steps in this direction. In both cases the idea of in-between is still limited to the simple handling of spatial relationships and is represented by the semipublic plazas within the buildings. The inner court of the City Hall is an interim zone between the two wings of the administrative offices and conference rooms, and in addition serves as a visual and physical connection between the street in front and nature—in this case the hills behind the building (256, 257).

The multistory space under the huge tablelike structure of the Fukuoka Bank plays a similar role and provides, in Kurokawa's words, an "urban

255. The Shinkoden Reception Office and Museum of the Izumo Shrine features expressly traditional forms (Izumo, 1981, K. Kikutake).

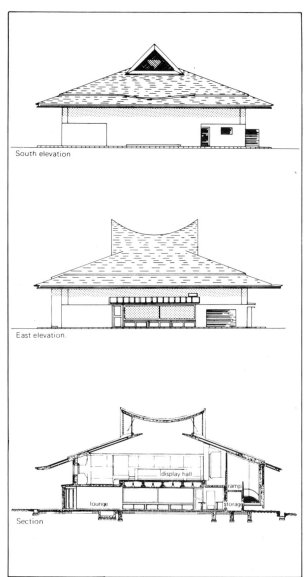

South elevation

East elevation.

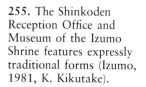

Section

256–257. The two wings of the Wagi City Hall are connected by two overhead bridges that form the huge gateways to a semipublic plaza within the building (Wagi, 1975, K. Kurokawa).

258. Like a gigantic table, the Home Office for the Fukuoka Bank features an urban hall under an urban roof (1975, K. Kurokawa).

259. The covered plaza of the Home Office for the Fukuoka Bank, with an outdoor sculpture garden, is situated on top of an underground auditorium.

260. The Head Office of the Japan Red Cross Society is a collection of various ideas from Kurokawa's Metabolist architecture and a collection of various fragments from the old headquarters building as well (Tokyo, 1977, K. Kurokawa).

261. The lobby of the Head Office of the Japan Red Cross Society has an appealing spatial effect.

hall" under an "urban roof" between inside and outside and private and public realms. The street-level plaza over the underground auditorium is a small park with trees, benches, and a tiny pool. It also serves as an outdoor sculpture exhibit (258, 259). The building's prototype is easily Kevin Roche's Ford Foundation Building in New York (1967). However, while the similar space in Roche's building is enclosed by huge glass walls, in Kurokawa's bank it is open to the adjacent streets.

Kurokawa needed considerably more time to come to more satisfactory terms with his new concept of coexistence. The intermediary zones in his Head Office of the Japan Red Cross Society (1977) in Tokyo, for example, seem to fail in connecting the parts into a whole, especially where the interior is concerned. Kurokawa here included many restored fragments of the old headquarters. The historic windows, door frames, and other interior elements remain a loose collection of originals and copies, creating an impression far from persuasive (260, 261). In this respect at least the exterior of the building is more successful than the interior.

Eventually Kurokawa did succeed in avoiding a lapse into superficial eclecticism and back into a hard-line Modernism. Even if a certain degree of pretentiousness and sterility surround his National Ethnological Museum (1978) in Osaka, with this building he once again proved his professional capabilities and talent. The museum is one of his most mature designs so far (262–264). Gone is the extravagance of his capsule architecture in the Nakagin Tower, yet the capsule idea is retained in the large individual quadratic units (265). The building's volumes are shaped in a simple but elegant manner in which details and materials are handled with the same attention and skill seen in Shirai's designs; not surprisingly, they also have some of the same qualities found in that architect's work.

Explaining the overall gray color of the building through its roots in Sen no Rikyu's philosophy, Kurokawa refers to the ambiguous character of Buddhist Japanese culture. "My interest in this color is concentrated on the nonsensual, continuity condition resulting from permitting two contradictory elements to collide and mutually cancel

262–265. A significant and successful transformation of Kurokawa's original Metabolist architecture characterizes his National Ethnological Museum (Suita, Osaka Pref., 1978, K. Kurokawa).

263. The videothèques
are audiovisual
information capsules.

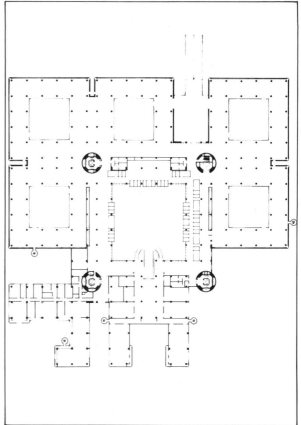

264–265. The capsule
idea is also recalled in the
large quadratic units of
the different exhibition
halls with their inner
sculpture gardens. The
central court is called
"Relics for the Future."

each other, in a way that two colors mutually cancel each other in this particular [gray] shade."[15] The entire building is covered with gray ceramic tiles. Different shades of the color appear in other materials, like aluminum, the cobblestones, granite, and so on. Thus, in addition to the ambiguity of spaces, surfaces, and details, even the applied colors have a vague, "undefined" disposition. This appears to be similar to Isozaki's ambiguous and uncertain images generated by "twilight" when sight slowly dims, and when reality and rationality give way to imagination and illusion. Yet Kurokawa's execution of his developing nonrational philosophy differs significantly from Isozaki's. Kurokawa is not a Mannerist architect; his Ethnological Museum and Isozaki's Kamioka Town Hall of the same year are opposite poles within the post-Metabolist attitude. In this sense the two architects were even arch rivals at that time. Their latest buildings also manifest their differences.

Kurokawa's hesitant gesture toward a less rationally determined architecture started, in fact, with the first application of the Rikkyu-Gray idea in his Fukuoka Bank, where polished dark gray granite slabs cover the whole building. This is continued at his Ishikawa Cultural Center (1977). Here the exterior bluish gray tile skin and the rough granite base walls, which are set in a surrounding moat, find meaning in the context of nearby Kanazawa Castle.

Several details of the Ethnological Museum show, however, that the Metabolist idea did not vanish entirely from Kurokawa's architecture at that time. Proof is found in the *videothèques,* in the audiovisual information boxes that are shaped and installed like capsules. Their high-tech futuristic effect recalls best the Osaka Sony Tower (263). The quadratic space units of the exhibition halls are arranged in a lattice system to permit further expansion of the museum; this has in fact occurred. Each unit includes an inner courtyard or exhibition patio to exemplify Kurokawa's in-between spaces.

The most unusual is the central patio covered with a stepped sculpture entitled "Relics for the Future" (264).

The last five years have witnessed another though partial reshuffling of the directions of such architects as Kurokawa, Maki, and Isozaki. Both Kurokawa and Maki have shifted further away from the relatively simplistic rational lines they had followed as Metabolists and as post-Metabolists. Though the underlying philosophy of intermediary region remains the same, in the Shoto Club (1980) and the Saitama Prefectural Museum (1982) Kurokawa has for the first time employed autonomous lattice walls and trabeated pergolas as space-structuring devices rather than as structural elements. In addition, both buildings, though their qualities differ, incorporate an intermediary courtyard, which in the museum appears as an attractive multistory space (266–269).

The latest works of Kurokawa attest that Metabolism plays an even less important role than before, or none at all, in his architecture. He admits this by writing: "In the future, I will no longer use the word Metabolism to describe my thought because I feel it sounds far too narrow to encompass what I mean by harmonious coexistence. I am already undergoing transformation, and Metabolism is only part of what I have to say."[16] In fact, in a recent dialog with Isozaki, he has even taken a step further. He voiced his denial of the function of signs, in terms of semiology at least. As Matsunaga explains, Kurokawa "intends to assemble signs without emitting any significance, and he insists this is the concept of *le poétique.* The extraordinary diversity of his recent works . . . could be clarified by this somewhat elusive notion of *le poétique.*"[17] As is evident, Kurokawa now aims at an architecture that has its philosophical origins in French-born post-Structuralism. Many of his recent works—the National Bunraku Theater in Osaka, the Yasuda Fire Insurance Building in Fukuoka, the Roppongi Prince Hotel and the Wacoal

Building in Tokyo (all 1984)—can be explained by his adoption of this philosophy (270). His discovery of similarities between Japanese Oriental traditions and recent post-Structuralist thought in Western philosophy is undeniably correct; it remains to be seen, however, whether his future buildings will demonstrate this direction more convincingly than his recent works have.

On the other hand, by implementing elements similar to some of Isozaki's and even Carlo Scarpa's Mannerist vocabulary, Maki has enriched his architectural language so that at the same time he has been able to reinforce his own increasingly sensitive Contextual approach and reach a new level of maturity.[18] This means first of all that he has avoided superficiality in spatial and formal articulation. The intangible qualities of his spaces and images are not only derivatives of tangible material substances, the tectonic entities of his building; they are also consistently rooted in the carefully interpreted local conditions of the site. In other words, his Contextual architecture has acquired a more explicit concern for creating place. Maki correctly explains that "a place, in a broader sense, is the product of a regional society and must be continually recreated."[19]

His recent buildings have been designed with this intention. While the stepped pyramidlike aggregate forms of the Keio University New Library (1981) continue along a line marked by such projects as the Tsukuba University Central Building, the National Aquarium in Okinawa, and the Iwasaki Museum, the articulate detailing of both the library's exterior and interior enable it to maintain a dialog with the old eclectic library nearby.

With respect to its spirit of place, one of the most remarkable buildings among Maki's recent works is certainly his YKK Guest House (1982) in Kurobe. Responding to the rural environment, Maki designed the building as both a spacious English country villa and an old-fashioned Japanese farmhouse, with articulate volumes, hipped and gabled roofs, a chimney, and above all with an inviting, intimate atmosphere. Fenestration, the bay windows, the careful elaboration of details, and the materials used play significant roles both inside and out in creating this milieu. Through his skillful investigations of the relationship between parts and the whole—wherein the aggregate of active parts that never conform to a formula generate the whole—Maki not only has built a place in its environment, but he has also done it so that it evokes both the Western and Japanese spirit as contemporary and traditional. This is most appropriate, since the guest house is used primarily for foreign guests and trainees of the YKK Company (271–274).

Maki knows that the expressive capabilities of Modernism have been exhausted; he also understands that a superficial manipulation of surfaces that merely dresses up an uninteresting structure may not solve architecture's present impasse. He finds the shaping of both image and substance equally important. The Fujisawa Municipal Gymnasium (1984) is his first project to employ curving forms so extensively. The forms of the two arenas, however, result largely from careful structural considerations. The large arena, with a roof that is a steel lattice structure of more than 80 meters and with pointed vaults and curving walls covered by stainless steel plates, was intentionally shaped to allude to the images of Japanese warrior helmets, the wooden gong (*mokugyo*) used in Buddhist ceremonies, the fencing masks of *kendo,* and many others, including perhaps even Tange's Olympic Stadium of twenty years earlier. Despite all the various forms and references of the parts, Maki was also able to give the building the distinct look of a general gymnasium (477, 478).

Unlike the cases of Kurokawa and Maki, the influence of contemporary American and European attitudes in Isozaki's architecture is at least on the surface significantly stronger and more explicit than a few years earlier. The Toga Small Theater (1980)

266–270. Kurokawa's latest buildings indicate that his architecture is shifting away from Metabolism.

266. Shibuya Shoto Club (Tokyo, 1980, K. Kurokawa).

267.

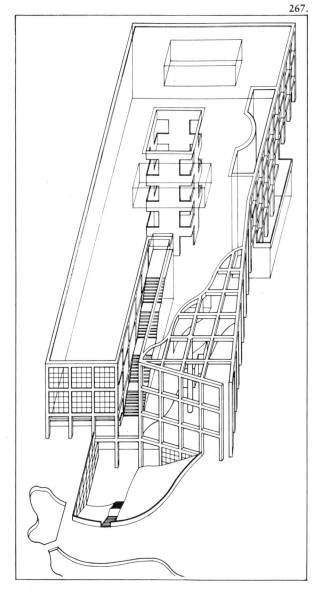

268.

267–269. Saitama Prefectural Museum (1982, K. Kurokawa).

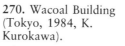

270. Wacoal Building (Tokyo, 1984, K. Kurokawa).

269.

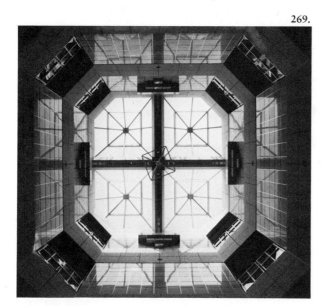

and the Tsukuba Center Building (1983) contain features that have seldom appeared in Isozaki's works before, yet the two buildings remain distinctly different from each other as well. An elongated pyramidal roof appears for the first time on the small Toga Theater; above and within the concrete base walls, wooden structural elements are exposed to the enclosed space below. Such solutions display the ample inspiration of the Japanese vernacular. Hiroshi Hara's influence is also apparent in the diagonal braces of the quadratic window frames and the primary importance of the stairway inside, while the overall image includes equal references to Aldo Rossi's Neorational architecture (275).

The Tsukuba Center comes much closer to the American populist Postmodernist interpretations of European Classicism, giving a heavy pastichelike dress to his own usual orthogonal structural skeleton (276–280). If Isozaki's works so far had been a subtle blend of foreign and Japanese quotations, in the details of this building, "Clichélike similes from historical styles are used extensively, not as vague suggestions, but directly," as Isozaki said.[20] Thus, beside the usual elements of Isozaki's ar-

chitecture—the orthogonal grid as substructure, the highly polished aluminum facades, the glass-block cylindrical volumes, visual tricks, the Marilyn Monroe curves, and so forth—we can see a large number of seemingly unrelated fragments, distorted and obvious quotations from many architects and ages, including classical times. The latter is most conspicuous in the rustication of the lower exterior walls in the manner of Ledoux and in the sunken courtyard fashioned after Michelangelo's piazza on the Capitoline Hill in Rome.

This conspicuous shift in Isozaki's architecture might have been triggered by his participation in the 1980 Tegel Harbor Competition in Berlin. In order to relate the new complex to Schinkel's Schloss Tegel of 1822, he designed the cultural and recreational center and the housing in a highly refined, expressly Neoclassical style—the quality of the urban context in Berlin.

But, consistent with the body of Isozaki's architecture and unlike most official Modernist and populist Postmodernist buildings, there is no consistent, coherent story within the Tsukuba Center; in fact, there is no center at all. In the plaza design

JAPANESE ARCHITECTURE TODAY   229

271–274. The images of a large English country house and a Japanese farmhouse are combined in Maki's YKK Guest House to create a pleasant homey atmosphere for the primarily foreign guests of the YKK Company (Kurobe, 1982, F. Maki).

274. Floor plans.

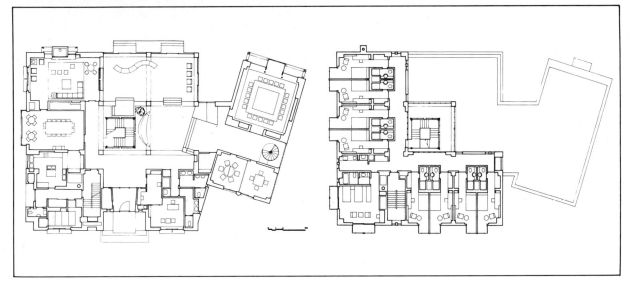

every possible relationship, motif, or form is inverted. While the empty plaza is, in fact, a visual or geometrical focal point, nothing attracts the viewer into descending to it. Omitted is a central symbol; here there is nothing like the statue of Marcus Aurelius on the original Michelangelo Campidoglio. In its place is the lowest point of the whole plaza where water flowing into it disappears into the earth and where, like in a whirl, everything else—line of vision, space, meaning, representation—is drawn into the abyss. In fact, with its central void, the plaza has been rendered a negative center itself or, alternatively, it symbolizes the loss, the absence, of center and perhaps the invisibility of the faceless ruler, the state behind the scene (278, 280). Yet, perhaps not accidentally, this absence coincides with the lack of the concept of an absolute center in the history of Japanese culture. Thus, the Tsukuba Center Building may turn out to be not only a critical inquiry into the nature of "center," but also, paradoxically, a questioning of the inevitable necessity and authority of such an absolute center.

In order to destroy further the clear organizing system of a "master narrative" usually preferred for institutional architecture, Isozaki has "deliberately called on things that have been made kitsch as long as they retain evocative powers but [has] employed counterbalances to prevent any one image from dominating."[21] The result is a complete mixture of everything wherein, as he writes, he "one by one . . . buried the limitlessly subdivided parts; and all that remains now is the recollection of the interminable nightmare."[22] In other words, this is a deliberate subversion of official representation, using this representation's own images and strategies. It is an attempt to win on the opponent's terms. Yet despite all these "unacceptable" and candidly admitted "sins," Isozaki's design mastery ensures that this nightmare, the subversion itself, is not only bearable but, as a lively mess, is also attractive. While remaining an essentially "Man-

275. The small Toga Theater annex incorporates elements from both traditional Japanese and Aldo Rossi's Neorational architectures (Gifu Pref., 1980, A. Isozaki).

276–280. Heavy clichélike rustication and other allusions to historical styles cover the deep-structure and characterize Isozaki's latest achievement at the Tsukuba Center Building. The allusions reveal a new direction in his Mannerist architecture (Tsukuba, 1983, A. Isozaki).

278. The sunken plaza as negative center.

280. Section and second-floor plan.

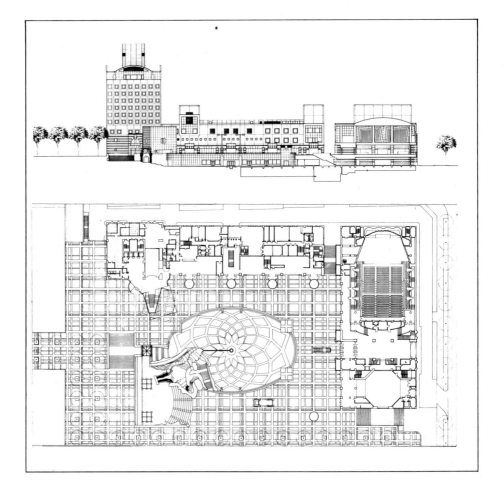

nerist-Symbolist" architect, Isozaki is seemingly entering a new phase. In this sense, the Tsukuba Center Building can be regarded as a very significant, if not entirely successful, further step toward a more consistently post-Structuralist and, perhaps, critical architecture in Japan.

The New Wave

In around the middle of the 1970s it became increasingly evident that Japanese architecture was undergoing a change of extraordinary variety that was thus genuine renewal. It came not from a modified Metabolism but from new ideas brought forth by a new generation of mainly young architects who opposed the idea of constant physical change and hence the need for interchangeability, and who for similar reasons also rejected the superficiality of ever-changing fashion manipulated by the commercially and consumer-oriented mass society. The exhibition entitled "A New Wave of Japanese Architecture" that toured the United States in late 1978 was not only a strong statement against these two trends but also the self-conscious manifestation of an evolving new Japanese architecture that offered a meaningful alternative and challenge to the ideal of technologically induced constant change and the reign of fashion. The developments since have shown that, as *New York Times* architecture critic Ada Louise Huxtable put it, "if there is an active avant-garde today, this is it."[23]

After the collapse of the already petrified Metabolist ideology and practice, the New Wave has erupted onto the scene with an ever-growing vitality and freshness stemming from released dogma-free creative energy. This architecture is as novel as it is powerful, yet naturally easy flowing and playful; concrete and poetically elusive; provocatively critical and simultaneously "silent." A cool neutrality toward it is not possible. The multifaceted sometimes truly esoteric personal philosophies and concepts behind and embodied by the works may still be puzzling or inaccessible to Western understanding and thus need thorough analysis.

Instead of harboring the obsession to reshape or revolutionize the cultural and social aspects of society, already proven impossible by positivist Modernism, these architects are better aware of their limitations. They are more inclined to carry out small-scale "subversions" in the face of the growing dictates of the anonymous process of instrumental production and consumption. They react against the ideological and political domination in contemporary society and aim to achieve sensible diversity and meaningful plurality. As "correctors" of the present situation, they intend to improve the living conditions of individuals by first of all restoring their identity through new relationships between man and architecture. More attention is paid to differences and details. There are more personal statements than general and empty phrases. Architecture is meant to be—and is looked upon as—a fabric of actual places in which man creatively dwells rather than occupies passively.

Many of these architects are motivated by the desire to free the individual from the mechanical, stereotyped, and distorted modes of experience inflicted by the everyday routines of contemporary life. They intend to provide, sometimes even to provoke, the conditions for regenerative moments of repose or self-renewal. They will do this by creating architectural spaces as refuge within the increasingly chaotic and destructively volatile urban environment. But since human life is extensively shaped by meanings perceived in the intricate web of relationships between man and his surrounding created world, renewal of self and the redefinition of existence may come from the redefinition of these very structuring relationships.

Thus existentialism is as essential today as it was in the architecture of the past. The past is alive and well again, but in a significantly different form; replacing often superficial expressive formalism, its spirit lingers in the works of the New Wave. Younger Japanese architects find it difficult to accept the usual Modernist and Western interpretations, like those of Taut and Gropius, of their traditional architecture as a mechanically flexible system of "transparent" spaces, an assembly of self-evident constituents within a strict functionalism conceived as a product of the super-rational devotion of the Japanese to the objective in the environment. In truth, as Chris Fawcett points out, this architecture "was in the end a response to a highly ritualized perception—for example, the parts of a Japanese house had to be sympathetically arranged owing to the various *Kami* . . . presiding over the site. Site configuration, location, accessibility—all were handled in ritual terms."[24] Indeed, these young architects have started to discover and incorporate another kind of tradition beneath the surface: the ambiguous symbolic qualities of space. These perceptual subtleties are among the deepest roots of the Japanese sensibility by which their traditional architecture was able to invoke and nourish the Oriental "spirit of place," in which the meanings of existence sprang from the shared identity between subject and object. It is through exactly this revitalized sensitivity that the architecture of the New Wave bypasses and challenges both Neorationalist and Neorealist populist trends in the contemporary international scene.

The first thing that strikes the viewer in these works is the architects' strong preoccupation with formal operations and their ability to deal with them, enabling the architects "to synthesize form into an incisive and powerful gestalt," as Kenneth Frampton observed.[25] There are two extremes among the wide range of possible approaches to the creation of extraordinary images and the generation of intangible qualities with forms and materials. One results in a more representational architecture in which the most various and often contradictory elements retain their original character while juxtaposed in a radical manner, yet gain new dimensions in the new contexts. The meaning, or rather the meanings of a building are derivatives of the new dimensions discovered in this way. This trend has its immediate tradition in the historically eclectic quality of the whole of Japanese culture, and beyond that one of its most extreme representations in Sei'ichi Shirai's bizarre and nonrational architecture. The other extreme, a largely abstract approach, is based on manipulations of simple geometric forms with the inherent intention of suspending and removing ordinary or conventional meanings from architecture. This esoteric and metaphysical use of a formally rational system is in spirit ultimately nonrational; it has its roots in Zen Buddhist traditions, and has been long represented by Kazuo Shinohara.

With its several idiosyncracies, contemporary Japanese architecture is an extremely varied mixture of these two different interpretations of existential issues. In most cases the emphasis is clearly on one or the other, but some works combine the two aspects to varying degrees. This has happened most consistently and successfully in Isozaki's designs. Greatly inspired by him, the New Wave focuses upon several aspects of his architecture individually, elaborates and varies them, gives them new dimensions, and sometimes even pushes them to extremes. Isozaki in turn shows signs of the influence of the generally younger architects of the New Wave.

COLORFUL BUILT DREAMS
Among those who positively reaffirm architectural and thus also existential meanings, Yasufumi Kijima (b. 1937) and Osamu Ishiyama (b. 1944) have to be mentioned first. They both speak a romantic language, yet in a contrasting manner. The plentiful decoration, form, and color inside and out contribute significantly to the delicacy of Kijima's architecture, but the same results in the "junk" ap-

281–283. In the White House, a colorful "dream," Kijima redefines the symbol of the "eternal column" (Tokyo, 1973, Y. Kijima).

283. Image drawing of the White House.

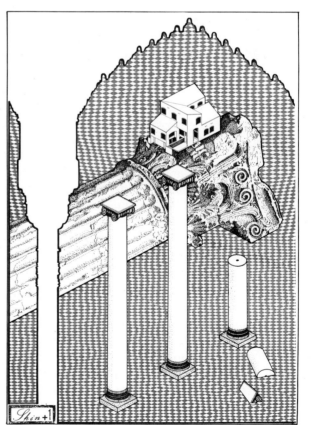

284. The Kamimuta Kominkan is a superimposition of several architectural surfaces and facades with different historical references (Kumamoto, 1975, Y. Kijima).

pearance of Ishiyama's. Interior and exterior are equally important in both their designs, and the two have similar modes of expression.

Kijima's architecture is a refined elite collection of foreign and Japanese images projected radically onto one another. All his houses, like the Villa on a Hill in Atami and the White House in Tokyo, both from 1973, or the Koike House (1975), also in Tokyo, have incorporated something from traditional residential architecture but more from the tiled and white-plastered *kura,* or storehouse, architecture. Their distinct features are mixed with elements of different ages and cultures spanning classical Greece and Rome, the Renaissance, and even the Viennese Secession. The willful superimposition of these styles in every case creates an extremely colorful, gay cavalcade, a romantic dream.

Kijima captures and introduces the dreams that characterize his buildings with "image sketches" drawn after the buildings are finished.[26] But a look at his beautiful drawings suggesting the buildings' cosmic or mythical associations leads one to assume that they depict images conceived in an early stage of the structures' design. The image sketch of the White House shows the inspiration to have been the classical column. Indeed, idealized white cylindrical columns appear everywhere: in the middle of the *tatami* room, lined up in the gateway, the entrance hall, and so on (281–283).

If the White House is a celebration of the "eternal column," the Kamimuta Kominkan (1975), a small daycare center in Kumamoto, is a celebration of layered and superimposed surfaces and facades.

The quasi-Palladian entrance appears under a colorful Secession-style roof before it continues in the central stairway that is implicitly Baroque in character (284). Kijima's technique of juxtaposition reaches its climax in the nearby Kamimuta Matsuo Shrine (1975). Here he brings together two buildings with basically different backgrounds: ancient Western and ancient Oriental. In front of a small renovated Shinto Shrine, Kijima has built a typically Western archetype, the classical Roman vaulted sanctuary; both are reflected in a surrounding pool that thus creates a harmonious composition. The only access to the Japanese shrine is through the colonnaded Western space (285, 286).

Indeed Kijima produces some cultural hybrids, one may even say products of a cultural schizophrenia; this is also suggested by his arresting drawings. The buildings and the sketches generate a hypnotic effect wherein the sense of place and time is lost; he succeeds in neutralizing both. For him history and time are not linear, but stagnant. For him the clock on the wall stopped long ago, or perhaps has never started.

Ishiyama's works, on the other hand, have very little to do with "history" directly and lie also completely outside the general stream of modern Western architecture. Instead they all comment on the absurdity of industrialism and its mass- and over-production. His "sewer pipe" steel tube houses are both lyrical recollections of industrial suburbs and real collections of readily available industrial products. Many of his buildings' components are in fact ordinary parts or by-products not intended for architecture. His latest houses, the Tower of

285. By juxtaposing two culturally different buildings in a radical manner, Kijima's design for the Kamimuta Matsuo Shrine reaches the level of cultural schizophrenia (Kumamoto, 1975, Y. Kijima).

286. Image drawing of the Kamimuta Matsuo Shrine.

the Hoped-for Winds (1981), and the Land Ship—1 (Iris) (1983) incorporate fishing boat and automobile parts. The admitted intention here—or an attempt at rational explanation—is the use of the surplus production of industrial societies. Ishiyama thus rescues whatever "junk" he finds and compiles it in an *ad hoc* fashion within the new contexts, yet with the result that his houses are always turned into poetry, or rather Japanese fairy tales of a counter-culture.

Ishiyama has built a large number of small buildings with corrugated steel tubes, the metal sheets of which are normally used in ground excavation and civil engineering construction. The steel tube, as in the Fantasy Villa (1975) in Omi,

is sunk into the ground and closed at its two ends, the elevation walls broken by entrances and decorated with stained-glass windows. Within the thin shell, the interior is converted with the help of "light, color, shadow, sounds and odors" into a small, symbolic universe complete with a two-story living room and an airy, arched Japanese bridge that connects the upper level with the elevated front door (287–289).

BUILDINGS WITH FACES

Ishiyama's easygoing, playful, and spectacular houses have a quality that reappears in various forms in the works of several young Japanese architects. It leads through the world of children,

287–289. The Fantasy Villa is an ad hoc collection of industrial byproducts and surplus in new contexts, creating a lyrical impression of industrial slums or the statement of a counterculture (near Omi, 1975, O. Ishiyama).

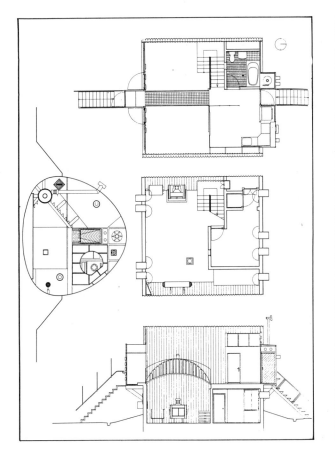

288. The interior is a special world.

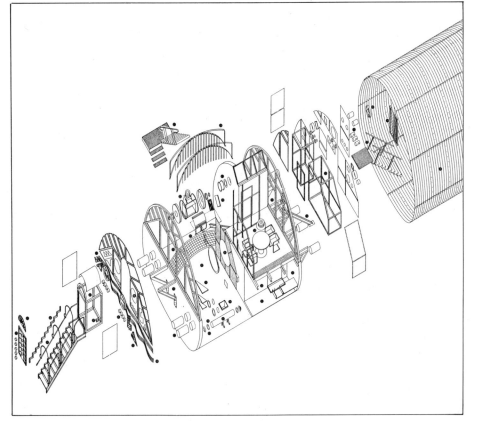

289. Plans, sections, and axonometric drawing.

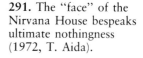

290. Yamashita's pop design, the Face House, laughs at the surprised visitor in Kyoto (1973, K. Yamashita).

291. The "face" of the Nirvana House bespeaks ultimate nothingness (1972, T. Aida).

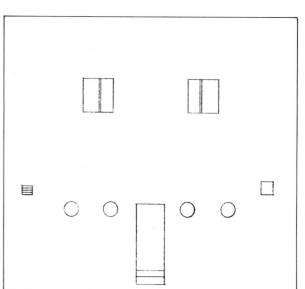

paying tribute to the rites of play. It is not really difficult to see that the Fantasy Villa was designed and put together with the imagination of a child, a child who lives in every adult no matter how it is suppressed by the grownup self-consciousness. Ishiyama and other architects in the Basara—an informal group of friends that includes Kazuhiro Ishii, Kijo Rokkaku and Monta Mozuna—in addition to many others not belonging to the group like Takefumi Aida and Kazumasa Yamashita descend into a playful world from time to time. They attempt to prove that adults need not forget or be ashamed of the *homo ludens* within themselves. Playing is more than self-amusement and time-killing, an escape from "reality"; for a child it is a serious self-creating act by which he actively participates in the world and thus affirms his own existence. One characteristic of the child, as of primitive man, is his identification with self in what he does. He is not yet alienated. He sees himself in his creations—his works, his drawings, and so on. He humanizes them, often by basing their forms on the shape of his own face and body.

This anthropomorphism is present in Ishiyama's works, and obvious in the front facade of the Fan-

tasy Villa. The round roof, the two circular windows, and the protruding entrance and stairway in the middle suggest a face; it is as if the spirit of the forest in which this summer house is located had its watchful eyes on us. But the sense of a living being's gaze is more subdued and more implicit here than in some other cases—for instance in Yamashita's Face House (1973) in Kyoto and the Pegasus Building (1978) in Tokyo. The Face House overstates the underlying anthropomorphism so much so that the building can be seen as pop architecture as well. Every element of the facade has been designed to correspond unmistakably with the parts of a human face. Windows become the "eyes" of the house, the entrance adequately opens up as the mouth, and the ventilation outlet (what else?) stands appropriately for the nose. But—where are the ears? No matter. This strangely laughing face makes one smile too, and perhaps also wonder what this univalent pop image has to do with the context of Kyoto (290).

In contrast to Yamashita's readily accessible design, the "faces" in the designs of Takefumi Aida, Shin Takamatsu, and Shinohara are deliberately esoteric and transcendental. The delicate

292. From the facade of the Hinaya Home Office a strange, prehistoric monster gazes down on the passersby (Kyoto, 1981, S. Takamatsu).

293. The clownish face of the Police Box watches the traffic at a busy Ginza intersection (Tokyo, 1982, K. Yamashita).

and wise "smile" of Aida's Nirvana House (1972), for example, is a subtle reference to the emotionless blank expression of Buddha statues, symbol of ultimate nothingness or nirvana (291). The notion of void is essential to the quality of the House in Uehara (1976) as well. The vaulted and corrugated iron upper section of this house is similar in solution to the Fantasy Villa, but while Ishiyama's circular windows seem to greet the visitor with a friendly wink, Shinohara's windows are empty eyeholes in a skull gazing back from a world beyond this (287, 433). The polished red granite facade of Takamatsu's Hinaya Home Office (1981) then suggests a monstrous prehistoric creature (292).

Between the two extremes, popular and esoteric, there are several ways to introduce anthropomorphic elements. Yamashita is one of those who experiments with the idea most. The face motif in his two recent buildings in Tokyo is more refined than in the Face House. In the case of the Pegasus Building it does not appear on the elevation but as part of the floor plan. The undulating line of a balcony takes on the shape of the client's enlarged profile, giving this office building floor a personal identity. The most successful work of Yamashita

294.

296.

294–296. Expressly Renaissance references characterize the facades of a few recent buildings.

294. Alumnae Hall for the Sacred Heart Women's College (Tokyo, 1977, S. Toki).

295. The tripartite main elevation of the Sanwa Building with an emphasis on the *piano nobile* (Kikuchi, 1977, S. Toki).

296. Kodama House (Tokyo, 1980, K. Ishii).

295.

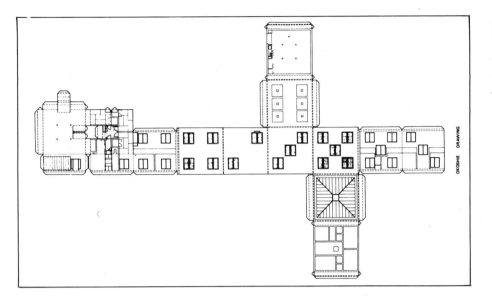

OKOSHIE DRAWING

297. A huge "toy," the House like a Die was designed by applying the traditional *okoshie* drawing method of Japanese carpenters (1973, T. Aida).

in this respect, however, is a small Police Box (1982) that faces a busy intersection in the Suki-yabashi area on the Ginza. Capped by a high pyramidal roof, the two-story building features a quadratic design that emphasizes the diagonal. The entrance and the small cylindrical balcony above it are part of the corner looking toward the streets. The box, which has some remote affinity with the simple, rational designs of Aldo Rossi's Teatro del Mondo, reveals its clownish face from the direction of this corner. Granted its purpose, it might seem that the building—not only the policemen inside— was keeping a watchful yet friendly eye on the crowd and traffic around it (293).

In all these examples, anthropomorphism has meant primarily a special emphasis on the facades. But even without anthropomorphism, an increased concern with facades is a strong feature in New Wave works in general. This is most evident in Isozaki's more recent works, in Minoru Takeyama's pop buildings, in Kazuhiro Ishii and Shin Toki's Renaissance-inspired designs, and in Toyo Ito's false facades.

According to Shin Toki (b. 1937), a former disciple of Tange, "the facade is the face of the building," and thus he attributes utmost importance to the expression of these "faces."[27] His approach is clearly historical, more precisely Renaissance, probably due to the influence of his long working experience in Italy. The Alumnae Hall for the Sacred Heart Women's College (1977) in Tokyo is a small but representative example of this (294). The elevation of his Sanwa Building (1977) in Kikuchi is concave and semicircular, recalling in addition

to Mannerist designs, some Baroque solutions as well. The deliberate historical reference includes the tripartite arrangement of this strictly symmetrical building, where the second floor acts as *piano nobile*, the main story. This is indicated by the two ceremonial curving stairways (295). Toki's Villa K (1975) has a more direct prototype in Palladio's Villa Giovanile and Villa Foscari. It has also a close affinity with Venturi's Chestnut Hill House, for which too the models were Palladian Villas. The original models in both cases, however, have obviously been distorted.

Nor are historic references strange in the works of Ishii (b. 1944), as in the colonnade of his Naoshima Gymnasium (1976) or the oval courtyard in his "Jazzy Baroque" House (1982) in Tokyo; in two other buildings, the references are more explicit. The Kodama House (1979) has high pitched roofs and an asbestos-cement shingle skin of two colors that recall both the striped facades of the Italian Romanesque including those of the Orvieto Dom and the Basilica in Siena, and the pop motifs of Isozaki and Takeyama's facades (296). The Gable Building (1980) in Tokyo reinvents the stepped gable roofs of Dutch Renaissance urban architecture. But as usual Ishii plays with the classical elements of arched entrances, base and pediment, balcony tabloids; he distorts or transmutes them or makes variations on their themes. In the Gable Building, which is typical of many similar examples, these rather trivial manipulations remain strictly within the plane of the facade, which is only a decorative mask that has "nothing" to do with the building behind.

ARCHITECTURE AS TOY

The playful, fairy-tale quality is only one characteristic of these designs. Another important aspect is that many buildings themselves are turned into toys. Such architecture appears in several of Aida's houses, for example. One explanation behind this phenomenon is again in the traditional architecture, the carpenter's old drawing method called *okoshie*. During the design phase of a building, the various elements—floors, ceilings, exterior and interior elevations—are laid out in one composite plan similar to the way small children cut a joining pattern out of paper before folding and gluing it into a three-dimensional form like, say, dice. Aida followed a similar method in designing his House like a Die (1973). The house is one single perfect cube that looks as if it had been thrown and "by chance" landed on its six-spotted side over a pilotis. The spots on the other sides of the die make up the appropriate number of square windows (297).

In his latest buildings Aida returns again to children's toys, but to different ones. The numerous buildings in the Toy Block House series in Hofu, Yokohama, and Tokyo have been conceived and built in the same spirit since 1979. The building components are reduced to the simplest geometrical solids—triangular and rectangular prisms, cylinders, stepped forms—and thus are identical or similar throughout the series. The houses are put together so that these "toy blocks" both create the overall forms of the buildings and retain their identity, just as children build different compositions from the same set of blocks. The world of children and elements of rational Western and traditional Japanese architecture (particularly the Shinto architecture of the Ise Shrine) are equally represented by the images of these houses. In addition, the Toy Block House No. 3 in Tokyo is a tribute to Mondrian's art—the two-color surfaces of the blocks follow a pattern similar to those in the painter's works (298–300). Despite its playful episodes, Aida's architecture has a definitely abstract some-

298–300. Toy Block Building No. 2 (Yokohama, 1980, T. Aida). Aida's recent buildings in a series have been designed in the playful manner of children as giant building blocks.

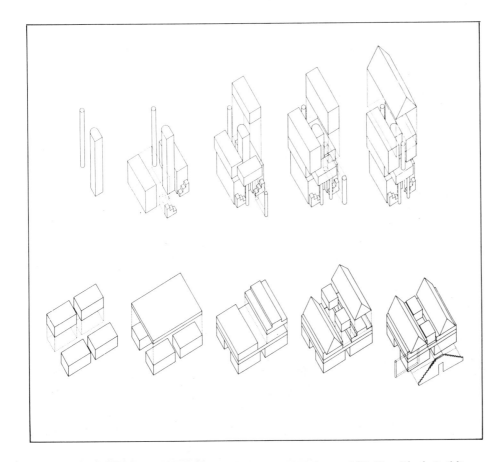

299. Conceptual drawings of the Toy Block Buildings No. 2 and No. 1 (Hofu, 1980, T. Aida).

300. Toy Block Building No. 3 (Tokyo, 1982, T. Aida).

301–302. Designed with
"54 Roofs," the Takebe
Nursery School is not a
single building but in fact
a small village for
children (Takebe, 1979,
K. Ishii).

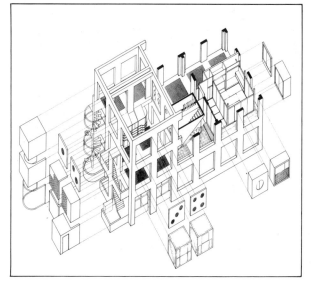

303–305. A residence and a private clinic, the House with 54 Windows is an "endless" variation on the meaning of one architectural element, the window (Hiratsuka, 1975, K. Ishii).

305. Axonometric drawing.

times even absurd quality, which, as he says, often places it in the "silence" of a transcendental world.

Aida's architecture invites the viewer to join in private, serious play, while Kazuhiro Ishii's architecture assures a happy, almost joking atmosphere that brings his buildings much closer to the affairs of children. With the Takebe Nursery School "54 Roofs" (1979) he goes beyond the usual idea of a school as one building to create in fact a small fairy-tale village within the surrounding real village. These scaled-down houses, represented by their real or symbolic roofs, are arranged in rows around a courtyard as the central plaza. The whole design is based on one reinforced concrete frame repeated fifty-four times, but this same frame is used in many different ways: it is the structural device, makes up the shape of the roofs, acts as a set of false facades or gables, and as a set of gates to and within the compound. The small building units themselves add further variety to the scheme. Their elevations, which fill the frames, are all more or less different. Thus the standard uniformity of the framework is consistently challenged by the identity of its components. As this structure indicates, Ishii shares some of Maki's concerns in architecture: the aggregate forms of the nursery successfully represent the idea of a building as a small city or, conversely, the notion of a small city as a large house.[28] It also reveals Ishii's interest in the larger social context: this building can be regarded as a comment on the difficult relationship between the individual and mass-society (301, 302).

The House with 54 Windows (1975) is Ishii's early investigation in this direction. As he quite often does, here he picked an order, a regular framework, and a certain architectural element, then tried to play as many variations and find as many meanings as possible within the limits of the selected scheme. The orthogonal structural skeleton of the house and small private clinic is filled with fifty-four different windows to form a colorful cavalcade both outside and inside. In this building Ishii again shows close affinity for several of his fellow architects like Isozaki, Fujii, Miyawaki, and Aida, yet he is still able to redefine or play other games with the cube form of which the house is composed. Though the philosophy behind the design is not as deep and esoteric as in the works of those other architects, the 54 Windows surpasses them in its easy-flowing manner and friendly, playful effect (303–305).

As in Aida's previous house, one of the ideas inherent behind the windows is the die. The colored, spotted sides, here fragmented, are aspects of a celebration with windows. However, as is not the case with Aida, here the celebration takes place all through the building, outside and inside alike. Shin Toki, probably influenced by Ishii's design, employed a similar approach in the Togane Central Clinic (1979). The quadratic space frame of the building features glass-block walls and windows with different formal solutions, but with a less impressive overall result (306).

Ishii, one of the youngest of the new generation, is unequivocally anti-Metabolist, yet he applies certain of its elements, though in a different context. The most apparent are the redefinition of the capsule idea and the importance of structure. A small but good example of this, the elevation of his Takahashi Residence (1977) in Tokyo is made up of one of the house's vierendeel trusses standing in front of the building as a "structural" false facade (307). In the Naoshima Municipal Gymnasium (1976) and Junior High School (1979) manipulations of the structure in another manner create a rather playful atmosphere. For the simple volumes of the gymnasium and the school, he designed a series of boxes above a continuous colonnade as a softly curving elevation that connects the two related institutions. The line of same-sized cubes provides uniformity, but as in his 54 Windows the details show a wide range of variation, among them openings of different sizes and the omission of a few "capsules" that are replaced by other elements.

306. In his Togane Central Clinic, Toki combines elements of Ishii's and of Ando's architecture (1979, S. Toki).

These elements include the gable roof of ancient Shinto shrines, here serving as the entrance to the training hall for traditional martial arts. Ishii's design is another example of how the Japanese "japanize" a Western idea or prototype, this time the Renaissance colonnade.

In addition to variations, Ishii turns the happy mood here into a real joke. A close look at the pillars reveals clearly that they are not identical either. What is more, at some places pairs of "structural" columns are left out, as if forgotten. On the other hand, certain of the columns receive special reinforcement. Ishii deliberately breaks the syntactic rules of construction to create a more cheerful effect (308, 309). It is obvious that in his hands, as well as those of Ishiyama and Aida, technology and structural solutions have become not only tools but also toys. Yet, these architects do not deny the importance of architecture's structural aspects; they "share the desire to use technology, while remaining aloof from it."[29]

Kijo Rokkaku (b. 1941), another member of the Basara group, uses "technology as toy" almost literally, yet also rather poetically, in his Zasso Forest School (1977). In other projects like the Ishiguro House (1970) and the House of the Tree Root (1980) this marks a further step toward joining the rites of playing and the rituals of living through architectural celebrations and thus also marks a further attempt to affirm human existence. The young Japanese architects quite often express this attempt at affirmation by celebrating with the innocence of a child some natural or created phe-

307. The Takahashi Residence is a small private house with a vierendeel truss structure (Tokyo, 1977, K. Ishii).

308–309. Beyond their simple variations on architectural solutions, the softly undulating colonnades of the Naoshima Municipal Gymnasium and Junior High School surprise the visitor with real jokes (Naoshima Island, 1976, 1979, K. Ishii).

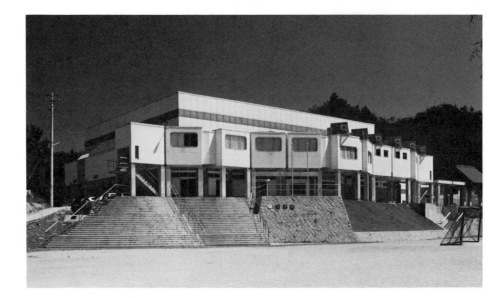

310. In the Zasso Forest School, Rokkaku introduces a natural phenomenon to children in a charming, playful manner through what he calls "wind-games architecture" (near Kyoto, 1977, K. Rokkaku).

nomenon. The phenomenon rediscovery and its multiple redefinition provide the theme for the design.

Rokkaku's Forest School, like many works of the New Wave, is a kindergarten. It is located in the midst of beautiful wooded hills near Kyoto. Its seven towers of varying height are an implicit reference to the urban forms of the Italian town of San Gimignano and perhaps to an enchanted castle but this castle has very little to do with those found in Disneyland. The charm and poetry here are rooted in the way a natural phenomenon, the wind, is introduced to the children. But how to "catch the wind"? How to make the invisible visible? Rokkaku chose the playful manner of displaying wind through the motion it generates. The collaborating sculptor, Susumu Shingu, designed several wind sculptures; each tower features one at its top. Their forms and translucent yellow surfaces of tensile fabric permit a range of associations: outstretched hands trying to reach the windy skies; radar antennas or radio telescopes scanning the waves of the ether; hoisted sails on a boat ready to set out; kites flying in the air; weathervanes revolving with the rising breeze. This "wind-games

architecture" and its symbolic toys culminate in the playschool, a separate building in the compound. It is covered by a pyramidal glass roof with a windmill (propeller?) on its peak. The windmill's moving blades and axles transmit the motion and energy created by the wind into the playroom under the roof. Toys in the room can be plugged into the outlets on the walls and under the floor connected to the revolving terminals (310). The wind is then perceived as it drives suspended small airplanes and other toys, thereby also stimulating "children's dreams and . . . curiosity about the world of nature."[30]

No matter how similar it may look, Minoru Takeyama's (b. 1934) Atelier Indigo (1976) has been conceived in a spirit unlike that of the Zasso School. The atelier, Takeyama's own design office in Sapporo, is a toy of a different breed. The school assumes its meanings and *raison d'être* by dramatizing man's poetic coexistence with a natural force, the wind; the atelier, in contrast, is "empty," a possibility yet to be filled with meaning. The affinity between Takeyama and Isozaki lies in "emptiness" as a point of departure. It is evident from the atelier plans that the cube and the cylinder played dominant roles in the design, suggesting it was inspired by Isozaki (311). Another feature can be likened to Isozaki's space-manipulating robot at the Osaka Expo-70 Festival Plaza. The spaces in the atelier feature almost endless possibilities for alteration and combination. These physical changes are performed with the help of mechanical devices. Meaning itself is dependent on such mechanisms. There is an *ad hoc* quality in the various installations and the "equipmentalized" furniture of the interior, but it is most notable in the rooftop boxes, a kind of kinetic space toy. All these features suggest an offering on the altar of Metabolism, yet the building is instead a parody of it. There is some weak utilitarian purpose behind this flexibility, but Takeyama's main intention is to generate and manipulate meaning. The "toy" consists of eight cubic rooftop boxes hinged together along their edges. This allows them to be folded into different configurations using manpower only. The whole device serves "as a space synthesizer performing in an *ad hoc* fashion the constantly altering combinations of architectural language" (312).[31]

CELEBRATION WITH ARCHITECTURE

Takeyama is not a one-sided architect. Even if some of his buildings, like the atelier or the Iwakura Residence (1974) in Tomakomai, represent a different approach from Kijima, Ishii, Ishiyama, or Rokkaku, other of his significant works come surprisingly close to theirs. It is a deliberate "heterology"—as he calls it—that best characterizes his architecture. Takeyama has arrived at this via his investigations of meaning in architecture. He has been the undeclared leader of and spokesman for ArchiteXt, the first counter-Metabolist group that looked upon architecture as a metalanguage. The ArchiteXt name itself indicates the underlying intention of trying to make architecture and the human environment in general, legible along the principles of semiotics, with buildings perceivable and interpretable in many ways. But this intention is

the end of the similarity among the members of the group—Minoru Takeyama, Mayumi Miyawaki, Takefumi Aida, Takamitsu Azuma, and Makoto Suzuki. Like the architecture of its architects, the group itself was a paradox. Formed in 1971, ArchiteXt issued no joint memorandum or manifesto at its first and only exhibition in Tokyo. This reflected the fact that these architects had followed no common line. Indeed, with their individual approaches, they aimed exactly at the opposite, emphasizing the different ways and multiplicity of architecture. The "group" had hardly come into being when it stopped functioning as a group. It has remained ever since an informal gathering of friends.

Takeyama declares the "common philosophy" he shares with ArchiteXt to be a "discontinuous continuity," which undoubtedly refers to Pluralism. Along with the paradoxes in their works can be found elements of humor, irony, and parody. They were the first to introduce such notions into contemporary Japanese architecture as "pop architecture," "defensive architecture," "vanishing architecture" then, what Azuma aims at, a "polyphony in architecture," and also what Aida calls the "architecture of silence." While their works with practically no exception are unique dashes in the urban environment, the intended meanings and conveyed messages differ significantly from architect to architect. Thus ArchiteXt can be regarded as representative of the whole New Wave.

Though Takeyama oscillates between various symbolic modes, his early period is clearly marked by an emphasis on a festive mood—a celebration of human activity related to its created environment. His Ichiban-kan (1969) and Niban-kan (1970) buildings in Shinjuku, one of Tokyo's amusement centers, are exuberant celebrations of pop functions—eating, drinking, gambling, and so on (313, 314). The Hotel Beverly Tom (1973) in Tomakomai and the Pepsi Cola Bottling Plant (1972) in Mikasa are similar in concept but different in symbolic content. The main functions in both are arranged along a cylinder from which one quarter has been removed. The cylindrical tower at the hotel accommodates the guest rooms and opens up to reveal its inner "secrets" to the background of residential areas and hilly, wooded areas. The cylinder's other side permits the building to blend successfully into the industrial facilities of the huge port nearby—silos, cranes, and the like (315, 316). These features make Takeyama's approach here comparable to Maki's Contextualism, especially as seen at the Osaka Prefectural Sports Center (158).

The festive mood of the whole building reaches its climax at the top of the cylinder, which is covered with a huge crystal geodesic-type dome. Conceived in the spirit of Buckminster Fuller, this dome is nothing more than a network of metal bars without any real cover. One metaphor generated by the overall form is what Takeyama describes as a phallic image, intended to symbolize the potential and vitality of this fast-growing industrial town in Hokkaido. The spatial arrangement also seems to promote this, wherein the urban space flows through under the cylinder that is raised on pilotis and at the same time enters and soars up inside the vertical tube, finding fulfillment in the dome from where it radiates toward the sky.

The dome in addition undeniably suggests a planetarium. This is true even in daytime, but it becomes "reality" at night, when the countless lightbulbs mounted at the joints of the structural grid are lit. Now the dome resembles the "starlit sky" even when the actual sky is cloudy. The building's extensive dark metal skin brings other associations to mind as well; it provides, for example, not only an industrial high-tech image but also a surrealist vision, of which perhaps the best other example is Sei'ichi Shirai's Noa Building in Tokyo (247).

The similar use of the cylinder in the Pepsi Cola plant seems less appropriate and arbitrary (317). Form and function are turned into two in-dependent matters. This is a feature common in the architecture of the New Wave, but in most examples it is more successful and convincing than here.

The ArchiteXt and Basara groups have several points of intersection, and this is nowhere else so conspicuous as in the similarity between Rokkaku's House of the Tree Root (1980) and Miyawaki's Blue Box (1971) in Tokyo. Both are built around a group of trees that, of course, symbolize nature. Yet the two houses express two different statements on the man-nature relationship that is so crucial to the Japanese. Miyawaki's building envelops a few tall bamboo trees on a steep hillside, and so living nature penetrates architecture as much as architecture is melted into nature (318, 319). Rokkaku's house, in contrast, seems a reflection on the spirit of nature after its "death." Indeed, in the form of three fourteen-meter tree trunks, only the spirit is enshrined here, as in Ise. The tree is always a living being for the Japanese; even after it is cut its spirit is kept alive in the "material wood" of the house.[32] The trunk of the tree and therefore the wooden pillar has a spiritual quality and mythical power; Amaterasu the Sun Goddess of Japan is enshrined in the form of a tree trunk or Heart pillar.[33] Long trunks and parts of unearthed roots are incorporated into Rokkaku's design for the Root House in two different ways. Two as horizontal beams play a traditional supportive role in the structure, while a third cuts diagonally across the interior space and is presented almost as some religious ceremonial or ritual object. Rokkaku has in this work drawn the parallels among the essences of house, temple, and museum and defined them well (320, 321).

With almost the same understanding, Monta Mozuna then practically turned the small Ainu Ethnic Museum (1982) in Hokkaido into a mysterious place of worship that simultaneously recalls the ancient earth-mound houses of this rapidly shrinking ethnic group. The seven freestanding

311–312. Takeyama's own studio, Atelier Indigo, features a "kinetic space toy" or "space synthesizer" on its rooftop (Sapporo, 1976, M. Takeyama).

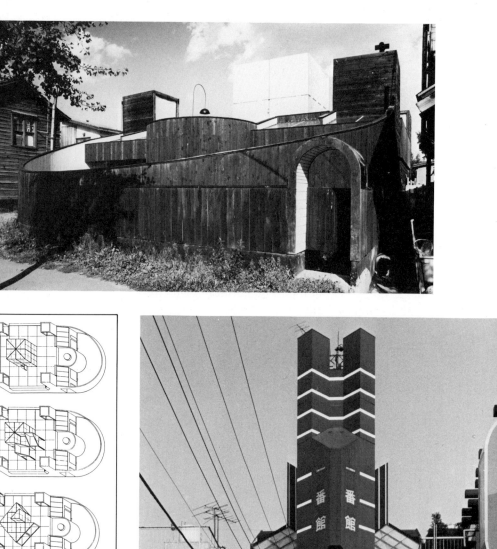

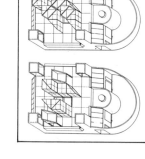

313–314. With their unorthodox geometrical forms, colorful super-graphics, and signboards, the Ichiban-kan and Niban-kan buildings in Tokyo are among the first representatives of pop architecture in Japan.

313. Ichiban-kan (1969, M. Takeyama).

314. Niban-kan (1970, M. Takeyama).

315–316. The Hotel Beverly Tom has been designed so that it fits into its industrial as well as residential environment, in addition to suggesting some unexpected metaphors (Tomakomai, 1973, M. Takeyama).

concrete columns in front of the building and the thirty-one wooden obelisks inside symbolize trees and by extension a forest, the historical place of Ainu homes. The whole ensemble, as Mozuna writes, "is redolent of the mystery and superstition of the old Ainu religion and suits the needs of a space in which to exhibit remnants of a dying way of life."[34] In this sense the Ainu museum can eventually and sadly become a mortuary chapel in which a whole culture lies in state (322).

The House as Religious Retreat

The interpretation of the house as a religious place and museum has never been foreign to the Japanese. Traditionally and in the present day, most homes have some Buddhist (*butsudan*) and Shinto (*kamidana*) altars dedicated to the family Buddha, house gods, or the spirits of the ancestors. Festivals are plentiful in Japan. Very often, as on the eve of the annual Gion Festival in Kyoto, they are accompanied by ceremonies in the home during which the household's most distinguished heirlooms are put on display, usually for the family and guests, but sometimes for public as well. In other words,

though the Japanese are not really dogmatic believers, the rituals that structure their lives and domestic environments are extremely numerous and complex; Chris Fawcett discusses these at length in *The New Japanese House.*[35] By understanding and intuitively or willfully relying on these aspects of the Japanese mentality, many architects in the New Wave have produced a large number of buildings that appear to be some religious sanctuary or place shaped intensively by cosmic forces. Besides Rokkaku's works, those of Hiroshi Hara (b. 1937), Shin Takamatsu (b. 1948), Toyokazu Watanabe (b. 1938), and Monta Mozuna (b. 1941) should be mentioned as good examples. Behind the intentions of these architects, nevertheless, very often lie also the dilemma and frustration of modern man who, in reaction to the increasing disorder of the external world of contemporary life, is trying to find some internal autonomous order to live in, but in so doing inevitably faces isolation and loses the common ground in which meaning is ultimately rooted. In the face of this dilemma, the playful and happy world of the child turns into the serious or, in Fawcett's word, the "tragic" environment

317. Form and function are independent matters in the case of the Pepsi-Cola Bottling Plant (Mikasa, 1972, M. Takeyama).

318–321. Two small residential buildings incorporate and celebrate a group of trees in two different ways.

318. The simple geometric forms of the Blue Box envelop a few bamboo trees (Tokyo, 1971, M. Miyawaki).

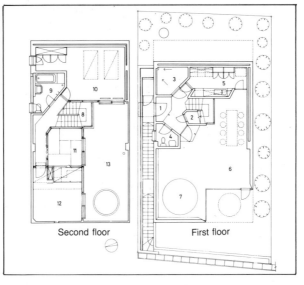

Second floor   First floor

319. Floor plans.
1. Anteroom. 2. Storage.
3. Mechanical room.
4. Lavatory. 5. Kitchen.
6. Living room.
7. Conversation pit.
8. Stairway. 9. Bathroom.
10. Bedroom. 11. *Tatami* room. 12. Child's room.
13. Terrace.

320–321. In the House of the Tree Root three large tree trunks organize and give meaning to the design. 1. Bedroom. 2. Children's room. 3. Roof. (Numata, 1980, K. Rokkaku; photograph courtesy of Kijo Rokkaku).

in which the adult seeks desperately for a fixed point, a justification of his own existence. "The tragic is an elliptical route through the existences and events occuring without relationship to oneself, but whose route forges a link, however artificial."[36]

The intense attempt to establish stability and order with architectural spaces reaches one of its extremes in the tiny private houses of Hara and Mozuna. "The dwelling should possess a nucleus capable of generating a high degree of order in opposition to the external disorder," writes Hara, and in order to attain this condition, his recent buildings, the so-called Reflection Houses, are meticulously symmetrical in design.[37] The ordinary and, as in the Kuragaki House (1977), somewhat shabby and dark clapboard wooden exteriors correspond not only with that of the similar *kura* or storehouse in Japanese vernacular architecture, but also with the cramped external environment; yet they conceal rich and solemn white interiors, where one is inclined to whisper (323, 324). The entranceway is usually very narrow and leads to a central space or, rather, a flow of central spaces, around which the rest of the house is organized. In the Awazu House (1972), his own Hara House (1974), and the Kuragaki House, these spaces are lit through skylights, long and narrow vaulted glass surfaces (325).

Spaces undulate, pulsate, and overlap both horizontally and vertically along the spatial flow. Their strongly symbolic yet ambiguous quality permits multiple readings. They recall carefully carved out caves, suggesting Hara's method of working "from outside in" (326, 327); indeed, Hara has such a strong concern for holes in architecture that he has declared that "the basic nature of architecture is in its holes," and he has even designed a City of Holes.[38] On the other hand, his highly sculptured interiors also appear as the "ordered exterior," as if the house itself were turned outside in. Hara buries the city within the house; thus the central space, so to speak, takes on the character of a city

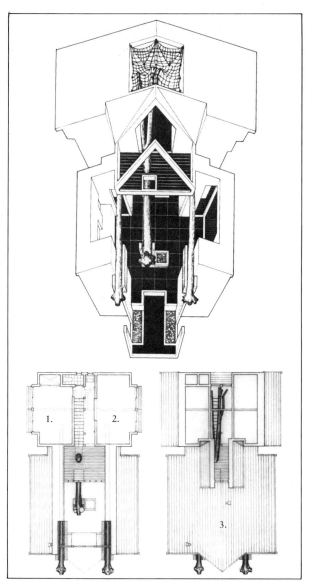

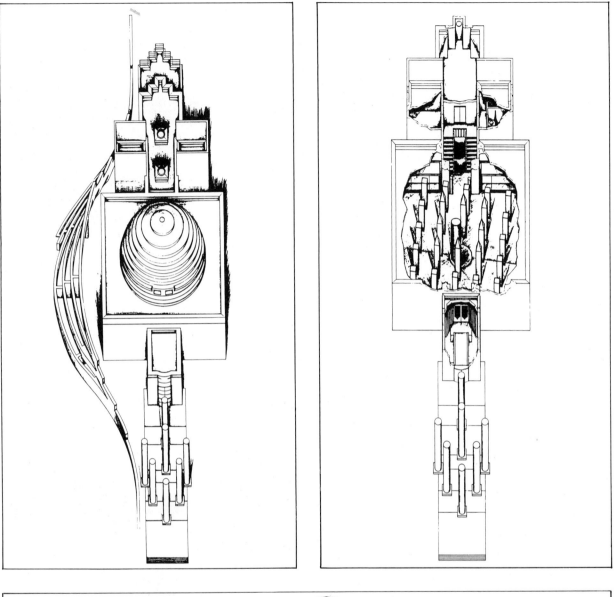

APPROACH

EXHIBITION HALL

OFFICE

STORAGE

322. The Ainu Ethnic Museum "is redolent of the mystery and superstition of the old Ainu religion" and commemorates a dying way of life (Hokkaido, 1982, M. Mozuna).

323–324. The ordinary exterior of the Kuragaki House conceals a highly ordered central interior space that plays the role of a miniature urban plaza (Tokyo, 1977, H. Hara).

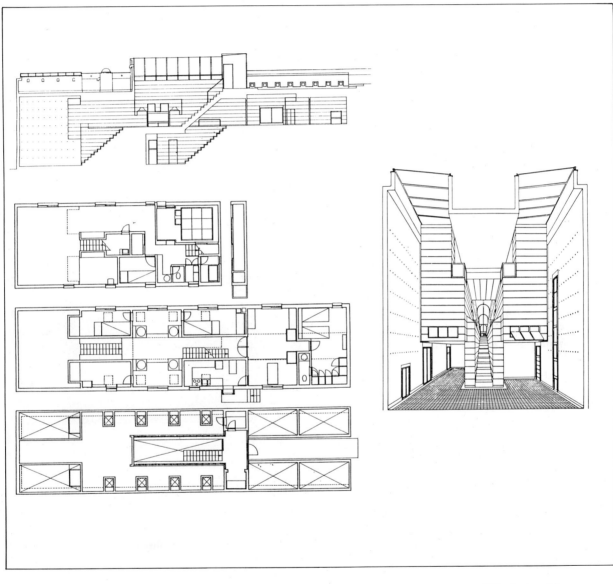

325. Awazu House
(Kawasaki, 1972,
H. Hara). The solemn
spaces in Hara's
symmetrical "Reflection
Houses" are usually lit
through glass vaulted
skylights.

center. The chain of narrow passages, "endless" stairways, the fragmented and elusive spaces with curving, shiny surfaces become a kind of processional path for pilgrimage, transforming one into a participant in a relentless, almost religious ritual, the "eternal return" (328–330).

The small houses of Yuzuru Tominaga (b. 1943) resemble Hara's designs in some respects. The most important is the ritualistic mode in which much of the interior in each of these houses is put together. The undulating white and shiny surfaces, however, are complemented by elements that characterize Shinohara's architecture as well. Columns with diagonal braces crowd the essentially void spaces of the House for a Newlywed Couple (1979) in Odawara and his own Tominaga residence (1983) in Kawasaki. But, as in the buildings by Shinohara, Hasegawa, and Sakamoto, the blank expression is most evident in the outer appearance, in the facades of these buildings. Tominaga obviously combines two opposite interpretations of architecture but holds both the overly ritual and the overly absurd at bay by playing them against each other (331, 332, 474–476).

A similar duality characterizes the architecture of Toyokazu Watanabe (b. 1938) and Shin Takamatsu (b. 1946). A deliberate disparity between exterior and interior and between forms and function is also evident in several of their works. Watanabe's Nakauchi House (1975) in Nara, like many Hara houses or Kijima's Koike House in Tokyo, takes the form of the traditional Japanese storehouse, the *kura*, but inside turns out to be a tiny Western "chapel." The six-column, basilica-type second-story "sanctuary," however, remains inaccessible even after the long journey of purification (or apotheosis) through the house; this space can be looked at, but, as with the innermost sanctuaries of Shinto shrines, cannot be entered (333, 334). The order is almost reversed in Takamatsu's Hinaya Office Building (1981) in Kyoto. The front of the building creates the strong sense of a religious center

326.

for some new Buddhist sect. But after passing the strange facelike facade and going through the huge ceremonial gate and into the multistory entrance hall, the effect inside is less dramatic, though surely unusual for the premises of a wholesale kimono dealer (292). The undoubtedly strong affinity with Sei'ichi Shirai's bizarre architecture continues in Takamatsu's designs for a small tea parlor, the Ponto-cho Ochaya (1982) in Kyoto. It also extends to private houses, inasmuch as the interiors of the otherwise toylike House at Shugakuin (1981), the House at Shimogamo (1982) in Kyoto, and the Takahashi Residence (1983) in Osaka resemble the unearthly places of some demonic cult or, perhaps, mortuary chapels (335–337).

Yet the most unreal buildings by Takamatsu

326–327. Entrance and dining hall of the Akita House (Tokyo, 1977, H. Hara). Hara usually starts the spatial flow in his houses with narrow entranceways and continues through a sequence of spaces that resemble carved-out caves.

327.

so far are unquestionably the two dental offices called "Ark" (1983) and "Pharaoh" (1984), both of which are also the dentist's residences in Kyoto. Here the mysticism of religion gives way to the mysticism of the machine "a kind of mechanical darkness or industrial despair," as Fawcett described the clinics.[39] With these buildings, made of unfinished concrete and steel elements, Takamatsu comments on the matter of death rather than affirms existence. This is reflected in the too readily suggestive gas-chamber or incinerator forms of Pharaoh, while the huge horizontal cylindrical third floor and ten tower- or, perhaps, lanternlike skylights of Ark suggest a strange robot or a derailed monstrous steam locomotive that has just overrun the owner and his residence. Takamatsu's expla-

nation (pretext?) for the absurdity of the Ark building is its location adjacent to a private railway station (338–340).

COSMIC ARCHITECTURE

It is Mozuna, however, who most consistently frees himself from earthly things and the events of everyday life, and who shifts the scope of his activity into the sphere of the "skies." In his strongly symbolic and often equally absurd architecture everything happens according to his idiosyncratic cosmology, his interpretation of the eternal interplay between various opposing cosmic forces, and not as the result of some mundane and rational considerations. The shapes of these buildings are explained by Mozuna solely in terms of the ancient

328–330. The
longitudinal entrance
hall—along continuous
flights of stairs—and
the living room in his
own Hara House best
represent the sanctuary-
like central spaces
in Hara's designs
(Machida City, Tokyo
Pref., 1974, H. Hara).

330. Plans and elevations.

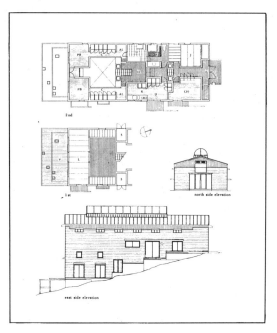

331–332. House for a Newlywed Couple (Odawara, 1979, Y. Tominaga). Tominaga combines the qualities of both Hara's and Shinohara's architecture.

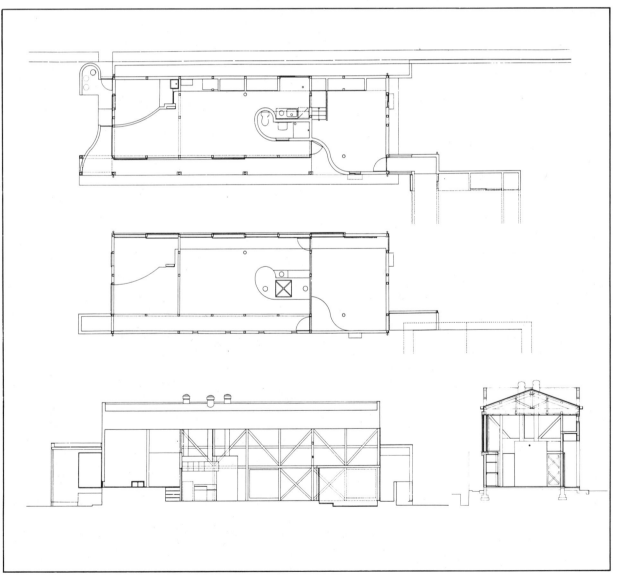

Oriental philosophies and myths, including Tantric mysticism, which is a highly ritualized esoteric Buddhism, and mandalas, the mythic diagrams of the cosmos. The House with Architecturalized Yin-Yang Symbols (1975) in Kushiro embodies the fundamental Chinese concept of two conflicting elements, Yin and Yang, present in all that exists; they "interact with and control each other, thus enabling existence."[40] Accordingly, every detail in the house corresponds to one of the two elements either in harmony or even more in conflict with the other, resulting in several visual ambiguities. The east front is an example: it seems as if another section of the house had been demolished and the interior inner facade acts as exterior; or, put another way, as if this elevation were turned inside out (341, 342).

Architecture based on cosmic beliefs or images is by no means new. Through the ages in all different cultures architecture followed some kind of perceived heavenly order that guided many important earthly aspects: location, orientation, form, the spatial organization of buildings and even of cities; it is called geomancy. Thus structures and the man-made world were mirror images of a particular cosmic order. The eighteenth-century Enlightenment in the West and the subsequent development of science, technology, and the rational modern mind, however, all served to dismiss these archaic and "superstitious" aspects of architecture. The mythical determinations of heaven have been replaced in the Western World by the rational laws and control of the Machine.

Geomancy in Japan, which evolved through Chinese influence, is called *kaso*. It is a very complex system, the elements of which are derived from religious beliefs, compass points, zodiac signs, Yin-Yang considerations, topographic conditions, climatic characteristics, and so on. Its influence has diminished significantly, but it is surprising how often this nonrational theory still plays a strong, and influential role in design. At the owner's request,

Rokkaku designed the Ishiguro House (1970) completely in accordance with *kaso*. Thus everything in the house—the top-lit central concrete dome, the entrances, windows, the configuration of the rooms—correspond to cosmic constellations (343). But despite all the restrictions (perhaps even because of them) Rokkaku has managed to create a real home for everyday life. This capacity of his appears to be the major difference between Rokkaku and Mozuna.

Mozuna remains aloof from the rituals and requirements of daily activity. For example, he designed his first house as an Anti-dwelling Box (1971). His architecture is a strong protest against the so-called rational modern mind and thus against modern architecture. Indeed, nothing is further from Mozuna than the simplistic functionalist reasoning of the late Modern Movement, and he never misses an opportunity to mock and laugh about it. Every element in his designs gains its meaning from outside, from above, as it were, having some supreme reason, a cosmic dimension. His architecture, which may be called cosmological, is the small-scale embodiment of celestial rules, the laws of heaven,

333.

334.

333–334. In the
Nakauchi House, the
ordinary exterior covers
an extraordinary interior
with an explicit quality of
the sacred (Nara, 1975,
T. Watanabe).

335–340. Most of Shin Takamatsu's small buildings are designed to resemble some bizarre "religious" place.

335.

336.

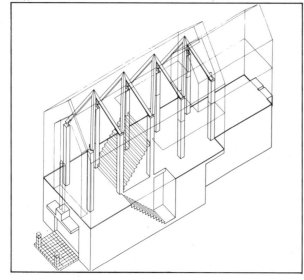

337. The Takahashi Residence is called the "Lost Tower" (Osaka, 1983).

335–336. House at Shimogamo (Kyoto, 1982).

338–339. Ark: Nishina Dental Clinic (Kyoto, 1983).

338.

339.

340. "Pharaoh" Dental Office (Kyoto, 1984).

341–342. The ancient Chinese philosophy of opposing cosmic forces constitutes the basic idea of the House with Architecturalized Yin-Yang Symbols (Kushiro, 1975, M. Mozuna; photograph courtesy of Monta Mozuna).

342. Floor plans.
1. Storage. 2. Utility.
3. Bedroom. 4. Entrance.
5. Kitchen. 6. Living and dining. 7. Boiler.

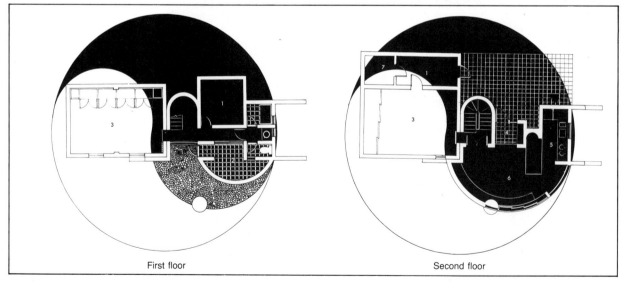

First floor

Second floor

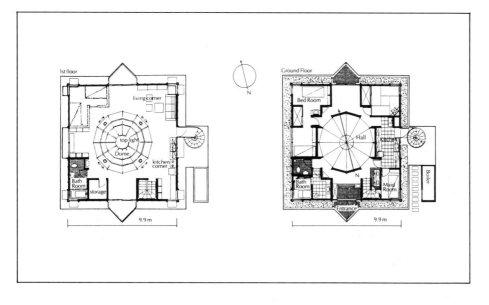

343. Rokkaku designed the Ishiguro House according to the ancient principles of geomancy, the *kaso* (Tokyo, 1970, K. Rokkaku).

terrestrial forces, and the like, that he wishes (or pretends) to believe govern our awareness. The Constellation House (1976) in Wakayama is a case in point. It was designed to resemble a star formation, and so the layout of its seven columns follows the configuration of the Big Bear. Mozuna also calls this building "The Celestial Aspect" in his architectural cosmos. It contains Yin and Yang volumes as well (344, 345). To complete his trinity, two other works: a meeting hall on Mt. Koya (1976) and the Terada House in Kyoto (1977) represent "The Terrestrial Aspect" and "The Human Aspect."

Mozuna's "outlook on the universe" continues in his other buildings as well. The Eisho-ji Zen Temple (1979) in Tokyo is actually a double symbol. It is a miniature, 1 : 100 scale, symbolic representation of the processional path of the famous Zen temple in Kyoto, the Myoshin-ji. Consistent with the Taizokai mandala, Myoshin-ji features the system of signs and symbols that organizes architectural and natural scenery into a chain of phenomena called "ten limits" or *jukkyo,* and Mozuna's design incorporates these Zen symbolic elements in condensed form. The sequence of experiences along the path to the temple, which is tightly squeezed between ordinary residential buildings, starts with the first gate (*somon*) at the street. The unfinished-concrete frame, which is said to resemble both an old *torii* gate and a Greco-Roman gate, is broken; with the two halves failing to reach each other, it looks as if Mother Earth's forces had some strong impact. This suggestion is furthered by the "ruined" colonnade lining the path (*sando*), which is a remote

reference to the remains of the Forum Romanum (346).

The series of unexpected events and the blending of Occidental and Oriental architectural symbols continue inside the building too, where the main idol (*honzon*), a statue of Buddha, is enshrined within an additional aedicule and between two mirrors on facing walls. The aedicule with its "magic square" plan is a building within the building. It has its own pyramidal roof over a sliced and stepped dome, supported by four gigantic cylindrical columns. To reach the altar on its high podium, it is necessary to climb a wide, circular stairway that starts from the symbolic "garden of the void" represented by the lower level of the main hall. The inclusive interpenetrating, and opposing forms all around refer again to the Yin-Yang philosophy. The mystical quality of the space is ultimately the result of the intricate natural and artificial light effects that, together with the numerous optical illusions, give everything inside a metaphysical dimension (347).

The inclusion of one building within another continues in Takamatsu's Saifuku-ji (1982) in Gifu—coincidentally another subsidiary temple of the Myoshin-ji headquarters of the Rinzai Zen sect in Kyoto—and contributes to a similarly strong mystic quality of the interior. The simple gable-roofed exterior concrete shell enveloped the longitudinal space of the main hall and the sanctuary, a space emphasized by the massive truss structure of a dark wooden roof work. This additional roof is supported by six pairs of independent columns and has curvilinear profiles like the roof, over tra-

344–345. The Constellation House has been laid out according to the star configuration of the Big Bear, represented by the arrangement of the house's seven columns (Wakayama, 1976, M. Mozuna).

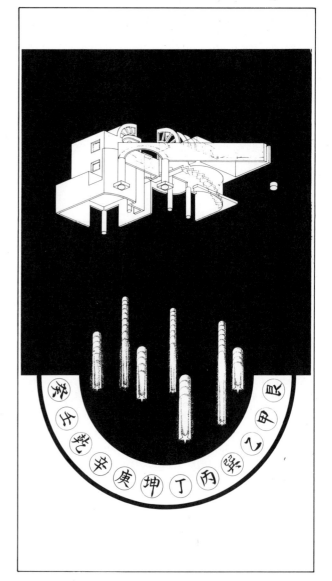

ditional Buddhist temples. Yet the explicitly morbid quality that characterizes many of Takamatsu's designs is not absent here. With its countless overhead ribs, the interior makes one feel buried alive or as if one had been swallowed up by Moby Dick (348). Both Mozuna's Eisho-ji and Takamatsu's Saifuku-ji easily recall Kijima's Matsuo Shrine in Kumamoto, with its juxtaposition of two different buildings side by side (285), but in these temples the two buildings are contained in one structure as if telescoped into each other.

Similarly, the idea of box-in-box forms the bases of Watanabe's design for a "Haunted House" (1982) in Nara City. Like the artist owner of this house, Watanabe believes the Shinto teaching that one shares one's home with the spirits of ancestors and even their animals. Accordingly, the interior of the "Haunted House" has been shaped as a sequence of inclusive and layered attics that evoke the eerie image of a grotto (349, 350).

The "cosmic horizon" is often extended into the realm of larger public buildings as well. In this respect, Team Zoo, a group of young architects—graduates of Waseda University in Tokyo and influenced by their famous mentor Takamasa Yoshizaka—has done pioneer work.[41] Their early buildings, most of them small houses, were designed according to biological or, as the name of the group indicates, zoological analogies. The Domo Celakanto (1975), for example, was built as a "living organism" of mysterious, monstrous fish of the sea (351). In more recent works, cosmic forces play more important roles than the biological ones. These buildings include such projects as kin-

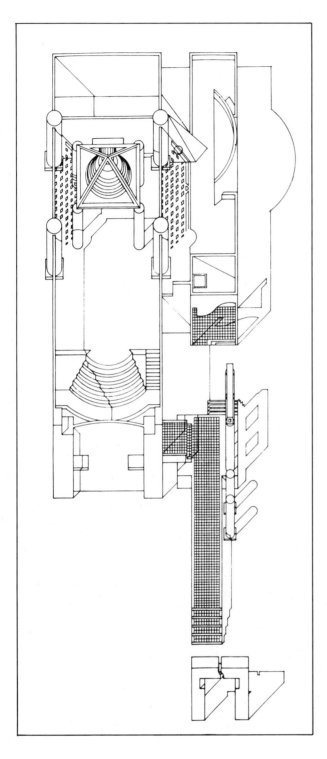

346. The Eisho-ji Zen Temple is a symbolic recollection of the procession path of the famous Myoshin-ji temple in Kyoto, but with Western architectural references (Tokyo, 1979, M. Mozuna).

dergartens, schools, and municipal civic centers. Representative of the shift in the direction of Team Zoo is the Miyashiro Municipal Center (1983). It is laid out in a concentric pattern to create what can be called mythical landscapes of ruined, archaic cultures (352–355). Unlike many works of Takamatsu and Mozuna, the buildings of Team Zoo manage that with and within them architectural forms and the lives of people mutually enhance each other.

In extending architecture into the sphere of metaphysics or, as Mozuna says, "creating the myth of architecture," he relies primarily on two principles: "architecture in architecture" and "twin architecture," which Mozuna defines as "the architecture of realization in which the phenomena of inside and outside, front and back, and (topologically) right and left, are dependent on optical illusion."[42] This is one reason behind many of his "mirror" symmetrical projects, including the Kushiro City Museum (1984) in Hokkaido and, most especially, the Mirror Image Hall (1980), a small private house in Niiza City near Tokyo. The house itself is not symmetrical at all; symmetry is created, as the name implies, through a mirror image of the interior. The house is somewhat awkward outside, an unfinished concrete box that seals the inner "cosmos" from the outer one. The entrance hall contains a surprising gigantic wooden stairway that occupies the total width of the house. It connects the first floor with the second but seems to seek beyond, toward the sky and stars. This unusual stairway alone could well be the main theme of the house, but it is doubled in the huge mirror that covers the entire two-story opposite wall. Shinto mythology regards mirrors as windows to the world of *kami;* thus they were often objects of worship and placed in shrines. Mozuna also believes that "the image of the mirror is the key to the secrets of the cosmos."[43]

Charles Jencks pointed out another possible influence on this house; the huge, long flights of stone stairs found in historical India's astronomical observatories.[44] Stairways have always had special significance in Japanese traditions as well. The long approaches to Shinto shrines and Buddhist monasteries in their remote mountain locations sometimes feature almost endless stairways; climbing them is part of the pilgrim's religious purification process. Whoever has once climbed the continuous flights of stone steps leading to the Kotohira-gu shrine, which spans a total elevation difference of 185 meters, can attest to the endurance involved.[45] There is in this a good explanation for the preoccupation of so many Japanese architects with stairs, among them Isozaki, Hara, Aida, Ando, and others. Both Indian and Japanese mythologies are incorporated in Mozuna's Mirror Image Hall to create the extraordinary interior. The effect is based on illusion. Yin and Yang in the carefully designed positive and negative stairstepped forms both contrast and complement each other. Reality and illusion overlap and are further mixed by the "unnoticed" glimpse of the outer world through the narrow, sensually curving, window slot vertically cut through the middle of the mirror, enhancing the ambiguous quality of this tiny space (356, 357).

The other principle in Mozuna's metaphysical world, "architecture in architecture," is best represented in his first notable work, the Anti-dwelling Box (1971) in Kushiro. Wrapped in some black humor, its design is a strong challenge to any idea of bourgeois comfort. The house, which really looks like a botched piece of junk, is a single box, a "transparent" cube that enshrines two similar, smaller cubes within each other in succession. The middle box, a multipurpose room, practically floats in the space of the bigger one, while the smaller is actually a piece of furniture that rolls on casters within this room. The arrangement pushes Hiromi Fujii's concept of box-within-a-box and the traditional Japanese idea of space layering to the extreme. Mozuna describes the smallest one as "the skin reaction box," the middle one as "the body response box," and the biggest one as "the environmental code box"; he also describes them as the "architecture of the parent and child."[46] And indeed, it is possible to see this inclusive series of boxes so that the outer one corresponds to the skin as the periphery of the body, and the second box can be seen as the womb pregnant with the fetus—the third box—of its own race. Mozuna is highly interested in the cosmic aspects of birth—the Birth of the Cosmos, Mother Earth, the "Universal Ovum"—a concept he calls *Uchu-an* or "cosmic hermitage." Yet the successive boxes of the Antidwelling House can also exemplify the notion of his "twin architecture," since one perceives the inside together with the outside, the front together with the back, and so on. The tenant, Mozuna's mother, lives in this hermetic world, inside and among the boxes (358, 359).

THE GEOMETRY OF DEFENSIVE ARCHITECTURE

One of the most conspicuous features of the New Wave is the recurrence of a hard-surfaced geometry. This appears in the use of the simplest Platonic solids: the cube, cylinder, trilateral prism, and their projections, the orthogonal grid or trabeated pergola, and so on. This can be seen in many recent works but for some conceptual architects it becomes a matter of almost exclusive reliance; among these are Hiromi Fujii, Tadao Ando, Takefumi Aida, Mayumi Miyawaki, and Kazuo Shinohara, who represent another extreme approach to existential issues. Their vocabulary is thus reminiscent of some aspects of the earlier Modern architecture. Indeed, the consistent use of unfinished concrete structural elements is associated so much with Le Corbusier, Neobrutalist, and even Metabolist architecture that its reappearance could easily be misleading. Though there certainly does exist a preference for simplistic forms, these forms cover, sometimes quite literally, a radically different approach to the meaning of architecture, to the quality of spaces, or rather, to the "spirit of places," and thus also to the quality

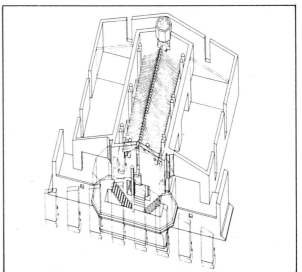

347. The extraordinary design of the Eisho-ji Zen Temple sanctuary also represents the idea of "building in building" or "architecture in architecture." (Photograph courtesy of Monta Mozuna.)

348. The Saifuku-ji Zen temple has a small Buddhist sanctuary within a simple concrete shell (Gifu, 1982, S. Takamatsu).

of human experience. Geometry serves as a deliberate tool to reestablish the *genius loci* within their structures, mainly small houses. This process coincides with a strong intention of redefining human existence. Beyond their purposes, their manner of execution is what distinguishes these architects from the rest of the New Wave.

Most of these buildings project a defensive character; like bunkers or bombshelters, they turn their backs to everything around them. In such extremes there is little if any communication between the inside spaces and the outside world. The architect hermetically seals off the inhabitant from the disturbing external environment in order to provide the conditions for moments of "silence," as Aida says, in which the individual can recreate himself physically and spiritually.[47] There is no doubt that the emphasis is on the "inner world" behind the hard shells, a "hermetic microcosm" concealed within the buildings. Tadao Ando's Row House at Sumiyoshi (1976) and Town House at Kujo (1982) are extreme examples of this trend. The rough concrete box of the Row House has one simply cutout opening, the entrance, as the only link to the urban environment. Yet inside,

these two tiny houses by Ando feature multistory courtyards with open-air stairways and walkways as small bridges (360–364). Then, carrying the notion of "silence" even further, comes Aida's PL Institute Kindergarten (1973) in Tondabayashi. It is in the form of an ancient Imperial burial mound; the building is a flat reinforced concrete pyramid that "disappears" under the earth and grass that cover it. Architecture itself here has vanished, becoming but a formation of nature. The unusual exterior covers an interior more appropriate to the affairs of children; it is organized around a central courtyard and playground (365).

The disparity between exterior and interior started with Isozaki's early Metabolist-Mannerist works of the mid-1960s—the Oita Prefectural Library, the Oita Medical Hall, and so on—and continued as defensive architecture within the activities of ArchiteXt. "We are now in a season," wrote Miyawaki, "in which we must do all we can to protect from outside."[48] In an age when the manmade urban environment is increasingly confronting its citizens with congestion, traffic, noise, and pollution, it is the duty of the architect to provide protection. Consequently, the "primary

349.

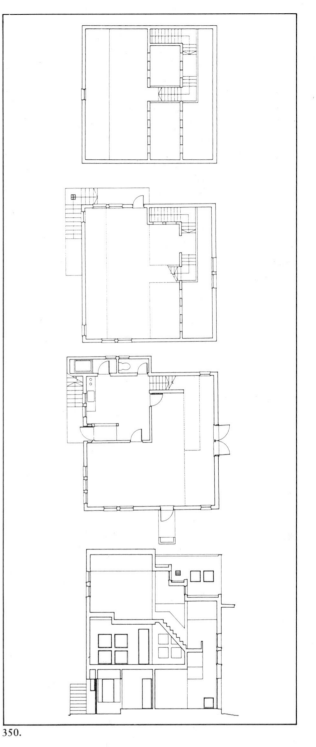

350.

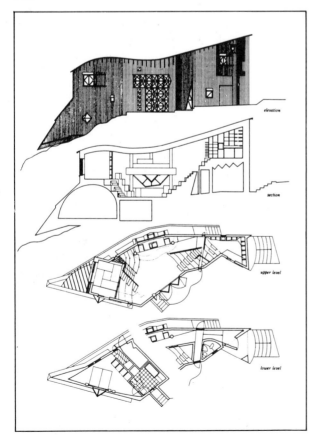

349–350. With the idea
of box-in-a-box,
Watanabe designed a
Haunted House (Nara,
1982, T. Watanabe).

351. The Domo Cela-
kanto takes the shape of
a large fish (1975, Atelier
Zo).

352–355. The Miyashiro Municipal Center recalls mythical landscapes of "ruined ancient worlds" (1983, Atelier Zo).

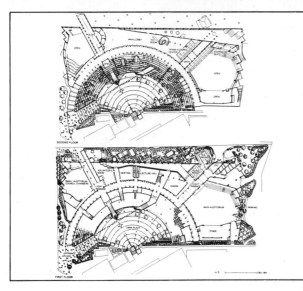

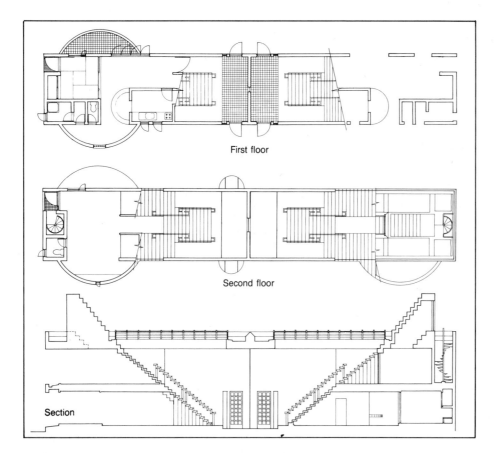

First floor

Second floor

Section

356–357. A huge, overblown wooden stairway and a continuously stepped concrete skylight are reflected in the two-story mirror wall, creating an optical illusion and a quality of cosmic dimension within the Mirror Image Hall, a small private residence near Tokyo (Niiza, 1980, M. Mozuna).

358. The house of the Anti-dwelling Box (Kushiro, 1971, M. Mozuna). The cosmic aspects of what Mozuna calls "Universal Birth" are represented by a series of similar cubic enclosures concealed within one another. (Photograph courtesy of Monta Mozuna.)

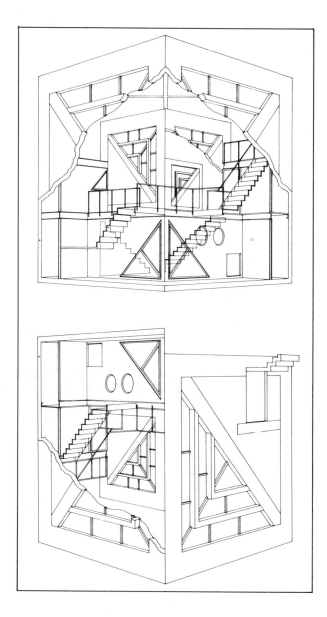

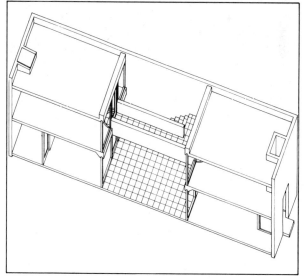

359. Axonometric drawing and plans for the Anti-dwelling Box.

360–364. With only one simple opening toward their urban environment and organized entirely around tiny inner courtyards, many of Ando's small private residences have become hermetic microcosms and new versions of old row houses.

360–361. Row House at Sumiyoshi (Osaka, 1976, T. Ando).

362–364. Town House at
Kujo (Osaka, 1982,
T. Ando).

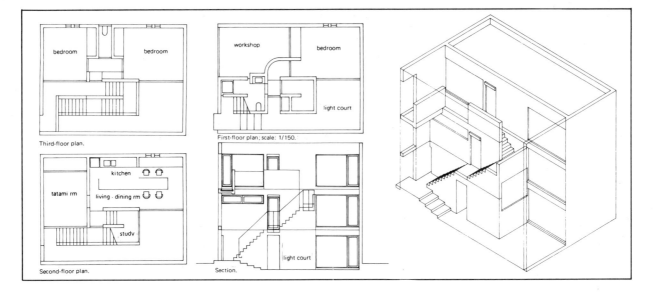

bedroom   bedroom

Third-floor plan.

workshop   bedroom

light court

First-floor plan; scale: 1/150.

kitchen

tatami rm   living · dining rm

study

Second-floor plan.

light court

Section.

365. Aida's "architecture of silence" reaches its epitome in the PL Institute Kindergarten, where the building disappears under the covering earth, as under an ancient burial mound (Tondabayashi, 1973, T. Aida).

architecture" of Mayumi Miyawaki (b. 1936) is characterized by hard exteriors and soft interiors, where solid concrete boxes of a simple geometric form and primary color enclose surprisingly pleasant interiors rich in both form and color. Openings in the defensive shell, which have special significance for Miyawaki, are kept to a minimum. They either highlight a particular event or are the events themselves, as can best be seen in the Blue Box and the Green Box No. 2. In addition, the openings mark the beginning of a festive atmosphere inside (318). The Morioka (1970) and Honjo (1973) branches of the Akita Sogo Bank are excellent examples of the latter. The Honjo bank is cut open by a skylight and a huge entranceway that continues as an inside promenade or a strangely shaped tunnel through the whole building and appears in both its front and back. But upon entering this "tunnel" one is welcomed by a warm and friendly small inner world. As opposed to the cold and dark purple of the exterior, everything inside is light: pale yellow, ochre, cream, and white. The steel structural skeleton, recalling a series of superimposed Shinto *torii* gates, similar to the ones at the Fushimi-Inari Shrine in Kyoto, is painted red (366–368).

Miyawaki's primary geometry is expressed in two ways. In several of his earlier buildings geometric forms penetrate the exterior surface more extensively than in his later ones, and the intricate manipulation of the primary forms contributes significantly to the rich quality of the interior spaces. In the Futatsui Branch Office (1971) of the Akita Sogo Bank, two concrete boxes—the exterior one containing a diagonally inserted smaller one—provide the basis for the impressive spatial experience. Thus certain of Miyawaki's solutions with innovative geometry, like the idea of box-in-box here, come close to the works of Isozaki, Fujii, or Ando; but with these architects the application of geometry gains deeper, more metaphysical meanings (369). Another expression of Miyawaki's sensitive use of geometric forms is also found in his best works. In these, he quietly celebrates episodes of everyday life. Through architecture, he tends toward an affirmation of human existence. This aspect of celebration he shares with Takeyama and Azuma.

Miyawaki's architectural philosophy of, what he calls, "parallel opposites" has developed over the years so that the interiors of his boxes are increasingly more radically distinct from the exteriors.[49] The differences are expressed not only in material, color, surface texture, shape of the installations, and so on, but also in structural solution. The latest houses, including the impressive Matsukawa Box No. 2 (1978) and Yoshimi Box (1979), contain independent wooden structural systems and wooden finish within the unfinished concrete shells. This polarization of inside and out, however, increases the danger of producing primarily ordinary, or simply convenient and less inspiring interior spaces wrapped in abstract geometric forms. And in fact, this has gradually become a serious temptation for Miyawaki.

Continuing the line of a defensive architecture, some designs by Ishii, Toki, and especially Kunihiko Hayakawa (b. 1941) provide additional variations on the positive use of geometry. Ishii's House with

366. The simple concrete box of the Akita Sogo Bank Morioka Branch Office Building, with only one opening to the outside, turns its back on the urban environment (Morioka, 1970, M. Miyawaki).

367–368. Akita Sogo Bank Honjo Branch Office Building (Honjo, 1974, M. Miyawaki). While the exteriors in Miyawaki's "primary architecture" are hard, providing very little communication with the outside world, the interiors are cozy, accommodating, and rich in form and color.

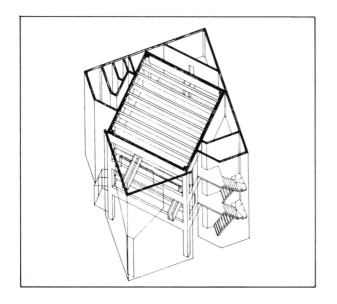

369. Axonometric drawing of the Akita Sogo Bank Futatsui Branch Office Building (1971, M. Miyawaki). Miyawaki's geometric operations with primary forms enable him to create spatial complexity.

54 Windows (1975) is based on a series of perforated cubes and the Takahashi House (1977) on a series of orthogonal frames of vierendeel trusses. In the latter, the structural geometry generates a street facade "on exhibit," highlighting the process of entry into the building (307). Almost the same description applies to Toki's own house. The difference here is that the concrete geometric frame in front neither penetrates the primary box of the building behind nor plays any structural role. It acts only as a screen. Thus Toki's application of geometry results in a House with an Independent Facade (1978) (370).

Perhaps the most successful application of a "defensive geometry" is represented by Hayakawa's architecture. Two of his recent houses in Tokyo, the House at a Bus stop (1982) and the House in Seijo (1983), respond to the hazards of the city by filtering and reducing the traffic noise of the busy streets in front through layering the elevations in an intricate way. This is done so that the punctured structural concrete wall planes and the carefully lit spaces in between provide a gradual transition between outside and inside and signify also the ritual of entry into these houses. Hayakawa notes that "exterior walls which enclose interior spaces also function as the interior walls of urban spaces . . . . This dual nature of building walls is one of the primary characteristics of architecture in an urban context."[50] In these works, Hayakawa is able to combine the best of Miyawaki and Maki, and even Ando (371–375). Yet another interpretation of structural geometry appears in Ando's "minimalist" architecture, while the use of surfaces

and facades is also present in Toyo Ito's "superficial, collage" architecture.[51]

DECONSTRUCTIVE GEOMETRY AND "QUINTESSENTIAL ARCHITECTURE"

Not all the solid concrete boxes of defensive architecture conceal such "cozy" and, so to speak, popular spaces as in the designs of Miyawaki and many others. More radical architects see this as architecture that protects its inhabitants physically but offers an inner environment of stereotypes that arouse only a range of automatic responses: routine perceptions and habitual associations and thought leading to usual and uniform self-awareness. They believe that architecture should enter the awareness of the user and create new existential conditions through "new relations between the space and the person," as Ando says.[52]

How are these new relations, the renewal of the self, brought about? The Japanense Conceptualists answer this question by their intention to efface old, conventional, everyday meanings and to generate new ones. Following Isozaki's lead, they turn to the overall application of Cartesian geometry, with an emphasis on the orthogonal grid. In brief, geometric operations generally play an important role within the New Wave, but with the Conceptualists they have a particularly special purpose. "Geometry . . . does not commit itself to reality," writes Hiromi Fujii (b. 1935).[53] And, indeed, he assigns to it "the ultimate goal of stripping architecture of its mundane functions . . . [of] transforming the world, that is, . . . [of] re-introducing the *primordial condition of man*" (italics added).[54] The simple and small concrete boxes within Fujii's most extreme and provocative architecture appear to have been penetrated by a three-dimensional infinite orthogonal grid that results in a network of squares on every possible surface inside and out, including installations and furniture. This network is not only an underlying modular system controlling the design but also a clipped-on "applique." The Miyajima Residence (1973) in Tokyo is a case in point. Its solid, windowless walls feature aluminum-joint grids applied all around the exterior, and square plywood panels of the same size on the interior, with similar patterns on the ceilings, floors, doors, and so on (376, 377).

With the overwhelming geometric grid Fujii aims at suspending architectural form and the meanings automatically associated with it. "He presents us with an objective denial of any representation," as Chris Fawcett wrote.[55] The absence of meanings is in turn meant to induce a purely existential relationship between subject and object, approaching a state devoid of dichotomy. As he correctly explains, meaning is not the inherent quality of the object but the product of its changing and multifarious relations with the subject, the person. The nonperceiving subject with its suspended intellect thus is prompted to become more intensively involved in establishing new existential meanings intuitively, whereby the subject is dissolved or alternatively is able to recreate its own self but only temporarily (378).

Fujii's frigidly abstract architecture, despite several common features, differs from and goes beyond Isozaki's "transpersonal" Mannerism. Isozaki is more of a lyricist and illusionist, while Fujii is a mathematician or alchemist, who executes his pure nonrational philosophy with the precision, consistency, and rationality of the laboratory. It may be said that Fujii works toward a condition wherein his buildings lose their character as objects and become nonobjects or, using his own term, "negative objects." He considers the negative object

370. Toki designed his own House with an Independent Facade (Kashiwa, 1978, S. Toki).

371–375. Two houses by Hayakawa protect the residents from the noise of the city by filtering the sound through carefully layered wall planes.

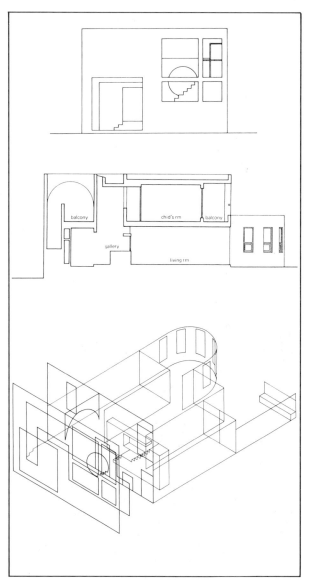

balcony

chid's rm

balcony

gallery

living rm

371–373. House at a Bus Stop (Tokyo, 1982, K. Hayakawa).

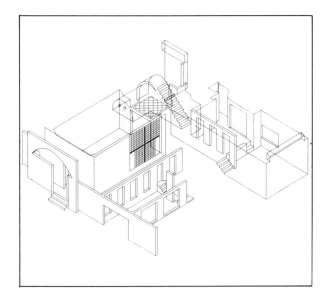

374–375. House in Seijo (Tokyo, 1983, K. Haya-kawa).

376–377. The orthogonal geometric grid as appliqué pervades the whole building at the Miyajima Residence, inside and out (Tokyo, 1973, H. Fujii).

377. Floor plans and section. 1. Entrance. 2. Living room. 3. Dining room. 4. Kitchen. 5. Balcony. 6. Bedroom. 7. Bathroom. 8. Study room. 9. Office.

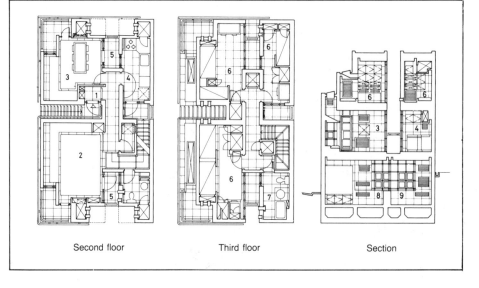

Second floor   Third floor   Section

as absolute existence, which is impartial, neither objective nor subjective, neither rational nor irrational.

Fujii's intentions with geometry run somewhat parallel to those of Ando and Shinohara, but his approach is based exclusively on operations with cubes consonant with the concepts of "repetition, multitiered structure, distance, and divergence" plus similarity, connotation, junction, and so on (379). At the three-story Marutake Doll Company (1976) office building in Konosu, the nest of boxes within the interior of the twelve cubes is presented only implicitly. The windows and doors are variations on the themes of window-in-window and door-in-door, an idea present in Ishii's House with 54 Windows (380). What Project No. 5 and the Marutake Building only touch upon, the boxes-in-box arrangement of Todoroki House (1976) in Tokyo builds very explicitly (381, 382). The house is one big cube in itself, constructed of eight smaller ones of equal size. In several of these small cubes other even smaller ones appear one after the next. Interestingly, this arrangement alludes to the intricate space-layering of the traditional Japanese house and the ambiguity of *oku* as well. In the Todoroki House, as in Mozuna's Anti-dwelling Box, everything is ordered by the sequential layers of inclusive cubic structures, the symbolic skeleton of existence.

Fujii's earlier works using cubic volumes were rather static; in them the cube is usually the final outcome of his geometric operations. In the late 1970s, Fujii began to extend these concepts. The cube, as in the Tandooki House, becomes the point of departure for various transformations, signaling the beginning of his investigation of spatial structures. His designs gain an additional dimension, that of time. A series of works entitled Metamorphosis Projects (1978–80) exemplifies Fujii's new concern for an "architectural metamorphology." In these projects, while the plans originate from square or cubic forms, the wall planes begin to move in and out, deviating from the Platonic order of the cube. Fujii's goal now is to transform this order, the code of architecture itself. Thus, various two-dimensional planes not only occasionally undulate, but acting as independent elements, they also interpenetrate in an intricate system wherein exterior walls are often found in the interior and vice versa. The Miyata Residence (1980) in Chofu, Tokyo, is Fujii's first building to realize this. In this design two "cubes" are collided such that the resulting impact deforms them both to a certain extent. This deformation creates a well-conceived spatial tension in the design while accommodating the notion of a controlled accident (383–385).

PHENOMENOLOGY OF MINIMALISM

At first glance Fujii's architecture and that of Tadao Ando (b. 1941) resemble each other. Their buildings, usually small houses, are conceived and built as systems of reinforced concrete structures that have an explicitly defensive character. Ando, like Fujii, aims at stabilizing human life but in a manner different from Fujii's. In the often chaotic and destructively volatile conditions of consumer-oriented present urbanism, he is determined to create architectural spaces with a new and elementary feeling of existence. For this reason he also gives primary importance to the relationship between architecture and human existence. He writes: "I want to charge architecture with a sense of life and feeling of substantial existence by creating simple geometric forms with materials as limited as possible at present."[56] This strong commitment to austerity brings him close not only to the conceptual architecture of Fujii and others, but also to the traditional Japanese aesthetic inspired by Zen Buddhism, in which the meanings of existence spring from a sense of identification between subject and object. In other words, substantial meanings are generated when existence is "vectorial"—that is, inspired by an active, creative participation of the self—not when it is carried by delusions and effortless, passively received, sensation.

378. Project E-1 (1976, H. Fujii). The mesmerizing visual effect of the overwhelming three-dimensional grid is intended to efface conventional and pragmatic meanings in order to induce new ones based on new existential relationships between subject and object.

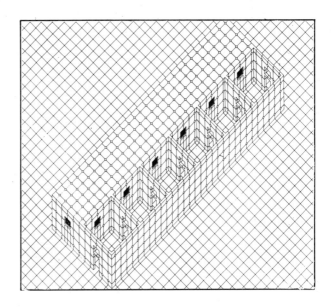

379. The idea of "similarity, connotation, and junction" as it appears in the Project No. 5 and the Todoroki House first-floor plan (1976, Hiromi Fujii).

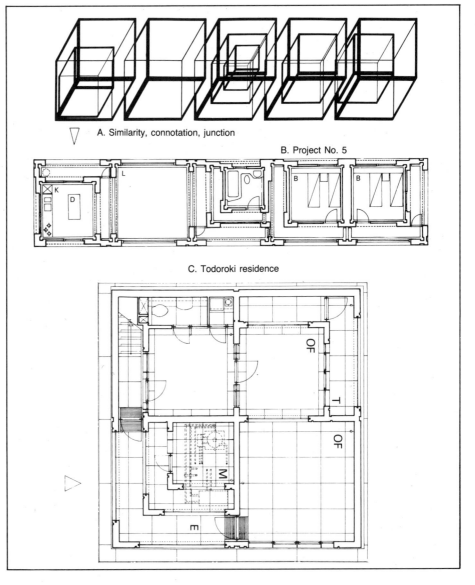

A. Similarity, connotation, junction

B. Project No. 5

C. Todoroki residence

380. The three-story building of the Marutake Doll Company is made up of the superimposition of twelve concrete cubes, featuring variations on window-in-window and door-in-door (Konosu, 1976, H. Fujii).

381–382. The box of the Todoroki House is composed of eight cubes of identical size and several smaller ones inside in sequence, which layer the interior in a manner similar to the traditional Japanese house (Funabashi, 1976, H. Fujii; photograph courtesy of Hiromi Fujii).

383–385. Two cubes within the Miyata House collide and as a result one of them is deformed, shifting the kitchen and other secondary rooms out of the overall orthogonal grid system (Fuchu, 1980, H. Fujii).

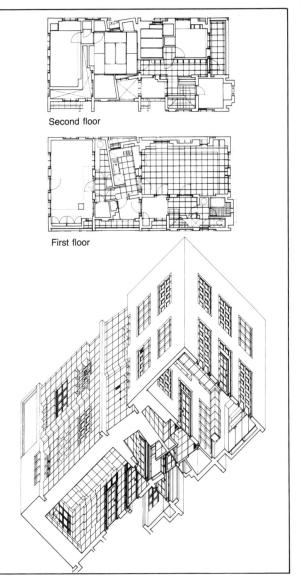

Second floor

First floor

Fujii calls his architecture "Quintessential," which on the subconscious level is supposed to carry existential meanings for man who in turn is required to "relinquish" or, in the best case, transform his ordinary self in order to experience a new feeling of existence. In such awareness, reminiscent of the benumbed state of Zen Buddhist meditation, "the eye of the subject capable of reading the meaning is patently absent."[57] With Ando's architecture the case is somewhat different.[58] Though it too requires a certain amount of self-denial for its full appreciation, self-denial here means primarily the checking of strong preconceptions, in other words, suspending the functions of the rational and assertive mind. Ando admits this: "I came to understand relations with actual architecture, not with my mind only, but with my whole experiencing being."[59] And indeed, with his sensitive use of materials and light-and-shadow effects with their resulting poetic images, his architecture appeals to the deepest human emotions. His formal architectural vocabulary also incorporates probably unintended, and therefore indirect, historical references, whereas works like the Wall House (1977) reexamine the architecture of classical Greece and Rome, Renaissance and modern architecture, while basically rejecting them all (386–389).

Ando's use of solid boxes, walls, the orthogonal frame or the trabeated pergola, in some cases the cylinder, and the vault, is close to obsession. His geometry of reinforced concrete could be likened to Fujii's or Isozaki's, while the poetry of his empty spaces brings him closer to Shinohara. But as opposed both to Fujii and Shinohara, and further, Ito, Hara, Aida, and Isozaki in some respects, Ando conceives his buildings not so much as volumes or forms but as highly structured spaces. He is interested in structural considerations as far as they help him set up "new relationships" between matter and matter, man and matter, and, finally, man and man. It is evident that his architecture, which he considers an antithesis to orthodox modern concerns, is not primarily the product of technological, production, economic, or even functional considerations. His buildings are visual images of a metaphysical order.

Many of his houses appear to be protective concrete shells that isolate the residents from a disturbing urban environment. In extreme examples like the Row House at Sumiyoshi (1976), the Town House at Kujo (1982), and the Glass-Block House (1978), the buildings are, so to speak, hermetic microcosms centered around tiny open courtyards. The prototype for this is the traditional row house (*nagaya*), the urban dwelling of the Osaka region, where Ando lives and works (360–364, 390–393). These courtyards play an extremely important role in Ando's architecture. In his attempt to reintroduce nature into the house and protect the "sense of the light, wind, and rain that is being lost in Japanese cities, the light court becomes the nucleus of the lives of the inhabitants."[60] Ando seeks this implicit regionalism consciously and designs even his small commercial buildings with atriums. The Rose Garden (1977), a shopping mall in Kobe, is designed with four solid walls that envelop the inner courtyard and plaza, which are filled with open pedestrian galleries and staircases. To blend the building into its Western-style vicinity, Ando covered the exterior walls with brick tiles and abandoned the flat roof (394, 395).

Although elements of a small inner world are consistently present in all of Ando's architecture, where the friendlier urban landscape allows it the hard boundaries soften and open up more toward the external world. Most of his buildings show this cautious duality. It is with this careful opening up, his way of handling the transition between macrocosm and microcosm, that Ando's architectural intentions are coupled with his greater talents and most skillful techniques, resulting in the most substantial meanings (396–398). For him openings are not merely devices for direct visual contact with the surrounding landscape but are more im-

386–389. The massive solid concrete walls and vaults and the trabeated pergola of the Wall House, built in a quasiclassical order, are in strong opposition to the natural environment. They exemplify best what Ando calls the "catabolism of the landscape" (Ashiya, 1976, T. Ando).

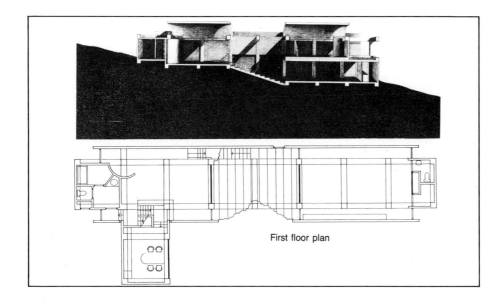

First floor plan

portantly intricate sources of light. The quality of light, whether the dramatic sharp contrast between direct light and shadow or the softly dispersed light filtered through translucent glass-block surfaces, reveals the essential darkness and radiant calm of his interiors. The careful modulation of light and shadow also enhances his spatial orders and transforms them into poetic images similar to those evoked in the ancient *haiku,* attempting to capture the elusive, transient nature of existence. Where silence and light intersect, the "dual nature of existence," the "disconnected time-space," find the way to new, higher, and more meaningful spheres.[61]

The sensitive treatment of unfinished concrete, a material that he converts into delicate and luxurious surfaces, is revealed and can be fully appreciated in the ever-changing light that sweeps across these surfaces. Many of the elements in his architecture—stark walls with narrow slots, trabeated frames, and so on—are set up only with the purpose of exploring light-and-shadow effects and, further, to evoke a profound feeling of spatiality. The concrete he employs in these elements does not create the feeling of rigidity or weight. When their surfaces agree with his aesthetic image, walls and other elements are transformed into thin, "immaterial" membranes; they "become abstract, are negated, and approach the ultimate limit of space. Their actuality is lost, and only the space they enclose gives a sense of really existing."[62] With respect to light, no one else is better compared with Ando than Louis Kahn, who had a similarly strong devotion to this essential architectural element (389, 407, 408, 412, 419, 421).

The presence of a large variety of light effects is not the only indication of Ando's ability to create delicate relationships—or "thresholds," as Fumihiko Maki put it—between outside and inside, between the building and the urban environment.[63] Another of his instruments, which reinforces the first, is the technique of space layering; the ambiguous character of Japanese traditional architecture—with special regard to the *sukiya-zukuri*—has always been based on this. In order to resuscitate the spatial and aesthetic qualities of tea houses and *sukiya* residences, Ando evokes their spirit rather than employing their direct formal or stylistic attributes (399, 400). "His skillful handling of the traditional Japanese concept of *ma* within the porous matrix which his framework creates is particularly noteworthy," wrote Maki.[64] This "porous matrix" is evident in the ubiquitous courtyards. Whether they are within the hard shell, as in the Row House, the Glass-Block House, and Kojima Housing (1981), or without but still within the framework—as in the Wall House, the Tezukayama House (1977), the Koshino Residence (1981)— they are in fact "roofless living rooms" (401–413). But rooms—especially *tatami* rooms—may be arranged within yet another room, as in the Glass-Block House and the Okusu Residence. In many cases independent wall planes or frame elements are used to make gradual transitions between spaces of different character. These planes can be looked upon as introductory elements, the beginnings of the whole underlying spatial composition, as in for example the outreaching frame of the Onishi Residence (1979), the small glass-block wall of the

390–393. Through its translucent interior surfaces within a solid concrete shell, the Glass-Block House opens up only toward its inner court (Osaka, 1978, T. Ando).

Matsumoto Residence, and the separate concrete walls of Kojima Housing (414, 415).

Within his buildings, Ando often brings into collision different formal systems or, like Isozaki and Fujii, deliberately deviates from rational order so that both deviation and system mutually define each other through opposition. One wall of the Tezukayama House and also of the Rose Garden is shifted out of the uniform orthogonal system. The diagonal staircase in the Kojima Housing is one of the most recent examples of this method of deviation from a system's "norm" (394, 401, 404, 409). But in many cases the opposition is tamed into a two-way dialog, as seen between the walls and frames. The Hirabayasi Residence (1976) and the Wall House, for example, are designed as the interpenetration of a two-story skeleton and a hard-surfaced shell; a similar operation is evident in the Matsumoto Residence (1980; 416–418).

In Ando's architecture the longitudinal "left-over" interstice spaces and the overlapping transitional areas between two systems are assigned the role of communications channels: long narrow passages and stairways. As opposed to Isozaki, Hara, Aida, and Mozuna, in most cases Ando's stairways and passages are found along the periphery of the buildings. However, sometimes they are so important that the entire design concept "centers" around them. A small shopping center in Takamatsu is laid out along continuous flights of stairs, hence its name: "Step" (1980; 419). The Okusu Residence (1978) in Tokyo is hardly more than a long L-shaped processional path full of stairs and corridors. The Wall House, Tezukayama House, the Matsumoto and Koshino residences also embody this processional quality (420–422). To emphasize its intermediary role, the diagonal staircase in the Kojima Housing is arranged to interpenetrate both interior and exterior and, with the planes of "independent" walls, the staircase serves to layer the transition between inside and out.

Ando uses a large variety of devices to shape the movement within his buildings in an attempt to heighten the experience so that one is conscious of participation and involvement in architecture through the kinetic impetus of the body, as well as in other ways. Aside from stairs and corridors, bridges are such devices. In the Row House and Matsumoto Residence, for example, narrow bridges

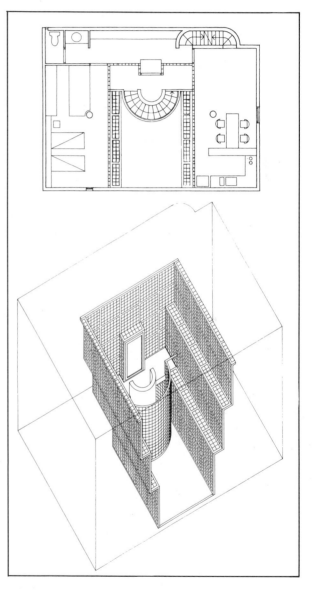

392. The semicircular stairway in the courtyard.

393. Axonometric drawing and second-floor plan.

394–395. The four brick-covered walls outside and the central mall inside the Rose Garden, a small commercial center in Kobe, create an atmosphere appropriate to a district with numerous Western-style buildings (1977, T. Ando).

connect different sections in an open courtyard and a large two-story entrance hall (361, 417). Because of their special arrangement, these spaces can be experienced in two different ways. In addition to their actual setup, they could also appear as, respectively, an externalized interior room and an internalized exterior courtyard.

Ando's latest and so far largest projects, the Rokko Housing (1983) in Kobe and the Festival (1984), a multistory commercial center in Okinawa, are consistent with his earlier works. Both are excellent examples of Ando's sensitive architectural response to the topographic and climatic conditions of the site as well as to the collective, public nature of the buildings. The Rokko complex is carefully integrated into the difficult steep southern slope of Mount Rokko. The twenty apartments are lined up along an open-air stairway that follows the slope. In addition, there is a variety of smaller stairs within the four different types of multistory residential units. Small bridges again appear to connect residences to their terraces, which are placed on the rooftops of the lower blocks in front. The common yard between the north and south sections is visible to all the inhabitants and in fact acts as

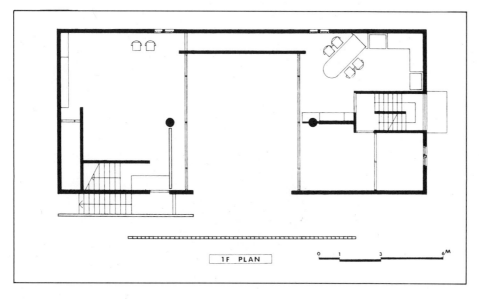

396–398. In the Glass-Block Wall house, the courtyard opens up toward the street but is screened by a translucent surface (Osaka, 1978, T. Ando).

1F PLAN

0 1 3 6ᴹ

399–400. Tea ceremony room in the annex of Soseikan House (Takarazuka, 1984, T. Ando).

an urban space or public plaza. Every unit has an excellent panoramic view of the Kobe Harbor in the farther distance. Ando's real achievement in this housing is that he not only successfully applied his usual rectangular-solid unfinished-concrete frame—here 5.4 by 4.8 meters—in a significantly larger building, but also provided an outstanding variety of individual apartments that retain privacy and individuality in the overall composition (423–427).

In the Festival, Ando's main concerns were to protect the interior spaces from the strong tropical sunshine, to ensure good natural ventilation, and to integrate this public building into its busy urban environment. Accordingly, he filled his usual orthogonal frame with many perforated concrete block walls, as well as multistory atriums, open-air walkways, bridges, and escalators to create attractive plazas and a network of "three-dimensional streets" continuous with the outside boulevard.

In Ando's buildings, as in these two examples, bridges and stairways are frequently located within the outdoor courtyards so that movement inside the building is exposed directly to the weather. The tenant of his Sumiyoshi or Kujo town houses has to cross outside spaces in order to reach the bedroom or bathroom, for example. For a Westerner this is a serious functional deficiency. Yet in Japan, where until very recently homes in the cramped suburbs did not have their own baths and the residents had to walk some distance to a public bath (*osento*), this may not be considered so unusual.[65] Agreeing with Ando, several of his clients still consider the direct contact with nature and natural phenomena more important than convenience. Ando is determined to resist the often hedonist and conformist bourgeois attitudes of contemporary society. He notes that today the individual, following his increasingly unrestrained ambitions for materialist trappings, "enters a neverending cycle and becomes dominated by his own excessive desires." He adds, "My approach is to

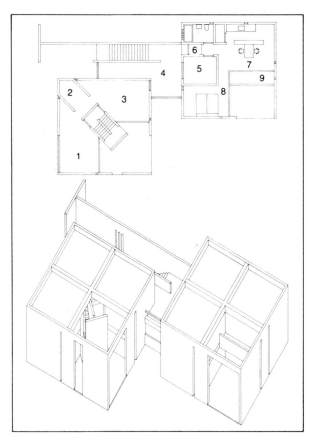

401–404. The two quadratic concrete boxes of the Kojima Housing feature "roofless" living rooms within the shells, creating a delicate transitional zone between inside and out (Kurashiki, 1981, T. Ando).

404. Floor plan and axonometric drawing.
1. Spare room. 2. Closet.
3. Study. 4. Court.
5. Spare room.
6. Entrance. 7. Living/dining room. 8. Bedroom.
9. Terrace.

405.   406.

405–409. Beyond the usual exterior concrete shell and the trabeated pergola, the main compositional element in the Tezukayama House is a solid wall cutting diagonally across the orthogonal skeleton, generating spatial tension and various light-and-shadow effects in the interior (Osaka, 1977, T. Ando).

407.

408.

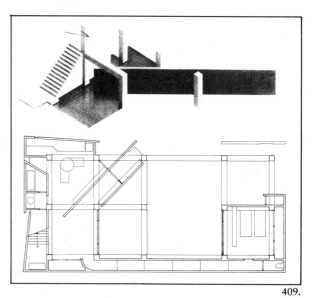

409.

410.

410–413. Between two volumetrically different "inorganic concrete boxes" with an underground connection, the wide stairway and the sloping courtyard of the Koshino Residence symbolize "the intrinsic nature of the site." Carefully arranged openings are sources of dramatic light effects (Ashiya, 1981, T. Ando).

411.

413. Floor plans. First floor: 1. Living room. 2. Lobby. 3. Child's room. 4. *Tatami* room. Second floor: 1. Entrance. 2. Study. 3. Bedroom. 4. Roof terrace.

413.

412.

415.

414.

416.

414. Part of the structural skeleton serves as an introduction to the spatial composition while it also signifies the entrance to the Onishi Residence (Osaka, 1979, T. Ando).

415–417. The Matsumoto Residence is a variation on the theme of interpenetration (Wakayama, 1980, T. Ando).

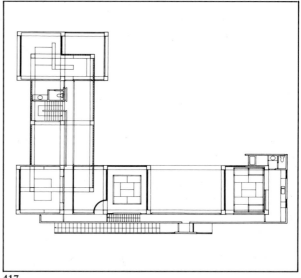

417.

418. Axonometric drawing of the Hirabayashi Residence (Osaka, 1976, T. Ando). The spatial and structural composition is brought about by the inter-penetration of a solid concrete shell and a three-dimensional skeleton.

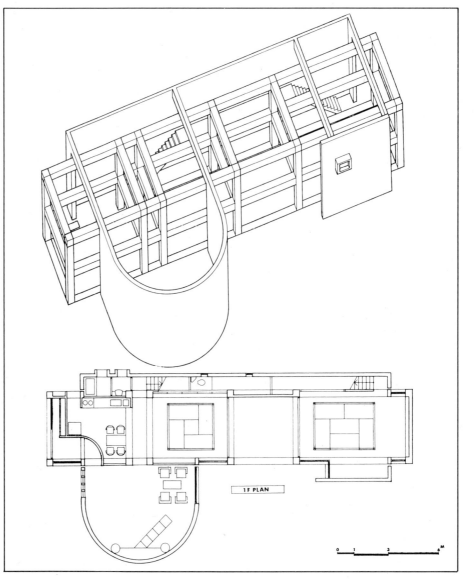

1F PLAN

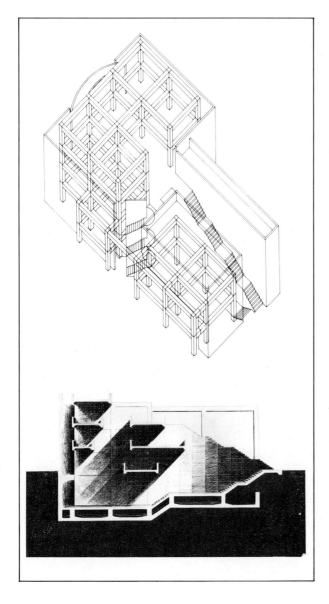

419. Axonometric drawing of the "Step" Shopping Center, which combines the organizing role and spatial dynamics of a multistory atrium and a long exterior stairway (Takamatsu, 1980, T. Ando).

pursue more than superficial comfort. I want to try to recapture and reexamine one by one the truly enduring and essential elements of the human residence, many of which have been abandoned in the course of rapid economic growth: basic relations with nature, direct dialogue with materials, the small discoveries and surprises people can detonate in their daily-life spaces, the pleasure and aesthetic uplift to be had from creative initiative in a simple way of life."[66]

This extreme sensitivity to the local conditions and values of a regional culture within the general norms of contemporary life on the one hand, and yet a consistently critical attitude by which he resists the alienating and destructive tendencies of this same modern life on the other hand, make Ando one of the most significant architects of the New Wave. He writes: "It seems difficult to me to attempt to express the sensibilities, customs, aesthetic awareness, distinctive culture, and social traditions of a given race by means of the open internationalist vocabulary of Modernism."[67]

As a result of Ando's skillful handling of pure and abstract geometry as well as material (largely limited to concrete) and light, space is reduced to its bare essentials, to an innermost feeling; as its entity converges to nothingness or *mu,* it corresponds to the universe. It is important here to remember that for the Japanese nothingness or void is not a derogatory "nihilistic" state or quality, but the very essence of existence to which everything relates, giving life its eternal richness. With this understanding, Ando's buildings, the microcosms themselves, "give the impression of being details," as Maki observed, while his details, the architectural elements, appear to gain macrocosmic quality and significance.[68]

CHOREOGRAPHY OF ABSENCE AND VOID
Ando shares this poetically rich minimalism with Kazuo Shinohara (b. 1925), whose philosophy and architecture, which have developed through various

420–422. One of Ando's most ingenious designs, the Okusu Residence is a stretched-out procession path filled with various entrances, tunnels, stairways, narrow corridors, interiors of mystic quality, and so on, on an extremely cramped urban lot in Tokyo (1978, T. Ando).

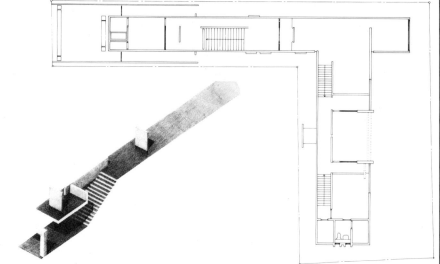

422. Axonometric drawing and second-floor plan.

423–427. At the Rokko Housing, Ando for the first time employed his uniform concrete-frame system in a large-scale project. He has achieved both privacy and individuality for the various apartments and for the tenants as well.

426. Section and axonometric drawing.

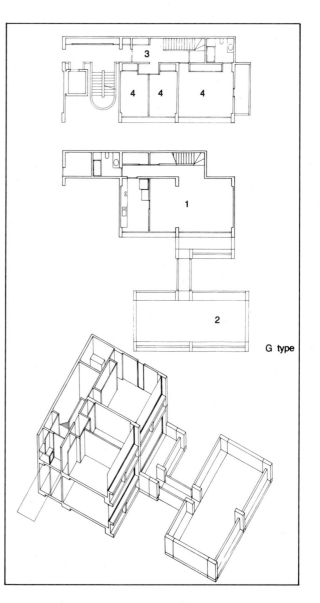

427. G- and I-type apartments: plans and axonometrics.

G-type:
1. Living room.
2. Terrace. 3. Entrance.
4. Bedroom.

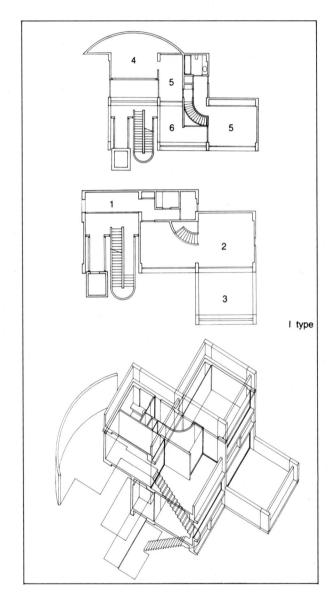

I type

I-type:
1. Entrance. 2. Living room. 3. Terrace.
4. Storage. 5. Bedroom.
6. Terrace.

phases since the early 1960s, run parallel with those of the New Wave. Shinohara is an enigma even in today's diverse situation. If the phenomenology of architecture is essential to Ando and his generation in general, it is equally essential to Shinohara. His architecture is a phenomenon in itself. Where the extraordinary in architectural experience leaves off, Shinohara's architecture begins to take shape. His abstract and "naked spaces" of transcendent purity are created for reasons beyond easy comprehension. They defy any rational expectation and explanation even if sometimes they are so explained. But while they leave the rational mind stuttering, they "conform to the deepest levels of human emotions" and promote spiritual purification.[69] Shinohara has an obviously Zen Buddhist awareness that keeps emotions well under control and "silent" on the surface. Like myths, the puzzles of his architecture can never be solved and yet have to be interpreted and encountered each time in order to be able to confront and live with the phenomenon and not overcome by it. This "creative difference" or "gap," as he calls it, between the impossibility of explaining the puzzle and yet the need to do so plays a special role in Shinohara's designs. "The way in which the architect can manipulate this concept [of "gap"] in the act of creating is not within the province of the observer, who is restricted to experiencing the built form *phenomenologically* as a text [italics added]" wrote Yasumitsu Matsunaga about him.[70]

Shinohara, who started his career as a mathematician, designs only small private houses that he uses as instruments in a long series of experiments devoted to symbolizing the purest themes. The works of his first creative phase, in the 1960s, were under the spell of the traditional architectural heritage. The houses of this time, though already abstract, always featured elements of the Japanese house. They all had tiled, pitched roofs with large overhanging eaves over simple spaces and raised floors. His second phase, in the 1970s, grew out of the first, and traditional architecture's influence was still evident. The formal aspects of his previous phase were denied, however, and abstract geometric forms, shaped of unfinished concrete began to dominate. Even the occasional slanting roof became a solid pyramid over hard boxes. This architecture was solely inward-oriented and preoccupied with such concepts as "repetition of 0 and 1," "indecision in decisiveness," "undulation and inversion," "from machine to savagery," and so on. These were subtitles of the houses from this period. Each work receives special meaning in the context of the others of the same phase, while remaining individual and independent.

Fujii and Shinohara are, in one respect, identical in their approaches. They both attempt to make architectural meaning converge to zero and in so doing to provide man with the possibility of creating new meanings and thus new aspects to his existence. This intention again has its roots in traditional Japanese mentality. The Japanese, says Shinohara, "have often chosen to rob [the material] elements of their vitality, thereby reducing them to inorganic matter. This insatiable commitment to simplification, however, has always been rewarded with the resuscitation of the given object as something new."[71] In a similar way Shinohara believes that "Value can be achieved from elements that have lost meaning and have been reduced to zero degree."[72] He picks these "empty words" and creates a syntax for them so that each of his houses becomes an "empty page" to be written on eventually by the "reader," inhabitant. He has recognized that between substantive meaning and void or nothingness there exists a nonrational line that can only be perceived intuitively. He even risks equating the two, which he admits when he writes: "Because I have taken a long time pondering meaningful space, there has appeared within me a 'meaningless' meaningful space."[73] As a result, Shinohara's architecture, more than that of any of his contemporaries, is able to induce the rare sense of

that delicate threshold between existence and nonexistence.

Fujii and Ando both systematically organize space, place, and meaning by the repetition of identical forms and elements in a "Mannerist" way. In contrast to them, Shinohara sets up a mere theoretical scheme behind the simplest geometric forms. In other words, his geometry is a nonregular type, and is often "out of order." Consider for example the House in Karuizawa (1975), where a rectangular volume is cut through by an irregular undulating courtyard that is an open-air walk-through gallery; or the House on a Curved Road (1978), where the heterogeneous exterior concrete shell is of a totally different geometry on the first, second, and third floors, approximating a continuum between apparent disorder and sophisticated order (428–431). With the exception of the House in Itoshima (1976), the exteriors of the defensive concrete houses from his second phase are rather ordinary, at least when compared to their extraordinary interiors. The spaces inside, where most surfaces are painted white, are not only pure but also ethereal and elusive. With the uncertainty of perception they tend to lose their materiality and appear only as shadows. But in this atmosphere of virtual sensory deprivation there are always elements that disquiet, sometimes even disrupt the motionless space, and thus the senses, to create the "gap between disorder and orderly space."[74]

His House in Ashitaka (1977) is a symmetrical building with monotonously alternating story-high openings and wall columns as the "repetition of 0 and 1." But in the large living room, reminiscent of the powerful images of Stonehenge, under the high-pitched and hipped concrete roof, the balance is deliberately out of kilter. Each facing facade is an opposite projection of the other: where one has a solid wall plane the other has a corresponding opening. This results in the subtle tension that characterizes the space (432).

Shinohara has an admitted devotion to columns

carried over most probably from his first and traditional period. For him columns have a mythical quality that makes the encounter a spiritual experience. This is not to say the numerous columns that appear consistently in many of his designs are not supporting elements or are fake. But it certainly means that beyond their structural function they play other, special roles. Their effect and immediacy of presence are catalysts that activate space and turn it into "progressive anarchy" or "savagery," in Shinohara's words. In the House on a Curved Road the irregular shell envelopes a massive latticework cube, the active heart of the microcosm inside, which gathers and unites the spaces. The four reinforced concrete columns and eight beams consistently penetrate the body of the house on all four levels and appear within. They dominate the multistory living room, bedrooms, and so on. The House in Uehara (1976) also has an irregular shape; its unusual structural and spatial solution of six concrete columns with two different diagonal braces determines the geometry of the house (433–436).

Shinohara's preoccupation with this forked type of column started earlier in his Tanikawa Residence (1974), where he designed such columns of wood to support the roof over the unusual sloping floor of beaten earth. The columns return in the large second-story living room of the House in Hanayama No. 3 (1977). Here the two columns have slightly different forms, yet both are similar to those in the Tanikawa and Uehara houses. This house also amply exemplifies Shinohara's effort to create the feeling of uncertainty in the course of spatial experience. The spatial sequence is filled with surprises, starting with the deliberate rotation of the horizontal axes. The second floor here is shifted out of the layout of the first by 90 degrees. Most of his interiors contradict the exteriors, and so the actual experience differs significantly from what would normally be expected. The exposed 45-degree braces and pitched roofs generate inside a perceptual field that con-

tradicts the usual notions of vertical and horizontal. The tension or "gap" between vertical and diagonal geometries reaches its epitome in the small study of the Higashi-Tamagawa Complex (1982), where the whole space is tilted along a 45-degree angle. The feeling of disorientation is reinforced by the similarly slanting upper edge of the door to this room. It is only the window's relationship to the sloping surfaces that helps reestablish the image of a pitched roof overhead and thus a feeling of certainty—yet it does so temporarily (449). In the Hanayama House No. 3 the smooth, white columns undergo a metamorphosis during the changing light of the day, moving between substantial existence and almost transparent nonexistence, thereby eventually transforming the space into a metaphysical one, as Matsunaga described it (437, 438).[75]

This metaphysical quality is present in practically all of Shinohara's interiors, rarely in the exteriors. The House in Itoshima (1976) is one in which the exterior does tend to take on that characteristic. The major element of its design is a series of outdoor spaces bisecting the building along its axis of symmetry. The house is located on the edge of a steep hill along the sea near Fukuoka City; the main axis of the approach to the entrance "aims" at a small island far off the shore, giving an almost cosmic order to the composition. Such cosmic dimension was not completely foreign to Shinohara's earlier architecture but it remained latent. The endless openings in the House in Ashitaka celebrate the sun and its setting as Stonehenge does, while a small roof window, a skylight of sorts, frames the polar star on clear nights. At the House in Uehara one observes what Matsunaga describes as a "spectrum of infinite gradations from light to dark introduced through the skylights and the triangular windows. . . . The passage of time can thus be seen as inscribed through a play of light and shadow." This suggests Shinohara's conscious attempt to engage form and space "with

428. The House in Karuizawa is cut through by an irregular courtyard that divides it into a residence-studio and a gallery block (1975, K. Shinohara).

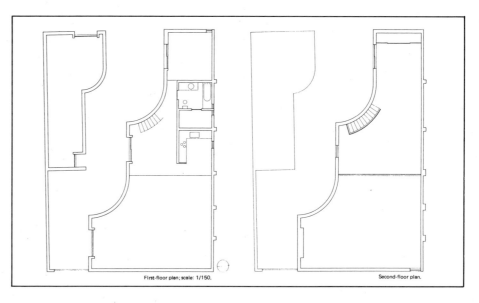

First-floor plan; scale: 1/150.　　　　　　　Second-floor plan.

429–431. The sturdy, almost brutal, reinforced-concrete skeleton gains a new metaphysical existence while giving substantive meaning to the elusive "dematerialized" spaces inside the House on a Curved Road. Shinohara in this way attempted to achieve "unity through savagery" (Tokyo, 1978, K. Shinohara).

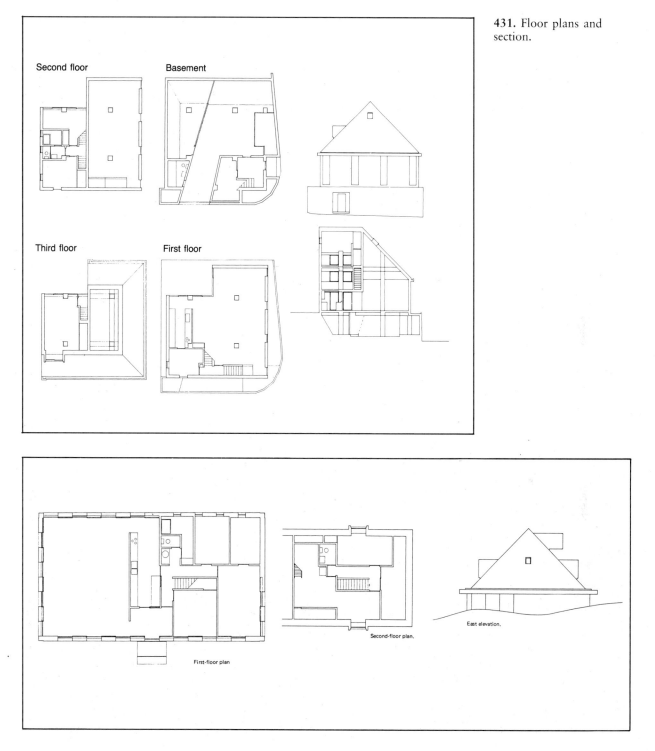

431. Floor plans and section.

Second floor   Basement

Third floor   First floor

432. House in Ashitaka: floor plans and East elevation (Ashitaka, 1977, K. Shinohara).

First-floor plan

Second-floor plan.

East elevation.

433–436. Shinohara's metaphysical architecture can only be understood phenomenologically. The carefully designed and constructed composition of the House in Uehara invites a wide range of possible interpretations (Tokyo, 1976, K. Shinohara).

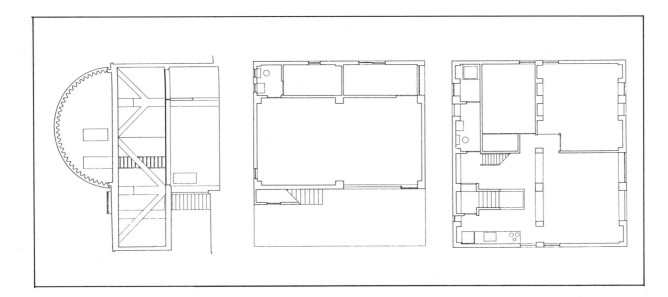

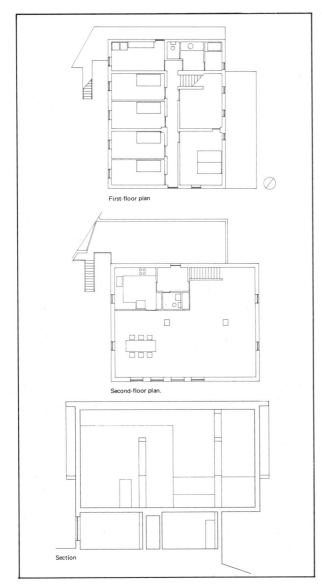

First-floor plan

Second-floor plan.

Section

437–438. Designing the House in Hanayama No. 3, Shinohara rotated the axis of the second floor ninety degrees out of the first-floor axis (Kobe, 1977, K. Shinohara).

the rotation of the earth and the flow of celestial movement."[76] In Itoshima, this engagement is obvious again yet on a different scale and in a different manner. Here Shinohara responded to an environmental phenomenon and framed the sight of the island, the infinity of the sky, and the sea all within an "artificial space," thereby converting the landscape itself into an architectural element.[77]

The Itoshima house thus has some affinity with Mozuna's "cosmic" architecture, but more so with Louis Kahn's design for the Salk Institute at La Jolla, California, where the central court is arranged in a similar way. Taming the natural or urban landscape and then turning it into a part of his architecture has become an important aspect of Shinohara's third phase. Structures designed recently, like the House in Hanayama No. 4 (1980) or the House Under High-Voltage Lines (1981), open up more toward the external world. Outer landscapes assist the inner ones, though in an artificial way (439-440). The roof of the House Under High-Voltage Lines, for example, is dented to create the distance required between the building and the two nearby cables. As if pushed in by the emanating electromagnetic force, the awkwardly trimmed forms of the house respond to given circumstances by incorporating the high-voltage lines into the composition. The curving surfaces appear in the interior as well, on the second and third floors (441–443).

This house signals the beginning of Shinohara's increased attention to surfaces apart from his responsive transmutations of geometric forms. Like colored surfaces, glass-block and flush-mounted half-reflective glass walls and windows are new in his architecture. The House Under High-Voltage Lines and his latest works, the Ukiyoe Museum (1982) in Matsumoto and the addition to the House in Higashi Tamagawa (1974, 1982) in Tokyo are based largely on the use of these materials. Stainless steel appears on the small gable-roofed section of the second floor of the Tamagawa House addition

as well (444–449). Shinohara sums up his recent concerns by saying: "The concept of 'surface-ness' and 'fragmentation,' as well as that of 'discreteness' (the central idea in the Ukiyoe Museum) intertwine to form the basis of 'progressive anarchy' and 'zero-degree machine,' which are currently my fundamental themes."[78]

Despite his increased interest in both a fragmented relation and a "mediated unity" between the house and its surroundings, most of Shinohara's interiors are self-contained, enclosed, and are timeless worlds that correspond with his intention "to carve out eternity in spaces."[79] As such, they are the strongest protest against consumerist architecture. Following a trail blazed almost solely by his own unique philosophy, Shinohara's architecture shows little sign of having been influenced by the changing architectural events and trends around it. His changes are self-inspired. On the other hand, his influence on his contemporaries and disciples was undeniably strong, particularly after the 1970s and thus the so-called Shinohara school was born.

The contribution of Itsuko Hasegawa (b. 1941) and Kazunari Sakamoto (b. 1943) to the school is significant (450–452). They both studied and worked with Shinohara before setting up their own offices. Again, the use of abstract geometry characterizes their architectures and also provides another lyrical interpretation of the Japanese notion of "absence," especially with Hasegawa. Her small buildings incorporate the simplest primary forms and use the simplest materials, while the intensity of the naked structures indicates her strong attempt to escape from the abused and ultimately meaningless semantic world of the amorphous urban environment in which the houses are inescapably set. The Silver Triangle House (1976), for example, makes extensive use of naked metal elements, plates and bars; in the Kuwahara House (1980) in Matsuyama polished metal sheets and punched aluminum screens are used, which turn the house into a surprisingly elegant "showroom" for the steel

439–443. Some of the latest buildings by Shinohara respond more to the external environment than his earlier buildings had.

439–440. House in Hanayama No. 4. (Kobe, 1980, K. Shinohara).

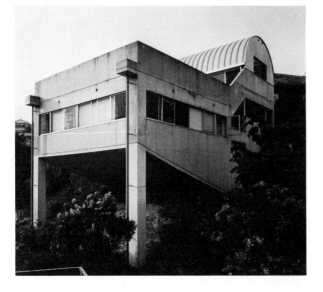

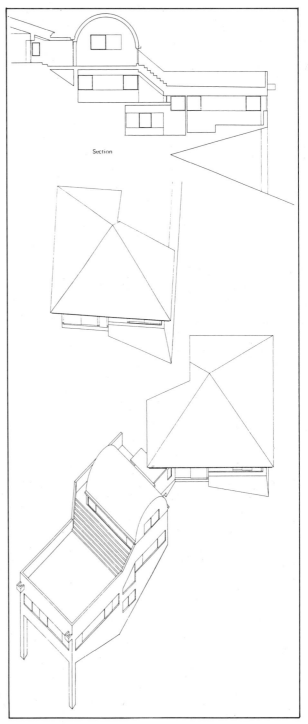

Section

and nonferrous metal products its owner sells as a dealer (453, 454). A series of industrial metaphors continues to dominate her latest projects as well, including the Nakano Housing (1984) in Tokyo. The seemingly arbitrary assemblage of forms, elements, and materials of this four-story building reflects equally well the effects of legal restrictions, site conditions, and the anarchic character of the surrounding cityscape (455–457).

Most of her designs have as remote prototypes the pitched-roof farmhouses (*minka*). Hasegawa molds her versions of these in concrete or metal. The Stationery Shop (1978) in Yaizu, the Tokumaru Children's Clinic (1979), and the Aono Building (1982) in Matsuyama—which represents a partial departure from the more abstract style she has followed so far—are examples of this connection (458–460). These buildings have a certain affinity with Sakamoto's "meaningless" and ordinary houselike forms. The works of Hasegawa in which "each element, . . . structure, opening, wall, and the like, has a peculiarly autonomous and fragmentary quality," on the other hand, closely resemble Ito's architecture of fragmented collage.[80]

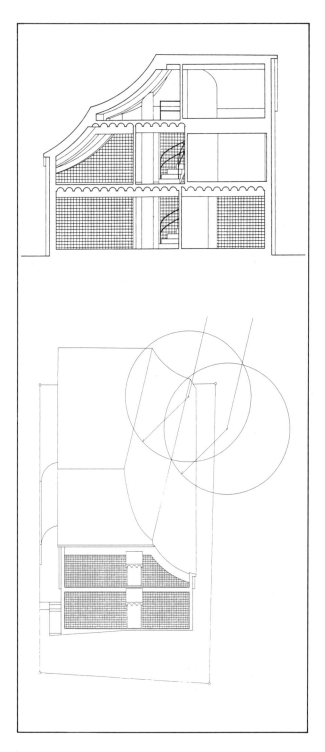

441–443. House under
High-Voltage Lines
(Tokyo, 1981, K. Shino-
hara).

444–449. The Ukiyo-e Museum and the Higashi Tamagawa Complex are characterized by the application of new materials: metal plates, reflective glass, and so on, as well as by the concepts of "surface-ness" and "fragmentation."

444–445. Ukiyo-e Museum (Matsumoto, 1982, K. Shinohara).

446–449. Higashi-
Tamagawa Complex
(Tokyo, 1974, 1982,
K. Shinohara).

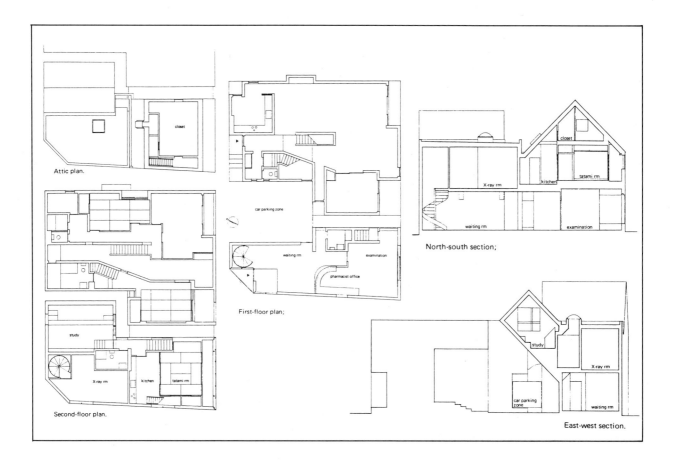

Attic plan.

First-floor plan;

Second-floor plan.

closet

car parking zone

waiting rm

examination

pharmacist office

study

X-ray rm

kitchen

tatami rm

North-south section;

closet

X-ray rm

kitchen

tatami rm

waiting rm

examination

East-west section.

study

X-ray rm

car parking zone

waiting rm

COLLAGE AND SUPERFICIAL URBANISM

Though Toyo Ito (b. 1941) did not study or work with Shinohara, he shares several of Shinohara's concerns, with special emphasis on the expression of void. "My intention is to destroy the realm of ordered imagery and to construct a more open, autonomous architecture," Ito writes.[81] For this purpose he uses pure, abstract forms and manipulates architectural surfaces. To his mind, it is ultimately surfaces that carry the meaning and the quality of space; breaking these surfaces into something unidentifiable, therefore, may result in a space that does not resemble anything in memory or previous experiences, thus eluding any analogy. Blankness and the suspension of rational awareness become possible. The House in Nakano (1976) is a huge, solidly built U-shaped building in which spatial reality eludes the observer. The space in the white U formed by two smoothly curving parallel concrete walls has no center, no clear direction, and no end. Nothing is fixed, nothing is absolute. The light penetrating through a slot in the slanting roof and through the one and only window to the empty courtyard—the negative center—destabilizes the reference system of usual perception. The soft light bouncing on the surfaces washes the interior into nonmaterial existence (461, 462).

In addition to undulating the surfaces, Ito also fragments them. In the House at Kamiwada (1976) many of the interior painted walls are either S-curved or densely staggered to create what he calls a "white labyrinth in a cube"; in the Hotel D (1977) the fragmentation is on the horizontal surfaces, so that virtually no flat, horizontal ceiling can be found. When everything is dismantled this way, Ito juxtaposes the fragments, which he calls "morphemes," into a collage while stripping any meaning from them. The overall image of the space is either of nothingness or else seems completely open, or indefinite. For the first time at the hotel, elevations also reflect this intention. They are comprised of discordant formal elements and are all different in character (463–465). In connection with this building, Ito writes: "Perhaps this design has supplied me with a further hint toward the development of the pluralistic architecture that has heretofore remained latent in me."[82]

The same concepts underlie the PMT Building (1976) in Nagoya. Here "fragmented juxtaposition" or collage is complemented by superficiality. The

450–452. Kazunari Sakamoto, following Shinohara's path, designs small and ordinary houses with "meaningless" forms.

450–451. House at Minase (Tokyo, 1971, K. Sakamoto).

452. House in Soshigaya (Tokyo, 1983, K. Sakamoto).

453–454. Kuwahara House (Matsuyama, 1980, I. Hasegawa). The skillful use of ordinary materials and form have resulted in a surprisingly elegant house.

454.

455.

457.

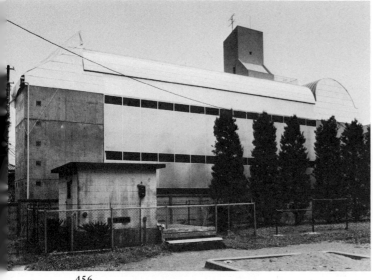

456.

455–457. The extensive
use of such industrial
products as punched alu
plates continues in
Hasegawa's latest design
for the Nakano Housing
(Tokyo, 1984,
I. Hasegawa).

458–460. With their pitched roofs, both the Tokumaru Clinic and the Aono Building have their remote prototype in Japanese farmhouses (*minka*), here molded in concrete and oxidized alu panels respectively.

458. Tokumaru Children's Clinic (Matsuyama, 1979, I. Hasegawa).

459–460. The colored elevation patterns of the Aono Building recall the spirit of previous buildings on the site (Matsuyama, 1982, I. Hasegawa).

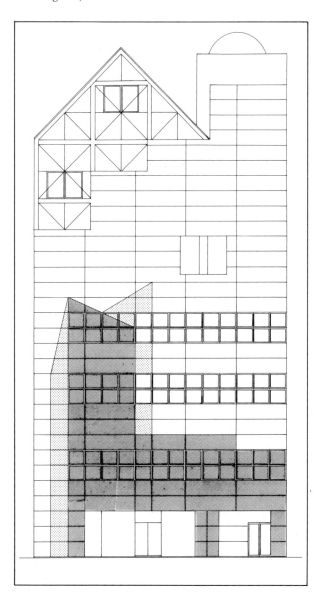

surfaces that only started to depart from the tectonic body of the Hotel D become here a completely independent aluminum skin beautifully and weightlessly undulating in front of and even above this small office building. The violence latent in many works of Shinohara and the New Wave has been modified and tamed into a sensitive lyricism. Explaining the insubstantial materiality of the elevation as a mask or thin membrane similar to a newspaper or flag blown about by the wind, Ito refers again to the quality of the Japanese urban facade. This enveloping infinite, thin surface—crowded with a forest of heterogeneous icons—carries "messages" toward people, building up a superficial and disordered realm of symbols while simultaneously hiding and revealing the empty reality behind.

Ito admits that he wishes to attain "a certain superficiality of expression in order to reveal the nature of void hidden beneath."[83] And indeed, behind the paper-thin membrane of the facade, the PMT Building has a standard "empty" space frame. The reason behind Ito's purpose of creating ambiguous and unclear forms, that is to say nonforms, is that they are less likely to degenerate into another of the countless consumerist codes in the city. When the communications industry, hand in hand with the strictly profit-oriented advertising industry, floods the market and practically every segment of contemporary life with mass-produced consumable images and with ruthlessly manipulated meanings, then a break in the line, a blackout or "silence," may be a welcome alternative, an initial step toward checking the process of overall devaluation. The PMT Building is a direct rejection of the instrumental sign, and in this sense it points beyond Isozaki's undulating "Marilyn Monroe" metal skin facades like those of the Kamioka Town Hall. It brings Ito closer to the Japanese syntax of space, with a result that differs even more radically from the American Postmodernists' stage-set architecture and Venturi's propagation of the "main street [as] almost all right" (466, 467).[84]

Two of Ito's recent houses deserve special attention. The House in Kodaira (1983) near Tokyo and his own Ito Residence (1984) in Tokyo were designed and built with a straightforward handling of ordinary industrial materials. While the use of ordinary materials is not unknown in his architecture, their dominance is certainly new. It is a feature that he now shares with Hasegawa and even Ishiyama. But Ito's approach still emphasizes, as it did before, the surface qualities of architecture. This has also become one of Shinohara's recent preoccupations. And, like Shinohara's new buildings, Ito's houses respond more willingly and perhaps even more poetically to the surrounding environment than previous works do. The House in Kodaira opens up to the south to let in ample sunshine and air; his own residence incorporates an inner courtyard that is not only a negative center, but also a lively, active (though somewhat surreal) place, a focal point as opposed to his U-shaped house in Nakano located nearby (468–473).

These two buildings by Ito emphasize once again the particular attention many New Wave architects pay to plain, industrially mass-produced materials in their pursuit not only to reveal, but also to resist, the alienating forces of industrial society. Rather than dismissing such products in the name of a wholesome or luxurious design, these architects use them readily, but in a way that endows these ordinary materials with a unique dimension; they become extraordinary—at times, poetic expressions in the "architecture of opposition." Of course this is a paradoxical relationship between architect and contemporary society. Jiro Murofushi expresses this very succinctly: "The realization of an industrialized society may be symbolized by words like *pollution* and *devastation*. Clearly, distortion has occurred in man's physical and mental aspects. In a consumer society that presumes such industrialization, the architect inevitably falls into the self-contradictory position of having to use materials that are the product of

461–462. The elusive
inner spaces in the
U-shaped House in
Nakano evoke a feeling
of uncertainty and void
(Tokyo, 1976, T. Ito).

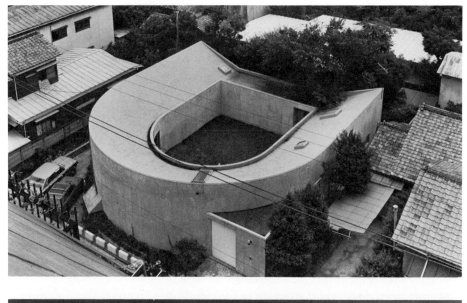

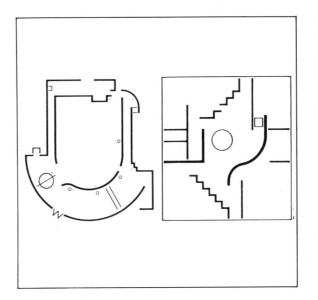

463. Spatial diagrams of the houses in Nakano and at Kamiwada. The arrangement of the fragmented walls in the House at Kamiwada results in a "white labyrinth in a cube" (1976, T. Ito).

464. In the Hotel "D" just about everything—exterior facades and interior surfaces—are fragmented "to destroy the realm of ordered imagery" (Nagano Pref., 1977, T. Ito; photograph courtesy of The Japan Architect Co. Ltd., Tokyo).

465. Cross-sections of Hotel "D."

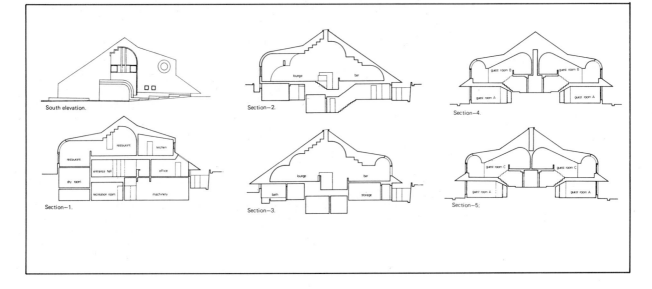

South elevation.

Section—2.

Section—4.

Section—1.

Section—3.

Section—5.

industry in his attempts to create things that in one way or another oppose industrial society."[85] Beyond the numerous, already mentioned works of Ishiyama, Ando, Shinohara, Hasegawa, Sakamoto, and many others, several designs by Tominaga and even Maki are worth mention. In many of his small houses, including his own residence (1983), Tominaga seems to be interested in discovering aesthetic value in cheap, readily available materials. His interiors often make extensive use of such products as metal, plastic, and Formica (474–476, 331, 332). Specially selected materials have also always played an important role in Maki's designs. He has increased the range of industrial materials he uses with the inclusion of stainless steel sheets that cover the entire exterior surface of his unusually constructed and shaped Fujisawa Municipal Gymnasium (1984). Undoubtedly, the unique application of this material contributed greatly to the significance of the project (477, 478).

While Ito's main concern is to use surfaces to decompose and reconstruct spaces and their meanings, Takefumi Aida uses solid "blocks" to do the same. This suggests that he too has been influenced by the Italian master Aldo Rossi's "analogous architecture." Aida's designs for the houses of the Toy-block series reveal this well, both inside and out (298–300). His attempts to generate meaning with solid forms began much earlier. In his Stair-stepped Platform House (1976) Aida comes surprisingly close to Ito's method of fragmentation. The staggered forms of the roof are fragmented surfaces inside and also broken volumes seen from outside. Looking at the building, one is compelled to ask: Is this house not yet completed, or is it already being demolished? As usual with Aida, here again, forms, spaces, functions, and existence are submerged into the blankness of silence. Says Aida, "Architecture of silence must be pure. Within pure forms there must be multiplicity of meaning. . . . Silent spaces are not seen with the eye, they are felt with the heart. For this reason, they must

be considered as metaphysical, not physical" (479, 480).[86]

His involvement in the realization of this Oriental philosophy is also reflected in the names of his buildings: Nirvana House, Annihilation House, and the like (291). On the other hand, the Toy-block House No. 3 (1981) or the more recent No. 7 (1983), both in Tokyo, emphasize the playful effects of architectural form and color. At the request of the client, a musician, the No. 3 house also conforms to the peaceful phase of *kaso,* the Japanese geomancy. Aida's architecture, like that of Isozaki, Ando, Mozuna, Hara, Tominaga, and Takeyama, connects the positive and "negative" aspects of architectural and human existence (481).

Ito's pursuit highlights the dilemma of his contemporaries in architecture; it raises the issue of the New Wave's relation to the city, to urbanism. It is quite clear that the pluralistic works of Post-Metabolism, including those of the New Wave, have little to do with one another; they lack a common denominator. Hermetic entities, they do not relate to a general or larger-scale urban pattern. Even those with Contextual implications are oftentimes "out of place." But it might safely be said that this is due to the special urban conditions of what may be called "Japan-the-city," in which no clear or rational patterns exist. Ito correctly defines this by saying that the Japanese "do not comprehend urban space"—as Americans and Europeans do— through a grid pattern or a radiating network, "but rather through collage or the empirical composition of symbols discontinuously scattered about."[87] Contemporary megalopolitan development has successfully exploited this and now in the Japanese urban environment any new element necessarily becomes part of a "contextless context." Thus the young Japanese architect in search of context has no choice but to add another element to the restless image. It may occur through a positive effort (Maki, Ishii, Takeyama, Yamashita, Kijima), which often results in a superficial facade archi-

466. The softly
undulating thin surfaces
of the aluminum facade
of the PMT Building
depart from its body to
create a delicate super-
ficiality (Nagoya, 1978,
T. Ito).

467. Axonometric
drawing of the PMT
Building.

468–473. Plain and ordinary industrial materials dominate Ito's latest buildings, which still emphasize the surface-ness of his architecture.

468–470. With the incorporation of ample sunshine and air through the large openings, the House in Kodaira responds more willingly to the outer world than do Ito's earlier buildings (Tokyo, 1983, T. Ito).

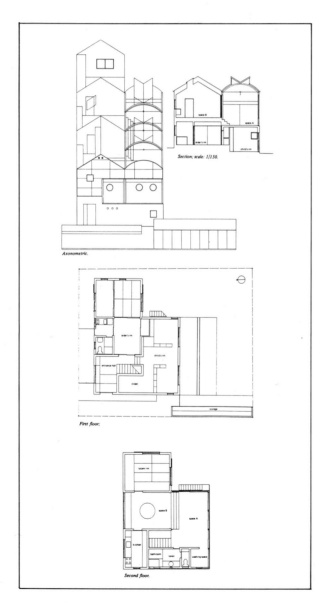

Axonometric.

Section; scale: 1/150.

First floor;

Second floor.

471–473. Vaulted volumes suggest small individual houses (or shacks) around an enclosed courtyard as the "urban plaza" in Ito's own residence (Tokyo, 1984, T. Ito).

474–476. Tominaga Residence, or House in Musashi-shingyo, Kawasaki (1983). Tominaga's small houses, which often were influenced by Shinohara's designs, include the extensive use of cheap, readily available materials such as Formica.

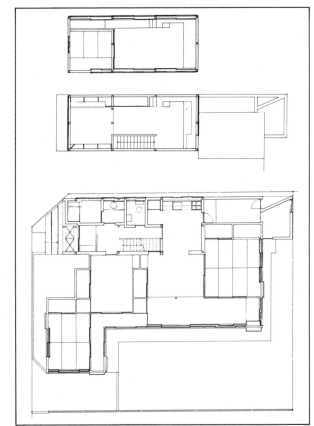

476. Floor plans and sections of the Tominaga Residence. These also show the old house of which Tominaga's design is an extension.

477–478. Fujisawa Municipal Gymnasium (F. Maki, 1984). The overall curving forms of the two arenas are accentuated by the stainless steel sheeting that covers the roofs, evoking a range of associations.

tecture with the void beneath (Ito, Toki, Isozaki) or through an attitude of indifference (Takamatsu, Hara, Aida, Shinohara), which often turns out to be a deliberate "antiurban" approach as best seen in the hermeticists (Ando, Fujii, Hasegawa, Sakamoto, and so on).

Yet, even if it often appears to be a deliberate retreat from the city, the new Japanese architecture is inevitably urban in the sense that the city is in the back of every architect's consciousness and behind every building. For the Japanese the city, beyond its physical and formal attributes, also acts as fantasy or, rather, myth. Upon initial interpretation, the city as myth is alive, well and flourishing; upon second interpretation, it is meaningless and empty. Yet, interestingly, most architects' concerns span both and move between the two. This is a condition wherein *yes* can turn out to be *no* and vice-versa. The architecture of Isozaki, Hara, Ando, Hasegawa, Sakamoto, and even Shinohara are cases in point, with special emphasis on Ito's "superficial urbanism."

Today, writes Ito, "Tokyo's old resilience is being covered up by a rigid frame. The city itself is gradually rigidifying. While modernizing and becoming more and more controlled, Tokyo [still] preserves, if only latently, a resilience and flexibility that accounted for its wonder and charm, and that are not to be found in Western cities. How much longer it will be able to preserve these qualities is a moot point. The rigidifying process is proceeding every day. Afraid of it, people surround themselves with consumer code items in the form of decorations. And the heavier the ornament, the emptier."[88] Numerous works of the New Wave attempt both to reveal and to resist today's manipulative and violent urban trends by assuming through their outer appearance an indifferent or negative stance toward the megalopolis. Yet they are also meant to re-create within the boundaries of architecture another urban environment, a more meaningful order of the city, a sort of microcosmic enclave

inside the building. This is an act in which deconstructing the megalopolis and reconstructing the city often takes place simultaneously and on a basis different from the strictly formalistic operations of a speculative and positivistic rational urbanism. As Hara says, "The city today can no longer be understood in terms of formal construction and must instead be interpreted in connection with . . . experience. The relations among consciousness, experience, and space cannot be clarified analytically. Planning the parts of the city architecturally is a problem of diverse definitions. We are now in transition from the stage of prephenomenal interpretation to one of prephenomenal planning of architecture and cities."[89]

Several Japanese architects aim both at "embedding architecture in the city" while "burying the trove of the city" in architecture.[90] This is done through the reduction of scale and the redefinition of elements, that is to say, through a poetic miniaturization generally symptomatic of the whole Japanese culture. For example, in Hiroshi Hara's Reflection Houses such urban elements as streets, intersections, "nodes," landmarks, tiny individual "city centers," and so on, are introduced. Their spaces are filled with the "reflection of air and sound" as well as with the "reflection of light in the inner cores," which expresses as well the designer's sensitivity to the natural environment.[91] Urban implications are reflected in a similar way in Ando's houses, with their courtyards or atriums, long corridors, the outside and inside stairways and bridges. The fissure spaces—a kind of street-architecture—in Shinohara's Uncompleted House (1970) or his Repeating Crevice House (1971) are spaces that, as Toyo Ito observed, also "symbolize the absence of the 'symbolic' in the city."[92] Isozaki's urban scheme for the Tsukuba Center Building features a public place from which the center itself is missing. As in the whole of Japanese culture, here the essence of an absolute center is absent. Both Hasegawa and Sakamoto's structures are

479–480. A small pyramid, the Stepped Platform House was built with fragmented surfaces and volumes, thus also conveying the fragmented or erased meanings of silence (Kawasaki, 1973, T. Aida).

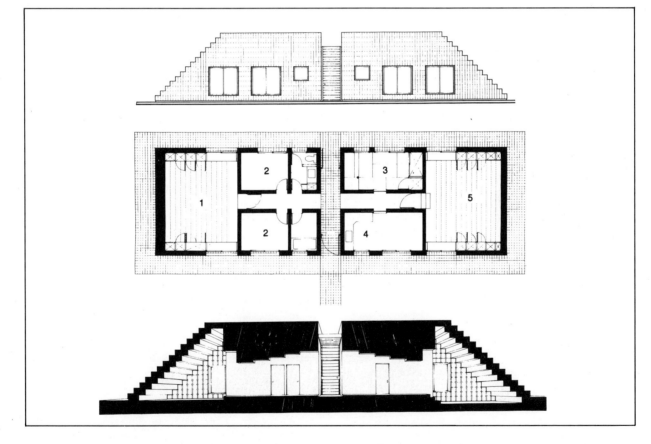

480. Plan, section, and elevations. 1. Bedroom. 2. Children's rooms. 3. *Tatami* room. 4. Kitchen. 5. Living room.

481. Toy Block House
No. 7 (Tokyo, 1984,
T. Aida).

characterized also by an ambiguity of design that is both an assimilation of the city and a contrast to it rather than just a one-way operation of defamiliarization. These are paradoxical models of the city; in a reevaluated form, the city is regenerated and continued also in its autonomous buildings through what Ando calls the "catabolism of landscape."[93] Then, says Yatsuka, "the elimination of meaning is nothing other than a demonstration that on both an architectural and urbanistic level, the cruelty of control and the cruelty of the absence of control are equally absurd."[94]

If one agrees with Chris Fawcett's apt remark that, by and large, "the new Japanese environment by virtue of its ecstatic and delirious dreams of itself, by virtue of its sheer guts and determination, by virtue of its watchfulness and probity, is both positive affirmation and consumation of the Japanese metropolitan project," then, through the increasingly critical attitude of the New Wave, as Kenneth Frampton says, the "ceaseless inundation of a place-less, alienating consumerism" within this project will "find itself momentarily checked."[95]

NOTES

1. Jürgen Habermas, "Modernity—An Incomplete Project," in Hal Foster, ed., *The Anti-Aesthetic: Essays on Postmodern Culture* (Port Townsend, Washington: Bay Press, 1984), p. 6.
2. Jürgen Habermas and Kenneth Frampton are cited by Hal Foster in "Postmodernism: A Preface," in Foster, ed., op. cit., 1, p. xii.
3. Kenneth Frampton, "Towards a Critical Regionalism: Six Points for an Architecture of Resistance," in Foster, ed., op. cit., 1, p. 16. It should be made clear that here I use the term *Pluralism* differently from the way it is usually used. In most Postmodern literature and criticism it generally designates an overall populism and the notion that in culture and politics all positions are now open and equal. I use it in its philosophical sense as "Any metaphysical view holding that the world must be composed of more than one or two basic kinds of entities. The latter views would be termed Monism or Dualism" (William L. Reese, *Dictionary of Philosophy and Religion: Eastern and Western Thought* [New Jersey: Humanities Press, 1980], p.

445). *Pluralism* herein therefore refers to a mode of thinking that opposes the dogmatism of a single truth.

4. Foster, op. cit., 2.

5. Heidegger, op. cit., Chapter 2, 52.

6. Kazuhiro Ishii and Hiroyuki Suzuki, "Post-Metabolism," *The Japan Architect* (October-November 1977), p. 9.

7. Larry W. Richards, "Letters from Readers," *The Japan Architect* (January 1979), p. 6.

8. "After Modernism: A Dialogue between Kenzo Tange and Kazuo Shinohara." *The Japan Architect* (November-December 1983), p. 9.

9. Kenzo Tange, "My Experiences," op. cit., Chapter 4, 11, p. 188.

10. Kenzo Tange in "After Modernism," op. cit., 8, p. 11.

11. Kazuo Shinohara in "After Modernism," op. cit., 8, p. 10.

12. Kiyonori Kikutake, *Concepts and Planning* (Tokyo: Bijutsu-Shuppan-sha, 1978), p. 243; and Kiyonori Kikutake, "Equipmentology," *The Japan Architect* (January 1978), p. 5.

13. Hiroshi Watanabe in the article on Kiyonori Kikutake in Muriel Emanuel, ed., *Encyclopedia of Contemporary Architects* (New York: St. Martin's Press, 1980), p. 423.

14. Kisho N. Kurokawa, "The Techniques of Coexistence," *The Japan Architect* (September 1977), p. 23.

15. Kisho N. Kurokawa, "Rikkyu Grey," *The Japan Architect* (January 1978), p. 32.

16. Kisho N. Kurokawa, "Japanese Culture and Postmodernist Architecture," *The Japan Architect* (April 1983), p. 6.

17. Yasumitsu Matsunaga, "Towards Post-Structurism—Kisho Kurokawa's Recent Work," *The Japan Architect* (May 1984), p. 4. See also Kisho Kurokawa, "The Philosophy of Symbiosis—From Internationalism to Interculturalism," "Le Poetique in Architecture: Beyond Semiotics," and "Karakuri: The Metastructural Machine," *The Japan Architect* (February 1985), pp. 12, 25, and 38.

18. Beyond his longstanding sympathy with Louis Kahn's "simple" architecture, Maki has, in recent years, shown greater interest in the more manneristic complexity of Carlo Scarpa's architecture.

19. Fumihiko Maki, "Modernism at the Crossroad," *The Japan Architect* (March 1983), p. 21.

20. Arata Isozaki, "Of City, Nation, and Style," *The Japan Architect* (January 1984), p. 13.

21. Ibid.

22. Ibid.

23. Ada Louise Huxtable, "The Japanese New Wave," *The New York Times* (January 14, 1979).

24. Fawcett, op. cit., Chapter 1, 1, p. 16.

25. Kenneth Frampton, "The Japanese New Wave," *A New Wave of Japanese Architecture*, Catalogue No. 10 (New York: IAUS, 1978), p. 5.

26. Yasufumi Kijima, "Making an Image Sketch after the Building is Finished," *The Japan Architect* (October-November 1977), p. 48.

27. Shin Toki, "Sanwa Building," *The Japan Architect* (May 1978), p. 52.

28. See Chapter 4, 41.

29. Kazuhiro Ishii and Hiroyuki Suzuki, op. cit., 6.

30. Susumu Shingu, "Play School Windmill," *The Japan Architect* (May 1978), p. 24.

31. Minoru Takeyama, "Atelier Indigo," *The Japan Architect* (January 1978), p. 21.

32. When building a house, carpenters "installed the milled lumber in the direction in which it grew, root end down," thus paying respect to the spirit of the tree. Even today Japanese store lumber vertically as opposed to Westerners, who do so horizontally. Kiyoshi Seike, "A Culture of Wood," *Japan: Climate, Space, and Concept. Process Architecture No. 25* (1981), p. 23.

33. For further details, see Chapter 2.

34. Monta Mozuna, "Ainu Ethnic Museum," *The Japan Architect* (January 1983), p. 38.

35. Fawcett, op. cit., Chapter 1, 1.

36. Ibid., p. 122.

37. Hiroshi Hara, "Anti-Traditional Architectural Contrivance," *A New Wave of Japanese Architecture*, Catalogue 10 (New York: IAUS, 1978), p. 39; and Hiroshi Hara, "On the Form of Reflection Houses," *GA Document* (Special Issue 1970-1980), p. 228.

38. Hiroshi Hara is quoted in Fawcett, op. cit., Chapter 1, 1, p. 85.

39. Chris Fawcett, "Architecture: The Essential Scandal," forthcoming.

40. See Chapter 2, 73.

41. Team Zoo was formed in 1971 by Koichi Otake (b. 1938), Tsutomu Shigemura (b. 1946), Reiko Tomita (b. 1938), Hiroyasu Higuchi (b. 1939), and Kinya Maruyama (b. 1939). It has two ateliers, the Atelier Zo and Atelier Mobil.

42. Monta Mozuna, "Theory of the Cosmic Architecture," *A New Wave of Japanese Architecture*, Catalogue 10 (New York: IAUS, 1978), p. 81.

43. Ibid., p. 80.

44. Charles Jencks, ed., *Post-Modern Classicism* (London: Academy Editions, 1980), p. 97.

45. The Kotohira-gu shrine (Kompira-san), built in the fifth and sixth centuries and rebuilt in 1870, is located in Kagawa Prefecture on Shikoku Island.

46. Monta Mozuna is quoted in Hiroshi Watanabe, "Nine New 'Wrinkles on the Water,'" *AIA Journal* (November

1979), p. 61. Mozuna, op. cit., 42.

47. Takefumi Aida, "Silence," *A New Wave of Japanese Architecture*, Catalogue 10 (New York: IAUS, 1978), p. 14; also *The Japan Architect* (October-November 1977), p. 52.

48. Mayumi Miyawaki, "In the Season of Protection," *The Japan Architect* (July 1977), p. 54.

49. "Mayumi Miyawaki—Architect of Parallel Opposites," editorial in *The Japan Architect* (August 1981), p. 7.

50. Kunihiko Hayakawa, "Circuit of Expression," *The Japan Architect* (May 1984), p. 17.

51. See *Tadao Ando—Minimalisme* (Paris: Electa Moniteur, 1982). Toyo Ito, "Collage and Superficiality in Architecture," *A New Wave of Japanese Architecture*, Catalogue 10 (New York: IAUS, 1978), p. 68.

52. Tadao Ando, "New Relations Between the Space and Person," *Japan Architect* (October-November 1977), p. 44.

53. Hiromi Fujii, "Architectural Metamorphology," *The Japan Architect* (November-December 1980), p. 26.

54. Hiromi Fujii, "Existential Architecture and the Role of Geometry," *A New Wave of Japanese Architecture*, Catalogue 10 (New York: IAUS, 1978), p. 29.

55. Chris Fawcett in the article on Hiromi Fujii, in Emanuel, ed., op. cit., 13, p. 268.

56. Ando, op. cit., 52.

57. Fujii, op. cit., 54.

58. The paragraphs on Tadao Ando's architecture that follow in the text are partially based on the author's "Latest Work of Tadao Ando," *Architectural Review* (November 1982), p. 68.

59. Tadao Ando, "From Self-enclosed Modern Architecture Toward Universality," *The Japan Architect* (May 1982), p. 9.

60. Tadao Ando, "Townhouse at Kujo," *The Japan Architect* (November-December 1983), p. 52.

61. Tadao Ando, "The Genealogy of Memories and the Revelation of Another-Scape," *A New Wave of Japanese Architecture*, Catalogue 10 (New York: IAUS, 1978), p. 21.

62. Ando, op. cit., 59, p. 12.

63. Fumihiko Maki in discussion with Fumitaka Nishizawa, quoted in *Space Design* (June 1981), p. 3.

64. Ibid.

65. The public bath system in Japan is fully operational today. Even those people with a bath at home often use an *osento* for a variety of reasons, sometimes only with the purpose of socializing. When visiting *osento*, people dress in their bathrobes (*yukata*), wear wooden clogs, and carry their own towels and soap and, when it is rainy, also an umbrella.

66. Tadao Ando, "Introduction," in *Tadao Ando: Buildings Projects Writings*, ed. Kenneth Frampton (New York: Rizzoli, 1984), p. 24; and Ando, op. cit., 60.

67. Ando, op. cit., 59.

68. Maki, op. cit., 63.

69. Kazuo Shinohara, "The Savage Machine as an Exercise," *The Japan Architect* (March 1979), p. 46.

70. Yasumitsu Matsunaga, "Architecture as Text—Kazuo Shinohara in His Third Phase," *Kazuo Shinohara*, Catalogue No. 17 (New York: IAUS, 1982), p. 4. Shinohara's use of *creative difference* and *gap* in describing many of his buildings is an indication of Jaques Derrida's influence on him. Derrida defined these concepts first and used them extensively in his critical writings, including *Speech and Phenomena*, trans. David Allison (Evanston, IL: Northwestern University, 1973); and *Writing and Difference*, trans. Alan Bass (Chicago: University of Chicago, 1978).

71. Kazuo Shinohara, op. cit., 70, p. 115.

72. Kazuo Shinohara, "Towards Architecture," *The Japan Architect* (September 1981), p. 30; also op. cit., 70, p. 15.

73. Kazuo Shinohara, "Now and Function," *Space Design* (January 1979).

74. Shinohara, op. cit., 72, p. 13.

75. Matsunaga, op. cit., 70.

76. Matsunaga, op. cit., 70.

77. Kazuo Shinohara used these words to describe this house. Shinohara, op. cit., 70, p. 90.

78. Kazuo Shinohara, "Higashi-Tamagawa Complex," *The Japan Architect* (November-December 1983), p. 36.

79. Shinohara, op. cit., 69.

80. Yatsuka, op. cit., Introduction 7, p. 25.

81. Ito, op. cit., 51, pp. 68, 69.

82. Toyo Ito, "Hotel D," *The Japan Architect* (May 1978), p. 38.

83. Ito, op. cit., 51.

84. Robert Venturi, Denise Scott Brown, Steven Izenour, *Learning from Las Vegas* (Cambridge, MA: The MIT Press, 1977), p. 6.

85. Jiro Murofushi, in an interview with him, *The Japan Architect* (April 1982), p. 22.

86. Aida, op. cit., p. 52.

87. Ito, op. cit., 51.

88. Toyo Ito, "In Search of a Context, 1971-," *The Japan Architect* (April 1982), p. 55.

89. Hiroshi Hara, "A Style for the Year 2001: A Commentary," *The Japan Architect* (March 1984), p. 40.

90. Itsuko Hasegawa, "Embedding Architecture in the City," *Shinkenchiku* (June 1978). Hara, op. cit., 37.

91. Hara, op. cit., 37.

92. Toyo Ito, "Kazuo Shinohara," *Shinkenchiku* (special issue on houses of the Showa Period), 1976.

93. Tadao Ando, "Ryoheki House: Catabolism of Land-scape," *A New Wave of Japanese Architecture*, Catalogue No. 10 (New York: IAUS, 1978), p. 26.
94. Yatsuka, op. cit., Introduction, 8, p. 28.
95. Fawcett, op. cit., Chapter 1, 1, p. 24. Frampton, op. cit., Introduction, 11, p. 162.

6. Conclusion

After a long journey through its many regions, corners, labyrinths, secrets, and rites, the new Japanese architecture still appears incomprehensible, thwarting attempts at explanation, categorization, and analysis. Since these works continually reveal yet another of their "changing faces" and "thousand eyes," any attempt to come to terms with them objectively fails or rewards one with partial understanding at best. The tangible and intangible qualities form a unity in which the best of these works are rooted, proving once again that a mere formalistic or semiotic explanation of architecture—that is, "architecture as language"—has serious limitations. Such explanations can hardly go beyond the logic and rational consciousness of an outside observer. These works, with their intangible qualities and poetic images generated in actual experience, eventually transcend the level of visual or verbal communication and reach the deeper subconscious regions of perception whereby we are compelled to approach them through an internal or intuitive understanding while being immersed in them. At this deepest level they do not stand for anything; they are only themselves hermetically closed within ourselves. This is a primordial ontological condition, a point where architecture steps out of space and time, and the "terror of history" is suspended. Here the past as much as the future is real and permanently exists.

At its best, the new Japanese architecture is the result of poetic inspiration and sentiment rather than a merely problem-solving or scientific analysis; its unique qualities defy quantitative measurement and evaluation. It successfully attempts to resist the nightmare of "progress" by refusing to surrender unconditionally to the rationale of an accelerating technological and industrial development; too often the market for the products of such development is artificially created, and the quality of human life becomes increasingly dependent solely on economic growth.[1] The new Japanese architecture attests to the fact that Pluralism, as both ideology and practice, does not necessarily have to represent an entertaining "take it easy," "fun" attitude that offers an effortless cozy complacency, supplying to the masses what they want, easily and without their involvement on the one hand, while cleverly manipulating these desires on the other. It is the

343

strongest statement against a market-oriented architecture that degenerates into virtually another consumer product, another form of investment, and thus also only a salable commodity.

Instead of reinforcing the *status quo* of the present human condition rooted in a superficial and false self-involvement or self-consciousness, instead of promoting mediocrity, the new Japanese architecture challenges it. It makes one remember rather than forget. Its aim is not the forgetful "good life" but to supply man's inspiration to rethink and redefine the world and himself in it, regardless of the effort and inconvenience. It strips away masks and protective pretentious images until one is forced to face not only present realities, but the internal forces of logic behind these realities. It values the multitude of self-creating human experience, wherein meaning is not preexistent or predetermined but is created and discovered simultaneously through the multitude of physical, spiritual, and symbolic interactions between man and his built world, as well as between man and man in the public realm. They mutually define, create, and respond to one another. The "spirit of place" and that of existence—the phenomena themselves—are evoked continuously in the process of the "performance" or experience of this man-world and man-society interaction. It is an interaction that calls not only upon creative imagination, but also upon critical awareness to appeal to the deepest human aspirations.

The new Japanese architecture is a meditation on the ultimate nonrationality of existence and thus conveys a continuous insistence on the necessity of the *poetique* in human life. It convincingly demonstrates that the increasingly rationally determined contemporary life must have a limit, must be checked in order not to lose the poetry and dignity of human existence. But it also proves that in our age of increasingly instrumental reason, optimized production and consumption, and fast-disappearing public realm, poetry and criticism are necessarily complementary. The sense of poetics cannot be evoked and cultivated without simultaneously being critical, without, as Ando says, cutting "one wedge after another into the circumstances" of today.[2] In other words, the new Japanese architecture proves that there is no aesthetic experience outside the domain of ideology and that what is necessary today is *not* the aesthetics of affirmation but the aesthetics of resistance. The New Wave does all this with inexhaustible urge and creativity and both micro- and macrocosmic sensitivity to poetic spirit and imagery, while—like traditional *haiku*—remaining consistently devoid of passive sentimentality.

To evoke the poetry and phenomenology of architecture, Japanese architects often obviously disregard several functional aspects, the rationale of maximum comfort or convenience, and rely on a minimum number of devices and also a minimum amount of space. Limited space is an absolute precondition for most Japanese designs; however, exactly this tightly limited condition—anywhere else a handicap—is what these architects turn into an advantage. It is the basis of their extraordinary compositions, oftentimes created with traditional methods. Kenneth Frampton comments that the New Wave architects, "with their acute awareness of change and fragility, have become preoccupied with the precise definition of architectural entities or 'archemes'—that is, with phenomenological 'nouns,' which by virtue of their precise definition may be used to expose form to the unpredictable play of changing action."[3]

"If we accept that poetry is always a particular use of a given language, in our case the elements of architecture, and thus it is a deviation from ordinary communication and experience, challenging the status quo of habitual or pragmatic meaning, then it is also a 'defamiliarization' of a taken-for-granted reality. It is a way of probing into the 'life of things', as well as a way of revealing the everyday human condition whereby we become not only aware of this reality and condition, but are also able to discover other modes and meanings of our existence."[4] It is precisely this line of critical ontology that underlies the majority of the New Wave's design intentions.

The new Japanese architecture is impressive in its ability to act as a catalyst, to generate the sense that man and his architecture should enhance one another; together they can be sublime, something more than present reality. In so doing, it provides us with the rare experience of traveling through a constantly shifting "space-time," engendering simultaneously a feeling of eternity and a heightened awareness of transitory existence. Clearly it has an edge—it is a challenge to us all.

NOTES

1. Norman O. Brown, *Life Against Death* (1968), quoted in Fawcett, op. cit., Chapter 1, 1, p. 17.
2. Tadao Ando, "A Wedge in Circumstances," *The Japan Architect* (June 1977); Frampton, op. cit., Chapter 5, 66, p. 134.
3. Frampton, op. cit., Chapter 5, 25, p. 3.
4. Botond Bognar, "Ando's Opposition," *Progressive Architecture* (May 1985), p. 105.

Bibliography

Architectural Design Profiles: Arata Isozaki. London: Architectural Design, 1977.

A Guide to Japanese Architecture. Tokyo: Shinkenchikusha, 1971. Revised Editions, 1975, 1984.

A.I.A. Journal. Washington, D.C. (November 1979). The issue deals with the "New Japanese Architecture."

A New Wave of Japanese Architecture, Catalogue 10. New York: The Institute for Architecture and Urban Studies (IAUS), 1978.

Architecture and Urbanism (1975–present).

Arendt, Hannah. *The Human Condition*. Chicago: The University of Chicago Press, 1958.

Banham, Reyner. *Theory and Design in the First Machine Age*. New York: Praeger, 1960.

Barthes, Roland. *Empire of Signs*. Richard Howard, trans. New York: Hill and Wang, 1982.

Basho, Matsuo. *A Haiku Journey: Basho's Narrow Road to a Far Province*. Dorothy Britton, trans. Tokyo and New York: Kodansha International, 1974, 1980.

Benedict, Ruth. *The Chrysanthemum and the Sword*. Tokyo: Tuttle, 1946, 1954.

Binyon, Laurence. *The Spirit of Man in Asian Art*. New York: Dover Publications, 1965.

Bognar, Botond. *Mai Japán Épitészet* (Japanese Architecture of Today). Budapest: Müszaki Kiadó, 1979.

———— "Ando's Opposition." *Progressive Architecture* (May 1985): 251.

———— "Arata Isozaki's Mannerism: or How to Put Humpty-Dumpty Together Again." *Reflections: The Journal of the School of Architecture, University of Illinois at Urbana-Champaign* 1, no. 1 (Fall 1983): 42–57.

———— "Tadao Ando: Latest Work." *Architectural Review* 172, no. 1029 (November 1982): 68–74.

———— "Tadao Ando: A Redefinition of Space, Time and Existence." *Architectural Design* 51 (May 1981): 25–34.

———— "Typology of Space-Constructions in Contemporary Japanese Architecture." *Japan: Climate, Space and Concept—Process Architecture No. 25* (1981): 135–160.

Boyd, Robin. *New Directions in Japanese Architecture*. New York: Braziller, 1968.

Bring, Mitchell, and Josse Wayembergh. *Japanese Gardens*. New York: McGraw-Hill, 1981.

Chamberlain, Basil Hall. *Japanese Things (Being notes on Various Subjects Connected with Japan)*. Tokyo: Tuttle, 1975.

Chang, Ching-Yu. "Japanese Spatial Conception." *The Japan Architect*, nos. 324–335 (April 1984–March 1985).

Cram, Ralph Adams. *Impressions of Japanese Architecture and the Allied Arts*. New York: Dover Publications, 1966.

Czaja, E. Michael. "Antonin Raymond, Artist and Dreamer." *Architectural Association Journal* 78, no. 864: 57–120.

Dalby, Liza Crihfield. *Geisha*. Berkeley: University of California Press, 1983.

Domus, no. 618 (June 1981). The issue is dedicated to contemporary Japanese design.

Drew, Philip. *The Architecture of Arata Isozaki*. New York: Harper and Row, 1982.

Drexler, Arthur. *The Architecture of Japan*. New York: The Museum of Modern Art, 1954.

Eagleton, Terry. *Literary Theory*. Minneapolis: University of Minnesota Press, 1983.

Eliade, Mircea. *The Myth of the Eternal Return, or Cosmos and History*. Princeton, NJ: Princeton University Press, 1954, 1974.

Emanual, Muriel, ed. *Encyclopedia of Contemporary Architects*. New York: St. Martin's Press, 1980.

Fawcett, Chris. *The New Japanese House: Ritual and Anti-Ritual Patterns of Dwelling*. New York: Harper and Row, 1980.

Foster, Hal, ed. *The Anti-Aesthetic: Essays on Postmodern Culture*. Port Townsend, Washington: Bay Press, 1983.

Frampton, Kenneth. *Modern Architecture: A Critical History*. New York: Oxford University Press, 1980.

Frampton, Kenneth, ed. *Modern Architecture: The Critical Present*. New York: St. Martin's Press, 1982.

———— *Tadao Ando*. New York: Rizzoli, 1984.

Frederic, Louis. *La vie quotidienne au Japon a l'époque des Samourai 1186–1603*. Paris: Librarie Hachette, 1968.

Fujioka, Michio. *Japanese Residences and Gardens*. Tokyo and New York: Kondansha International, 1983.

Fukuyama, Toshio. *Heian Temples: Byodo-in and Chuzon-ji*. Tokyo and New York: Weatherhill, 1976.

GA, Global Architecture Houses. "Japanese Houses 1,"

no. 4 (1978); "Japanese Houses 2," no. 14 (1984).

Glasenapp, Helmut von. *Die fünf Weltreligionen*. Köln: Eugen Diederichs Verlag, 1972.

Gropius, Walter, Kenzo Tange, and Yasuhiro Ishimoto. *Katsura: Tradition and Creation in Japanese Architecture*. New Haven: Yale University Press, 1960.

Habermas, Jürgen. *Toward a Rational Society*. Boston: Beacon Press, 1970.

Habraken, N. J. *Supports, an Alternative to Mass Housing*. London: The Architectural Press, 1972.

Hall, Edward T. *The Hidden Dimension*. New York: Doubleday, 1966.

Hayakawa, Masao. *The Garden Art of Japan*. Tokyo and New York: Weatherhill, 1973.

Heidegger, Martin. *Poetry, Language, Thought*. Albert Hofstadter, trans. New York: Harper and Row, 1971.

Herbert, Jean. *Shinto: At the Fountain-head of Japan*. London: Allen and Unwin, 1967.

Higuchi, Tadahiko. *The Visual and Spatial Structure of Landscapes*. Cambridge, Massachusetts: MIT Press, 1983.

Hirai, Kiyoshi. *Feudal Architecture of Japan*. Tokyo and New York: Weatherhill, 1973.

Hitchcock, Henry-Russel, and Philip Johnson. *The International Style*. New York: Norton and Company, 1932, 1966.

Illik, Drahoslav. *Traditionelle Japanische Architektur*. Prague: Artia Verlag, 1970.

Irie, Takaichi, and Shigeru Aoyama. *Buddhist Images*. Osaka: Hoikusha, 1973.

Isozaki, Arata. *MA: Space-Time in Japan*. Catalogue to the exhibit at the Cooper-Hewitt Museum, New York, 1979.

Itoh, Teiji. *Space and Illusion in the Japanese Garden*. Tokyo and New York: Weatherhill, 1973.

———— *Traditional Domestic Architecture of Japan*. Tokyo and New York: Weatherhill, 1974.

The Japan Architect (1965–present).

Jacobs, Jane. *The Death and Life of Great American Cities*. New York: Random House, 1961.

Japan's Construction. Tokyo: Shinkenchiku-sha, 1974.

Jencks, Charles. *Late-Modern Architecture and Other Essays*. New York: Rizzoli, 1980.

———— *Modern Movements in Architecture*. Garden City, N.Y.: Doubleday, 1973.

———— *The Language of Post-Modern Architecture*. London: Academy Editions, 1977.

Jencks, Charles, and George Baird, eds. *Meaning in Architecture*. New York: Braziller, 1970.

Kawasaki, Ichiro. *Japan Unmasked*. Tokyo: Tuttle, 1974.

Kawazoe, Noboru. *Contemporary Japanese Architecture*. Tokyo: Kokusai Bunka Shinkokai, 1965.

Kazuo Shinohara, Catalogue 17. New York: IAUS, 1982.

Kikutake, Kiyonori. *Concepts and Planning*. Tokyo: Bijutsu Shuppansha, 1978.

———— *Works and Methods 1956–1970*. Tokyo: Bijutsu Shuppansha, 1973.

Kodansha Encyclopedia of Japan, vols. 1–9. Tokyo and New York: Kodansha International Co., 1983.

Koike, Shinji. *Contemporary Architecture of Japan*. Tokyo, 1956.

Kulterman, Udo. *New Japanese Architecture*. New York: Praeger, 1961, 1967.

———— *Kenzo Tange 1946–1969: Architecture and Urban Design*. New York: Praeger, 1970.

Kurokawa, Kisho N. *Capsule*. Tokyo: Bijutsu Shuppansha, 1970.

———— *Metabolism in Architecture*. Boulder, Colorado: Westview Press, 1977.

Leitch, Vincent B. *Deconstructive Criticism*. New York: Columbia University Press, 1983.

Lüchinger, Arnulf. *Structuralism in Architecture and Urban Planning*. Stuttgart: Karl Krämer Verlag, 1981.

Maki, Fumihiko. *Investigations in Collective Form*. St. Louis: University of Washington Press, 1964.

———— "Japanese City Spaces and the Concept of *Oku*." *The Japan Architect* (May 1979): 51–62.

———— "Some Thoughts on Collective Form." In Gyorgy Kepes, ed. *Structure in Art and in Science*. New York: Braziller, 1965.

Maruyama, Masao. *Studies in the Intellectual History of Tokugawa Japan*. Mikiso Hane, trans. Tokyo: University of Tokyo Press, 1974.

Masuda, Tomoya. *Living Architecture: Japanese*. New York: Grosset and Dunlap, 1970.

Matsumoto, Michihiro. *Haragei*. Tokyo: Kodansha International Co., 1984.

Mikes, George. *The Land of the Rising Yen*. Middlesex: Penguin Books, 1973.

Mizuno, Seiichi. *Asuka Buddhist Art: Horyu-ji*. Tokyo and New York: Weatherhill, 1973.

Moles, Abraham A. *Information Theory and Aesthetic Perception*. Urbana: University of Illinois Press, 1966.

Moloney, James Clark. *Understanding the Japanese Mind*. Tokyo: Tuttle, 1973.

Morse, Edward S. *Japanese Homes and Their Surroundings*. Tokyo: Tuttle, 1885, 1974.

Muramatsu, Teijiro. "The Course of Modern Japanese Architecture." *The Japan Architect* (June 1965): 37–56.

Nakane, Chie. *Japanese Society*. Middlesex: Penguin Books, 1973.

Nitschke, Günter. " 'MA': The Japanese Sense of 'Place.' " *Architectural Design* (March 1966): 117–157.

———— "Shime—Binding/Unbinding." *Architectural Design*: (December 1974): 747–791.

Norberg-Schulz, Christian. *Existence, Space and Architecture*. London: Praeger, 1971.

———— *Genius Loci: Towards a Phenomenology of Architecture*. New York: Rizzoli, 1980.

———— *Meaning in Western Architecture*. London: Prager, 1975; and New York: Rizzoli, 1980.

Okamoto, Toyo and Gisei Takakuwa. *The Zen Gardens*, vols. 1 and 2. Tokyo: Mitsumura Suiko Shoin, 1968.

Okawa, Naomi. *Edo Architecture: Katsura and Nikko*. Tokyo and New York: Weatherhill, 1975.

Ooka, Minoru. *Temples of Nara and Their Art*. Tokyo and New York: Weatherhill, 1973.

Ota, Hirotaro, ed. *Japanese Architecture and Gardens*. Tokyo: Kokusai Bunka Shinkokai, 1972.

Paine, T. Robert, and Alexander Soper. *The Art and Architecture of Japan*. New York: Penguin Books, 1955, 1981.

Papinot, E. *Historical and Geographical Dictionary of Japan*. Tokyo: Tuttle, 1974.

Parent, Mary Neighbour. *The Roof in Japanese Buddhist Architecture*. Tokyo and New York: Weatherhill/Kajima, 1983.

Perez-Gomez, Alberto. *Architecture and the Crisis of Modern Science*. Cambridge, Massachusetts: MIT Press, 1983.

Perspecta: The Yale Architectural Journal, no. 20 (1983).

Pevsner, Nikolaus. *An Outline of European Architecture and Design*. London: Thames and Hudson, 1968.

Piggot, Juliet. *Japanese Mythology*. London: Hamlyn, 1969.

Plutschow, Herbert E. *Introducing Kyoto*. Tokyo and New York: Kodansha International Co., 1979.

Japan: Climate, Space and Concept—Process Architecture No. 25 (1981).

Reischauer, Edwin O. *The Japanese*. Cambridge, MA: Harvard University Press, 1977.

Ross, Michael Franklin. *Beyond Metabolism: The New Japanese Architecture*. New York: McGraw-Hill, 1978.

Rykwert, Joseph. *On Adam's House in Paradise*. Cambridge, MA: The MIT Press, 1972, 1981.

Sasaki, Hiro. "The Development of Modern Architecture in Japan." *The Japan Architect*, no. 109 (June 1965): 57–70.

Seidensticker, Edward. *Japan*. New York: Time-Life Books, 1968.

Saunders, E. Dale. *Buddhism in Japan*. Tokyo: Tuttle, 1964, 1972.

Seike, Kiyoshi, Masanobu Kudo, and David Engel. *A Japanese Touch for Your Garden*. Tokyo and New York: Kodansha International Co., 1964.

Seike, Kiyoshi. *The Art of Japanese Joinery*. Tokyo and New York: Weatherhill, 1977.

Seward, Jack. *More About the Japanese*. Tokyo: Lotus Press, 1971.

Seward, Jack. *The Japanese*. Tokyo: Lotus Press, 1971, 1974.

Smithson, Alison, ed. *Team 10 Primer*. London: Studio Vista, 1968.

Speidel, Manfred. *Japanische Architektur: Geschichte und Gegenwart*. Stuttgart: Hatje, 1983.

Suzuki, D. T. *Zen Buddhism*. New York: Anchor Books, 1956.

———— *Zen and Japanese Culture*. Princeton, NJ: Princeton University Press, 1973.

Suzuki, Kakichi. *Early Buddhist Architecture in Japan*. Tokyo and New York: Kodansha International Co., 1971.

Tadao Ando-Minimalism. Paris: Moniteur-Electa, 1982.

Tanaka, Ikko, and Kazuko Koike, eds. *Japan Color*. San Francisco: Chronicle Books, 1982.

———— *Japan Design*. San Francisco: Chronicle Books, 1984.

Tange, Kenzo. *Kenzo Tange + Urtec*, portfolio. Tokyo: 1975.

Tange, Kenzo and Noboru Kawazoe. *Ise: Prototype of Japanese Architecture*. Cambridge, MA: The MIT Press,

Tange, Kenzo. *A Plan for Tokyo, 1960: Toward a Structural Reorganization*. English edition: Tokyo: Shin-kenchikusha, 1961.

"Tokyo 1964." *Architectural Design* 34 (October 1964): 479–613.

Tanizaki, Junichiro. *In Praise of Shadows (1932)*. Tokyo: Tuttle, 1977.

Treib, Mark, and Ron Herman. *Guide to the Gardens of Kyoto*. Tokyo: Shufunotomo, 1980.

Varley, H. Paul. *Japanese Culture*. Tokyo: Tuttle, 1974.

Venturi, Robert. *Complexity and Contradiction in Architecture*. New York: The Museum of Modern Art, 1966.

Vogel, Ezra R. *Japan as Number One*. New York: Harper Colophon Books, 1979.

Watanabe, Yasutada. *Shinto Art: Ise and Izumo Shrines*. Tokyo and New York: Weatherhill, 1974.

Yagi, Koji. *A Japanese Touch for Your Home*. Tokyo and New York: Kodansha International, 1982.

Yatsuka, Hajime. "Architecture in the Urban Desert: A Critical Introduction to Japanese Architecture After Modernism." *Oppositions* 23 (Winter 1981): 1.
——— "Textual Strategy and Post-modernism." *SD, Space Design* 232 (January 1984): 182–186.
Yoshida, Mitsukuni, Ikko Tanaka, and Tsune Sesoko, eds. *The Compact Culture: The Ethos of Japanese Life*. Hiroshima: Toyo Kogyo, 1982.

Index

Page references in *italic* indicate illustration figure numbers.